THE NEW ECONOMICS ONE DECADE OLDER

JAMES TOBIN

"From the bright hopes of the Kennedy years came the 'new economists' —Keynesians disrupting the cobwebs of complacency and static economic indicator gazing. In these three essays, Tobin, a member of the Council of Economic Advisers under Kennedy, recalls the exhilaration and the advent of unforeseen problems. . . . Tobin defends the record—he discusses the political clashes that prevented the 1963 tax cut, and he insists that it was the Indochina War that collapsed prosperity. . . ."—*The Kirkus Reviews* $6.50

THE POLITICAL CHARACTER OF ADOLESCENCE

The Influence of Families and Schools

M. KENT JENNINGS and RICHARD G. NIEMI

To show how and to what degree specific agents shape the political character of adolescents, M. Kent Jennings and Richard G. Niemi draw on a set of large, interrelated, nationwide samples, including interviews with 1,669 high school seniors, and supplementary information gleaned from the students' parents, classmates, social studies teachers, and school officials. The study shows how response to these agents varies according to sex, race, and other factors, and how political learning changes through the life-cycle and across generations. "An exceptionally important contribution to the political socialization literature—one of the rare books which produces more in the way of firm evidence than it claims."—Fred I. Greenstein $12.50

THE FASCIST PERSUASION IN RADICAL POLITICS

A. JAMES GREGOR

How valid are the assertions of contemporary radicals who insist that they are "Marxists"? A. James Gregor measures the distance that separates today's radicals from the belief system of Marx and Engels, and offers a new conceptual framework for the analysis of contemporary totalitarian movements and established regimes. "This book develops at length an incisive, original, and significant interpretation of 'paradigmatic' Italian fascism and contemporary radicalisms."—Stanley Payne $15.00

THE SURROGATE PROLETARIAT

Moslem Women and Revolutionary Strategies in Soviet Central Asia, 1919-1929

GREGORY J. MASSELL

Women in Moslem societies were segregated, exploited, and degraded; thus they were a structural weak point in the traditional order—a surrogate proletariat. This study of the interaction between central power and local traditions relates the Soviet authorities' attempts to bring about revolutionary modernization by the mobilization of women. *Written under the auspices of the Center for International Studies, Princeton University* $18.50

now in paperback . . .

PRESIDENTS, BUREAUCRATS, AND FOREIGN POLICY

The Politics of Organizational Reform

I. M. DESTLER

For this paperback edition, the author has provided an epilogue which takes into account foreign policy developments since 1971. He considers the implications of the appointment of Henry Kissinger as Secretary of State and deals with some of the larger issues raised by the events of the past two years. "Destler's book is a valuable contribution to the ongoing debate about American foreign policy. The issue confronting this country is not only what should our policy be, but how should it be conducted."—Zbigniew Brzezinski Cloth, $12.50; paper $3.45

VOLUME 414   JULY 1974

THE ANNALS

of The American Academy *of* Political
and Social Science

Richard D. Lambert, *Editor*

Alan W. Heston, *Assistant Editor*

USA-USSR: AGENDA FOR COMMUNICATION

Special Editor of This Volume

MARVIN E. WOLFGANG
President
American Academy of Political and Social Science
Professor of Sociology
University of Pennsylvania
Philadelphia, Pennsylvania

PHILADELPHIA

The articles appearing in THE ANNALS are indexed in the *Reader's Guide to Periodical Literature,* the *Book Review Index,* the *Public Affairs Information Service Bulletin,* and *Current Contents: Behavioral, Social, and Management Sciences.* They are also abstracted and indexed in *ABC Pol Sci, Historical Abstracts, International Political Science Abstracts* and/or *America: History and Life.*

International Standard Book Numbers (ISBN)

ISBN 0-87761-179-3, vol. 414, 1974; paper—$3.00

ISBN 0-87761-178-5, vol. 414, 1974; cloth—$4.00

Issued bimonthly by The American Academy of Political and Social Science at Prince and Lemon Sts., Lancaster, Pennsylvania 17604. Cost per year: $15.00 paperbound; $20.00 clothbound. Add $1.00 to above rates for membership outside U.S.A. Second-class postage paid at Lancaster and at additional mailing offices.

Editorial and Business Offices, 3937 Chestnut Street, Philadelphia, Pennsylvania 19104.

CONTENTS

BOOK DEPARTMENT

PAGE

INTERNATIONAL RELATIONS AND POLITICAL THOUGHT

AFRICA, ASIA, AND LATIN AMERICA

EUROPEAN HISTORY AND POLITICS

UNITED STATES HISTORY AND POLITICS

SOCIOLOGY

ECONOMICS

PREFACE

At the Seventy-eighth Annual Meeting of the American Academy of Political and Social Science, eight hundred members and delegates were present. Despite the travel budget cuts of many organizations and universities, the attendance at our sessions was between five and six hundred, and the audience's enthusiasm and interest in the topic were surely as evident as ever. Our theme for the 1974 Annual Meeting was meant to convey the need for continued dialogue between the two super-powers in recognition of the importance of their reaching an international relationship of cordiality.

The papers presented at the meeting and prepared for this issue are the products of careful and erudite thought of scholars and officials from the United States and the Soviet Union. However some remarks may be perceived by participants from either country, the tenor of the entire meeting was characterized as conciliatory and cooperative. In private conversations with representatives from both countries, I felt their strong desire to communicate, and the language of discourse was that of a new awareness of our commonality.

While I do not wish to sound unrealistically sanguine, I am now further convinced, as a result of this Annual Meeting, that the US-USSR relationship will continue to reflect cooperation rather than conflict—no matter which political party controls Congress or the White House. As I indicated in my remarks at the opening session of the Seventy-eighth Annual Meeting, our two countries stand on the edge of tomorrow—with hands shaking not in terror or anger, but in friendship—and, together, face many of the major crises of humanity, from famine in Africa to the challenges of outer space. For this reason, the theme of our meeting was both timely and timeless.

Our meeting was not in the old mode of coexistence with confrontation, but in the style of men and women of varying political, economic and social persuasions living together as a family of nations. As our technology reaches out to fill the earlier abstractions of our imaginations in space and in the sea, we are learning to control our aggression, to speak with frankness and honesty and to measure our integrity by our capacity to promote social justice and harmony within, and between, nations.

That men with quite contrary views can often speak across their differences and voice similar thoughts can be illustrated by comments from Adam Smith and Karl Marx. Either could have endorsed the other's statement:

The real price of everything, what everything really costs, to the man who wants to acquire it, is the toil and trouble of acquiring [*Wealth of Nations*, 1776];

In proportion as the antagonism between classes within the nation vanishes, the hostility of one nation to another will come to an end [*Manifesto of the Communist Party*, 1848].

Thus, an agenda for communication began, with focus on trade and economics, arms control and disarmament, diplomatic relations and the exchange of scientific ideas and organizations. Both the members of the Academy and the delegates who attended the sessions will recognize the articles in this volume as the written and somewhat revised versions of the presentations of our speakers. Those who were present at our luncheon will recall with pleasure the enthusiasm and ebullience of Buckminster Fuller, whose remarks could not readily be abbreviated for publication in this issue of THE ANNALS.

I wish again to thank both our American and Soviet colleagues for their participation in a program which has further enhanced the dignity of the Academy and has helped to promote more international understanding.

MARVIN E. WOLFGANG

An American View of Economic Relations with the USSR

By HERBERT S. LEVINE

ABSTRACT: The current rise in US-USSR trade has its antecedents, which are discussed briefly in the first section of this paper. Attention is then focused on the basic economic reasons which might be adduced for the manifest increased Soviet interest in expanded economic relations with the United States. Special emphasis is given to the Soviet desire to import advanced Western technology. The salient issues in the current discussions of expanded US-USSR economic relations are indicated and examined. These issues include: the administration of Soviet trade, problems related to state trading, credits, most favored nation (MFN) status and potential advantages of expanded economic relations. It is concluded that, while the economic advantages for the United States as a nation are debatable, expanded economic relations may increase our political bargaining strength vis-à-vis the Soviets. Also, the commitment to detente should be preserved, as it is in the interest of us all that this be done.

Herbert S. Levine is Professor of Economics at the University of Pennsylvania and is a consultant to the Stanford Research Institute. During 1963–1964 he was resident fellow and Visiting Lecturer at the Russian Research Center of Harvard University. He was recipient of the Lindback Foundation Distinguished Teaching Award in 1965. Profesor Levine is co-editor of Mathematics and Computers in Soviet Economic Planning *and author of* "The Centralized Planning of Supply," in Comparisons of the U.S. and Soviet Economies.

The author is indebted to the Stanford Research Institute, Washington D.C., and the Russian Institute at Columbia University for research support.

Some of the material presented in this paper was presented earlier in testimony before the House Committee on Science and Astronautics and in the magazine *Enterprise* 23, no. 3 (Fall 1973).

IT IS by now commonplace to point out that trade between the United States and the Soviet Union has grown rapidly in the last few years. However, this recent upsurge of trade should not obscure the fact that trade relations between the United States and Russia go back a long time.[1] At the beginning of the nineteenth century there was already substantial trade between the two countries, and in 1837 they signed a mutual most favored nation (MFN) tariff treaty. By the period of the First World War, the United States was an important supplier of equipment—especially agricultural equipment—to Russia. It is also interesting to note that in 1911 the United States government abrogated the aforementioned MFN treaty in an attempt—which was unsuccessful—to pressure the Tsarist government into a policy of more humane treatment of Russian Jews.

A BRIEF HISTORY OF US-USSR TRADE RELATIONS

After the war and the Communist Revolution the first major United States economic involvement in the Soviet Union was the distribution of $20 million worth of grain to the Russian people by the American Relief Administration under the direction of Herbert Hoover. American firms played a fairly active role in the 1920s in the Soviet program of foreign concessions. Firms with such names as Harriman, Hammer and Ford, among others,

were involved in economic concessions granted by the Soviet government. In the early 1930s United States corporations were prominent in the surge of Soviet economic relations with the West which came with the first five year plan.[2] United States exports to the Soviet Union increased sharply, and the large purchases by the Soviets during these years, when the American economy was in a major depression, won powerful support in the business community for US recognition of the Soviet government. This came in 1933. In the following year the Export-Import Bank (Eximbank) was established with the direct purpose of financing Soviet-American trade. In the year following that— 1935—the United States granted MFN status to the Soviet Union, and a trade agreement between the two countries was signed.

The Cold War period, after the Second World War, was inimical to Soviet-American economic relations. The period was dominated by reduced interest in such relations on the Soviet side and by trade restrictions on the American side. The United States government put restrictions on the types of goods— related to national security—which American firms could export to either the Soviet Union or Soviet-bloc nations and arranged for similar export restrictions to be instituted by other North Atlantic Treaty Organization (NATO) nations and Japan. While the adherence to this policy by other Western nations and the policy's effect on the growth of the Soviet economy are matters of debate, there is no doubt that the policy did contribute significantly to the

1. Edward T. Wilson et al., "U.S.-Soviet Commercial Relations," in U.S., Congress, Joint Economic Committee, *Soviet Economic Prospects for the Seventies* (Washington, D.C.: U.S. Government Printing Office, 1973), p. 638; hereafter referred to as *SEPS*. Much of what follows in this section is based on this article.

2. The relevance of this to the international transfer of technology will be discussed below.

low level of US-USSR trade through the fifties and mid-sixties.

The current rise in US-USSR trade had its antecedents in various periods of thaw in the 1950s and early '60s, when attempts were made to reduce restrictions and to improve Soviet-American economic relations. Yet, it was not until the mid-sixties that substantial progress in this direction was made. At that time many items were removed from the export control list; furthermore, in 1967 and 1969 East-West trade bills, with MFN recognition— by then already granted to Yugoslavia and Poland—were introduced into Congress, but were not passed. Negotiations undertaken in 1971 culminated in (1) preliminary agreements on certain trade issues at the Moscow summit in May of 1972, (2) in the trade agreement worked out between United States and Soviet representatives in October 1972 and (3) in several protocols relating to economic relations signed at the Washington summit in June 1973.

The actual dimensions of the growth of US-USSR trade in the last few years are rather remarkable, reflecting both the previous political suppression of trade between the two countries in the postwar period and the recent change in the political atmosphere to one encouraging the development of trade and other forms of economic relations.[3] The total volume of US-USSR trade during the 1950s was below $50 million per year. During the period 1960 to 1968 it was below $110 million per year, with the sole exception of 1964 when the trade turnover soared to $184 million—Soviet imports, $163 million—as a result of massive Soviet grain purchases; trade volume fell to below $100 million the following year. The rapid climb in trade began in 1969, when the turnover grew to $177 million from a level of $99 million the previous year—an increase of almost 80 percent. The trade volume grew moderately in 1970 and 1971 and then tripled in 1972, to a level of $462 million. It then more than doubled in 1973, reaching a level of about $1,500 million.[4] Much of the increase in the last two years is a result of the large Soviet grain and soy bean imports from the United States which were contracted for in the summer of 1972. These came to about $420 million in 1972 and $800 to $850 million in 1973.[5] However, a substantial increase in United States exports of machinery to the Soviet Union has also been of importance. In 1971 the Soviet Union placed orders for $239 million worth of plant and equipment in the United States, and in 1972, for $465 million worth.[6] These orders gave rise to actual United States exports of machinery to the Soviet Union of $62 million in 1972 and of approximately $200 million in 1973.[7] This latter figure alone was more than the total US-USSR trade

3. Sources for the data are as follows: 1950–1959: Leon M. Herman, "Soviet Foreign Trade and the United States Market," in U.S., Congress, Joint Economic Committee, New Directions in the Soviet Economy (Washington, D.C.: GPO, 1966), p. 943; 1960–72: John T. Farrell, "Soviet Payments Problems in Trade with the West," in SEPS, pp. 698, 693; 1973: U.S., Department of Commerce, preliminary data.

4. Ekonomicheskaia gazeta 15 (April 1974), p. 20.
5. U.S., Department of Commerce, preliminary data.
6. Farrel, "Soviet Payments Problems," p. 693.
7. U.S., Department of Commerce, preliminary data.

turnover in 1970. Also, Soviet exports to the United States increased by 50 percent in 1972 and more than doubled in 1973, attaining a level of $215 million—including Soviet exports to the United States of $75 million worth of oil.[8] However, while in the years 1960 to 1971 United States exports to the Soviet Union were commonly twice the level of United States imports from the Soviet Union, in the last two years they were more than five times as high—in 1964 the ratio was eight.

SOVIET INTEREST IN EXPANDED ECONOMIC RELATIONS WITH THE UNITED STATES

There are, clearly, many reasons —political, military and economic —which might be adduced for the manifest increased Soviet interest in expanded economic relations with the United States. I will restrict my discussion, first of all, to the economic reasons and, within that set, to a limited subset of major factors.

The basic economic factor concerns recent Soviet growth and productivity. Dividing the postwar period into subperiods of decreasing growth of Soviet output —gross national product (GNP)— one observes a relationship of great importance. According to Western recalculations of official Soviet data, Soviet GNP grew at the following average annual rates: 1950 to 1958: 6.4 percent; 1958 to 1967: 5.3 percent; 1967 to 1973: 3.7 percent.[9] The official Soviet data shows higher rates, but the same

trend: 10.9 percent; 7.2 percent; 6.4 percent.[10] However, while the rates of growth of output were declining, the rates of growth of inputs into the economy—labor and capital—were remaining almost completely constant over the entire 1950 to 1973 period, with a slight decrease in the rate of growth of capital stock during the period 1967 to 1973.

That is, while the Soviet economic authorities were able, through the various means at their disposal, to maintain the rate of growth of the flow of labor and capital inputs into the economy, they were not able to maintain the rate of growth of output; the reason for this has been a decline in the rate of growth of factor productivity. Indeed, when a statistical comparison is made between the rates of growth of output and of combined labor and capital inputs, it is seen that total factor productivity grew at the following rates: 1950 to 1958: 1.7 percent; 1958 to 1967: 0.7 percent; 1967 to 1973: −0.7 percent.[11] These data indicate a steady decline in the rate of growth of factor productivity. In fact, in the most recent period inputs into the economy grew more rapidly than output—thus, the negative rate of growth of factor productivity.

This decline in the growth of productivity has clearly been a matter of grave concern to Soviet leaders. The growth of factor productivity is a major source of economic growth in developed industrial economies. Its decline in the Soviet Union is seen as possibly leading to decreased world esteem for the Soviet economic system; also, and of more substance, it is seen as an erosion of the effectiveness of the

8. Ibid.

9. Sources of data are as follows: Abram Bergson, "Toward a New Growth Model," *Problems of Communism* 22, no. 2 (March-April 1973), pp. 1–9; *SEPS* and preliminary U.S. government estimates.

10. *Narodnoe khoziaistvo SSSR v 1972g.* (Moscow: Statistika, 1973), p. 531; and *Pravda*, 26 January 1974, p. 1.

11. Ibid.

Soviet growth model, which—in a somewhat oversimplification—called for the Soviet authorities to concentrate on increasing the supply of inputs into the economy with the assumption that this would lead to a concomitant increase in output. Furthermore, the decline in factor productivity casts its shadow ahead. If this decline is not reversed and if the Soviets seek to achieve economic growth through the maintenance of the 9 percent rate of growth of capital stock, then the share of investment of GNP will, by the end of the 1970s, reach 50 percent.[12] Given the realities of the political situation in the Soviet Union today and the importance being accorded consumption, such a rate of investment is totally unacceptable.

The conclusion from this is clear. Something has to be done to improve productivity in the economy. There are a number of factors which are of relevance in this regard. But for the purposes of this paper, the role of technology and technical change is clearly dominant. One of the major aims of the economic reforms introduced in 1965 was to encourage the growth of technology. It is obvious by now that the results of the reform have, so far, been disappointing. Some, within the Soviet Union and outside in the West, argue that the reforms did not go far enough, that what is required for the reform to be effective is a significant increase in the degree of economic decentralization. Apparently, the Soviet leaders feel that such radical reform would involve economic and political risks which they are reluctant to assume. Instead, they appear to be placing major reliance on a program of im-

portation of advanced technology and capital equipment from the developed industrial nations. The Soviets are especially—although not exclusively—interested in American technology. They have a high regard for the high level of American technology, both for real and imaginary reasons. That is, United States technology is the world leader in a number of fields in which the Soviet Union is interested—for example, computers, integrated circuits. Also, the Soviets tend to regard the world in a bipolar sense, and this biases them toward things American. Yet, one aspect of this "two-giants" approach which is relevant in the borrowing of technology is the fact that the large scale of production usually found in the United States, but not so frequently in other developed countries, is appropriate to the Soviet scene.

SOME ISSUES IN US-USSR TRADE AND ECONOMIC RELATIONS

Before going on to an assessment of the potential Soviet success in improving the performance of their economy through the transfer of technology from abroad, let me indicate and briefly examine some of the salient issues in the current discussions of expanded US-USSR economic relations. These issues include: the administration of Soviet trade, problems related to state trading, credits, MFN status and potential advantages of expanded economic relations. These are discussed below.

The administration of Soviet trade[13]

At the top of the Soviet foreign trade system stands the Ministry of

12. Bergson, "Toward a New Growth Model."

13. There are a number of standard sources. See, for example: V. S. Vaganov,

Foreign Trade—primarily an administrative and regulatory body which does not normally directly engage in operational work on foreign trade transactions. Direct operation is performed by the foreign trade organizations, which are juridical, independent budget organizations having monopoly rights over export and import of defined groups of products. Currently, they number about fifty, over half of which are concerned with machinery, equipment and instrument products.

In principle—and normally in practice—they, rather than the enterprises which will eventually be buying and selling traded products, conduct all trade negotiations with foreign firms. Needless to say, this has turned out to be a cumbersome, generally inefficient way of conducting foreign trade, especially in regard to new technology where very specific information about the using enterprise's needs is required. Recently, in response to growing complaints from Soviet managers and others, there has been talk of allowing more direct participation by Soviet enterprises in foreign trade negotiations.[14] In the last year or so, the State Committee on Science and Technology has been more active in foreign trade negotiations regarding the importing of new technology—both of know-how and equipment.

To administer and encourage increased trade, a number of joint Soviet-American organizations—including the official joint US-USSR Commercial Commission established at the May 1972 Moscow summit and the US-USSR Council on Trade and Economic Relations—have been established. Also, the United States Department of Commerce has set up a Bureau of East-West Trade.

Problems related to state trading

There are numerous possible problems within this category. I will mention only a few.

To begin, many American businessmen are concerned about conducting business negotiations with government agencies which have, at least so it seems, a monolothic state bureaucracy behind them. The Soviets have on occasion "whip-sawed" competing United States firms in regard to their bids. It may turn out that some institution-creation on the United States side will have to be undertaken in order to deal with such problems.

Second, there is concern that the Soviets will be unstable trading partners, tying their purchases to temporary needs and shortages, rather than making such decisions on more basic factors and comparative economic advantage. If the Russians are not persuaded to agree to longer term purchase agreements, American producers in certain fields may in time become disillusioned and abandon the Soviet market.

Third, if economic relations are to be successful, United States firms will need more information about the Soviet economy than the Soviets have been in the habit of giving. This includes data which would reflect business and credit conditions and

Vneshnaia torgovlia sotsialisticheskikh stran (Moscow, 1966); Metodicheskie ukazaniia k sostavleniia gosudarstvennogo plana razvitiia narodnogo khoziaistva SSR (Moscow, 1969), pp. 681–690; and A. Brown and E. Neuberger, eds., International Trade and Central Planning (Berkeley, Cal.: University of California Press, 1968).

14. See, for example, Gosudarstvennyi piatiletnii plan razvitiia narodnogo khoziastva SSSR na 1971–1975 gody (Moscow, 1972), p. 327.

also the opportunity to conduct on-the-spot observation of relevant economic activity.

Fourth, until very recently the number of United States companies permitted to operate business facilities in Russia has been severely limited—Pan American and American Express. If trade is to flourish, American firms need office space in Moscow and other Russian cities. It appears that progress on this front is being made. In one of the protocols at the Washington summit in June 1973 it was stated that an additional ten United States corporations had been accredited to establish offices in Moscow. The Soviet government also gave assurance that, among other things, accredited United States businesses in Moscow would be authorized to acquire telex equipment and other such communication equipment and would receive prompt processing of visa requests. Moreover, plans to build a $110 million international trade center in Moscow were announced this past September. Construction will be under the supervision of Occidental Petroleum and Bechtel Corporation, with credit and financing through a consortium of United States banks headed by Chase Manhattan. The center will have office space for 400 business concerns, living quarters for their employees, a 600 room hotel and conference and exhibition facilities. Construction will begin in the spring of 1974; the planned completion date is 1977.

Fifth, there has been fear that massive Soviet sales in certain United States markets could disrupt these markets. In the October 1972 trade agreement, the Soviets agreed to discontinue sales of individual products if United States firms complained of market disruption.

Sixth, concern has been raised over legal methods for settling disputes. The Soviet government, in the trade agreement, has accepted third country arbitration.

Seventh, there have been questions about protection of United States companies' proprietary rights in products and processes. The Soviet government participates in world patenting and licensing arrangements and now, also, in copyrighting.

Eighth, the trade agreement included a number of provisions on maritime shipping, an issue of some importance to the American labor unions involved. Forty United States and Soviet ports to which access was guaranteed were listed. Also, shares for American, Soviet and third parties in the shipping business were established.

Credits

It is normally argued, by both sides, that if the Soviet Union is to increase purchases from the United States it will need substantial hard currency credits, at least for an initial period.

The first item which had to be settled to clear the way for Eximbank financing was the Soviet outstanding debts for post-World War II civilian goods delivered to it as part of the lend-lease program. In October 1972 the Soviets agreed to pay a total amount of $722 million: $48 million by mid-1975 and the remainder over a twenty-five year period, contingent upon the United States officially granting the Soviet Union MFN status. In addition, a separate "Agreement of Financing Procedures" was signed and will remain in effect even if MFN status is not granted by Congress. Under this agreement Eximbank will direct credits to the Soviet Foreign Trade

Bank on a case-by-case basis. The normal pattern for direct credit will be 10 percent down, 45 percent from Eximbank—at originally six, now seven percent interest—and 45 percent from commercial banks at negotiated interest rates.

Some business transactions being discussed will require massive financing. Natural gas deals may come to more than $5 billion. The total credit exposure of Eximbank is currently $16.5 billion with less than $1.5 billion to a single country. New approaches to financing, private and government, may have to be developed.

One of the questions raised in regard to the role of Eximbank in fostering trade with the Soviet Union is whether its activity will amount to the granting of preferential treatment to the Soviets. To the extent that this turns out to be so, the United States runs the risk of antagonizing our regular trading partners. For example, in an era of inflation and high interest rates, 7 percent loans could be considered subsidized credit and, while the Soviet Union will have to negotiate with private lenders for a good portion of its credit, Eximbank and its 7 percent rate might exert pressure on the market. In addition, there is concern that Eximbank will lean over backwards in its dealings with the Soviet Union and treat the Soviets differently from other customers. It has already been reported that Eximbank has not insisted upon receiving the usual balance of payments statistics and independently determined geological surveys and financial statements in its consideration of loans to the Soviet Union.[15]

Another frequent question concerns the credit worthiness of the Soviets—that is, their ability to repay the loans granted to them. In recent years the Soviet Union has been running a deficit in its hard currency balance of payments. Its estimated hard currency debt service ratio—debt payments divided by hard currency earnings—was about 20 percent, with the expectation that it would rise in 1972 to 25 percent.[16] Furthermore, the usual range of estimates puts the annual Soviet deficit at about $1 billion and its debt at the end of the 1970s at $7 to $10 billion, with a rise in its debt service ratio toward the 50 percent range. Finally, questions are being raised about what sorts of goods and in what quantities the Soviet Union could sell to the United States or other hard currency countries which could yield enough revenue to repay its debts.

In analyzing these questions, it should first be pointed out that a debt service ratio of 25 percent is quite an acceptable level; however, a 50 percent ratio is not. If it ever got to that level, it would be difficult for the financial community to grant further credit. Secondly, many of the business arrangements entered into, and proposed by, the Soviets are self-liquidating—that is, the Western seller agrees to accept the output of the plant or technology which he is selling in payment for the credit extended. Third, in addition to its staple raw material, nonferous metals and semifabricated exports to hard currency countries—including the United States—the Soviet Union is developing some manufactured goods exports, such as watches, television sets, hydro-

15. Marshall I. Goldman, "Who Profits More from US-Soviet Trade?" *Harvard Business Review*, November-December 1973, p. 86.

16. Farrel, "Soviet Payments Problems," p. 702.

foil boats and executive-size airplanes.

Fourth—and perhaps most important at this time—the demand for, and world prices of, two of the Soviet Union's important export products, oil and gold, have risen dramatically in the past year. This puts the Soviet Union's credit position in an entirely different light, at least for the time being. The Russian situation in regard to oil is actually rather complex. Currently, the Soviet Union is an oil exporter. It earned high revenues on this account this past year, and the expectation is that it will continue to do so for several years, but for exactly how long is the question. Its consumption of oil over the past few years has risen faster than its production; in the future, consumption will rise even faster. Furthermore, in the absence of major new oil fields, production growth will begin to tail off. Some specialists expect the Soviet Union to be a net importer of oil in ten to twenty years.

The current Soviet gold stock has been estimated at about 2,000 tons, with annual production of about 300 tons.[17] At the end of 1972 the free market price of gold was approximately $70 per ounce, which meant that the stock was worth about $4.5 billion and the annual flow about $0.7 billion. At the time of this writing—April 1974—the free market price of gold is about $175 per ounce, which means that the Soviet gold stock is now worth $11.2 billion and the annual production flow, $1.7 billion. Needless to say, this puts the Soviet Union in a much stronger position vis-à-vis the hard currency countries. Unofficial estimates are that the Soviets sold 300 tons of gold last year to help finance their hard currency purchases. Now, the expectations are that in 1974, with the rise in oil prices and the decrease in Soviet grain purchases—they had an excellent harvest in 1973—they might not have to sell much or any gold.

MFN

The Soviets have been vigorously pressing for the mutual granting of MFN status. They argue that the tariffs they now have to pay inhibit their ability to export to the United States and that on a diplomatic level, MFN status is a symbol of normalized relations similar to diplomatic recognition. Some in the United States argue that the types of goods, mostly unprocessed, which the Soviets export to the United States are not highly tariffed. Furthermore, they say, even with MFN the Soviets will have a hard time exporting highly processed goods to the United States, because in most cases they do not produce goods of sufficient quality, design, reliability of services and spare parts supply to be competitive in American markets.

Another issue stems from the fact that the USSR's grant of MFN status does not guarantee the US equal access to Soviet markets, since the Soviet government controls all trade. This basic asymmetry in the MFN situation has been one of the bases upon which many American political leaders pursue a *quid pro quo* in the political area in exchange for the United States granting MFN. The Soviets appear to be holding to the view that MFN is a test of American commitment to expanded economic relations. For example, in their five year plan for 1976 to 1980 the figures they include for Soviet-American trade may well depend on what we do with MFN.

17. Ibid., pp. 691–692, 702.

THE ABILITY OF THE SOVIET UNION TO IMPORT AND MASTER ADVANCED TECHNOLOGY

In this section I would like to discuss the possibilities of the Soviets achieving their major aim in the expansion of economic relations with the United States—that is, the acquisition of advanced technology. I will begin with a brief sketch of Russia's historical experience with the borrowing of technology, which is important in understanding the present situation.

At the risk of gross oversimplification, it might be said that all of modern Russian history—from the middle of the fifteenth century to the present day—has been dominated by the need perceived by Russian leaders to catch up with the more advanced nations of the West. An important part of this catching up process has been the importing and employment of advanced foreign technology. This occurred on a massive scale at the beginning of the eighteenth century under Peter the Great; he brought in not only foreign technology, but foreign technologists by the thousands, and built an economic base primarily for the support of his military, foreign policy ambitions.

Within the past hundred years there have been, on the part of the Russians, two major periods of concentrated effort to acquire advanced foreign technology; currently, a third major campaign is underway. The first of these in the past century was connected with the industrialization spurt in the 1890s. It was led, against the opposition of many among the Russian nobility, by the Russian minister of finance, Count Witte, whose policy was to encourage foreign capital and direct foreign investment in Russia. Foreign capital, especially French and Belgian, accounted for almost 50 percent of all new capital invested in Russia during the industrialization drive of the 1890s. In 1900 foreign companies owned more than 70 percent of the capital in mining, metallurgy and machine building in Russia.

As a result of this foreign investment not only was the capital stock of Russia greatly expanded, but also foreign technology was brought into Russia, in both the form of advanced capital equipment itself and in the form of human capital. Foreign technologists, experienced businessmen, managers and engineers came to Russia as foreign companies were set up within Russia. Direct foreign investment was thus responsible for the implantation of advanced techniques in several key industries. New technology was often brought with little or no adaptation. For example, the steel mills built in southern Russia after the mid-1880s were of the same technological level and size as those being built in Western Europe. Furthermore, in this period, with the continuing participation of foreigners in management, these steel mills kept up with Western European progress and remained in the mainstream of world progress in steel making. Moreover, the foreign firms competed with Russian firms inside Russia and forced the latter to be more efficient if they were to survive.

A second period of major importation of foreign technology occurred during the 1920s and, especially, the early 1930s. During the relatively free market-oriented period of the new economic policy of the 1920s, the Soviets attempted to import foreign technology through the program of foreign concessions in a number of different forms. The quantitative importance of this program is a matter of debate. Nevertheless, the actual number of business arrangements with foreign concerns was larger than has been commonly believed. [18] However, it was during the period of the first five year plan, 1928 to 1932, that major efforts were made to import foreign technology in connection with the industrialization program that was then being initiated.[19] With the emphasis on industrial capital formation, imports of machinery and equipment began to assume greater importance. By 1932 the imports of machinery and equipment rose to a level of more than half of the total imports of the Soviet Union, and imports of certain types of machines—turbines, generators, boilers, machine tools, metal cutting machines—accounted for between 50 and 90 percent of the growth in the supply of these machines during the period of the first five year plan. On the whole, imports of capital goods from abroad amounted to almost 15 percent of gross investment in the Soviet Union during this period. Furthermore, imports of certain basic industrial materials—lead, tin, nickel, zinc, aluminum, rubber—accounted for perhaps 90 to 100 percent of these materials consumed in the Soviet industrialization program.

After the completion of the first five year plan, Soviet involvement in this type of trade decreased. This was in large part a consequence of Stalin's policy of nondependence on the West—often erroneously classified as a policy of autarky—for major parts of Soviet economic materials and capital equipment. Also, there were certain financial developments associated with the relative price movements during the depression which made it much more difficult for the Russians to buy equipment with the grain which they were exporting; these developments contributed to a significant decline in trade. Furthermore, the inability of the Soviets to acquire foreign credits—which they felt they could afford—contributed to a decline in imports. In the next five year plan—that is, the period 1933 to 1937—imports of foreign capital goods fell to about 2 percent of gross investment. Dependence upon the West for major products decreased dramatically. Sometimes, imports of equipment fell rather suddenly. For example, imports of tractors in 1931 accounted for about 60 percent of the growth of the tractor stock in that year, and in the next year they fell to zero.

It is interesting that in both the 1890s and 1930s the imports of foreign goods, machinery and technology was paid for primarily through the export of Russian raw materials, such as grain, lumber and oil. This is, of course, true to a great extent currently, except for the grain.

In these past periods of importation of advanced technology—including the period of Peter the Great—the Russians were able, within a compressed period of time, to approach contemporary economic levels in the West and, to some extent, even the levels of contemporary technology in the West. Yet, in

18. See, Anthony C. Sutton, *Western Technology and Soviet Economic Development, 1917 to 1930* (Stanford, Cal.: Hoover Institution Press, 1968), vol. 1.

19. See, Franklyn Holzman, "Foreign Trade," in *Economic Trends in the Soviet Union,* ed. A. Bergson and S. Kuznets (Cambridge, Mass.: Harvard University Press, 1963), pp. 287–320.

the longer run, as the advanced nations of the West continued to develop new technology, the Russians were not able to maintain their relative position, and they fell back.

The first decade or so of the twentieth century did show signs of being different, but those developments were cut off by World War I and the Communist Revolution. For example, in the period 1905 to 1913 the management of many firms set up by foreigners in Russia was taken over by the Russians, themselves. There was a rather rapid development of a Russian managerial group and Russian engineering, technological and financial groups. By the beginning of World War I Russian banks, corporations and entrepreneurs were floating their own stock on West European stock exchanges and were raising their own capital in the international capitalist world. The Communist Revolution significantly removed, both directly and indirectly, this human capital from Russia. Thus, after the revolution this group of trained people was, for the most part, lost to the Soviets; to a great extent, the Soviets had to start over again.

A full identification and analysis of the historical reasons for the Russian failure to internalize the creation and diffusion of technology is beyond the scope of my paper. However, I would like to indicate briefly some of the economic institutions which affect the ability of the Soviet economy to absorb, master and create new technology.

One reason which has been well discussed in the literature of the Soviet economy is the incentive mechanism that has more or less dominated the Soviet scene since the 1930s. The Soviet economy is currently in a period of economic reform, and while the picture is not totally clear, this is still basically an economy where there is a target to be reached. In any situation such as this there are two ways of assuring success or of increasing the possibility of success: 1) performance; and 2) keeping that target within reasonable distance. The second aspect of target-type rewarding is detrimental to the innovation process. Innovation always involves risk. The compensation for risk, contained in the reward for possible over-plan fulfillment, is reduced by the fact that success today will mean a higher target tomorrow, and success in the system requires the rather regular meeting of targets. Thus, managers resist innovation and try to keep targets low. There is much discussion in the Soviet Union on how to get around this problem, but nothing very effective has been introduced so far.

A second factor involves the organization of research and development (R and D). A great deal of effort is put forth on research and development in the Soviet Union, but to a great extent it is separated from production. As a result, a fair amount of new technology is developed, but the implementation and the diffusion of it is limited, for the reasons just discussed: the managers of industrial enterprises try to keep new technology away because it will cause problems and will not lead to sustained rewards. Giving the control of R and D to the production managers is also not an acceptable solution, since the expectation is that they will not encourage the development of new products and processes.

A further factor concerns the creative destruction aspect of technical change—that is, when something new is done and it is successful, the old is destroyed. In a politicized, bureaucratized economy, those who operate the existing types of activities are much better able to protect themselves against the threat of new types of activities and new technologies. One of the operational advantages of a free enterprise system is that it does not internalize for the whole society the destruction of the old. The price paid for new technology is absorbed in individual elements in the society rather than the whole society.

In the Soviet Union creative destruction is limited by the bureaucracy; this is an important and difficult aspect of the whole process of technical change in the Soviet economy. In general, bureaucracies tend to possess a high degree of risk aversion and ability to protect themselves against the pains of change. This was true of the Tsarist bureaucracy; it is also true of the Soviet bureaucracy. Frequently, there appear men in leadership positions who are dynamic and who press for change—such a person, for example, is Dzhermin Gvishiani, the deputy director of the State Committee on Science and Technology. They are not, however, at the production level; thus, their influence is limited.

A final factor in the Soviet picture is that the Soviets have primarily imported foreign technology for domestic purposes rather than for exports which would have to be internationally competitive. Thus, once the new technology was in place, there was no pressure on those using it to keep it up to changing foreign levels, and the technology languished. An important element, then, in analyzing the current situation is the extent to which foreign companies have buy-back arrangements with the Soviets in which the foreign company agrees to buy back a share of output produced with the new technology, which it then markets in the West.

The technology transfer process is not a simple process. While it is true that the Soviets can import contemporary technology, often embodied in foreign capital equipment, it is not clear that they can operate this technology in the same way that it is operated abroad, nor is it clear that they can master the process of technology creation and renewal.

UNITED STATES INTERESTS

Although I am skeptical about the future mastery of technology by the Soviets, it is clear that in the short run they stand to gain a great deal from expanded economic relations with the United States. It is not so clear what we as a nation stand to gain. It would be nice to fall back on the market mechanism and say if something is privately profitable, it is socially desirable. Unfortunately, this is not necessarily true; as Marx might have said: "What is good for Occidental Petroleum is not necessarily good for the country."

What the United States stands to gain is debatable. Even the planned tripling of trade volume to $500 million or even one billion per year, it is argued, will only be on the order of 1 percent of total United States trade—approximately the level of trade with Spain and Switzerland. This can hardly have a significant aggregate effect. Yet, to put the matter briefly, I think it is in our interests to pursue expanded economic relations with the Soviets for economic and political reasons.

First of all, the expectation is that the United States will have a substantially favorable balance in expanded trade, and at the margin this will help our balance of payments. Second, even though we may not be getting goods we need from the Soviets, American businessmen will be making hard currency earnings which can be used, in normal economic channels, to purchase the goods and services we do need. Third, it is possible that in the longer run we could gain significant additions to our energy supplies from joint development of Soviet resources. Finally, there are the political issues and the issue of detente. While normalization of relations and increased economic relations do not guarantee peace between nations— as history clearly demonstrates—it can be argued that they increase the chances of peace.

This is perhaps especially true when an essential element of the economic relations involves international transfer of technology. The process of international transfer of technology is a people process. It will not be sufficient for the Russians to buy blueprints, machines or even turnkey plants. They will also have to import people who are familiar with the advanced pro-

cesses and who can help guide their implantation. Increased human contacts among Russian economic decision makers and engineers and American businessmen and technologists can contribute toward decreasing tension between the two countries; they might also make a modest contribution toward the opening up of Soviet society.

The Soviet desire for expanded economic relations within an atmosphere of detente makes possible a certain increase in our political bargaining strength vis-à-vis the Soviets. In the heat of the Mid-East crisis this may not have been readily apparent. However, in time, I think there will be agreement that Soviet behavior in this crisis was, to some extent, moderate.

In our economic relations with the Soviets we should be hard bargainers. We should pursue our own interests in economic issues and political ones. Yet, the commitment to detente should be preserved. It is in the interest of us all that this be done.

* * *

QUESTIONS AND ANSWERS

Q: Dr. Ivanov has indicated that dealings with any bureaucracy are essentially the same; thus, both the United States and the Soviet bureaucracies present the same problems for the businessman. The American businessman has been accustomed to dealing with primarily the military bureaucracy, in a way that allows him to come back and say: "Well, it cost me more than I thought it would. Would you please now reimburse me twice as much as I recently said?" I have serious doubts whether one could do that in the Soviet Union. I wonder if this is

the businessman's problem rather than merely dealing with bureaucracy.

My second question, Professor Levine, is: as an expert in economics, I'm sure you have the comparative figures for the second period GNP growth and labor-capital productivity of the United States and the Soviet Union. I would hope that you might share these figures with us.

A: I don't have the exact figures with me. However, my impression of the figures is that the rates of output growth are generally smaller in the United States than they are in the Soviet Union, although in 1972 and 1973 real growth in the United States was 6 percent per year. At the same time, the rates of input growth are also smaller—that is, our rate of growth of capital stock is nowhere near the size of that which the Soviets have. Therefore, my feeling is that the rate of growth of productivity exhibited by most Western nations in the recent period is quite a bit better than the rate of growth productivity in the Soviet Union.

As for your first question, let me take it in two parts: first, the bureaucracy; then, the cost plus. It's not sufficient to say that we all have bureaucracies. There is an essential difference: if I may use a Marxist phrase, there is a point at which quantitative difference changes into qualitative difference. That is, in the Soviet Union there is an all encompassing bureaucracy. Indeed, they claim that centralized decision making in the economy is their strength. General Motors is a big bureaucracy, but it still faces competition not only from internal producers, but from external producers. The companies, as big as they are in the United States, have to respond to this sort of competition. Therefore, the impact on technical change is quite a bit different from that to be found in the Soviet Union.

The government bureaucracy is another story. What is interesting is that in the defense field —where the government bureaucracy most clearly comes into the economy—in both the Soviet Union and the United States there is a fair amount —and many people fear an excessive amount—of technical change going on. This is one aspect of the Soviet scene where technical change does occur. There are many reasons for this, for example, priority allocations of men and materials. Also, it's one of those fields where, in a sense, the essence of the game is competition. No general is going to accept a horse-drawn cannon from producers on the grounds that it's the best damn horse-drawn cannon they've ever produced. The only sort of military equipment that's acceptable in the Soviet Union is that which is internationally competitive. On that ground, the two bureaucracies do well.

While I don't want to use the economists' line that everything is more complicated than it seems, cost-plus contracts, when the product is new technology, are not necessarily a kind of rape of the American public. The development of new materials and new methods is very hard to forecast. Thus, it is argued by people who look closely at the situation that if there were no cost plus, the government really wouldn't get the type of developments that it does get. Maybe the government shouldn't be getting those developments, but that's another issue.

I take it that your question is really one about the record of profitability: will the American company be able to make a profit with the Soviet Union, especially if the Soviet Union does not grant cost-plus contracts? This is an issue which the American companies are going to have to look at very carefully. The record of the '20s and '30s is a mixed one; in their dealings with the Soviet Union some companies made profits and a lot of companies did not.

Ultimately, I would argue that it is to the advantage of the Soviet Union to make sure that enough companies —that is, American and foreign companies—make profit, because in the long run they will not deal unless there's profit to be made. You may find that in the longer run the Soviet government will begin to make cost-plus contracts. These things are done if one wants the product being produced.

Q: Professor Levine came to the conclusion that trade and that MFN status would be in the self-interest of the United States. He has talked about gold, incentives, rewards and punishments and the fact that the Soviets would like to buy commodities and technology. However, if we look upon the fact that the Soviets are really architects of the Mid-East war, why should we reward them with MFN status and technology?

A: Let me speak directly to the issue which I think you're raising. I as an American Jew find that we are really not very sophisticated in our interpretation of world relations. We're not very sophisticated in our conception of the power client states have over the two great masters. The client states of both the United States and the Soviet Union do not dance to our bidding every time we bid; and the issues involved are really much less clear than many of us have tried to make them out to be.

I think there is no evidence whatsoever that the Soviet Union instituted the war. There is a great deal of evidence that the Soviet Union supplied arms to Egypt and Syria; we, also, supplied arms to Israel. This is the sort of action nations take under the pressure of war when they have client states which they wish to keep as client states. Indeed, our supplying Israel with arms during the war was the major factor allowing Israel to survive this crisis.

I would maintain that the situation in the Mid-East could have been more dangerous, both to Israel and

to world peace, without the possibility for the Soviets of economic advantages from detente. I think that in time most of us will come to agree that the behavior of the Soviet Union —given the pressures to which it could have responded—was rather moderate. The arming of Egypt and of Syria could have been much more destructive than it actually turned out to be.

Finally, there is absolutely nothing to gain in terms of improving the world situation and the situation in regard to Israel by cutting off relations with the Soviet Union. It may salve one's conscience and make one feel better or morally superior, but it doesn't help anyone. Quite the contrary, it would remove a possible source of leverage on Soviet policy.

Q: In his original remarks Professor Levine stated that there are, from the American point of view, political factors involved in attempting to establish closer trade relations with the Soviet Union in our very dangerous world. Also, as Professor Levine pointed out, the continuing increase in trade would tend to strengthen the present system in the Soviet Union and would eventually make the Soviet Union stronger in the world. In view of these facts, do we not have a moral and political obligation to encourage the Soviet government to develop a more humane approach toward its own people? Also, do we not have a political obligation to come to some sort of general understanding with the Soviet Union that they will not follow policies such as they might be following in the Middle East—policies which may even give them economic advantages, such as increasing the price of oil, and which may create serious political and economic problems for the United States?

A: These moral questions have been coming up, especially among the American left and American liberals. In terms of humane treatment of citizens within the Soviet Union, let me say that economic relations are only one part of an overall picture. One policy issue does not guarantee the achievement of all objectives. One has to work with a whole policy composed of many different elements.

I would like to make an observation: in terms of attitudes towards the Soviet Union we have come almost full-circle. Conservatives in the United States are now advocating closer relations, while liberals are holding out on grounds of differences of political systems, human rights and the way in which dissidents are being treated in the Soviet Union. I see this as part of a problem for those of us who work in this area, especially for those of us who take the position strongly favoring the development of economic relations. I must say that I see these issues as moral agonies. However, I think that we have learned one thing: we cannot control the entire world. We do have moral responsibilities, we do our bit and we try to help, but we do not have total power in these regards.

Soviet-American Economic Cooperation: Recent Development, Prospects and Problems

By Ivan D. Ivanov

ABSTRACT: The summit meetings between Secretary General Leonid I. Breznev and President Richard M. Nixon, *inter alia,* broke the economic isolation which existed between the USSR and the USA. The turnover in trade rose to $642 million in 1972 and to approximately $1.5 billion in 1973. This growth in trade reflects, without doubt, the economic potentialities of, as well as the wide scope for, mutual economic complementarity between the two countries. Interesting joint undertakings are already in sight. Yet, the primary problem of the future is the normalization of trade policy. The USSR cannot afford to pay a political price for normalization of trade. The fact that the USSR has not been extended most favored nation (MFN) treatment and difficulties in credit arrangements through Eximbank have put the Soviet Union in an inferior position in the United States market. Should this situation continue long enough, adjustments to real market conditions will appear to be necessary in US-USSR trade and the lend-lease package.

Ivan D. Ivanov has been Chief of the Economic Division at the Institute of United States Studies of the Soviet Academy of Sciences in Moscow since 1971. He was Economic Affairs Officer and First Research Officer to the United Nations Conference on Trade and Development during 1966 to 1971. Dr. Ivanov is author of The Common Market and the Competition between Two Economic and Social Systems, Decision-Making Process in Respect to Imports in the Socialist Countries of Eastern Europe, USA: R and D Management in Manufacturing Corporations *and of other books and articles.*

SOVIET economists have always paid due attention to the benefits embodied in the international division of labor. Moreover, we have always considered foreign trade to be very instrumental in promoting peaceful and good neighborly relations with other nations. From the very beginning these two essential issues were especially stressed by the founder of our socialist state, Vladimir I. Lenin. Accordingly, this position has determined all our subsequent foreign economic policy, including that toward the United States. For this reason, the interstate documents—which resulted from the last summits between the secretary general of the Communist Party of the Soviet Union (CPSU), Leonid I. Brezhnev, and the president of the United States, Richard M. Nixon—assign our mutual economic cooperation a most significant role within the entire complex of Soviet-American relations.

This meeting is attended by many well-known American economists, including those dealing professionally with foreign trade. Thus, this seems to be the right place to discuss the recent development in Soviet-American trade, particularly in view of the fact that there have been some remarkable achievements—while certain problems still remain unsettled—in this important domain.

FROM MARGINAL DEALS TOWARDS A LARGE SCALE ECONOMIC COOPERATION

The summit meetings, *inter alia,* broke the economic isolation which existed between our two countries through triggering a powerful impulse for the expansion of Soviet-American trade. From $200 million three years ago, the turnover in trade rose to $642 million in 1972 and to approximately $1.5 billion in 1973. This certainly constitutes one of the most rapid increases in any bilateral trade throughout the entire world market. This growth in trade reflects, without any doubt, the huge economic potentialities of, as well as the wide scope for, mutual economic complementarity between the two countries. In 1973 the United States took second place among our Western trade partners.

Indeed, even in its formative stage the US-USSR trade showed some very characteristic features: we dealt with rather big projects, even for the world-market scale. The Kama River Track Plant (KAMAZ) Procurement Commission, for example, managed to place orders amounting to about $220 million with several dozen United States corporations. Caterpillar Tractor was awarded with orders of up to $150 million; Monsanto, $100 million; Cross and International Harvester, both about $70 million. While being a big buyer, the USSR has been, at the same time, a major source of diamonds, palladium, platinum and even oil products for the United States economy.

Currently, however, we are going further than single transactions—whatever importance they may continue to have—and looking forward to establishing large scale and stable economic cooperation with foreign countries, including the United States, on a long term basis. To this end, the traditional ways and means of trading have been supplemented, step by step, with new, nontraditional arrangements based mainly on the internationalization in production and in research and development (R and D). For instance, joint investment schemes—shaped as export oriented, as far as the foreign partner is financially involved—

have been devised. The tapping of our oil, gas, potash, asbestos, timber, ores and other resources and the manufacturing of wood products, pulp and paper is proceeding with the participation of the Council of Mutual Economic Assistance (CMEA) and with French, West German, United States, Japanese and Italian business interests. Also, declarations of intentions were announced with two groups of United States interests pledging to share in the construction of the western Siberia-Murmansk and Jakutsk-Pacific long distance gas pipelines—with a view to export part of this gas to the United States. Preliminary contacts also took place with Atlantic Richfield, offering a collaboration in the development of the Sakhalin Shelf oil and gas resources.

The compensation deals appear to be instrumental, too. In these agreements machinery and technology provided by foreign partners are to be repaid in kind—including the products originating from the enterprise concerned. In addition to the well-known Hammer deal—which covered the exchange of chemical equipment for basic chemicals—the agreements with Monsanto and Lummus might be mentioned. In this case the payments for the polystyrene plant are to be made in raw materials and chemicals. Similar offers were tabled in General Tire, Boeing, PPG, Uniroyal, Kaiser and Gleasson.

Cooperation in R and D is growing even more quickly than it is in trade, both on intergovernmental and enterprise-to-enterprise levels. General Electric, Occidental Petroleum, ITT, Boeing, General Dynamics, Singer, Stanford Research Institute, Monsanto, Control Data, Brown and Root and others are our partners in a number of very promising joint projects already agreed upon, as well as in the exchange of information and experts. Thus, the facts are in favor of those who trust in the opportunities of Soviet-American economic cooperation as a whole and, particularly, in large scale collaborations. These targets, however, can hardly be assessed as a ceiling.

THE SOVIET ECONOMY: PROSPECTS UNTIL 1990 AND THEIR FOREIGN TRADE IMPLICATIONS

It is well known that for decades the environment for our foreign trade was rather hostile, thus forcing us to trade only far below our desires and potentialities. Any other, broader orientation towards foreign markets in our planning was not duly reliable to achieve our economic goals. However, things are moving. Today, the economy of the USSR—and of the world socialist system as a whole—has become powerful enough, and detente wide enough, to induce us to manage our economy as more and more open. In fact, we never were partisans of an isolationism or an autarky.

Within the CMEA, enjoying the socialist environment conducive to cooperation, the USSR commits itself to the most sophisticated form of international division of labor and economic complementarity—including complex, socialist economic integration. Some advanced forms have recently started to be used in our economic relations, both with developing, and with some developed, market economies. We are now trading with one hundred six countries around the world, and we have intergovernmental trade agreements in force with eighty-five of them. Soviet foreign trade, now truly worldwide and globally oriented, plays an important role in our national economic growth as a whole. As statistics show, during the last three consecutive five-year-plan spans our foreign trade turnover has risen faster than the gross national product (GNP) and, moreover, in 1971 to 1973 even faster than was originally planned—12 percent and 6 percent per annum. In 1973 it almost reached the 1975 planned level.

The growth in foreign trade has led to some far-reaching structural adjustments and to the emergence of trade-oriented sectors in the national economy—processing imports and producing exports. World markets are now the source of a wide range of products—such as rubber, wool, cotton, hides and skins, some nonferrous metals, tropical foods, tobacco, machinery and consumer goods—and technology which, for various reasons, are unavailable, scarce or unprofitable to produce at home. Furthermore, these products are assigned not merely to bridge temporary gaps in supply as was the case previously, but to supplement and even to replace domestic production if the imports are superior in terms of cost and quality. In supplying the Soviet far east and far north with basic products—such as grain, fruits and vegetables, salt, consumer goods, wines and spirits, fishing nets and trucks—there has also been a partial shift from costly transporting of these items from the central part of the country to importing them. At the same time, national plans allocate noticeable investments in setting up some extra, export-oriented capacities in both industry and agriculture. Exports represent a growing business for many well-known Soviet enterprises, such as Electrosila—generators—VEF—radios, telephones—AZLH, VAZ—automobiles. The export quota is particularly high in the mining, refining, timber, autotractor and machinery industries (see table 1).

In April 1973 the plenary session of the CPSU Central Committee drew the attention of planners to the necessity and advantages of strengthening the role of foreign trade in the Soviet economy. Relevant recommendations are under implementation now, including those

TABLE 1

FOREIGN TRADE-ORIENTED SECTORS WITHIN THE
SOVIET ECONOMY, 1971

EXPORTS AS PERCENT OF DOMESTIC PRODUCTION		IMPORTS AS PERCENT OF DOMESTIC CONSUMPTION	
Cameras	31	Oranges	60
Automobiles	29	Passenger carriages	45
Cotton	23	Tea	23
Newsprint	22	Rice	15
Oil	19	Electric locomotives	15
Iron ore	18	Cigarettes	14
Cardboards	18	Autobuses	13
Plywood	13	Cotton	12
Cycles	12	Steel pipes	11
Autograders	11	Soda	9–11
Paper	11	Footwear	10
		Motorcycles, scooters	10

connected with the recent shaping of the *General Perspective for the Development of the Soviet Economy for 1976 to 1990*. This perspective is still not expressed in definite figures. However, the foreign economic guidelines in its draft may be traced, to a large extent, with certitude. They are directly determined by the principal long term goals adopted by the Twenty-fourth CPSU Congress—namely, ensuring an intensive, rapid and balanced pattern of economic growth in the USSR; rapid technological progress; and, on this solid foundation, a steady improvement in the standard of living of the Soviet people.

In particular, Soviet economists suggest, for the period of 1976 to 1990, the following: (1) a growth of foreign trade surpassing that of GNP; (2) expansion of export specialization in the most advanced industries; (3) evaluation of new products and technology in comparison with world market requirements; (4) taking a major place in the world research-intensive exports; (5) assessment of imports as an alternative, while making decisions on domestic investment; (6) structural adjustments in the economy and assigning a larger share in expansion and modernization to imports; (7) incorporation of international exchange into technology and R and D plans and programs.

Under these circumstances, one may see new, promising opportunities for further enriching US-USSR cooperation through a cluster of traditional and nontraditional ways and means. For example, the United States is already the major outlet for our export of technology. Reynolds Metals and Kaiser have purchased licenses for pouring aluminum in electromagnetic field and processing aluminum oxide; Andko, for cooling furnaces; American Magnesium, for a method of magnesium extraction. We anticipate that our agreements on scientific and technological cooperation will also eventually generate commercial outcomes.

Some very interesting joint innovations are already in sight. For example, the Soviet institutions have made good progress with General Electric in blueprinting a high-power gas turbine, gas turbine locomotives, compressors and uranium enrichment; with Singer in developing textile machinery; and, with Armco Steel in designing drilling rigs. The Soviet foreign trade organizations cooperate with some well-established United States traders in marketing our products in the United States: Pepsico is in charge of marketing Soviet wines and spirits; Satra, of tractors; Patent Management and Williams of technology.

It is also important to note that Soviet-American trade is not necessarily a zone reserved exclusively for large corporations; we are also ready to deal with medium and small businesses. The possibility of our involving smaller firms in venture-capital arrangements is now under consideration. "Tiny Toms" may also be dynamic and technologically advanced—for example, Energy Science in the Boston area is taking care of sales of our ion-beam technology.

The USSR Ministry of Foreign Trade has announced our readiness to enter into joint patenting and licensing operations with American corporations—as well as into a variety of other long term business arrangement in third countries. The Soviet foreign trade organizations, considering American multinationals as a reality, are dealing with both their domestic headquarters and their foreign affiliates. The trade center, now being designed, is aimed to house more foreign business representations in Moscow.

Learning from my recent talks with United States businessmen, I may easily forestall the question of whether we are ready to allow the setting up of Soviet-American joint ventures within the Soviet Union. We know, of course, that these are a favorite way for United States business to operate abroad. Economists are studying the relevant experience. It would still be premature to suggest any definite formulas. However, we hope that this experience is multifaceted enough so that we may try to select or to shape certain techniques able to conform both to planned, socialist economy and foreign interests—even without giving them traditional portfolio control.

Summing up, the prospects and opportunities for cooperation are evident. Many United States corporations are very strong in economic and financial terms; many of them are technological leaders in the world. However, the further progress in Soviet-American economic cooperation depends heavily not only upon the objectives mentioned above and on the intentions of our business associates, but also upon the United States pursuing the normalization of the trade policy treatment now applied to the Soviet Union. Indeed, the recent situation here is rather complicated and vague.

THE PRIMARY PROBLEM: ACCOMPLISHING NORMALIZATION

You are surely well informed about the opposition still in force within the United States Congress against the ratification of the Soviet-American trade agreement. As a result, the USSR currently finds itself in a quite inferior position within the US market. We are still refused most favored nation (MFN) treatment, which the US extends to almost all of its other trade partners. Furthermore, there are some attempts to strip US-USSR trade of state credit support.

We regret that these decisions, which are purely politically motivated, create only artificial barriers to a further expansion of our mutual trade—and, one may add, not only to trade. In fact, we find ourselves pressed to pay a political price, even in the form of intervention into our domestic affairs, for trade normalization. We cannot afford such a linkage. It would be against the fundamentals of our sovereignty, as well as against the principles which the USSR and the USA agreed should govern our interstate relations. Thus, these trade policy issues are not merely purely commercial ones. They have become an important element in the very core of recent Soviet-American relations as a whole, a touchstone of the good will we need so much in order to further our historic efforts. For this reason, the trade policy issues—should they be normalized—could serve as one small step for the law, one giant leap for mutual confidence. Otherwise, there will be a victory for those who are intentionally trying to push history counterclockwise.

Turning back to trade itself, one may see that most of the damage has resulted from the inferior custom and credit treatment which is focused, first of all, in the diminishing opportunities for a diversification of Soviet exports, as well as in the fact that the support for large scale Soviet orders has been placed with Eximbank. It is no secret that the recent US-USSR trade turnover is in disequilibrium, with an abnormally large deficit for the USSR.

In a situation such as this we find ourselves invited to improve your balance of payments either through a deterioration in our own or through the transfer of our export proceeds from other countries to the United States. Under recent international monetary conditions these alternatives are rather impossible. In addition, for the time being we shall need some extra money to clean our recent debts with American corporations. Our exports—and only the exports to the United States—are the source to settle these odds. This implies, consequently, equal competitive opportunities for our goods, simply because one can never be competitive while paying 50 to 100 percent higher duties than one's rivals.

There are some opinions that the USSR may be lucky even without MFN treatment, because our exports consist of raw materials—which are either only moderately charged or duty-free. However, such a narrow exports composition is partly the result of discriminatory custom treatment, itself, hampering efforts to diversify our counter. For example, a lot has been done in the USSR to fit our research-intensive products—such as airplanes, helicopters, tractors, generators, transformers, machine tools, equipment for rolling mills, nuclear power stations, long distance energy transmission, compact automobiles, cameras and chemicals—to American requirements. Moreover, for the time being we are going to balance our trade with the United States noticeably with manufactures. However, the custom duties on the bulk of them is still rather prohibitive. The various nontraditional business arrangements are also sensitive to custom treatment, as far as they imply a mutual exchange in products or semimanufactures.

The detrimental effect of withdrawing state credit support is evident, because today about 90 percent of equipment is being sold on credit terms—which weigh heavily in competition. Consequently, the prospects for some large contracts agreed upon on the private level have proved to be uncertain. For instance, a $100 million petrochemical plant contract recently signed by Monsanto, Lummus and the Soviet Techmashimport is still under question because Eximbank has not given any commitment for $20 million direct credit and the guarantee for an additional $20 million to be financed from private funds.

One need not be a prophet to see that should this situation continue long enough, adjustments to real market conditions will appear to be necessary in US-USSR trade and the lend-lease package. While the United States is our major trade partner, it is only one among many partners, and our procurement activity will naturally tend to be concentrated in easier-to-sell and cheaper-to-buy areas. In view of this, some additional opportunities may emerge for business interests from other countries with more favorable trade regimes, and they are not sleepy.

Japan, for example, has already offered its own project for tapping the Sakhalin Shelf resources and is even ready to bid for the American share of the Tumen-Pacific oil pipeline. Tompson of France and Selenia of Italy are bidding against IBM and Reytheon for navigation equipment tender. Moreover, some United States corporations now transfer Soviet orders to their affiliates abroad, with a view to making the payments easier. Amtel signed a $110 million contract in French francs to be performed by its French subsidiary, Litwin. American Chain and Cable will supply KAMAZ with conveyers from its affiliate Fata in Italy, under credit arrangements in lire financed by Institute Mobil-iare Italiano at the interest rate of only 5.95 percent.

These are some of the principal problems we are now facing in Soviet-American trade. My interpretation was probably a provoking one, but only for the reason that it was my genuine desire to discuss the issues in the most unequivocal and constructive way possible at this high level professional forum. My intent was to contribute positively to a further improvement in Soviet-American relations—which are a matter of utmost importance for all of us and for the entire world.

* * *

QUESTIONS AND ANSWERS

Q: I am addressing my question to both speakers. Is it in the interest of the United States and international relations that Congress is trying to attach the issue of Jewish immigration from the Soviet Union to the trade bill?

A: I may only repeat what I have said. From our point of view the problem of immigration and the problem of trade are quite different and not relevant to each other. You know that the United States Congress is trying to merge these problems, to establish a sort of linkage between them. I think of trade as trade and of immigration as immigration. In this context such a linkage seems to me both artificial and politically motivated. Such a linkage will prevent further expansion of our trade relations—that is, it will only damage our trade relations.

A (Levine): I'd like to respond briefly to the question. On principle I do not object to tying political issues to trade issues. I think the argument which is generally made in the United States is that on certain issues there is no *quid pro quo*, and MFN is one of them. Since—as Dr. Ivanov has stated—the Soviet system is different and the Soviet government controls Soviet trade, the mutual granting of MFN has no meaning. I think other arguments can be made that we should look for some additional benefits in our relations with the Soviet Union. However, I object, specifically, to the Jackson Amendment, and other types of amendments like it, in that it is not the sort of tactics which I think will get any payoffs.

One of the things that economists bring to policy making is the whole question of opportunity cost. That is, when making decisions one decides not only to do a, but to give up b. I think that we should constantly pressure the Soviet leaders in our dealings with them. However, we should do so quietly, not openly—

especially if the situation is one in which they find it almost impossible to respond to the pressure. Since there are some advantages for the Soviet Union in economic relations with the United States, I think less open pressure can be effective. However, if political behavior is such that the American political scene is deeply affected, then, it's going to be very difficult to maintain economic relations in the way that they have been developing. What I am arguing for is a subtle handling of political issues rather than the sort of blunderbuss approach which destroys whatever leverage we can get over Soviet policy.

The Future of Soviet-American Diplomacy

By ANATOLY A. GROMYKO

ABSTRACT: An attempt to give a reply to the question of the possible directions which the development of Soviet-American diplomacy may take must incorporate a consideration of both objective and subjective factors. If the subjective efforts of individuals, especially those forming foreign policy, do not contradict the main, positive trends in the development of international affairs—which are determined by objective factors—then the relations among states will develop more or less smoothly. In the sphere of Soviet-American relations, at least one thing is clear: the competition between the USSR and the USA should be carried out only through peaceful means. The Moscow and Washington meetings are a significant step in the transition to an era of negotiation; detente is explained by the substance of the Moscow and Washington documents adopted at the highest level. Furthermore, the basic notion of detente, as seen in the Soviet Union, is that it is a process of relaxation of tension and peaceful coexistence. The scientific and technological revolution will have a profound impact on this process. While it is difficult to predict the possible lines and forms of the international effort in conditions of this revolution, one thing is quite clear: the lines and forms of international cooperation will steadily gain in scope and diversity.

Anatoly A. Gromyko is Minister-Counselor of the Embassy of the Union of Soviet Socialist Republics. He was Academic Researcher for the Institute of USA in Moscow between 1968 and 1973 and for the Institute of Africa between 1966 and 1968. Dr. Gromyko is the author of numerous books and articles on international relations, United States foreign policy and Soviet-American relations, including 1036 Days of President Kennedy, Africa in International Relations and USSR-USA: Relations Today.

I GUESS you will agree that it is impossible to embrace the unembraceable. Similarly, it is not an easy task to analyze—even in general terms—the possible ways, the future of the development of Soviet-American diplomacy. However, some of the points related to the subject under discussion not only might be analyzed, they must be. They, in my opinion, are of significant interest to us all.

OBJECTIVE FACTORS AND SUBJECTIVE FORCES

To a great extent the state of possible ways of development in international relations depends on the understanding of these ways by the responsible personalities in politics and science, both in the Soviet Union and in the United States. It is clear to all of us that the state of the international climate in the '70s in which Soviet-American interaction develops is dependent not only on objective factors, but also on the direction to be taken by certain subjective forces which influence this climate. Thus, I have already raised the question of an interplay of objective factors and subjective forces and their combined influence on international relations and Soviet-American diplomacy. This question is, I think, an integral part of the subject under discussion.

What are the objective factors which determine international relations and Soviet-American dialogue today? I believe that objective factors are related to the laws of development of human society. It is easy to agree with such a view, unless one does not believe that such laws actually exist. In that case, what makes the world go round? Is it the biological nature of the human being, or is it the power struggle in all of its manifestations? As I see it, it is neither the former nor the latter.

There are men who reject the natural laws of the development of human society. They usually take history to be a pile of casual circumstances, a confrontation of abstract notions of good and evil. They may feel, also, that history is molded by great personalities or heroes. In fact, this school of politicians and thinkers disregards the decisive role which objective factors play in the development of international relations. Moreover, this school declares that a philosophy which accepts the validity of natural laws in the development of international relations is unscientific.

One may well inquire what is meant by the objective factors in terms of their decisive influence upon the development of international relations. I will mention only a few: (1) profound contradictions between socialism and capitalism; (2) class struggle, which leaves a clear imprint on international life, as well; (3) struggle of the forces of the national liberation movement against policies of colonialism and neocolonialism; (4) balance of power between the USSR and the USA; (5) the nature of a nuclear war; (6) the impact of science and technology on international relations. Some of these factors, in their turn, are deeply rooted in one common problem which boils down to the following questions: (1) who is the owner of the means of production in a certain society; (2) what is the pattern of social relationships and relations among people; (3) in what way is wealth distributed; (4) in whose hands are the reins of power?

As is well known, the socialist and the capitalist systems give opposite answers to these questions. This is the reality of our days. and it may be observed by all. For this reason all kinds of theories—including those based on ideas of scientific and technological progress—of a convergence of the two systems are distinctly unscientific. One can neither reconcile the irreconcilable nor mix water and fire together. Due to this, it seems to me, any diplomacy which strives to achieve convergence of opposite social structures would end in failure. This does not mean, of course, that both opposite political and social structures cannot learn from each other, borrowing some experience in specific fields. However, there are clear-cut limits in such interaction which are set by the nature of the systems.

Let us go back, however, to the question of factors determining the development of international relations. The objective factors certainly are not the cause of all events; if they were, we would all have to become fatalists. These events are in their turn greatly influenced by subjective factors connected with activities of individuals or a group of individuals. If their subjective efforts do not contradict the main, positive trends in the development of international relations, which are determined by objective factors, then the relations among states will develop more or less smoothly. If, on the other hand, subjective actions go counter to the objective course of such a development process, then the temperature of the political climate of our planet will rise abruptly. Unwarranted conflicts will break out and dangerous crises will emerge.

Among the factors which influence the development of Soviet-American relations, one may cite the following: the balance of power existing between the Soviet Union and the United States of America. The balance of military might, as well as the influence of scientific and technological progress on the foreign policies of states, plays an especially great role in this complex. I am firmly convinced that the future development of Soviet-American relations will be influenced by the above-mentioned, very complicated factors—as well as, probably, by other objective factors.

An attempt to give a reply to the question about the possible directions of this development and the state of Soviet-American diplomacy is, of course, quite another matter. What new shapes might both the cooperation and the competition between states, such as the USSR and the USA, take? These are all very complex questions; naturally, I do not have the intention of giving comprehensive answers to them. Therefore, I will confine myself to expressing general considerations only.

At least one thing is clear: the competition between the USSR and the USA should be carried out only through peaceful means. It is the historic task of Soviet-American diplomacy to see that the shape of future interaction between our countries is governed by this very aim. The alternative is war. If wars are not once and for all excluded from the life of society, many cities and many people dear to us may burn in the conflagration. Who needs that? Who also needs local wars, which are hideous in nature, where naked force substitutes for reason? A particularly menacing alternative to peace is a nuclear war which, as a means of waging struggle, should be absolutely precluded from international life. The foreign policies of all states in the '70s and in the more distant future should be aimed at settling international disputes through negotiation, not through the use of arms. In this respect, both diplomacies should not waver, either today or in the future.

The great powers, however, must not settle international disputes at the expense of the interests of small countries. Such is precisely the policy of the Soviet government. Such is precisely the thrust of the Program of Peace and International Cooperation set forth by the Twenty-fourth Congress of the Communist Party of the Soviet Union (CPSU).[1] It is gratifying that many of the tasks set in this program have already been achieved. The process of invigorating international relations has gained momentum.

There is a considerable improvement of relations in Europe, where the results of World War II have been codified. There has been a substantial improvement in Soviet-American relations. The problem of limiting the strategic offensive arms race has been solved, if only on a temporary basis. An important conference on the problems of European security is taking place. The Cold War is gradually receding into the past. The policy of peaceful coexistence finds more and more advocates, and many worn-out cliches marring relations between the United States and the Soviet Union are being smashed. However, one may easily notice that there are still not a few opportunists who oppose the relaxation of tension and eagerly try to breathe new life into the old, Cold War witch.

Lasting peace today is not merely a phantom; its outline is becoming more and more visible. This outline became clearer after the historic results of the Moscow talks between

Soviet leaders and President Richard Nixon and the highly successful visit of General Secretary Leonid I. Brezhnev to the United States in June 1973.[2]

THE SIGNIFICANCE OF THE MOSCOW AND WASHINGTON MEETINGS

The Moscow and Washington meetings have become a significant step in the transition from an era of confrontation to an era of negotiation. The talks have graphically shown that, despite the differences between the social systems, improvement of relations between the Soviet Union and the United States is possible. The results of the talks dealt a mighty blow to those who, for a long period of time, have been anticipating the fruitless outcome of the Soviet-American summit.

For example, consider the concrete results of the negotiations in Moscow—that is, the agreements which the world press termed the "Moscow cascade." It is appropriate to begin with the document entitled "The Basic Principles of Mutual Relations between the Union of Soviet Socialist Republics and the United States of America." This far-reaching document formulates the essence of the international legal principles of relations between the two states. It is a sort of guiding star for the diplomacy of both countries. First of all, it sets forth the principle of peaceful coexistence of

1. See, *Materials of the Twenty-fourth Congress of the Communist Party of the Soviet Union* (Moscow: Publishers of Political Literature, 1971), pp. 23–30 and 191–196.

2. See, for instance, "Joint USSR-US Communique" and "Agreement between the Union of Soviet Socialist Republics and the United States of America on the Prevention Nuclear War," in *Second Round of USSR-USA Summit Talks: Main Documents of Leonid I. Brezhnev's Visit to the USA, June 18–25, 1973* (Reprints from the Soviet Press, 16, no. 13, 29 June 1973).

states belonging to different social systems. The fact that the Leninist idea of peaceful coexistence has been given juridical recognition in agreements on relations between states can truly be regarded as a sign of the times, an important result of the changes taking place in the world.

In general, one can say that this is a basic document specifying, in the precise terms of international law, the change from any Cold War manifestations—including the positions-of-strength policy and the vying for military superiority—to the relations of peaceful coexistence and mutually beneficial cooperation. Both sides agreed that:

They will proceed from the common determination that in the nuclear age there is no alternative to conducting their mutual relations on the basis of peaceful coexistence. Differences in ideology and in the social systems of the USSR and the USA are not obstacles to the bilateral development of normal relations based on the principles of sovereignty, equality, noninterference in internal affairs and mutual advantage.[3]

Another clause in the "Basic Principles of Mutual Relations" states that the USSR and the USA attach major importance to "preventing the development of situations capable of causing a dangerous exacerbation of their relations. Therefore, they will do their utmost to avoid military confrontations and to prevent the outbreak of nuclear war."[4] It was also agreed that differences between the two states should be settled by peaceful means through negotiations which would be conducted in the spirit of reciprocity, mutual accommodation and mutual benefit.

An important feature of the document signed in Moscow on the basic principles of mutual relations between the USA and the USSR is that both sides expressed their will, and agreed on appropriate means, to ensure that the main provisions of this document do not remain mere words. With this in view, the USSR and the USA expressed their intent to "widen the juridical basis of their mutual relations and to exert the necessary efforts so that bilateral agreements which they have concluded and the multilateral treaties and agreements to which they are jointly parties are faithfully implemented."[5] They stated their readiness to continue the practice of exchanging views on problems of mutual interest, including the exchange of such views at summit meetings. Both sides also expressed themselves in favor of promoting fruitful contacts between representatives of the legislative bodies of the two states. Indeed, the document of "The Basic Principles of Mutual Relations between the USSR and the USA" provided for extending old channels and developing new mechanisms in Soviet-American relations.

The principle of peaceful coexistence is now recognized by many as the main basis of relations between the socialist and capitalist systems. The world is turning gradually, although with some difficulty, from a long period of tension towards peace and businesslike cooperation. International crises sometimes erupt; however, as the general secretary of the Central Committee of the

3. "Basic Principles of Mutual Relations between the Union of Soviet Socialist Republics and the United States of America," in *USSR: Peace Program in Action: On the Results of Soviet-American Talks* (Moscow: Novosty Press Agency Publishing House, 1972), p. 15.

4. Ibid.

5. Ibid.

CPSU, Leonid Brezhnev, recently pointed out: "It is our basic conviction . . . that the major tendency in the development of modern international relations is the current turn from 'cold war' . . . to detente, from military confrontation . . . to the strengthening of security, to peaceful cooperation."[6] The agreements between the USSR and the USA concluded in Moscow and in Washington, especially the agreement on the prevention of nuclear war, signify major contributions to the development of that tendency. Thus, Soviet-American relations have every high-level-diplomacy prospect of growing from undeveloped, unstable relations into mature relations built on a firm and long term basis.

The results of the Moscow and Washington talks and the documents approved have a positive impact on international relations. In my opinion, they are also influencing the future of Soviet-American diplomacy in the most favorable fashion. Such results are very important for bilateral relations between our countries.

This is very important, indeed, because it is precisely the bilateral relations between the USSR and the USA which have stayed underdeveloped for a long time, especially in the economic field. In the past, Soviet-American negotiations were conducted mainly on international problems, not on the problems of bilateral relations. The negotiations on international problems are, of course, necessary if the world role of the two countries is to be taken into account. Today, however, we have reached the stage at which efforts to develop relations between the two countries, themselves, should be part of such negotiation. Such efforts

will help lay a more solid groundwork for interaction or, at least, will make it less delicate. This, in turn, will help cement the international structure, where destabilizing factors are numerous enough.

WHAT IS DETENTE?

For the present and future Soviet-American diplomacy, it is very important to have a clear understanding of the nature of detente. In our evaluations we proceed from the belief that our two countries—the most powerful on the globe, capable of eliminating life itself—find themselves in the situation, created by the logic of objective developments, in which there are no alternatives to peaceful coexistence or, as your president said some time ago: "We must either live together, or we will all die together."[7] This is a realistic statement, although one may differ on the survival issue—that is, on the possibilities of this or that country to function.

At the same time, we never believed that our relations—which exist only because they are objectively necessary—will become a sort of perfect accord or entente. As I have already mentioned, we represent different—or even opposing—social systems and hold different views on many issues. We live in a complex, changing world; we have our own friends and allies whose interests we must always take into consideration.

It is a pity, but some persons in merely noticing that the United States and the Soviet Union have taken a different or an opposing stand on a certain issue almost eagerly declare that the Soviet-

6. *Pravda*, 27 October 1973.

7. Presidential press conference of 25 February 1973, *Congressional Quarterly Weekly Report* 32, no.9, p. 556.

American detente did not pass the test. This is either wishful thinking or—and I say this in sorrow—quite often a deliberate attempt to mystify public opinion in a rather unsophisticated way. Frankly speaking, however, it is impossible to mystify any public on the question of whether the policy of confrontation or that of relaxation of tension with another nuclear power is in their interest. They will always choose the latter.

We also recognize that some subjective factors—for example, selfish needs of certain interest groups or personal ambitions of politicians—can deter and hinder the process of relaxation of tension. Certain minor setbacks in various fields are possible. Still, the question is: should we be totally desperate even if we allow them to happen? The answer is: no, we should not.

Of importance, among other things, is the clarification of the misconceptions regarding the so-called detente. One may sometimes feel that many people talk about completely different things while calling them by the same name, detente. The ambiguity of this word stems not only from its origin—it is neither an English nor a Russian word—but from intentional interpretations of it. Some people put forward "a narrowed conception of detente"; some, "humanitarian detente." Again, certain Americans talk about "the price of detente."

We think that detente is explained by the substance of the Moscow and Washington documents adopted at the highest level. One has only to read them in order to understand the real meaning of detente. It is a must for those who are trying to explain what detente is.

We in the Soviet Union do not use this word. We always talk about peaceful coexistence, the relaxation of international tensions or, in a definite way, the relaxation of tensions in Soviet-American relations and their further improvement. Thus, our basic notion of the so-called detente is that it is a process of relaxation of tension, not an accomplished phenomenon or an entity which has already taken shape. We do not passively admire it; nor, at any given moment do we hysterically and, at the same time, rather monotonously declare that it has broken up, as if it were some crystal chandelier which has already fallen to the floor and broken into a thousand pieces.

The relaxation of tension between the US and USSR is, first of all, the mutual agreement to avoid war, especially nuclear war. It is a recognition of the inevitability of peaceful coexistence between the two countries. At the same time, this is a first and very important stage in the process of strengthening cooperation and friendship and developing economic, cultural, scientific and other ties between the two nations. In a way, it is a constant uphill process without, probably, definite limit. Furthermore, we want this process to become irreversible.

Thus, the misconceptions about putting detente to the test reflect a simplified understanding of the whole idea of detente. At best, one can test by words or deeds only certain stages of detente; however, I doubt the wisdom of such tests, if detente is a mutual recognition to live in peace.

One often hears arguments to the effect that detente is a kind of tactical invention of Moscow, and fear is expressed that the United States can become a hostage of the Soviets if America goes the full way in cooperating with Russia. This is nonsense, of course. On our side, it is not a tactical maneuver. Peaceful coexistence is one of the pillars of our foreign policy.

There is another noticeable misconception so far as the improvement of US-USSR relations is concerned. It deals with the so-called price of detente which the USSR must allegedly pay. This price is usually connected with the internal affairs of our country. Those people who are demanding a price from the Soviet Union are, in fact, against the good feeling and friendship between our two nations; they are trying to put a price tag on peaceful life for both American and Soviet people—in other words, on their own peaceful survival.

As I have already mentioned, this is a futile effort. Fortunately enough, the political philosophy of political figures who shape the present developments of Soviet-American relations has nothing to do with a bazaar-level of thinking. So, to a large extent, the future of Soviet-American relations depends upon whether diplomacy will be able to withstand the corroding ideas of some detrimental unprofessional—in a diplomatic sense—propaganda approaches. We are of an opinion that it can, and will.

SCIENTIFIC AND TECHNOLOGICAL REVOLUTION AND ITS EFFECT ON SOVIET-AMERICAN DIPLOMACY

In recent years the scientific and technological revolution and its political, economic and social consequences have attracted the close attention of scientists in various countries. The influence of this revolution is being intensively studied, with good reason. The scientific and technological revolution is an active process not limited to one or two

important scientific and technical discoveries or inventions—as were, for instance, the invention of the steam engine or the practical use of electricity. Today, when important new developments and discoveries appear in science and technology on a steadily increasing scale, we have a qualitatively different situation.

Consequently, the scientific and technological revolution is not a one-time event; it is a dynamic process which has—not only today, but also tomorrow and, probably, to an ever growing extent—an immense effect on all aspects of human life, including politics, diplomacy and the entire system of present-day international relations. Without analyzing, to some extent, the influence of the scientific and technological revolution on international relations, we cannot grasp the complex picture of our times. Furthermore, we will not be able to identify either the new opportunities open to the states of the world—including the USSR and the USA—for establishing good neighborly relations or the hazards which, at the same time, the scientific and technological revolution may spell.

The scientific and technological revolution is changing many traditional concepts and notions about many spheres of social life, including the concept of the strength and might of states. This development will affect diplomacy, as such. Much of what was once considered to be the determining criteria of the strength and might of states—for instance, such factors as the availability of natural resources and developed industrial potential—today, while they retain great significance, are not the only ones capable to giving a true idea of the strength of a state or its possibilities in the sphere of foreign policy. Moreover, we may probably draw the conclusion that such showings as the scope of research, experimental and designing work, the level of the population's education, the quality of training, the number of scientists and specialists and the society's ability to introduce scientific innovations into production quickly and efficiently are steadily advancing to the fore.

It is clear that today the solutions to some of the most acute problems confronting the human race—such as overcoming poverty and hunger, defeating diseases, easing labor conditions, preserving the environment and promoting international cooperation on seas, oceans and in outer space, in short, serving to better life on the entire planet—as well as the solutions to a number of large scale problems of world importance, call for extensive international cooperation on a global and regional foundation. In this effort the role of our countries, as well as of diplomacies, cannot be underestimated. Cooperation, extending the international division of labor, can be organized only in conditions of peace, in conditions of steady improvement of the international situation—provided that the effects of many old, negative tendencies of the fifties and sixties, marked by conditions of confrontation and Cold War, do not only diminish, but are brought to nought. Also, such relaxation of international tension may take place despite the present objective contradictions in international relations, provided that these contradictions are resolved without armed conflicts, test of strength, confrontation, crisis diplomacy and international crises.

Today it is, of course, difficult to map, or even to predict, all the possible lines and forms of the international effort in conditions of the scientific and technological revolution—in which, one can presume, both of our countries will take part. One thing is quite clear: these lines and forms of international cooperation will steadily gain in scope and diversity. The Soviet Union has repeatedly declared, on the summit level, that it is prepared to foster relations of mutually advantageous cooperation with all states wishing to do so.

Important lines of international cooperation have been established in areas such as environmental protection, development of power and other natural resources, advancement of transport and communications, prophylaxis and elimination of the gravest and the most widespread diseases, exploration and use of outer space and the world ocean. International cooperation is absolutely essential, for instance, in the fields connected with weather and climate control. It is no less obvious now that without international cooperation no effective efforts can be made to keep up the earth's ecological balance, to preserve favorable habitation conditions on our planet and its future value for human life. Of particular importance to developing countries are the problems—such as the development of high-yielding varieties of staple foodstuffs, the food protein problem, the development of up-to-date progressive methods of fishing in open sea, the problem of agricultural pests and disease-carrier control and the water freshening problem—which they can solve only on the basis of equal cooperation with industrially developed countries. It is clear that all these immense potential possibilities for developing scientific, technical and economic cooperation among countries with opposite socioeconomic systems can be realized only if peace is preserved.

Here, one must lay special stress on the following factor: many states are known to have built up an immense military potential. My country has always come out in favor of bringing this military potential to nought.

The revolution in military technology is known to lead to a fast rate renovation of technical ideas and principles in designing armaments and to the steady expansion of technological possibilities for their production. In those cases when the arms race is supported by an influential sector of a country's economy, it follows its own logic of development, as it were. The strategic arms race cannot be limited or stopped by virtue of this technological logic being exhausted; this will hardly take place, because the possibilities for the technical perfection of weapon systems are infinite, as are scientific and technical thought. Consequently, such a race in the creation of deadly arms can be checked only by means of rational decisions and the plain, hard work of both politicians and diplomats who must reach beyond considerations of purely technological logic.

In order to promote the positive solution to all of these problems, it is essential to admit that today, in conditions of the scientific and technological revolution, there is a great need: (1) for the development of new legal standards which would perfect the juridical foundation of the interaction of states and (2) for establishing the rights and duties of states on land, on oceans and seas and in outer space. Here, an important contribution might be made by the Soviet Union and the United States, working bilaterally and through the United Nations— an organization which plays an extremely important role in strengthening international security. In conclusion, one can point out that there are really many spheres in which the interests of the Soviet Union and the United States concur or run parallel. This is an important, positive factor if one is thinking about the future of Soviet-American diplomacy.

* * *

QUESTIONS AND ANSWERS

Q: Dr. Gromyko talked about the price of detente, while raising the specter of a possible nuclear holocaust and conflagration. That is, he seemed to say that anyone who puts a price on detente, who suggests preconditions in terms of changes in Soviet internal affairs, is raising such a possibility. However, I think he ignores the many levels of detente, for example, nuclear detente and social and economic detente. Would he not agree that while nuclear detente should not be linked in any way to the internal affairs of our countries, social and economic detente is, indeed, necessarily linked with issues of this kind and, therefore, that we do have the right to set preconditions on detente with the USSR? I'm thinking specifically of MFN status and of the Jackson Amendment.

A: The question merely proves my point: detente as it is expressed in the United States has very different meanings for various people. The person who just spoke said we have an agreed upon nuclear detente. In fact, the nuclear detente, —or nuclear relaxation of tension —resulted from the agreements concluded by the Soviet Union and the United States. I think that the agreement on the prevention of nuclear war—one of the most, if not the most, important agreement made by our countries—is a historic achievement. At the same time, however, it is not the only agreement which we have concluded. If my memory doesn't fail me, in the past four years our important agreements totaled almost one hundred on the state level. The agreements were not only in the area of nuclear weapons, but in all kinds of activities which constitute interaction between the Soviet Union and the United States. Thus, the relaxation of tension is not a process which is connected to only nuclear detente, but to quite a number of other developments.

I would say that, of course, each side has the right to criticize the other. The bourgeois way of life, the capitalist society, is criticized in our country no less than our society is criticized here. However, our criticism should never interfere—that is, the most important problems should not be made dependent upon others —with the strengthening of peace on earth.

From my point of view, it would be extremely foolish to say that if the United States does not develop internally in a particular way, I will refuse to develop relations with the United States. Criticism is one thing, but relations between states is a matter of diplomacy and international law. And diplomacy is the art—perhaps, the science—of relationships among states, not among personalities. We have millions of personalities; we have all kinds of views— including such pessimistic ones as

those of Mr. Schwartz. However, these simply can not be incorporated into the relationship between states.

I don't think that anyone trying to run his family life would think it right for a neighbor, whose wife comes home at 6:00 PM, to tell him: "I don't like your wife coming home at eight o'clock in the evening."

I am, of course, simplifying the argument. Yet, I think that family life resembles, on the whole, state interaction; the main point is that if we are to preserve the future of the world—if we are to preserve such people as Mr. Schwartz and Mr. Gromyko, Jr.—we must find some way to get together without telling the other side what they are to do at home. I think this is one of the main principles of international law. I would not waiver from this position, nor would I give in to discussing the merits or the failures of the other side. I think it is up to the American people to deal with their own problems.

———

Q: Mr. Chaimran, my name is Paul Grimes. I am the *Evening Bulletin* reporter about whom Dr. Gromyko spoke so glowingly. I would like to ask Dr. Gromyko why he omitted a long section in the advance text of his report, as released by his embassy, in which he referred to basic, objective differences between capitalism and socialism and included these two sentences: (1) "One cannot reconcile the irreconcilable or mix together water and fire"; (2) "Due to this, it seems to me that any diplomacy which would try to achieve—would strive to achieve—convergence of opposite social structures would end in failure."

A: The text to which you refer deals with differences between capitalistic and socialistic systems. As far as I understand them, they do not depict internal situations, as such, in the United States. They were dropped from my oral delivery purely for the benefit of your time.

A (Schwartz): I would simply like to make a personal comment that Paul Grimes, who just spoke, is a former colleague of mine and that I've known him for years. He's a man whose journalistic ability and integrity and honor are exceeded by no one's.

Q: In his presentation Dr. Gromyko has put considerable emphasis on what he calls "the objective laws of social development," according to which we represent an obsolete order which is historically doomed. Of course, objectively, we would like to have a cooperative relationship with the Soviet Union; moreover, the Soviet government tells us that this relationship is possible and that it will serve our mutual benefit.

My question is: does Dr. Gromyko feel that such cooperation will hasten the objective of lawful, inevitable decline of our system or does he feel—as some people here have argued—that it will delay it?

A: Cooperation at the state level has nothing to do with the laws of the society, as such. Everything happening here or in my country is happening in accordance to the factors of internal development. As for the future of the United States, you know better than I how your society is developing.

In our interstate relations with the United States we are taking your entity—that is, your society—as it is and trying to find compatible and parallel interests to bring together the international situation and to create more favorable international situations in Soviet-American relations.

The developments which worry you are not happening because of what I say. I say these things because they are happening in objective reality. Anyone who studies philosophy knows that there is an objective reality. If you are worried about the objective reality, I can't help it.

The same is true if it is the trends which worry you. They were discovered not by me, but by Marx and Engels. What they said can be traced deep into the past to many French, English and German philosophers who explained things happening in the world in almost the same way as I did when I tried to explain the current situation by mentioning the objective factors of the two different social systems.

Of course, the two systems will compete. But the competition should be carried on in a peaceful way. I hope you will agree with me that there are a great many different ways to compete. There is a great difference, for example, between military means and peaceful means.

Q: Dr. Gromyko made some remarks on objective and subjective contradictions. I was somewhat unhappy about the emphasis which he gave to the contradictions between the United States and the Soviet Union and the West and underdeveloped countries.

As I understand Marxist-Leninist theory, contradictions are not logical contradictions which can be resolved through discussion or through changing people's minds. They are to be resolved through struggle, with some element of violence—in other words, the ruling class will not give up power by itself. If this is the case, wouldn't the Soviet Union then follow a policy of using violence and encouraging conflict—as it might be doing in the Middle East—wherever it is possible to gain advantage? Furthermore, if the Soviet Union could get strategic advantages in nuclear weapons, would they not use such weapons?

A: We are not in favor of violence, and we have proposed quite a lot of international agreements designed to create a structure of modern relationships in which there would be no international violence. For example, if one examines the documents of the last General Assembly session, one can see that we have proposed a resolution—which, by the way, the General Assembly approved—that all states should not resort to the use of nuclear arms or any other violent means—that is, conventional arms—for settling disputes. Nonuse of nuclear, and all other, force in the international arena is the principle of Soviet foreign policy. We want crisis diplomacy to step down from the international pedestal so that positive diplomacy can take over irreversibly.

Although some of the things mentioned may have seemed contradictory to you, I would say that, in effect, we did not go to war after World War II. One of the main reasons for such solid support of our system and our government in the Soviet Union is that we have been living in peace since the Second World War. We intend to do so in the future.

Q: Dr. Gromyko said that in the Soviet Union people tend to refer to the policy of detente as a policy of peaceful coexistence. As I remember

it, the policy of peaceful coexistence saw many agreements between the United States and the Soviet Union, including nuclear agreements, and many cultural exchanges. Here I beg to differ with the comment made by Dr. Schwartz that such agreements were impossible prior to detente. Furthermore, the policy of peaceful coexistence also solved the Cuban-missile crisis, which—as we know—has been the closest the world has come to a nuclear holocaust. In fact, when we speak of the Cold War and the bad old days of the Cold War, we are talking about Krushchev's policy of peaceful coexistence.

If this is the case, and if peaceful coexistence is compatible with Cold War, then I don't exactly understand why Dr. Gromyko makes the distinction between the present policy of detente and peaceful coexistence, which is what the policy was called under Krushchev during the period of the Cold War.

A: I would say that in the 1950s and 1960s we were striving for peaceful coexistence in the international arena. We proclaimed the policy of peaceful coexistence, by the way, in 1917. Thus, you can trace this policy further back into our history.

However, after the Second World War it was our understanding that the other side did not wish us to prosper. While some say that the Soviet Union was to blame for the Cold War, now many are of the opinion that the West at that time had doctrines and policies which were very hostile to our country. For example, in 1948 and in 1949—before we had nuclear weapons—the United States had preventive doctrines. Quite a lot of people said that the United States, under certain circumstances, should use nuclear weapons against the Soviet Union before Communist ideas and the Soviet way of life prevailed.

This talk receded with the development of Soviet might. Therefore, I would say that negotiation came into being in the late 1960s and matured in the beginning of 1970s. The negotiations culminated in the historic "Declaration of Public Principles," concluded by the United States and the Soviet governments. Both countries proclaimed that the basis for their relations was to be the principle of peaceful coexistence.

As for the Caribbean—not the Cuban—nuclear crisis, the Cubans were not responsible. Did it ever enter into your mind that the Americans created this Caribbean situation? It was actually a question of a military base being built not far from your shores; once you noticed it, you became very agitated—but keep in mind that we have quite a number of such installations not very far from our country.

For you, perhaps, Cuba seemed dangerous to the United States. For the Soviet Union this episode in our relations was a question of security. I hope you will admit that the Soviet government behaved most reasonably. We were really very worried about the situation and didn't want to draw either you or ourselves into nuclear exchanges. We had to compromise, but we didn't surrender. Socialist Cuba does exist, and we don't have our nuclear rockets there, simply because we don't need them there. However, the main point is that both governments have realized that such situations occur because both sides have tried, to a large extent, to defend their interests mainly by the use of force, on the presumption that the other side would use force. Currently, both state and public opinion in the United States—as in the Soviet Union—is in favor of relaxation of tension. And one may ask: what is the alternative to the policy of detente, of peaceful coexistence?

A:(Schwartz): Just a very brief comment. Dr. Gromyko has asked: "What is the alternative!" I would suggest that he poses the issue, should I say, in a rather defective way. I would really agree with the point of the questioner. That is, we have been engaged in peaceful coexistence, but rather rambunctious peaceful coexistence. Neither one of us wants to blow up the world, because we know we will be blown up along with it. However, we certainly are not living in peace and harmony and kisses. The honeymoon, let's remember, is just that of the Kissingers.

The Moscow-Peking-Washington Triangle

By Harry Schwartz

ABSTRACT. Two major factors in the world scene must be considered in any analysis of current Soviet-American relations: (1) the United States and Western Europe are, today, at the nadir of their effective political, military and economic power; (2) the specter of war with the People's Republic of China is in the background of all Soviet thinking. What has actually happened in the last few years is a sort of competitive wooing of the United States by the Russians and the Chinese. Each country is worried that the United States will team up with the other: for, while the United States does not have the political will to do anything major on the world scene by itself, the combination of American technological power and either Chinese or Soviet political power raises the most awesome possibilities. Thus, the recent historic changes—including those accomplished by President Nixon and Secretary of State Kissinger—have issued from the opportunities created by the Soviet-Chinese split. However, both in China and in Russia very real questions are being raised about the wisdom of the policy of the past. In view of this danger, in addition to the prospect of a major Constitutional crisis in the impeachment and trial of the president of the United States, American foreign policy must be at maximum alert.

Harry Schwartz, currently on leave from the Editorial Board of The New York Times, is Visiting Professor at Columbia University. He is also Distinguished Professor at the State University College, New Paltz, New York. Professor Schwartz is the author of numerous books on the Communist world, including Tsars, Mandarins, and Commissars: A History of Chinese-Russian Relations, Eastern Europe under the Soviet Shadow: Prague's Two Hundred Days and An Introduction to the Soviet Economy.

ON APRIL 5, 1974 the *New York Times* printed a story by its Moscow correspondent, Hedrick Smith, the essence of which is explained by the headline: "Soviet Attacks United States Press on Kissinger." Apparently, *Pravda* and other Soviet newspapers are extremely unhappy with certain stories which have recently appeared in the *New York Times* and the *Washington Post;* they have accused both newspapers of "indulging in irresponsible disinformation contrary to the facts," of trying to misrepresent the Moscow mission of Mr. Kissinger as a complete failure caused by the Kremlin's hard line

Whatever the *New York Times* and *Washington Post* did or did not do, I want to underline the fact that I am not speaking for the *New York Times*. Furthermore, I am not an employee of the United States government. The opinions—with which some Americans may agree, but with which other Americans may undoubtedly disagree—I express are simply my own.

I stress this point because I think that one of the great misfortunes in the efforts to create a Soviet-American dialogue is that there exists an asymmetry of importance. On the one hand, the United States is a tower of Babel. There are many different points of view, and they are expressed vigorously. In a sense, there is no American line which is accepted by all American citizens. Whatever Henry Kissinger may say in Moscow, there are many people in New York, Washington, Boston, Philadelphia and so on who disagree with him.

On the other hand, those who publicly speak for the Soviet Union are, as is Dr. Gromyko, employees or representatives of the Soviet government. They essentially follow the Soviet government's position as of the moment. In the past, as their government's mind changed, they have changed their positions; and as their government's mind changes in the future, they will undoubtedly do so again. The Soviet government demands from both its representatives abroad and from its citizens at home a degree of public conformity and unanimity which is simply impractical in the United States. If I may sum it up simply, there are no Soviet Daniel Ellsbergs, and we have no Soviet equivalent of the Pentagon Papers. It would, indeed, be fascinating to see the equivalent.

I would like to remedy, in part, the situation just described. It is ridiculous to assume that within an advanced, industrial nation of 250 million people, such as the Soviet Union, only one view and one opinion exist. This may have been true several hundred years ago when the overwhelming majority of the population—the ancestors of those who are now Soviet citizens—were illiterate serfs. However, today the Soviet Union is a major industrial, technological, economic and scientific power; it has tens of millions of intelligent people who—while unfortunately often systematically misinformed by their own press— do have the ability to weigh ideas and events independently. One must therefore assume that there are many opinions in the Soviet Union.

ALEXANDER SOLZHENITSYN'S VIEW

I think there is one opinion, different from the rather official opinion Dr. Gromyko has presented, which deserves special attention. I am speaking of an opinion recently voiced by the man who is, morally, the outstanding Soviet citizen alive today, Alexander Solzhenitsyn.

Last September Mr. Solzhenitsyn —who is, of course, presently in involuntary exile from his own country —expressed his own views in an open letter written to Soviet leaders. That letter, unfortunately, has never been published in the Soviet Union. The closest approximation of a response to it from the Soviet leaders was Mr. Solzhenitsyn's expulsion from the USSR. At the moment, as far as I know, the English translation of the letter has been made generally available only through its printing in the *London Sunday Times* of March 3, 1974. The full text of the letter has not yet appeared in the United States in English, although I understand it is being published as a separate book very shortly. I think this lack of attention is significant, and I regard it with sadness.

I do not bring up Mr. Solzhenitsyn's opinions to be unnecessarily provocative, but because I suspect that Mr. Solzhenitsyn, as a sensitive private citizen, is probably reflecting views which are widespread among the Soviet people—views which may even be widespread among the Soviet leadership. Furthermore, these views—perhaps for very understandable reasons—are not frequently articulated, particularly in public forums.

While I will not try to read the complete text of the Solzhenitsyn letter, I think it is very important to analyze, at least briefly, Mr. Solzhenitsyn's view of the world stage on which the diplomacy of the present moment is being staged.

The position of the West

Mr. Solzhenitsyn titled the first section of his letter to the Soviet leadership "The West on Its Knees." Through this title he makes a very important point, one which we all too often seem to forget in the United States. Dr. Gromyko is undoubtedly much too polite to refer to this point in his public utterances. In other words, Mr. Solzhenitsyn focuses attention on the fact that through a truly complex series of events the effective political and military power of the West—defining the West, for the moment, as the United States and Western Europe —is now at an all time low since World War II. The West has never seemed so confused, so divided, so leaderless and, therefore, for all practical purposes, so weak as it does in the present unhappy period.

The story in the paper this week about the twenty-fifth anniversary of the North Atlantic Treaty Organization (NATO) and the lack-luster way in which it was marked tells one something. This is, after all, also the week during which the president of the United States has been declared to be in default of almost a half-million dollars in income tax, which he has announced he will pay. The net result is that some people see more grounds for his impeachment.

For a great many reasons, the United States and Western Europe are today at the nadir of their effective political, military and economic power. They are rent by inflation. They are much more concerned with domestic tensions than they have been for many years. The great and dismaying recent symbol of the West's internal fissures was the readiness of the British coal miners to go on strike during the Arab embargo on oil exports.

Mr. Solzhenitsyn notes that the Soviet leaders—who are certainly intelligent and well-informed men —understand all this and, furthermore, understand that the Soviet Union today is the sole super-power of the world. It is the super-power of the world because today it alone has both the technical capability of using the most modern weapons and the political capability to do so if the need arises. For example, can anyone think that in the present climate —that is, after the Vietnam War, after Watergate— the United States or, for that matter, Britain, France or West Germany, would go to war in the foreseeable future for any other reason than to repel a direct attack.

On the other hand, it was not so long ago that we saw the Soviet Union, in collaboration with its immediate Eastern European satellites, engage in a direct, massive and unprovoked attack against a friendly country, Czechoslovakia. Without any effective world opposition, Moscow was able to occupy Czechoslovakia and to impose its will and the government it desired upon that country. One should also note that the Soviet Union had earlier signed numerous pacts guaranteeing the inviolability of Czechoslovakia's sovereignty and independence. That, too, is part of the historic record. The men who are now in rule in Moscow ordered Soviet troops into Czechoslovakia on the night of August 20, 1968. We forget that order and its consequences only at our peril, it seems to me.

Thus, Mr. Solzhenitsyn's first point: there is a new disequilibrium in the world. The Soviet Union— and I am paraphrasing him, of course —has both military power and the political capability to use it. The West, while it has much physical power—that is, modern weapons and the like—has essentially lost the political capability of using it. For example, it seems likely that if President Nixon tried to order American troops into any new conflict which any substantial segment of American opinion could regard as another Vietnam, he would have a mass mutiny on his hands.

The factor of the Chinese People's Republic

The second point Mr. Solzhenitsyn raises in his letter is one that Dr. Gromyko ignored completely, but which no serious student of Soviet-American affairs can ignore: namely, the factor of the Chinese People's Republic. Mr. Solzhenitsyn calls the Chinese "900 million ax handles." Of course, the great specter in the mind of every intelligent and informed Soviet citizen—and even among many who are neither very intelligent nor very well informed—is the specter of war with China. I do not think that it is questionable that in the minds of Soviet citizens Mao Tse-tung is seen as today's successor to Genghis Khan. All Soviet school children have learned about Genghis Khan, the Mongol invasion of Russia and the cruelties and barbarisms of the Mongolian yoke; the possibility of the repetition of history by Mao Tse-tung and the Chinese is very real in the fears of many contemporary Soviet citizens.

It is worth quoting Mr. Solzhenitsyn on his vision of a possible Soviet-Chinese conflict; he writes:

You [the Soviet leadership] will have against you almost a thousand-million people, the like of which have never yet gone to war in the history of the world. The time, since 1949, has evidently not been enough for this population to lose its high degree of fundamental industriousness, which is higher than ours is today. It has not lost its tenacity and submissiveness and it is firmly in the grip of a totalitarian system no wit less vigilant than ours. Its army and population would not surrender en masse with Western good sense even when surrounded and beaten. Every soldier and every civilian will fight to the last bullet, the last breath.

I would charge that this kind of apocalyptic vision of a possible future Soviet-Chinese war is in the mind of, literally, the great majority of the 250 million Soviet citizens alive today and that no one can understand the recent revolution in Soviet-American relations without realizing that this nightmare is in the background of all Soviet thinking.

Reassessment of Soviet foreign policy

Mr. Solzhenitsyn goes on to prescribe a policy path of his own. He believes that the basis of the Soviet-Chinese split is largely ideological and, therefore, he appeals to the Soviet leaders to abandon their ideology. He states:

Let China have a monopoly of Communist ideology; let them bear the burdens of encouraging the revolutions in South America; let them have all the worries we have been bearing all these years, and let us go and take care of our own.

His idea, of course, is to go off and develop Siberia at a tremendous clip.

Essentially, what Mr. Solzhenitsyn is saying is that today a rational Soviet policy would be a very fundamental change toward deep isolationism—if you will, a fortress-Russia concept—in which Russia would devote its primary energies to tilling its undeveloped soil in Siberia and in the European northeast of Russia, while letting the rest of the world go hang. Mr. Solzhenitsyn's vision is, I think, probably shared by many others.

The Russian author is also a very firm opponent to all of the energy deals which propose to make Siberian energy available to the United States, if only we invest a few billion dollars. He says that if the Soviet Union goes through with such deals, future generations will curse the names and memories of the present Soviet leaders. Thus, his argument is: Soviet energy for future Soviet generations, not for the Americans. I do not know how many Soviet citizens agree with the position Mr. Solzhenitsyn has expounded, but at least it is a different position and it has the virtue of candor and openness which one does not often find in, say, *Pravda* or *Izvestiya*.

Mr. Solzhenitsyn has also been influenced by Andrei Amal'rik's book, *Will the Soviet Union Survive until 1984?*[1] The author—who, as far as is known, is either in jail or in exile somewhere in Siberia—answers the question he raises with a dim prognosis, because he believes that the Chinese will beat the Russians when and if war comes. Mr. Solzhenitsyn asks why Mr. Amal'rik was exiled to Siberia rather than promoted to, perhaps, chief of the policy planning board of the Soviet Ministry of Foreign Affairs.

I think the question is very pertinent. We now have a tri-polar situation dominating international affairs. For most purposes—although not for all—there are three players. One can no longer speak about Soviet-American relations while isolating the factor of the Soviet-American-Chinese triangle. Certainly, Washington, Moscow and Peking no longer make that kind of mistake.

BACKGROUND OF CURRENT AMERICAN FOREIGN POLICY

One begins to understand the true nature of the recent historic changes in the world scene—including those accomplished by President Nixon and Secretary of State Kissinger—only if one realizes that even among

1. Andrei Amal'rik, *Will the Soviet Union Survive until 1984?* (New York: Harper and Row, 1970).

the top echelons of the Kremlin there are adherents to Mr. Solzhenitsyn's viewpoint. I say this feelingly, because in my book,[2] published about ten years ago, I suggested just such a view, and I am gratified to see that someone subsequently implemented a policy I urged. That is, Mr. Nixon and Mr. Kissinger realized that the appearance of a Soviet-Chinese split—which must be considered the major factor in world affairs this past decade or so—created opportunities for the United States which had not existed earlier.

These opportunities when perceived very realistically—and, again, I give my own view—gave us the opportunity to play the two sides against each other. If you will, not divide and conquer, but divide and make gains. Of course, this has been done in the brilliant American political maneuvering in recent years. Mr. Kissinger's trip to Peking, President Nixon's trip to Peking, President Nixon's visit to Moscow and Mr. Brezhnev's trip to the United States profoundly changed the entire face of international relations.

What has actually occurred in the past few years is a sort of competitive wooing of the United States by the Russians and the Chinese. Each country is worried that we will team up with the other. As I said before, the United States has the physical capabilities, but not the political will, to do anything major by itself on the world scene.

The Chinese, on the other hand, do not have the physical capability —in terms of abundant modern weapons—which we have. However, they have an obedient, hard-working and self-sacrificing population. There is little doubt that if Mao Tse-tung gave any order—including the order to invade the Soviet Union —it would be obeyed. Thus, from Moscow's point of view, the combination of American technological power and Chinese political power raises the most awesome possibility.

Similarly, the possibility of a Soviet-American alliance is threatening from Peking's point of view. The Chinese have often voiced their fear of a super-power deal to divide the world between Moscow and Washington. Such a deal, Peking believes, would see the United States give the Soviet Union permission to go ahead and settle its Chinese problem without interference from us, which means without interference from anyone.

In retrospect, I think that both the invasion of Czechoslovakia and what has come to be called the Brezhnev doctrine are major contributing factors to the current situation. The Brezhnev doctrine was enunciated in *Pravda* on September 26, 1968. It holds that the Soviet Union has the right to interfere in the affairs of other socialist states if, in the judgment of the Soviet leaders, socialism is in danger of being removed as a country's ruling system. Once that doctrine had been implemented in the invasion of Czechoslovakia, the question of when that doctrine would be exercised vis-à-vis China inevitably rose in Chinese minds. After all, it has often been proclaimed in the Soviet press and in the speeches of various Soviet leaders that the Chinese leadership has betrayed socialism and the working class of the Chinese People's Republic and even that the Chinese People's Republic has abandoned Communism for some kind of bloody Fascist rule headed by Mao Tse-

2. Harry Schwartz, *Tsars, Mandarins, and Commissars: A History of Chinese-Russian Relations* (Philadelphia, Pa.: Lippincott, 1964).

tung, whom Moscow sees as a modern-day Hitler.

With such a background in mind, one can hardly blame the Chinese for supposing that Czechoslovakia may have been a small scale dress rehearsal for some future invasion of China. Let us remember, further, that the consequent change in Chinese attitude was major: the shift was from the Proletarian Cultural Revolution in the late 1960s to the kind of atmosphere in which it was possible to receive Henry Kissinger, and, then, President Nixon in Peking.

AGENDA FOR FUTURE AMERICAN FOREIGN POLICY

I raise the question of what future American policy should be against this background, because it is clear that certain limitations to the original Kissinger-Nixon—or Nixon-Kissinger, however one wants to divide the credit—policy have begun to appear. Mr. Kissinger, himself, has obviously had a disappointing time in Moscow during his last visit. We must all be aware, of course, of the Aesopian character of much of the current discussion; after all, the statements in the *New York Times* and the *Washington Post* to which *Pravda* and *Izvestiya* have objected were statements made by officials on the Kissinger plane. But everyone knows that these anonymous officials are the venerable Dr. Kissinger, himself. In other words, the actual Soviet polemic is not with the *Times* or the *Post*, but with Henry Kissinger.

The Soviet barrage, nominally against the newspapers, is really a demand for more Kissinger concessions. There is a kind of Soviet-American confrontation going on

right now: Mr. Kissinger did not get his conceptual breakthrough on arms control in Moscow, and Moscow is still trying to sell its version. There is at least a kind of mini-crisis in Soviet-American relations, and exacerbating that mini-crisis is the fact that, undoubtedly, our Soviet friends are taking a second reading of the American political scene.

When Mr. Brezhnev was here last year I accompanied his party on the trip a bit and spoke to many of the Soviet journalists and Soviet officials who had come with the general secretary. They seemed to be incredulous about "all this Watergate nonsense." The question they constantly asked me was: "Will it go away?"

I think that by April 1974 it has finally dawned upon the minds of Soviet planners and policy-makers that Watergate probably will not go away and, if anything, there is a serious possibility that Mr. Nixon will go away, prematurely. Since Mr. Brezhnev has placed very substantial bets for his own political future on the staying power of Mr. Nixon and Mr. Nixon's policies, Mr. Brezhnev, I suspect, is understandably nervous and beginning to try to see if he should not hedge his bets. After all, who knows what the foreign policy of Gerald Ford might be? As a matter of fact, there have been rumors that Henry Kissinger might not even be secretary of state in a Ford administration.

On the Chinese side, there have been other, and in some ways more profoundly disquieting, developments. In China—and anyone who speaks of China must do so with humility and an open confession of ignorance—there have recently been some very ominous signs. There has been a renewal of public Xenophobia, and various public meetings have been held to create and in-flame hatred of foreigners. There are indications of an intense political struggle at the highest levels of Chinese power. How long Chou En-lai—and what I would regard as his rational foreign policy—can survive is now very much under question.

Therefore, the Kissinger-Nixon foreign policy—which in recent years has been so brilliant and has accomplished so much—seems to be in danger, both in Moscow and in Peking. It is thus a fateful moment: Mr. Kissinger is going to have to face these problems, as well as face the question of whether Mr. Nixon is going to be in power very much longer.

I suppose that apprehensive Americans, such as myself, can merely say this: we need to under-stand that neither the Soviet Union as it exists today nor the Chinese People's Republic as it exists today is a friend to the United States. The leadership of both countries is very deeply hostile to our country,

to our way of life, and looks for-ward with pleasure to what it regards as the historically inevitable de-struction of the political, economic and social system under which we live. Their willingness to be co-operative comes from their mutual fear of each other. The United States has been the beneficiary of the Sino-Soviet split.

However, both in China and in Russia very real questions are being raised about the wisdom of the policy of the past; there are dangers of major changes. I think this is a time for American foreign policy to be at maximum alert. We must realize that some swift and fancy footwork may be needed in the months just ahead—especially in view of the prospect that we may be caught up in a major Constitu-tional crisis in the impeachment and trial of the president of the United States. I would be less than candid if I did not say that I look to the foreign policy consequences of such a domestic crisis with more than a little trepidation.

* * *

QUESTIONS AND ANSWERS

Q: Historically, the relaxation of tensions between countries oc-curred when there was a free flow of information and ideas between those countries—that is, between the peoples of those countries. Un-fortunately, this situation doesn't exist today: there is no opportunity for the Soviet people to get a full-range of ideas, except in very censored form. Given that situation, I would ask how greater relaxation of tension can occur without a free flow of information.

A: The objective fact is that there has been some relaxation of tension,

even though there are still sub-stantial barriers to the free flow of information in the Soviet Union. Thus, I think that in the narrow sense the questioner is wrong: ex-perience has shown that there can be some relaxation of tension.

In the more basic sense, I would agree with the position of the ques-tioner—namely, if there is ever to be full confidence, trust and friend-ship between the United States and the Soviet Union, there must be a far greater degree of free flow of information in both countries, par-ticularly in the Soviet Union. How-ever, we have to realize that in the Soviet Union the prime goal is the maintenance of the power of the present ruling clique. As *Pravda* declared in 1956, the Communist Party is the sole master of the minds of the people of the Soviet Union. As long as the Communist Party feels that its mastery of the country requires mastery of the minds of the people of the Soviet Union, there will be no free flow of information in that country.

A (Gromyko): I would say that the Communist Party is the best, the most refined and the most liked party of our people—that's true. After the great Socialist Revolution we had not one, but several, parties in the government. On June 6, 1918, there was a very serious uprising in one of the parties; only after this did the government under Lenin decide that those parties which threatened Soviet power were to be controlled.

The Soviet Union is run by the Soviet councils; in these councils there are millions of people, beginning from the lower levels and going up to the Council of Ministers of the Supreme Soviet of the USSR. While stupid people may ask why we have a one-party government, the future society may be organized along this very principle. Can one envisage the future development of human society as a continuous conflict between different political parties trying to take the upper hand? The future of human society will be the future of generational decisions, based on the experience of all mankind, taken by some surviving citizenship body.

Sometimes people try to imply that the Soviet government has a monopoly on the rigid control of the minds of the people. This is not true, in the sense that the government is trying to create a Communist society. If you know the writings of Marx and Engels, you can easily see that they are striving to eliminate "stateage."

Furthermore, we have always been surrounded by capitalist states. We have been attacked many times, and millions of people died in these attacks. The American people sometimes do not realize that, for example, if a country is occupied or if it experiences the "intervention" of millions of soldiers on its own soil, no controls exist in such a state of siege. In the 1920s and 1930s the Soviet Union was really fighting against this threat, which was not only external, but also internal. Quite a number of people didn't like the Socialist way of life, established after the great October Revolution. They were deprived of incomes—some justified—and of the opportunity to use the labor of other people in order to earn money. Yet, we still think that everybody should receive according to his ability and according to his needs, now and in the future. This is a just approach.

Q: At this point in history we need a world government which would effectively outlaw war. Which nation and which forces within that nation are preventing this much needed change in international relations?

A: I daresay that in Moscow there would be no objection to a world government with headquarters in Moscow; and, no doubt, in Peking there would be no objections to a world government with headquarters in Peking.

While I would like a democratic world government, unfortunately, the divisions within mankind—political, economic and social divisions—are still so deep today that I don't see any world government arising in the near future. If anything, what I foresee is the disintegration of present governments. I would direct the attention of the questioner to the fact that in various countries, such as Belgium, Canada and even Britain, the strengthening power of local nationalism—for example, French-Canadians in Canada, Scots in Britain, the Flemings and the Walloons in Belgium and the Croats and Serbians in Yugoslavia—raises the question of whether even the current governments will survive. I'm afraid that the question of world government on a democratic basis is, unfortunately, extremely premature.

Q: I have two short questions for Dr. Schwartz. First, would Dr. Schwartz extend his statement about the United States not being able to wage war, even though we have the capability of doing so, to a situation in which the Soviet Union began a war in a part of the world where its immediate influence is not prevalent—that is, outside Eastern Europe, say, in the Middle East.

Second, I want to ask about Ford and Kissinger. It seemed to me that Dr. Schwartz suggested that Mr. Ford might not ask Mr. Kissinger to continue as secretary of state;

I wonder if he has any concrete reason for thinking so. Or does he have any concrete reason for thinking that Kissinger would not accept the position?

A: It is simply my judgment that, given the state of national demoralization which has been produced by the past decade of internal struggle—first over Vietnam and now over Watergate—it is now unthinkable that any national leader would order American troops into action for any purpose but the immediate defense of the United States. Therefore, I think that if the Soviet Union wants to take over the Middle East or Western Europe, this is an excellent opportunity to do so without risking the intervention of the United States. I think Mr. Solzhenitsyn shares my view of the situation, as evidenced in his use of the term "The West on Its Knees."

As for your second question, neither Secretary of State Kissinger nor Vice President Ford has made me a special confidant of his thoughts and hopes; I didn't mean to give that impression. However, there have been stories in the press—and this was all I was going by—which indicated that Dr. Kissinger had said to various people that if President Nixon goes, he will go, too. I'm simply referring to those stories in the press; I repeat, I have no inside information from Dr. Kissinger or Mr. Ford.

The USSR Position on Disarmament in the United Nations

By RICHARD S. OVINNIKOV

ABSTRACT: Inevitability of peaceful coexistence provides new opportunities for peace and disarmament. In accordance with the peace program of the Twenty-fourth Congress of the Communist Party of the Soviet Union (CPSU) held in April 1971, the USSR put forward at the last three sessions of the United Nations (UN) General Assembly three concrete proposals. These are proposals on the convening of a world disarmament conference, on the nonuse of force in international relations and permanent prohibition of the use of nuclear weapons and on the reduction by 10 percent of the military budgets of those states which are permanent members of the Security Council and utilization of part of the funds thus saved to provide assistance to developing countries. Implementation of the UN resolutions adopted on all three items would widen the geographical scope of disarmament and the trend towards reducing armaments and would substantially contribute to actual decrease of the burden of armaments and the danger of war.

Richard S. Ovinnikov has been Envoy Extraordinary and Minister Plenipotentiary of the Permanent Mission of the Union of Soviet Socialist Republics to the United Nations since 1970. He was Counselor to the USSR Foreign Ministry in 1966 to 1970 and First Secretary to the Permanent Mission of the Union of Soviet Socialist Republics to the United Nations in 1960 to 1966. Dr. Ovinnikov is author of Behind the Screen of Non-Intervention, The Authors of British Foreign Policy, 1957–1966 *and numerous articles.*

THE position expressed by my country in regard to disarmament issues at the United Nations (UN) is only one aspect of the whole spectrum. First, the United Nations does not embrace the politics of the Soviet Union in the full measure from the chronological point of view. The USSR has existed for more than half a century, whereas the United Nations has been in existence for roughly a quarter of a century; therefore, it cannot reflect the whole history of the USSR's struggle for disarmament. Second, the position of the USSR regarding disarmament and related issues is not limited to the United Nations forum. There are other forms, both bilateral and multilateral, which make it possible to consider and solve disarmament issues—if not all at once, then at least by undertaking certain measures to restrain the arms race. These forms became especially numerous in recent years. In this connection, one can refer first of all to the Soviet-American strategic arms limitation talks (SALT), as well as to the talks on mutual reduction of armed forces and armaments in central Europe. Therefore, it is natural that one should view the position of the USSR regarding disarmament issues at the UN in a broader context, both historically and politically.

A BIT OF HISTORY

The new Soviet system came into existence in, among other things, the struggle against the participation of Tzarist Russia in World War I. The first act by the Soviet state, born in 1917, was the Decree on Peace, signed by V. I. Lenin.

The arms race and wars are alien to our system. There are no population strata in the Soviet Union which would profit from the arms race. We have no unemployment which would force the masses to participate in this race as a paradoxical way of earning their living. However, it is said that there is an inconsistency in the politics of the Soviet Union. For example, if the USSR is against wars and for disarmament, then how does one explain the fact that, today, the Soviet Union is not second in quality of its armaments to the mightiest power of the capitalist world, the United States?

Let me remind you, then, in this connection of certain hard lessons in our history. The gist of these lessons is that the Soviet Union more than once had to defend, with arms, the right of our socialist system to exist. It is a fact that on the very emergence of the new system in Russia the West reacted with an armed intervention of fourteen states. By the way, the United States also participated in that intervention. Ten thousand American soldiers were among the first interventionists on the territory of the newly born Soviet Republic.

It is also a fact that for us World War II was started by the invasion of our territory from the West; Fascism had grown on Western soil. It was from the West that the hardest war in our history fell upon the Soviet Union. World War II cost the Soviet Union twenty million lives. We appreciate the sacrifices suffered by the American people in fighting against Fascism; however, it is difficult for the Americans, who lost about 300,000 of their sons, to imagine the proportions of our sacrifices. That war took one out of every five hundred Americans, but it took one out of every ten Russians—

that is, fifty times more. After World War II, and at the expense of such enormous sacrifices, it might have seemed that we had finally assured our right to existence. But, again, events began to develop in a very ominous direction.

We know that in your country—and in the West, generally—a particular view of the origin of the Cold War is advocated. The basis of this view was laid down by Mr. Churchill in the speech he made at Fulton in March 1946. The essence of that speech was that after World War II the Soviet Union was allegedly busy with preparations for an aggression against the West. It is true, however, that in your country a more sober school of historians has developed. You call them revisionists. This school considers the West to be responsible for the Cold War.

However, let us leave the solution of this dispute at this point. Let us forget, for some time—if it is at all possible—that it was not the Soviet Union that encircled the United Sates with bases, but the United States that encircled the Soviet Union with military bases. Instead, I would like to draw your attention to a certain published diary.

This diary is unique in its own way. It was written by Lord Moran, Mr. Churchill's personal physician. The title of the book is: *Churchill, Taken from the Diaries of Lord Moran: The Struggle for Survival, 1940–1965.* Being far from politics, Lord Moran did not see his task as one of concealing from the reader, in vague phraseology, the essence of what he heard from Sir Winston. He merely put down scrupulously what he heard.

On August 8, 1946—that is, five months after Churchill's Fulton speech—Lord Moran put down the following on Churchill's thoughts:

"We ought not to wait until Russia is ready. I believe it will be eight years before she has these bombs." His face brightened, "America knows that 52 percent of Russia's motor industry is in Moscow and could be wiped out by a single bomb. It might mean wiping out three million people, but they would think nothing of that."He smiled. "They think more of erasing a historical building like the Kremlin."[1]

Seven years later, in his entry on December 5, 1953, Lord Moran wrote:

The P.M. is less sure about things today . . . . Russia, acording to Ike [that is, Eisenhower], was out to destroy the civilized world. "Of course", said the P.M. . . . "Well, if we really think like that, perhaps we out to take action before they get as many atomic bombs as America has. I made that point to Ike, who said, perhaps logically, that it out to be considered."[2]

This is very instructive if one is considering the issue of who planned the war and against whom.

Now, let us come to the year 1954. On July 2 of that year Lord Moran, at last, wrote down in his diary the following new-look statement voiced by Mr. Churchill, who had just returned from Washington: "Ike has crossed a gulf of thought. He has taken a very important step. He has made up his mind that Communism is not something which we must at all costs wipe out, but rather something we have got to learn to live with, and alongside—peaceful coexistence."[3] The next

1. Charles McMoran Wilson Moran, *Churchill, Taken from the Diaries of Lord Moran: The Struggle for Survival, 1940–1965* (Boston, Mass.: Houghton Mifflin, 1966), pp. 337–338.

2. Ibid., pp. 537–538.

3. Ibid., p. 608.

day, on July 3, 1954, Churchill agains says: "Ike has crossed the gulf which separates a mission to destroy Bolshevism from living side by side in peace. I must admit that I myself have crossed the gulf."[4]

We, the Soviet people, read these historic notes as a proof of the fact that in mid-'50s we finally succeeded in implanting into certain Western minds our right to existence. This is why we needed, and why we still need, our arms. Furthermore, it also shows that it was not the Soviet Union that gave up aggressive intentions, which we have never harbored. The psychological gulf has been crossed by the Western powers.

Naturally, it was only the beginning of a new relationship of forces on the international arena which made peaceful coexistence possible. As you know, there were retreats; there were relapses of the Cold War. Yet, the basis of peaceful coexistence had already been laid down.

NEW AVENUES FOR PEACE AND DISARMAMENT

By the early '70s what was always considered a most important objective in the USSR's foreign policy had, on the whole, been achieved. The West gave up the idea of wiping out Communism militarily. The words peaceful coexistence—which for a long time were considered to be Communist propaganda—finally found their way to the West. It became an established factor in international life that there was no alternative to peaceful coexistence but a catastrophic nuclear war.

In this we, the Soviet people,

Communists, see new opportunities for mankind to achieve its age-long dream: peace and disarmament. If a military way of solving the historic dispute between the two systems is now proved unfeasible—as the USSR has always advocated—then the arms race becomes a completely senseless exercise in the waste of resources.

For this reason, the Twenty-fourth Congress of the Communist Party of the Soviet Union (CPSU) approved what became known as the Program of Peace and International Cooperation. It approved this program as the general course for the Soviet Union in a new, historic period and offered it to all other countries of the world.

Allow me to remind you of the basic provisions in this program which directly concern the subject under discussion today—that is, disarmament. As L. I. Brezhnev, general secretary of the CPSU Central Committee, noted in his speech to the Congress, the USSR views the basic, concrete tasks of the struggle for peace, strengthening international security and disarmament in the present situation in the following order:

First: repudiation of the threat or use of force in settling outstanding issues must become a law of international life. For its part, the Soviet Union invites the countries which accept this approach to conclude appropriate bilateral or regional treaties.

Third: to conclude treaties putting a ban on nuclear, chemical, and bacteriological weapons.

To work for an end to the testing of nuclear weapons, including underground tests, by everyone everywhere.

To promote the establishment of nuclear-free zones in various parts of the world.

We stand for the nuclear disarmament of all states in possession of nuclear

4. Ibid., p. 610.

weapons, and for the convocation for these purposes of a conference of the five nuclear powers—the USSR, the USA, the PRC, France and Britain.

Fourth: to invigorate the struggle to halt the race in all types of weapons. We favor the convocation of a world conference to consider disarmament questions to their full extent.

We stand for the dismantling of foreign military bases. We stand for a reduction of armed forces and armaments in areas where the military confrontation is especially dangerous, above all in Central Europe.

We consider it advisable to work out measures reducing the probability of accidental outbreak or deliberate fabrication of armed incidents and their development into international crises, into war.

The Soviet Union is prepared to negotiate agreements on reducing military expenditure, above all by the major powers.

Great progress has been made on the way to the implementation of this program. One of the most important results is the fact that the relations between the two leading powers of the modern world—the USSR and the USA—have been put on a more stable foundation. Even to enumerate all the positive changes which have occurred in the relations between the two countries becomes a difficult task in itself, although these are pleasant difficulties. I would only refer to two basic documents which regulate the relations between the USSR and the USA at this new, historic stage.

The first of these documents is the "Basic Principles of Relations between the Union of Soviet Socialist Republics and the United States of America." It was signed in Moscow on May 29, 1972, during the visit of President Richard Nixon to the Soviet Union. I believe that the following provisions of the

document—directly related to today's topic—are most relevant: (1) the common determination of the USSR and the USA to conduct their mutual relations on the basis of peaceful coexistence, since there is no alternative in the nuclear age; (2) the commitment by the parties to negotiate and settle differences by peaceful means; (3) the stipulation that the prerequisites for maintaining and strengthening peaceful relations between the USSR and the USA are the recognition of the security interests of the parties concerned, based on the principle of equality and the renunciation of the use or threat of force; (4) the obligation, undertaken by both parties, to continue their efforts to limit armaments on a bilateral, as well as on a multilateral, basis; (5) the stipulation that the USSR and the USA regard as the ultimate objective of their efforts the achievement of general and complete disarmament and the establishment of an effective system of international security in accordance with the purposes and principles of the United Nations Charter.

The other fundamental document on Soviet-American relations is the "Agreement between the USSR and the USA on the Prevention of Nuclear War," which was signed on June 22, 1973, in Washington during General Secretary L. I. Brezhnev's visit to the United States. In my opinion, the following, most important provisions of this agreement should be noted: (1) the commitment by the parties to act in such a manner as to prevent the development of situations capable of causing a nuclear war; (2) the obligation undertaken by the parties to refrain from the threat or use of force against the allies of the other party and against other countries; (3)

the obligation of the parties to enter immediately into urgent consultation with each other if there is a risk of a nuclear conflict and to make every necessary effort to avert this risk. These history-making documents lay down a solid foundation for strengthening world peace and security.

DETENTE AND THE POTENTIAL OF THE UNITED NATIONS

While my country is attaching great importance to its relations with the United States, we never intended to confine improvement of relations to that country alone— however significant the US role might be in the contemporary world. For stabilizing detente in international relations so as to secure a crucial turn towards peace it is essential that: (1) the number of states which would be involved in, and would benefit from, such detente be radically increased to the widest possible extent; and (2) detente be made more profound and more specific, primarily by complementing the political detente with military detente.

From this viewpoint, the United Nations provides considerable additional opportunities. As far as disarmament issues are concerned, the UN was earlier addressed as the widest and most representative forum. Suffice it to recall, for example, the 1959 proposal of the Soviet Union on general and complete disarmament. It is common knowledge that the United Nations has already taken specific steps promoting, inter alia, wider application of the Moscow treaty of 1963 banning nuclear tests in three environments and the treaty on non-proliferation of nuclear weapons. Yet, we believe that this use of the United Nations with regard to disarmament has been only the start.

In the light of detente, new horizons open up before the United Nations. For this reason, the Soviet Union has intensified its efforts for disarmament in the United Nations in recent years, putting forward proposals to all states of the world on various aspects of limitation of armaments, strengthening peace and disarmament. I will refer only to the latest three sessions of the UN General Assembly, during which the Soviet Union—in accordance with its peace program—brought before the organization three far-reaching proposals.

TWENTY-SIXTH SESSION OF THE GENERAL ASSEMBLY: WORLD DISARMAMENT CONFERENCE

The United Nations has yet to make use of one of the possibilities for promoting peace: the convening of a world disarmament conference for comprehensive consideration of the disarmament issues in their entire scope. In 1971 the Soviet Union submitted the world-disarmament-conference item for consideration by the General Assembly at its twenty-sixth session. In making this proposal, the Soviet Union proceeded from the belief that it met the interests of the overwhelming majority of the world's population.

As is known, the idea of convening a world disarmament conference was suggested by the nonaligned countries a decade ago, at their second conference in 1964. On the initiative of those countries, the General Assembly adopted Resolution 2030 on this matter at its twentieth session in 1965. In this resolution the idea to convene a world disarmament conference was approved, as was the recommendation to conduct necessary consultations with all countries, with a view to establishing a preparatory committee for convening the world disarmament conference no later than 1967. However, the question of convening the world disarmament conference then faded away.

In again bringing this question to the twenty-sixth session of the General Assembly, the Soviet Union proceeded from the conviction that the development of events on the international arena made desirable further intensification of efforts by all the countries of the world—both nuclear and nonnuclear—to solve disarmament problems. It is the view of the Soviet government that this objective would be met by convening the world disarmament conference—a forum in which all countries of the world, without exception, could comprehensively consider the disarmament problem in its entirety and could try to find practical and generally acceptable ways for its solution. We did, however, attach a special importance to securing the participation of the states with considerable armed forces and armaments.

In putting forward this proposal the Soviet Union did not expect prompt success or immediate results in solving such a complex and important matter. Nevertheless, the consideration of this issue resulted in adoption of Resolution 2833, in which the General Assembly approved the need to consider the question of convening, after appropriate preparations, a world disarmament conference open to all states. The General Assembly also requested that all the states submit their opinions and views on issues related to the conduct of such a conference. On this basis it became

possible to make the next step at the following, twenty-seventh session of the General Assembly. In accordance with the then adopted Resolution 2030, the General Assembly established a special committee to consider all views which the governments expressed about convening the conference and related problems. In other words, the preparation of the world disarmament conference was moving towards actualization.

It was significant that one nuclear power, the United States, preferred to abstain—in complete isolation—from voting on this resolution. Another nuclear power, China, after voting in favor of the resolution, later spared no effort in undermining the special committee; two other nuclear powers, Britain and France, did not participate in the work of the special committee. Yet, while the preparation of the world disarmament conference could be delayed, it was already impossible to stop the drive, since the idea of convening the conference was supported by the overwhelming majority of the member states of the United Nations.

The committee for the world disarmament conference was revived as a phoenix from the ashes at the twenty-eighth session of the General Assembly by Resolution 3183. This time, the composition of the resolution was somewhat enlarged; it created conditions for the normalization of the work of the committee and for the commencement of practical preparations for the conference. We do not expect prompt progress in the work of the committee at this stage, either, for the preparation of such a conference is a complex and delicate matter. However, the Soviet Union— together with the majority of the

United Nations member states—is resolute to proceed with this work; as do the other states, we believe that the world disarmament conference is in the interests of the overwhelming majority of the population of the globe.

TWENTY-SEVENTH SESSION OF THE GENERAL ASSEMBLY: NONUSE OF FORCE

In developing the initiative towards strengthening international peace and security, the Soviet Union put the following item on the agenda of the twenty-seventh session in 1972: "nonuse of force in international relations and permanent prohibition of use of nuclear weapons."

First of all, we feel it important to secure the assurance that no force is used in relations between states. How can this be done? So far, no way out has been found from a certain contradiction: prohibition of threat or use of force in relations between states has been considered separately from banning the most formidable type of weapons—that is, nuclear weapons. The essence of the Soviet proposal in this connection is that the renunciation of any use of force in settling international disputes should include the employment of nuclear weapons, as well as those types of weapons which are usually called conventional. The realistic nature of this proposal lies in the fact that, in case it is implemented, the security of every state would be assured on an equal basis—that is, no one would gain unilateral advantage at someone else's expense. Furthermore, the Soviet Union proposed to formulate the renunciation of any

use of force, including use of nuclear weapons, in such a way that no state could evade its strict observance.

For this purpose the USSR brought before the General Assembly a concrete proposal which suggested: (1) that the General Assembly solemnly declare, on behalf of the UN member states, their renunciation of both the threat and the use of force in international relations and the permanent prohibition of the use of nuclear weapons; and (2) that the Security Council take appropriate measures to give a binding force to the declaration of the General Assembly. The proposals by the Soviet Union in no way prejudiced the right of a state for self-defense against aggression. Their adoption would, however, create more favorable conditions for halting the arms race and achieving disarmament.

On the basis of the Soviet proposal, twenty-three states—including representatives of all five regional groups of the UN member states—submitted the relevant final draft resolution. This draft was adopted by a majority of votes as Resolution 2936. The results of voting upon this resolution were very significant. Negative votes against this resolution were cast by the Republic of South Africa and Portugal—thus obviously trying to reserve a possibility to use force against African peoples and countries. Votes against this resolution were also cast by China and Albania. Such voting by China was not unexpected, because reliance on the use of force underlies China's foreign policy. There are those, perhaps, who believe that China's liking for the use of force can be turned against only her immediate neighbors; however, such hopes are already proving to be short-sighted.

The analysis of the states abstaining from voting on this resolution is no less significant. Israel refused to approve this resolution, while an overwhelming majority of seventeen Arab countries voted for it; only two Arab countries—Tunisia and Morocco—abstained. It is also very symptomatic that all members of the North Atlantic Treaty Organization (NATO), including the United States—and excluding Portugal, which explicitly voted against—refused to support Resolution 2936. On the other hand, socialist countries, including the USSR, voted in favor of the resolution. The conclusion to be derived from this voting is clear. Unfortunately, there are still a number of countries, including countries of the NATO military bloc, which do not like the idea of renunciating the use of force in international relations and of permanently prohibiting the use of nuclear weapons.

The adoption of Resolution 2936 does not exhaust the duties of the United Nations in this respect. It is well known that this resolution recommended that the Security Council take, as soon as possible, appropriate steps for the full implementation of the solemn declaration of the General Assembly on the renunciation of the use of force and the permanent prohibition of the use of nuclear weapons. Therefore, the task of the Security Council is to take action which would give a binding force to the renunciation of the use of force in international relations and the permanent prohibition of the use of nuclear weapons. The Soviet Union has done, and will continue to do, its best to ensure that the Security Council adopts a positive decision with regard to this matter.

TWENTY-EIGHTH SESSION OF THE GENERAL ASSEMBLY: THE REDUCTION OF MILITARY BUDGETS

In 1973 the Soviet Union brought before the twenty-eighth session of the General Assembly the question of: "reduction of the military budgets of the States permanent members of the Security Council by 10 percent and utilization of part of the funds thus saved to provide assistance to developing countries." What were the motives of the Soviet Union for bringing this proposal before the United Nations? First of all, the USSR proceeded from the same necessity to consolidate political detente in interstate relations by supplementing it with military detente. The realization of the Soviet proposal would provide an opportunity to turn considerable funds from the arms race to peaceful economic development. Finally, the realization of the Soviet proposal would enable a wide range of states, including developing countries, to enjoy the benefits of detente in international relations.

The proposal of the USSR to reduce military budgets was primarily focused on five states— that is, the permanent members of the Security Council. It is quite understood that "The Big Five" consists of the militarily largest states with the greatest military expenditures. The proposal of the USSR was based on regard for the interest of equal security of all five permanent members of the Security

Council, because it provided for the reduction of their military budgets for 1973 by an equal portion—10 percent. According to the proposal of the USSR, the utilization of part of the funds thus saved to provide assistance to developing countries would also have a practical character. The USSR specifically suggested that 10 percent of the funds saved by reducing military budgets be used for these purposes. We also proposed to set up a General Assembly special committee on the distribution of the funds released as a result of the reduction of military budgets. These funds would supplement the assistance already provided to such countries through existing channels.

Unfortunately, Western states opposed the Soviet proposal. Sir Alec Douglas Home—foreign secretary of the United Kingdom's conservative government—foretold that this proposal would result in failure, saying that fifteen years before—in 1958—a similar proposal of the USSR had not been approved by the General Assembly. Our answer to his statement was that while the resolution had not been approved in the past, the situation had changed since then. Life itself has shown that the Soviet Union was right. The proposal we made was approved by the General Assembly as Resolution 3093 A. Yet, again, the same countries turned out to be either explicit or tacit opponents of our last proposal. China and Albania voted against the reduction of military budgets, while member countries of NATO—including the United States—abstained.

SOME REFLECTIONS

Thus, during the last three sessions of the General Assembly the Soviet Union brought before the United Nations a number of key proposals for the solution of problems of disarmament and other relevant questions. It is difficult to believe that serious-minded men in the West could view them as propaganda motions. While bringing these questions before the United Nations, my country is fully convinced of the correctness of the course towards the widest possible geographical spreading of the trend towards the limiting of the arms race. Unfortunately, the negative attitude of the United States and other Western powers towards these questions brings one to the conclusion that they do not share this approach, but that they favor the geographical limitation of this process. This is one of the objective contradictions of contemporary international life.

Another contradiction is that the Soviet Union, on one side, is ready to go further and further in the practical reduction of armaments. Our support for disarmament is demonstrated, for example, by our proposal for the reduction of military budgets of the permanent members of the Security Council. The United States and other Western powers, on the other side, are not ready for it. After the adoption of the convention banning bacteriological weapons, the United States seemed to have lost the taste for other practical steps in the field of disarmament. For example, the United States does not care for any agreement banning the production of chemical weapons and providing for the destruction of stockpiles of chemical weapons. Moreover, the United States has not ratified even the 1925 Geneva Protocol—which next year will be half a century old—banning the use of chemical weapons. Thus, the United

States still considers it desirable to limit the disarmament process in its substance.

You are, probably, more aware of the factors which motivate this position. However, one cannot but pay attention to certain articles in the American press which develop a rather curious theory. As this theory goes, the United States could not sophisticate the most modern weaponry during the war in Vietnam; thus, after the end of this war, enormous funds should go to improving weaponry. On the whole, an impression is created that a military-industrial complex—as President Eisenhower once called it—has its own stable, if not perpetual, interests and that this complex should be fed regardless of any other considerations. So, when one direction of arms production is exhausted or when one door is closed, another door to open is sought.

Where can all this lead? The curbing of the arms race and reduction of armaments covering only several countries cannot but have its own limits. It is impossible to imagine a situation in which some countries infinitely reduce and limit their armaments while others accelerate the arms race. Also, an arms limitation which barely scratches the tip of an iceberg of enormous stockpiles of weaponry and still makes it possible to repeatedly replace outdated armaments by new ones does not lead to a stable peace. The continuation of this situation brings about the danger of a new and unprecedented spiral in the arms race. As Mr. Dent—United States secretary of commerce—put it it the other day, a new spiral in the arms race would cost the United States $100 billion annually, in addition to the more than $80 billion which are spent at present. All that has been said makes one doubt whether the present-day position of the United States in the United Nations and in the contemporary world with regard to both the limitation of the arms race and disarmament is far-seeing and realistic.

The Soviet Union considers the contemporary detente in the world arena not as a fleeting moment, but as a possible turning point. However, it cannot be reached if enormous arsenals of the means of mass destruction are preserved and replenished with more and more dangerous weapons. If all the states are interested in the consolidation of detente, then substantial arms reduction and actual disarmament should become the pivot of detente and the guarantee of its irreversibility. These issues should be in the USA-USSR agenda not only for communication, but in the USA-USSR agenda for cooperation.

* * *

QUESTIONS AND ANSWERS

Q: This is, of course, in no sense a debate, but would Dr. Ovinnikov like to comment on anything that Dr. Shulman had said?

A: First of all, I would like to say that I share the constructive approach of Dr. Shulman to the program of disarmament. It seems to me that a positive aspect, in itself, is the serious attitude of both our countries that somehow, at a certain stage, there will be an end to this mad armaments race. The reason for such a policy is, of course, that there is no alternative.

My second thought is that I'm sorry Professor Shulman somehow misconstrued my presentation. My point was that Americans have been continuously misinformed about the causes for our involvement in the arms race. I simply wanted to present the psychology of our motive. Moreover, it's very difficult to make a final judgment of who is right and who is wrong in a dispute. Thus, my point was that the majority of the countries in the world should somehow be judges.

For this reason, the Soviet Union brought these questions to the United Nations. While one could view this as merely propaganda, the UN has adopted our proposals. Could the majority of countries be considered fools? I think there must be a better explanation. They can make their own judgments; they can see their own interests.

The whole purpose of our introducing proposals connected with disarmament at the three sessions of the General Assembly was, and is, our interest in spreading this trend throughout the globe. The United States will profit from such a worldwide process, as will the Soviet Union.

Q: Dr. Ovinnikov has spoken very forcefully about Russia's desire to reduce armaments. However, as the old saying goes, actions speak louder than words. Why is the Soviet Union in the process of increasing, to a large extent, their naval forces while the United States is substantially reducing theirs?

A: I do agree with you completely on the point that deeds are much more important than words. Thus, about deeds: on December 14, 1973, the Soviet Union reduced its military budget by 250 million rubles—which is more than $300 million.

I think you know what the trend is as far as the United States military budget is concerned.

About the Soviet fleet: you ask why the Russians are sending warships to this or that point in the world. We have our interests—which I think are legitimate—all over the world; we have our friends all over the world. Take, for example, such a case: in 1971, when Bangladesh history was developing, one fleet was sent to that area. You can judge whether our intentions were friendly or unfriendly. The Soviet fleet isn't sent to any country where there is a kind of internal revolt or civil strife.

Q: There has been some recent writing in this country, as well as in Europe, on the topic of nonviolent national defense. A recent example is Professor Gene Sharp's *The Politics of Nonviolent Action*. I wonder if Dr. Ovinnikov can tell us whether there has been any consideration—which, granted, is in only the very early stage of exploration—of this topic within Soviet circles. Has any consideration been given to the idea of adapting the so-called Ghandian peaceful techniques—which would involve doing away with military arms—to national defense? I think we all agree with the need to abolish arms; yet, people do need to feel there is a defense technique available to them.

A: While, frankly, I haven't read the book, I'll try to answer your question. I believe I understand, by implication, the gist of this theory of nonviolent defense. However, it is only on the basis of my understanding of the theory that I can comment.

It seems unrealistic to me to speak in terms of a nonviolent defense for a state in the present world. As soon as major political conflicts develop between any two countries, there is always a risk that this conflict will inevitably develop into a military confrontation. So, I for one do not believe in a theory of nonviolent defense of states. Our point is that in the present world armaments do exist and that all the countries of the world should somehow do away with them.

Q: Dr. Ovinnikov called for United States participation in the chemical warfare treaty. I think his point was well taken. Yet, even when such treaties are ratified, the question of how to control perhaps well-intentioned military leaders who attempt to violate these agreements still remains. I say this in view of actual violations, by both the US and the USSR, currently justified in the name of "research."

To put the question in another way, how can the political leadership of the Union of the Soviet Socialist Republics effectively control their own military to make it comply with ratified treaties?

A: A very simple reply to this question can be offered. We can control our military, as evidenced by the fact that they were not the first, but the second, to create an atomic bomb; they were the second, not the first, to create the hydrogen bomb. So, they have been controlled, and they are being controlled. They do not display any initiative in the international arena.

Q: Dr. Ovinnikov advanced the thesis that while there was a disparity in military power between the United States and the Soviet Union, the risks of war were greater and that once there was parity in military power, the risks of war were reduced. In view of his advancing the theory, I wonder if he could apply it to relations between the Soviet Union and China. Does he think the chances for war would be reduced if China had parity?

A: As is widely known, the Chinese are lagging seriously in the arms race. We are confident that before they reach our level the relationships between our two countries will be restored.

Arms Control and Disarmament:
A View from the USA

By Marshall D. Shulman

ABSTRACT: While the interests of the United States and the Soviet Union are in many respects competitive, they do overlap in one important respect: namely, the avoidance of nuclear war. Yet, the fact is that despite the strategic arms limitation talks (SALT), the competition in strategic weapons continues and may even be exacerbated by these negotiations. For numerous and varied reasons—which are discussed—we have reached the point at which both countries are acquiring war-fighting capabilities. The crisis can be offset only if people take the trouble to study, to learn and to seek to understand the problems and, then, to make their voices heard.

Marshall D. Shulman is Adlai E. Stevenson Professor of International Relations at Columbia University and has been Director of the Russian Institute of Columbia University since 1967. He was Professor of International Politics at the Fletcher School of Law and Diplomacy (1961–1967) and Associate Director of the Russian Research Center at Harvard University (1954–1962). Professor Shulman, who is a member of the Council of Foreign Relations, the International Political Science Association and the American Political Science Association, is author of Stalin's Foreign Policy Reappraised *and* Beyond the Cold War.

THE operative word in the title of this paper is the article a—that is, "A View from the USA." Any resemblance between what I have to say and the official view of the United States government will be purely coincidental.

It was with great sadness that I listened to Dr. Ovinnikov. I felt that the situation may not have changed as much as we had hoped. It seems to me that the subject of arms control can be addressed at several levels. One can try to address the present problem and try to resolve the misunderstandings; or one can go back over the events of the past, over the origins of the Cold War, the intervention, the rise of Fascism and its various explanations, as Dr. Ovinnikov has done. I think the net effect of such an approach is not very productive. I do not think it serves the interests of the USA-USSR agenda for communication—which is the title of our discussions—to approach a subject as serious as this in propagandistic terms. However, my intention is not to enter into a debate.

Moreover, I do not feel that either country—the Soviet Union or the United States—is in a position to wrap itself in the cloak of self-righteousness. There is blame enough for both countries in the history of these sad, even tragic, negotiations. If we are to make progress, I think we have to approach these issues with honesty, understanding and self-criticism.

What is at stake here is nothing less than the question of peace or war. The main objective of the rocky road to coexistence is here in this subject. At the present we find ourselves in the first phase of a limited detente, of which the central and most urgent aspect is to reduce the danger of nuclear war.

CAUSES OF CONTINUED STRATEGIC ARMS COMPETITION

While the interests of the Soviet Union and the United States are in many respects competitive, as we have seen illustrated, they do overlap in one important respect: namely, the avoidance of nuclear war. Rationally, the logic for limiting the strategic military competition is compelling; there can be no advantage for either country in an unregulated competition in nuclear weapons. There can be no doubt that both countries—and the rest of the world—would be more secure if the level of Soviet and American strategic weapons were half of what it now is.

Yet, the fact is that despite the strategic arms limitation talks (SALT), competition in strategic weapons continues and may even be exacerbated by these negotiations. Why is this so? What I propose to do is to suggest what seem to me to be some of the present difficulties we have in understanding each other and in understanding the problem.

Complacency

I think the first problem we have is that there exists a false sense of complacency about the danger of war. We have grown accustomed to living with nuclear weapons, and because their scale of destructiveness is so difficult to comprehend, we find the thought of general war inconceivable. However, there are reasons, it seems to me, that this general complacency is not justified. In fact, the possibility of nuclear war is such that it ought to be in the forefront of our consciousness and of our efforts.

We are in a period in which the prospect of the spread of nuclear weapons to other countries, and even to groups of people, is still a real possibility which, furthermore, has not been sufficiently addressed. We face the possibility of unauthorized use of weapons. We have to take account of the possibility that local conflicts may easily escalate into a general war, without either the United States or the Soviet Union wishing this to happen.

Spread of conventional weapons

We see in this period the blurring of the line between so-called conventional and nuclear weapons and the elimination of some of the inhibitions in the use of, or at least in the deployment of, tactical nuclear weapons. We see about us the increased danger of war involving conventional weapons. There is a widespread unregulated sale and transfer of conventional weapons, the development of greater mobility and fire power of these weapons and the existence of many situations of political instability around the world which may lead to conventional military involvement.

We see technological innovations coming on the scene which have the effect of increasing the instability of the present nuclear balance. At the same time, the best we have been able to develop so far for the preservation of peace is a balance of mutual deterrence which rests upon the assumption, or perhaps the hope, of rationality on the part of decision makers. Yet, we live in a century which has amply demonstrated how little we can safely repose our confidence in the rationality of nations or in the leaders of nations.

Lack of communication

Some of the difficulties arise from problems of communication, of per-

ception, of misunderstanding. This is, perhaps, a particularly fortuitous moment in which to be addressing this problem. In my view, we now face a fateful moment in SALT, in the effort to reach the next stage of strategic arms limitation agreements, because of these difficulties of perception and misunderstanding. Deployment decisions to be taken by the United States and the Soviet Union in the next few months will determine whether there will be a stabilization in the strategic competition or another round of higher competition in weapons—which will be ever more complex, more costly, more unstable and more productive of tensions.

Technological complexity

We have difficulties which simply grow out of the complexity of the problem of knowing how to define what a military equilibrium means; for, the two countries have different kinds of weapons and different geographical situations. It is difficult for us to know what equal security means, what parity means, in concrete terms. This difficulty is illustrated in the present stage of the negotiations. Although both countries have a genuine interest, I think, in limiting the widespread deployment of multiple warhead missiles, the United States in these negotiations finds itself concerned about the total weight and the number of Soviet launchers, while the Soviet Union is concerned about the number of United States warheads. It has been difficult to find a common ground between these two sets of apprehensions in order to define what an equilibrium means in practice.

Political and ideological pressures

There are also differences in strategic doctrines between the two countries. The official American doctrine has tended to emphasize the notion of deterrence, although in practice it has sought to hedge against the possibility that deterrence might break down. The Soviet Union has not made the same distinction in its writings. The result of this unclarity between the two countries in defining the basis upon which their military postures are built has been a movement, within the last few years, away from a reasonably stable and moderate level of deterrence. We have reached the point at which both countries are, in the jargon of the trade, acquiring war-fighting capabilities—that is, more diversified arsenals on both sides.

There are, moreover, uncertainties about the intentions of the other side. There is, of course, the residual mistrust—based on years of aggravated, hostile relations—which will take a long time to dispell. In part, the persistence of this residual mistrust is based upon lack of information. Given the need to plan many years in advance, because the complexity of weapons imposes what is called a long lead time—that is, perhaps five, seven, ten years between the design of weapons and their availability—the tendency has been for planners to operate on the basis of their most prudential assumptions. Most prudential means, in practice, an assumption that the other side would do the utmost of which it is capable. This excess of prudence may do us in. It has provided a dynamism for the arms competition, and it has resulted in the paradox that the more both countries have armed, the less secure we have become.

The negotiating process itself has become an exacerbating factor. In preparing and strengthening their positions for the bargaining negotiations, both countries have undertaken actions which have had the consequence of stimulating the military competition.

Also, in the thinking of both sides there is a concern about the political effects of weapons; this issue is still unclarified. That is, although we have told ourselves that there is no military advantage in striving for superiority in strategic weapons, there has remained the unclarity of whether there may be political advantage in the disparity of arsenals between the two countries. Indeed, at times statesmen appear to be making an effort to draw some political advantage from a presumed superiority in one category of weapons or another. This has also created difficulty in the attempts to stabilize this phase of our relationship.

Research and development programs

One needs to add to this catalogue some of the technical factors involved. There is the tug of new technology. The uncertainty about potential breakthroughs has led each side to hedge against these possibilities by instituting very large research and development programs. These programs develop their own momentum. Once the weapon system is developed and made available, it then becomes quite difficult to argue against its entry into the arsenals of the two countries. This new and ever more complex technology makes it increasingly difficult for the civilian political leadership to know how to make decisions, to choose from among conflicting technical advisers, to keep control over the process and to exert a common sense judgment in the midst of these increasingly complex technical negotiations.

Some of the new technology now making its appearance has the effect of increasing the instability of a nuclear balance. The developments of the last few years in accuracy, in multiple warheads and in other areas have once again been stimulating anxieties about the possibility of a first strike by either country against the other. Although it seems apparent that an effective disabling first strike is not a feasible action by either country, ambiguous actions on the part of either country give rise to these apprehensions and serve to stimulate military programs.

Internal tensions

I think we must realize that in these negotiations there are really three sets of ongoing negotiations. There are those between the United States and the Soviet Union. There are also negotiations which are taking place within each country— that is, within the United States and within the Soviet Union. Within each country there is an interplay of pressures between institutional groups which have different interests with regard to security problems. There are strong pressures which come from those who have responsibility to their governments for professional military services, but who come to represent, instead, the parochial interest of the various services; I think that this is true for both countries. The political leadership will have the problem of exerting an overarching political judgment over these parochial interests and of defining the real security interests of their respective countries.

There are, I believe, unresolved differences within each of the countries in understanding their own real security interests under modern conditions. There has been a persistence of anachronistic views on the real meaning of security and of the tendency to try to achieve it by piling on ever more weapons. It ought to be clear to us that, given the nature of modern weapons, security cannot be achieved by the pursuit of superiority by either side and that the interests of both countries would be served by the achievement of a stable equilibrium at moderate levels through negotiations. This implies an integration of arms control considerations into the defense policies of both countries.

In the case of the United States, the technical brilliance of United States strategic planning has not been matched by equal common sense in the political realm. There has been a false reliance on the games that strategists play, on a specious precision of misapplied mathematics which—however logical within the finite, but insane, world of nuclear strategy—takes leave of sanity and common sense in relation to the world as a whole.

In the case of the Soviet Union, the articulation of strategic notions is largely in the hands of the professional military services. There is relatively little public discussion and debate to be observed regarding alternative policies. This obscurity about the development of Soviet thinking and the extreme secrecy with which these matters are developed has been, as I have suggested, a factor in exacerbating the arms competition. I believe it to be true that if the Soviet minister of defense were to publish a posture statement similar to that published by the United States secretary of defense, it would help greatly to remove some uncertainties regarding Soviet intentions.

THE AGENDA FOR FUTURE LIMITATION OF STRATEGIC ARMS

This leads me to a few conclusions, in the form of some recommendations. I think we—and by we I do not mean the professionals, but the concerned public—need to seek a more enlightened understanding of our respective security interests under present conditions. I think that understanding will lead us to the acceptance of two principles: (1) that a military equilibrium is necessary for international stability; (2) that the optimum security interest of both countries would be served by having that equilibrium at as stable and as moderate a level as can be made possible through negotiations.

This will require, on the part of both countries, a top level political commitment, expressing an overarching judgment over the parochial interests—particularly those of the military pressures in our respective countries—to move in the direction of a stable, moderate level equilibrium. This will also require a radical acceleration of the SALT process, which is moving at such a pace that it is not able to keep up with the increasing development and deployment of new weapons.

In the present development of what I earlier called the first stage of a limited detente—which involves multiple levels of interaction between the two countries—

we ought to recognize our interests in the stabilization of the strategic competition as a semiindependent aspect of the total relationship. That is to say, the mutual interests of the two countries should require stabilizing the military competition, whatever the level of political competition between the two countries.

I think we also need something which might be called CALT—that is, conventional arms limitation talks—at the highest level. Although, obviously, the destructiveness of strategic weapons makes them a problem of great urgency, there is also great urgency in the imminent possibility of conflict arising through the increasing capabilities of the two countries in conventional weapons. The situation may be further exacerbated if local areas of great instability draw us against our will, against our judgment, into a conflict which can begin at the conventional level and may not be subject to any nation's control.

Finally, as part of this agenda of communication we need to develop public interest and public understanding. We need to develop a public constituency for this set of problems—despite their complexity and the sharp, effective pressures of the involved interest groups. The crisis can be offset only if people take the trouble to study, to learn and to seek to understand the problems and, then, to make their voices heard.

* * *

QUESTIONS AND ANSWERS

Q: Dr. Shulman, I admit that the Soviet speaker's speech was more propagandistic than I had hoped. However, all the charges which he raises can't simply be dismissed as propaganda. One hundred nations in the General Assembly expressed desire for a world disarmament conference. Presumably, they don't all want it for the purpose of scoring propaganda points against the United States. Similarly, with the Geneva protocol of 1925: it is a fact that the United States has not agreed to ban gas warfare, for example. These issues should be addressed, I think. Could you try to do that in a few minutes?

A: DR. SHULMAN: As I say, I do not speak as a representative of the United States government. However, it happens that on the first question posed—that is, the one about a world disarmament conference—I agree with the position of United States government. I do not think that the proposal is constructive. I think it is one way of evading serious discussion on these matters. My impression is— particularly in regard to the control of strategic weapons—that the urgent business now is primarily bilateral, at least in the first instance. There is immediately before us a requirement for the United States and the Soviet Union to address themselves to the matters on the table in SALT and to resolve them.

There are some questions which do involve other countries. For example, the questions of European-based forces are properly discussed in the forum of the mutual balanced force reduction discussions. The questions involving nuclear proliferation do, of course, involve those nations which are potential nuclear powers.

Yet, I think the results of a world disarmament conference would, unfortunately, be predictable. It seems to me we've had too much of that kind of futile discussion. That is not the way to make progress, in my judgment.

Now, on the second issue, however, I disagree with the position of the United States government.

I do think we ought to have signed the protocol. I hope we will do so.

———————

Q: This is not merely an agenda for communication between American academics and Soviet academics, or else we could all lean back and enjoy it. It is a dialogue between American academics and representatives of the Soviet state— a very serious matter, indeed. It is most dangerous for Soviet representatives to misunderstand the American people. It's a danger, I think, to our peace. For example, Harry Schwartz earlier said that since the American people are so demoralized, they would not react if the Soviet Union intervened in the Middle East or elsewhere in the globe. I think that's a dangerous idea to tell the Soviet representatives. Furthermore, I don't think it's true. I just hope someone will straighten out the Soviet representative.

A: We have seen in this country —largely, I think, as a result of the Vietnam experience—the contending of two trends in public opinion. One is the continuation of rather strong military pressures—which I have noted—which I think are not peculiar to the United States. The other is a very strong feeling of revulsion against military matters altogether, against the military buildup and against the large military budget.

My impression is that, to some extent, the Middle East war put a punctuation mark at the end of the immediate post-Vietnam-war phase of American policy. I think it had the effect of bringing home to many people the importance of a military equilibrium as a basis for international stability.

I believe it to be true, therefore, that the American people would indeed support the maintenance of the military equilibrium at whatever level is required. This is embodied in the secretary of defense's posture statement, in which he said: "We hope that it will be possible to level off at present levels. If, however, the Soviet Union, in the deployment decisions it faces in the period ahead, should increase its deployments in a way that we regard as destabilizing, we will keep pace with it." My reading of the present American political temper is that this would be the reaction of the American people.

A (Ovinnikov): My first remark is to question what is so bad if Soviet representatives speak here? What's so bad if their counterparts are professors? I happen to be a doctor, too. Could it be interpreted that I was given this degree by the Soviet government specially for this particular occasion?

My second point is a more serious one. I see that the man who asked the question—or, rather, who delivered a kind of presentation— seems irritated that we, the Soviets, are somehow suspicious. You tell us all the time that you are suspicious of us. We have our reasons for suspicion, too. This is the situation. So, let's step by step remove these mutual suspicions. Also, please do not substitute the phases I put forward for your own phases, as if I castigated the American people. This is not a matter for serious discussion.

———

Q: It is evident that the nations of the world have armed, and continue to arm today, in search of security. According to the reports I have seen,

the United States has spent $1 trillion, 300 billion for armaments since the Second World War. We have built hundreds of military and air bases around the world. Can you say that we are more secure today than we were twenty-five years ago?

A: The answer is clearly: no, we are not. And I'm very much in sympathy with the sentiments implied and expressed in your question.

It's clear, I think, that we have been guided by what I feel are anachronistic conceptions of security. Perhaps, we have sought to build upon the old frontier traditions, when security rested in the six-shooter on one's hip. This feeling was strengthened over many years when this country had superiority in nuclear weapons. We may now be in a period of psychological adjustment, at which point we must learn what parity means and what a military equilibrium means. I do not underestimate the difficulty of our absorption of that notion as a people and as a government. However, I must say that the process of negotiation has not made it any easier to find concrete solutions to these problems.

To attempt to answer the question of who has the greatest blame, I don't know the answer. As I said, I think all governments now share responsibility for the situation, including the two leading powers in the world. We must do what we can in this country, and we must hope that we will find responsiveness in the Soviet Union. I don't think it is profitable to assess who is more to blame.

———

Q: Some young people today are saying that they believe the non-violent approach, rather than wars, should be used in international relations. Theories have been advanced that war is not an instinct, but a learned way of responding and that peaceful methods of responding can also be learned. If this nonviolent approach can be learned, how can we best apply it to achieve peace? It seems to me that there are peace-loving people among the population of all nations.

A: There have been, as probably many of you know, many interesting studies of the very tormenting question of whether war is rooted in human nature, whether it's related to an instinctual drive of man toward conflict, toward hostility, toward aggression. Those studies have not been altogether conclusive. Furthermore, the question is ever more complicated by the development of weapons which remove war-making activities from the direct combat involvement of the individual. The remoteness, for example, of a pilot from the people who are the victims of his bombs is such as to create a separation between the act in warfare and the immediate physical consequences of it. It's quite possible for a bomber pilot or a bombadier to discharge his weapons with-

out any feelings of aggression whatsoever—especially in an age of missiles when the remoteness of the target from the individual tends to dehumanize the process, as well. Indeed, this is one of the dangers: the means of warfare become separated; they become too professionalized.

In fact, what we find as we grapple with the question of arms limitation and control in an effort to reduce the danger of war is a world increasingly involved not so much with the bellicosity of individuals, but rather with the complex problems in the behavior of large bureaucracies and large organizations whose dynamics we very little understand. This situation presents quite different problems from those posed by controlling war at a time when war meant essentially individual combat and the expression of individual aggressiveness.

I think it is true, as the speaker said, that the people of this country and the people of the Soviet Union are certainly not disposed towards war. Our problem is how to translate that sentiment in such a way that governments respond to the same sentiment.

The Exchange of People and Ideas

By ALLEN H. KASSOF

ABSTRACT: In this paper attention is focused on long term exchanges of individuals, because this is the area in which interaction is most significant and in which there are the best possibilities for serious communication on the complex issues of Soviet-American cooperation. For the United States the exchanges provide indispensible access for hundreds of scholarly specialists who conduct research on Russian and Soviet life and culture. The majority of Soviet participants are in scientific and technical fields. For both sides the exchanges provide the less tangible benefits of mutual understanding which can come only from personal involvement and exposure. There are, however, various obstacles to maintaining and broadening the exchange program: quantitative and practical problems, the securing of access to Soviet scholars on an individual basis, the lopsided imbalance of fields represented in the exchange and the working conditions for visiting scholars. While recent success and innovations illustrate the potential of the exchange program, worrisome questions about its future must be faced now; for, it is unlikely that the long range accommodation being sought by the USA and the USSR will take place without such an exchange program.

Allen H. Kassof has been Executive Director of the International Research and Exchanges Board since 1968. He was Associate Professor of Sociology and Assistant Dean of the College of Princeton University (1965–1968). Dr. Kassof is the author of Soviet Youth Program: The Administered Society *and editor of* Prospects for Soviet Society.

WHAT are the prospects for Soviet-American cooperation in education, research and scholarship? Hopes for such partnership are so identified with the recent move towards detente that many are surprised to learn that our exchanges of scholars have already been going on for seventeen years. In lean times that small, but steady, flow of professors and researchers was often the only sustained, intensive contact between Soviet and American life; in good times it will continue to be the most important channel for the exchange of people and ideas. The lessons learned from this mutual experience are instructive and should help us to shape and to expand our future relationship.

The principal United States exchanges are conducted by the International Research and Exchanges Board (IREX) with the USSR Ministry of Higher and Specialized Secondary Education and with the Soviet Academy of Sciences. Each year they currently involve some one hundred young Soviet and American researchers in all fields, about fifty senior scholars and almost seventy teachers of the Russian or English languages. There is also a long-standing exchange of scientists between the United States National Academy of Sciences and the Soviet Academy of Sciences. Recently, a few small exchanges administered by various government bureaus or agencies have been instituted in specific areas of cooperation, such as transportation, environmental quality and medicine; a number of special projects in "big science" and in space exploration are planned or are underway.

All of these new efforts can be expected to have significant and beneficial effects on the larger Soviet-American relationship. However, I focus here on the long term exchanges of individuals—that is, those lasting for an academic semester or more—for this is the area in which interaction is most significant and in which there are the best possibilities for serious communication on the complex issues of Soviet-American cooperation.

LONG TERM EXCHANGES OF INDIVIDUALS

Although the exchanges have been hampered from the beginning by some very serious limitations and shortcomings—to which I shall return—they have already made substantial contributions. It would be worth mentioning some of the important ones before turning to the question of a future agenda.

For the United States the exchanges provide indispensible access for hundreds of scholarly specialists who conduct research on Russian and Soviet life and culture. Their work is immeasurably enriched by their access to original sources, by direct consultation and collaboration with Soviet colleagues and by living and participating in the culture which they are studying. In turn, their students share in this enriched experience, and the public at large benefits from the growing fund of accurate and sensitive interpretations of a society with which American interests are, for better or for worse, increasingly intertwined. Those who were engaged in Russian and Soviet studies before 1958, when the exchanges finally opened long closed doors, and who had to struggle to conduct their research from a distance and with skimpy secondary sources will fully appreciate the magnitude of the achievement.

The benefits on the Soviet side are in some ways comparable—although they have a somewhat different profile, since the great majority of Soviet participants are in scientific and technical fields and relatively fewer have come to study aspects of the American experience. Nevertheless, inasmuch as science and technology are no less a part of contemporary culture than are the social sciences and humanities, communication in this sector also has great transnational significance. Moreover, contrary to a widespread popular misconception, the presence of Soviet scientists in the United States by no means implies a one-way process of technology transfer to the Soviet Union. In the majority of cases, as we know from their university hosts in the United States, Soviet exchange participants are outstanding specialists who contribute as much as they take. In other words, the relationship more often than not is a collaborative one, and the many individual successes are a useful reminder of the vast potential for Soviet-American cooperation in the future.

For both sides, too, there are the less tangible benefits of mutual understanding which can come only from personal involvement and exposure. Although most Soviet and American participants are likely to conclude that there is no place like home, all of them return with a deepened appreciation of life "over there" and a newly acquired incapacity to make simplistic moral judgments about the other side. Alas, it will take much more than this to resolve the tensions between the two superpowers, but it is not entirely naive

to suppose that experiences of this kind have real and salutory effects on cross-national perceptions and, potentially, on policy and behavior.

A catalogue of the successes and contributions of the exchange program would be very long indeed. If Soviet-American relations had remained fixed at their earlier stage, we could continue to take comfort from the fact that scholarly cooperation, although limited, was one of the few bright spots in an otherwise gloomy landscape. However, the changes of the last two or three years have placed new demands on Soviet-American exchanges. Thus, our expectations of them, quite rightly, have been raised. To write a fresh agenda will require, first of all, some frank criticisms of things as they are.

PROBLEMS OF, AND OBSTACLES TO, MAINTAINING AND BROADENING THE EXCHANGE PROGRAM

The most obvious problem is quantitative: the USSR and USA—with combined populations of almost half a billion souls and the most extensive research and university establishments in the world—are exchanging fewer than two hundred scholars a year and fewer than ten for purposes of lecturing and teaching. If we count only those whose visits last for at least a semester, the figure on each side is well under one hundred. The volume is now slowly increasing, but it will have to be multiplied many times before it can be considered anything but token.

There are some practical obstacles which need to be overcome, for example, financing—relatively easy to arrange—and language capability—which will take some time to achieve. However, the most important obstacle is the political factor. That is, Soviet-American exchange relationships from the beginning have been governed by formal agreements at the intergovernmental level. Unfortunately, the quotas have been treated as absolute ceilings rather than as starting points.

On the American side, this inflexibility sometimes took the form of insisting on a literal one-for-one reciprocal count, even when it served no obviously useful purpose. The policy has now changed substantially for the better as a result of pressure from academic interests and the general improvement in relations.

On the Soviet side, countless legitimate and worthwhile initiatives undertaken by United States individuals and institutions have been, and continue to be, turned away arbitrarily, because they are not enumerated in the official agreement. The use of the agreement format to minimize, rather than to facilitate, contacts between individuals and institutions is a doubtful device at any time. During a period of improving relations there is no conceivable warrant for it.

A related and still more vexing obstacle is the extreme difficulty—virtually, the total impossibility—of securing access to Soviet scholars on an individual basis, for example, so far as invitations are concerned. Our experience has shown almost without exception that Soviet scholars who are invited to teach, to lecture or to conduct research at our universities, even within the framework of existing agreements, and who wish to accept are routinely denied permission to do so by the authorities—who, to make matters worse, frequently offer gratuitous

excuses in the name of the recipient of the invitation. Sometimes it is illness, otherwise the press of other duties, even though the invitation may be proffered a year or two in advance. Recently a new reason has been cited: that the Soviet authorities are in a better position than the United States host to know who is worth inviting and who is not. It is important to emphasize that I am not speaking here of controversial figures—who pose a different question—but of Soviet scholars about whom there is no dispute. It is necessary to say in all candor to our Soviet colleagues that this practice, which was always puzzling in that it served no useful purpose, is a most serious impediment to the normalization of our communications.

Still another problem concerns the lopsided imbalance of fields represented in the exchanges. Both sides are responsible, although in different ways. In the program for young researchers, which is the largest Soviet-American exchange, United States applicants come overwhelmingly from the fields of history, language and literature, while those studying contemporary aspects of Soviet life—for example, economists, political scientists and sociologists—are severely underrepresented. There are also very few scientists on this exchange, but their needs are more appropriately met by the National Academy of Sciences program. If the figures for the latter are added to the total, the overall proportion of American scientists participating is reasonably representative.

The blame is in part attributable to the shortsightedness of the underrepresented disciplines, themselves, where the importance of Soviet studies has never been fully understood, but also to the difficulties of conducting research on current topics under Soviet conditions. In the past, specialists in these fields either have not been accepted by our Soviet exchange partners or, once they arrived, have found it all but impossible to gain access to information and reasonable research facilities beyond those already available to them in published sources at home. Accordingly, others were discouraged from trying at all and from making the substantial time investment in linguistic and other essential background preparation.

Recently some improvements have been registered: more participants are beginning to come from the underrepresented disciplines, in part as a result of a special preparatory program which IREX has organized for them. More scholars are now being accepted whose topics previously were thought to be sensitive by our Soviet partners. It is still too early to come to any conclusions about whether their research access will prove adequate and whether their experiences will encourage or discourage others from following.

The imbalance on the Soviet side stems from the fact that more than 90 percent of the participants in the basic exchange have come from science and technology. The point is not that the scientists and engineers are less warmly welcomed, but that virtually no room is left in the younger group for scholars whose work might contribute towards a clearer understanding in the Soviet Union of American culture, society and politics at a time when the prospect of intensified relations has made the need more acute than ever. The smaller senior exchanges are better bal-

anced in this respect, but they provide opportunities only for older scholars. One can understand the desire of the sending side in an exchange to choose participants whose work will reflect national priorities in scientific and technological development. Yet, we wonder whether a slate of fifty scholars which includes more than a dozen specialists in electronics and computers, but not a single student of American society—as is the case with the 1974-1975 exchange—constitutes a wholly legitimate understanding or use of the purpose of Soviet-American scholarly and cultural contacts.

Finally, there is the problem of working conditions for scholars once they have been accepted by the receiving side. Although marked improvements have occurred in recent years, some participants still run into difficulties and delays of many months in gaining access to Soviet archival materials. Each year there are the inevitable few whose research plans are utterly frustrated after they have waited for a whole academic year in futile hope of an opening. What is puzzling is that the materials in question are almost always historical or literary in nature and that their use by scholars could not possibly be problematic to the authorities. Perhaps the source of the difficulty lies less in any intention of ill-will than in the often formidable bureaucratic obstacles with which an overburdened Soviet exchange staff cannot always cope.

Whatever the reasons, they are no more consoling to the victim than is the news that such incidents are becoming less frequent. Those whose legitimate hopes and expectations have been raised and then dashed return home with gloomy reports—and rightly so—about their experiences in the Soviet Union. These negative accounts have an impact on academic and public opinion quite out of proportion to their actual part in the exchanges. Considering that corrective measures could be taken with so little trouble and at such great gain, it is difficult for us to understand why these problems are allowed to fester.

If I have paused on some of the disappointments in the exchanges, it is not to allocate blame, but to underscore the fact that it is high time to resolve them so that we can move on to more urgent matters which already have been delayed too long. The Soviet-American exchanges, which began as symbolic efforts at cooperation when there was very little else on which to cooperate, now have assumed an independent importance. They no longer only reflect Soviet-American relations, but influence them. It is all the more important, then, to see to it that they are conducted fairly and efficiently.

RECENT INNOVATIONS

A number of recent successes and innovations illustrate the potential of the exchange program. One of the most impressive is an informal program of contacts which began in 1971 with a number of institutes of the Soviet Academy of Sciences, whose work involves research on the United States, shares an interest in Soviet-American relations or in third areas where Soviet and American involvements meet. Among the institutes involved are the Institute for the Study of the USA, the Institute for World Economy and International Relations, the Institute of the World Labor Movement and the Institute for Sociological Research.

The result has been a series of intervisitations, lectures, consultations and exchanges of data between Soviet and American scholars which have proved useful to both sides and which continue to become more active each year. Moreover, as those involved become better acquainted with one another after repeated visits, the reserve which characterizes first-time contacts has given way to some very frank discussions on important matters among those whose research is followed with interest by policy makers on both sides. The creation of a regular and reliable channel for such contacts, which at the same time is an unofficial one, is therefore a welcome and significant development. There is no reason that such an approach cannot be extended to include a broader range of concerns.

In contemplating further developments on the basis of this successful model, we would also like to urge on our Soviet colleagues the inclusion of provisions for future extended exchanges to and from these institutions of younger scholars who are still in training. Thus far, contacts have been more or less the exclusive domain of senior personnel; however, both sides would stand to benefit if, for example, students at about the dissertation stage or its equivalent could spend an academic year at a corresponding institution on the other side. There is a great shortage of Soviet American specialists and American Soviet specialists who are able to understand nuance and context in the other society. Therefore, we ought to give at least a few of our most promising young people oppor-tunities to associate intensively with their opposite numbers while they are still in the formative period of their scholarly lives.

One of the most striking gaps in Soviet-American cooperation has been almost total absence of col-laborative research beyond the level of consultation between indi-vidual exchange scholars and their hosts. Yet, such cooperation is an utterly essential part of Soviet-American communication, not only because joint work provides the most effective means of establish-ing durable and consequential rela-tionships, but because the modern world has become so complex that even the superpowers cannot ig-nore the need for an international division of scholarly and scientific labor.

A beginning has finally been made in the sciences and technol-ogy, although much of the pro-jected collaboration still remains on the drawing board. In a sense, collaboration in this area is the easiest because it is the most obvi-ous: science has an internal agenda which offers rich choices for joint work that does not necessarily raise or touch on political issues as such. A more challenging task will be to reach agreement on joint work in areas which impinge on the basic Soviet-American relationship or which, indeed, specifically concern the subject.

It is perhaps a measure of the growing confidence in Soviet-American communications that a decision has now been taken to create a Joint Commission on the Social Sciences and Humanities. I am pleased to make today the first public announcement of its estab-lishment. This fourteen-man com-mission will have as its task the identification and facilitation of col-laborative work in all the social-scientific and humanistic disciplines. It will encourage joint and parallel research, ad hoc ex-changes of individuals and groups engaged in topic- or problem-oriented research and the exchange of data and experience.

The commission will meet for the first time early in 1975 in the United States and thereafter will meet periodically, alternating between the two countries. It will be sponsored on the American side by the American Council of Learned Societies and in the Soviet Union by the Academy of Sciences. It will be up to the commission itself, of course, to chart an agenda. Yet, it is perhaps not too soon to express some hopes concerning its work. No doubt it will wish at the beginning, when cooperative under-takings are still in the experimental stage, to concentrate on joint ef-forts which are important, but relatively noncontroversial. In the long run, however, there is no reason that it should not address some of the tougher questions con-fronting us.

Indeed, such a backlog of un-conducted business has accumu-lated during the years of tension that the possibilities are staggering. The problem will be as much one of knowing where, as one of how, to begin. Both countries share, be-cause of their size, complexity, rank in world production and strategic position, an exceptional number of overarching problems to which they sometimes adapt in similar, and sometimes in quite different, ways. Master questions of resource allocation, the impact of continuing modernization and urbanization on social existence, problems of edu-cation and the identification and nurturing of talent, adaptation to the changing contours of life as we move into the postindustrial era, take their place beside more immediate and urgent questions of war and peace and of conflict and accommodation between the United States and the Soviet Union. To be sure, it is easier to mention these themes than it is to translate them into specific collaborative researches, but what is important is that for the first time in the Soviet-American relationship it is realistic to expect that we can and shall do so.

AGENDA FOR FUTURE EXCHANGES

I do not need to belabor the point that the prospects for significant improvements in scholarly exchanges between our two countries—indeed, the very possibility of speaking seriously of an agenda for communication—did not come about spontaneously. They have depended upon the posture of political detente which has come to characterize, at least in part, Soviet-American relations during recent years. Those who are concerned with the administration of exchanges on both sides can rightly claim some credit for gradual and piecemeal improvements, but there is no doubt that the possibilities for a major breakthrough are associated with the development of a favorable international climate. I mention this obvious connection because it also raises some worrisome questions about the future which we ought to face now.

For many years we have argued with our Soviet colleagues that such forms of communication as scholarly exchanges should pro-

ceed and should flourish independently of the temperature of Soviet-American relations at a given time. These communications, we argued, have an independent significance which, if anything, grows during times of tension when other channels are closed or abandoned. Our partners have replied—and still reply—that, on the contrary, improvements in, or expansion of, such exchange relationships can follow only from improvements in political relations.

In fact, events have overtaken the argument as the prevailing atmosphere of detente has stimulated the exchange of people and ideas. However, we should be under no illusions that the question has been answered. Perhaps it would be better to raise it again now, while relations continue to be cordial. The stakes are substantial.

It could perhaps have been predicted—and is now confirmed—that the road to Soviet-American accommodation is neither easy nor straight. Detente is a vague concept and a fragile reality, with no guarantees; no one can safely predict its future course. It is not only possible, but virtually inevitable, that we shall suffer setbacks, some of them serious.

It is all the more vital, then, to avoid the destructive practice of treating—as we have in the past—communications and exchanges as though they were rewards for good behavior or a barometer of state relationships. Contacts among scholars and systematic collaboration on problems of mutual concern to the two countries are not gifts to be dispensed as tokens of approbation, but a permanent necessity in a complicated and dangerous world. The current atmosphere of detente makes possible only the first steps towards establishing the kind of communication between the USA and the USSR which should have existed long ago, and the work is only beginning. To allow ourselves to be drawn back into the old pattern because of future, and perhaps inevitable, disappointments on the political level would be just as irresponsible as to suppose that scholarly and scientific collaboration, once underway, can be turned on and off as a matter of governmental convenience without grave and lasting damage to the enterprise.

It may well be that these anxieties concerning the future course of Soviet-American relations are unfounded and that our communications will become even more intensive—we can surely hope so. However, prudence suggests that accommodation is not likely to be a linear process and that it would be realistic to expect at least some periods when the initial enthusiasm will be insufficient in itself to carry us through. In that case, we shall have to recognize that the basic need for exchanges of people is irreducible. The long range accommodation which is now being sought by the two countries will hardly be brought about by such exchanges alone, but it is unlikely to take place without them.

* * *

QUESTIONS AND ANSWERS

Q: In the presentation on the exchanges of scholars, I was happy to note that there was some discussion of joint work. However, I'm wondering whether the procedures being developed for a full cooperation will take into account the fact that in the American academic community there have been basic structural changes. Important scholar-contributors are now located not only at the leading, more famous universities, but at a number of state and smaller colleges. This question carries with it the implication that those who benefit from detente may be leading corporations and outstanding individuals and that the participation may be limited—that is, it may exclude a number of the people not at the very top levels of our society.

A: The exchanges have always been open to individual applicants, and there is no reason for the procedure to change. The number of places available in exchange programs with the Soviet Union —for reasons which I mentioned earlier—has always been rather limited. Thus, the competition has quite naturally tended to focus on the selection of people of the highest quality. I don't expect that this will change, but as the exchanges expand, there will be room for more and more people. In any case, the exchanges have never been mediated through individual academic institutions; therefore, academic affiliation is not really an issue in the exchange. It hasn't been and won't be.

As for Soviet participation and placement at American universities, it is perfectly understandable that Soviet scholars tend to be interested in leading institutions, simply because these institutions make superior facilities available to them. We have taken great pains to point out to our Soviet colleagues that there are more than a handful of famous institutions in the United States which offer worthwhile facilities. I think we are gradually succeeding in distributing Soviet and other exchange scholars to a larger number of institutions.

Q: Since the title of Dr. Kassof's presentation was "The Exchange of People and Ideas," I wonder whether he would comment briefly on the exchange of documentary and published materials. It seems to me that, since all of the people who might usefully go çannot go abroad, the free flow of materials can serve an important purpose.

Secondly, can Dr. Kassof comment on American access to some of the archival documents which deal with the long concern that the Russians have had in the past, and the Soviets have had more recently, in the field of China studies?

A: First, with respect to the exchange of materials, this normally has taken the form of exchanges of books, manuscripts and other information among Soviet and American libraries and institutions. Most American centers which have major collections of Slavic materials have one or more exchanges with Soviet institutions. These exchanges continue to be a general problem, because the quantities of material to be exchanged are so vast and so complicated. We're trying to make some contribution towards the solution of the problem, for example, by sponsoring meetings between American archivists and Soviet archival authorities. These contacts are going on, and we're hopeful that there will be some useful result.

With respect to China studies, there is a perfectly understandable and very live interest on both sides in exchanges of scholarship and materials. I should estimate that not fewer than a dozen American and Soviet sinologists have spent time with one another over the last couple of years. The Soviets are very interested—I think for obvious reasons—in finding out what American research is being done on both historical and contemporary China.

The Soviets, as you know, have immense repositories of materials of Chinese historical significance. I am confident that when we have prepared a sufficient number of young American specialists who are not only sinologists, but who are linguistically equipped to work in the Soviet Union, we will, in fact, be able to tap the material profitably. It's a very promising area.

Q: In making his strong point about the validity of semester-long visits by scholars in the ongoing exchange between the Soviet Union and the United States and about the less tangible, but equally important, significance of exchange on the individual and personal exposure level in mutual understanding, I wonder why Dr. Kassof neglected to mention the international effect of cultural exchange, which has been inspired by people of high calibre?

A: I would not have neglected it, except that the time is, after all, limited. Furthermore, it has generally been my feeling that the actual impact on national behavior and policy making is likely to be more substantial if it occurs through the exchange of people who share working relationships in areas of common concern. Cultural—as opposed to scholarly —exchanges, while they are immensely important, tend to be presentational and to involve display rather than an exchange as such. For example, a Soviet scholar coming to the United States goes home with quite different ideas about his work and about the United States; the same is true in the case of an American scholar returning from the Soviet Union. Ballet dancers, however, are usually too busy with other things—namely, dancing. Thus, the degree of contact tends to be limited and passive, although much prettier.

Q: Hitler, fortunately, is dead. However, assuming for one moment that the Nazis were still in power in Germany, I doubt whether sensible Americans would advocate any kind of benefits to the Nazi regime, because we wouldn't want to strengthen them. My question is, Dr. Kassof, why do you support exchange programs with the Soviet Union, in spite of the following facts: Krushchev threatened to bury us; Lenin promised to conquer the whole world for the Soviet Union; and so far nobody in Moscow has seen fit to retract his statements—which implies that the Soviets still have these purposes. Why, then, are we giving them advanced computer technology in exchange for Russian folk songs? I am very much afraid that the Soviet Union is benefiting greatly, while we are ultimately contributing to the end of civilization as we know it and cherish it. I hope that Dr. Kassof can alleviate my fears in this respect.

A: Your accusation is so intense that I don't think I can alleviate your fears. I am not sure that I agree with either your estimate of the state of Soviet-American relations nor of the procedures involved in improving them.

One of the major contributions which the exchanges have made, and continue to make, is the modification of the kinds of extreme and one-sided apocalyptic views which you have attributed to the Soviet leadership. I am confident that the presence in the United States of an increasing number of Soviet specialists, who come to understand the full complexity and subtlety of American society and politics, will make an important, lasting and long term contribution towards the modification of the kind of position which you have described. At the same time—as I have suggested in my address—the presence in the Soviet Union of Americans, who have opportunities to work with their Soviet colleagues and to become more closely associated with Soviet life and culture, leads to a modification of the kind of simplistic view which, if you will forgive me, I think you have expressed.

Aspects of Sharing Science and Technology

By LOREN R. GRAHAM

ABSTRACT: Before 1972 the exchange of science and technology between the United States and the Soviet Union was limited to the very small program administered in accordance with official agreements which dated back to 1958. The tempo and scale of the exchanges in technical areas were dramatically altered by the eight separate agreements signed at the 1972 and 1973 summit meetings. These agreements were reached as a part of foreign policy considerations pointing toward detente and were thus not given specific content. While progress in each of the exchange areas has been slowed by numerous delays in making the original agreements more concrete, the prospects for the future appear to be good. Yet, a most sensitive problem plagues Soviet-American scientific relations: that of political or human-rights issues as factors influencing the course of the exchange program. Among American scientists there is a full spectrum of opinion on these questions. Dealing with this dilemma can be facilitated by making several important distinctions, starting with one between protests by American individuals and those by official administrators. We are now entering a period of optimism tempered by realism in which the rate of expansion of exchanges will rest on the willingness of both countries to face problems openly and to find solutions to them emanating from a spirit of accommodation.

Loren R. Graham is Professor of History and Staff Member of the Russian Institute at Columbia University. He was Research Fellow of the History of Science Department at Harvard University—1972–1973; member of the Institute for Advanced Study—1969–1970; and a Guggenheim Fellow—1969–1970. Professor Graham is author of numerous scholarly articles and books, including Science and Philosophy in the Soviet Union, which was nominated for the 1973 National Book Award.

AS a result of the 1972 and 1973 summit meetings between President Nixon and Chairman Brezhnev, the exchange programs in science and technology between the United States and the Soviet Union have blossomed. Although some of the new projects are still in early stages, already enough has actually been accomplished to indicate that an entirely new and highly promising period in Soviet-American relations in these fields has been initiated.

Perhaps the most spectacular of the new cooperative efforts will be the linking of Apollo-type and Soiuz-type space vehicles and the resulting visit of astronauts to each other's spacecraft. The event is being prepared now and is scheduled for 1975. This specific feat can be described both figuratively and literally as the exchange of scientific personnel on a very high level. Its accomplishment will have great symbolic significance and, hopefully, will lead to further cooperation in space. However, its total scientific value is considerably less than the expansion of exchanges in other fields, which will attract little attention in newspaper columns.

If, in the years before 1972, we could speak of official scientific exchanges between the two countries involving, at most, visits by several dozens of specialists from each country annually, we can now speak of several hundreds every year.[1] An even greater growth in the near future is possible. This increase in the number of technical specialists has been accompanied by a truly vast expansion of the subject areas

and specific topics upon which cooperation is either projected or underway. All of this encourages one to predict significant advances for world society through the promotion of science resulting from increased contacts between scientists and engineers of these two leading nations.

At the same time that this impressive growth in scientific relations has occurred, we have come to recognize that a great many difficulties still remain. In fact, the very increase in volume of scientific and technological exchanges has brought to light a series of new problems or has underscored old ones—some of which are of a technical or administrative nature, while others are political or even ideological in character. Several of these difficulties—to which I will return later—are sufficiently serious to introduce in the minds of some scientists and engineers genuine reservations about the validity or desirability of the expanded scientific and technological exchange program. However, taking both the encouraging signs and the trouble spots into consideration, it is my opinion that we are justified in remaining optimistic and even enthusiastic about continued expansion of exchanges in science and technology, while at the same time remaining aware that further painful difficulties are likely.

A BRIEF HISTORY OF US-USSR SCIENTIFIC AND TECHNOLOGICAL EXCHANGE

Before 1972 the exchange of science and technology between the Soviet Union and the United States was largely limited to the very small, but highly valuable, program administered in accordance with the series of official exchange agree-

1. See, annual reports of the Office of Soviet and Eastern European Exchanges, *Exchanges and Cooperation with the Soviet Union and Eastern Europe* (Washington, D.C.: Government Printing Office).

ments which dated back to 1958. Other Western nations signed similar exchange agreements with the Soviet Union in the late 1950s and early '60s. France, in fact, led the way in technological and scientific cooperation with an agreement in 1957 and, throughout the '60s and early '70s, conducted a more extensive cooperation with the Soviet Union in these fields than the United States or any other Western country.[2]

On the American side, the science and technology exchanges between the US and the USSR in the '60s were administered primarily by the National Academy of Sciences (NAS) and secondarily by the International Research and Exchanges Board (IREX)—before 1968, the Inter-University Committee on Travel Grants—with the further cooperation and support of the American Council of Learned Societies. On the Soviet side, the primary coordinating bodies were the Soviet Academy of Sciences and the Ministry of Higher and Secondary Specialized Education. Each year in the late '60s and early '70s twenty to forty American scientists made research trips to the Soviet Union under the auspices of the exchange between the United States national academy and the Soviet academy, and a similar number of Soviet scientists came to the United States. Soviet and American scientists and engineers at a more junior level were also exchanged between Soviet and American universities in the '60s, but most American graduate students and young instructors who were interested in studying in the Soviet Union were in the humanities and social sciences. In addition to the academy and university exchanges, a small number of scientists were exchanged at the direct invitation of research institutions.[3]

The tempo and scale of the exchanges in technical areas were dramatically altered by the eight separate agreements affecting science and technology signed at the 1972 and 1973 summit meetings. The four agreements signed in Moscow in 1972 were: (1) environmental protection, (2) medical science and public health, (3) cooperation in space and (4) science and technology. In Washington in the summer of 1973 additional agreements were reached in: (5) agriculture, (6) studies of the world ocean, (7) transportation and (8) peaceful uses of atomic energy.[4] These new programs were not designed to replace the scientific and technical exchanges carried out under the older agreements, but to supplement them. In fact, a sepa-

2. Maurice Levy, "Scientific and Technological Cooperation with the Soviet Union: The French Experience" (Paper presented at the conference "Russia and the West: Cultural Contacts and Influences," Schloss Leopoldskron, Salzburg, Austria, 1 November 1974).

3. For an interesting report on an exchange predating the 1972 and 1973 agreements involving the National Accelerator Laboratory near Batavia, Illinois, the University of California at Los Angeles and the Soviet accelerator at Serpukhov, see, Jane Wilson, "A Russian Experiment," *Bulletin of the Atomic Scientists*, December 1972, pp. 29–31.

4. For the texts of the agreements, see, *Department of State Bulletin*, 26 June 1972 and 23 July 1973. See, also, "U.S.-U.S.S.R. Commission on Scientific and Technical Cooperation," ibid., 21 August 1972, pp. 214–217; and Philip Handler, "The Moscow Agreements and U.S.-Soviet Scientific Relationships," *News Report, National Academy of Sciences, National Research Council, National Academy of Engineering* 22, no. 7 (August-September 1972), pp. 8–11, and 22, no. 10 (December 1972), p. 1. Also, "U.S.-Soviet Accord Will Ease Joint Research," *Physics Today*, August 1972, pp. 69–71.

rate agreement in 1973 provided specifically for the continuation of the older exchanges. The NAS and the Soviet Academy of Sciences even agreed to a 50 percent increase in the older exchange program to accompany the creation of the newer ones.

The agreements of 1972 and 1973 represent such a quantum leap in the level of scientific exchange between the two countries—in addition to the expansion in so many different directions—that it is very difficult to provide a description of them which would not amount to a long and tedious list of separate topics. Furthermore, the problem involved in providing a description of the expanded exchange program is accentuated by the fact that the original agreements signed in 1972 and 1973 were phrased in very general terms. These agreements were reached as a part of foreign policy considerations pointing toward detente, not as a result of specific requests by scientists and engineers. As a result, a long period of separate negotiations and discussions among specialists was required before the summit agreements could be given specific content. That process is still underway and will, no doubt, continue throughout the entire life of the agreements.

In order to make the original agreements more concrete a joint commission was established for each of the eight exchange areas. The Joint Commission for Science and Technology has had two meetings since its establishment: the first during March 19 to 21, 1973, in Washington and the second during November 28 and 29, 1973, in Moscow.[5] The joint commission has

cochairmen—one from each country. For both meetings the United States chairman has been Dr. H. Guyford Stever, director of the National Science Foundation. The Soviet chairman for both meetings was scheduled to be academician V. A. Kirillin, chairman of the USSR State Committee for Science and Technology; however, as a result of his illness during the first meeting, he was temporarily replaced by his deputy, academician V. A. Trapeznikov.

From the beginning the Commission on Science and Technology had agreed to concentrate on six areas: energy, agriculture, computer applications in management, water resources, microbiology and chemical catalysis. Topics added later were scientific and technical information, forestry research and technology, science policy and electrometallurgy. Within each of these areas the joint commission has tried to elaborate lists of subtopics and to suggest institutions suitable for cooperative research.[6]

It soon became clear that the interests of the Soviet and American sides were not identical; each suggested topics which reflected its own interests and its perception of what the other side had to offer of the greatest value. The Soviet

5. For the report of the first meeting, see, National Science Foundation press release

73–131, dated 21 March 1973; or "U.S.-U.S.S.R. Scientific and Technical Commission Holds First Meeting," *Department of State Bulletin*, 7 May 1973, pp. 584–585. For second meeting, see, U.S., Department of State, Bureau of International Scientific and Technological Affairs, "Record of the Second Meeting of the U.S.-U.S.S.R. Joint Commission on Scientific and Technical Cooperation." The third meeting is scheduled to be held in the United States in October of 1974.

6. "U.S.-U.S.S.R. Agreement on Cooperation in Science, Technology: The Emphasis Is on Applications and on Practical Results," *Science* 180 (6 April 1973), pp. 40–41.

representatives, for example, expressed strong interest in computer technology and its application to industrial management, agricultural technology and deep-sea drilling research—three fields in which American experience has been extensive. The Americans, on the other hand, inquired about Soviet expertise in areas in which Soviet scientists and engineers were known to have done significant work—such as equipment designed for use in arctic regions, magnetohydrodynamic generating facilities and high powered lasers for thermonuclear reactions and fusion.[7]

Gradually, and with numerous delays, progress was achieved in most of these areas. In 1973 over 150 scientists and specialists were exchanged under the terms of the "Agreement on Science and Technology" alone—which is only one of the eight different agreements affecting scientific and technical exchanges. Furthermore, outside the specific exchanges named in these agreements, specialists from numerous private American firms visited the USSR, and over fifteen concluded technical cooperation agreements with the Soviet government.

It turned out to be easier to arrange exchanges between massive institutions on both sides—for example, between the United States Atomic Energy Commission and its Soviet counterpart—than it was between individual groups of scientists working in university or institute laboratories. The paradox of the ease of large institutional exchanges and the difficulty of small specialized ones can be explained by the fact that governmental bureaucracies, when instructed to do so, respond

more readily to the political movement toward detente than do individual researchers in laboratories; the latter may even be oblivious to trends in international relations and are often rather specific and even idiosyncratic in their requests for exchanges. The chemist working on biological synthesis of proteins in an American university laboratory may express disinterest in exchange unless he can be assured that he will be able to entertain in his own laboratory the specific Soviet scholars he names. So far, such guarantees have been rare, since—according to the agreements—each side has the right to nominate its own citizens for the exchanges rather than to invite specific persons from the other side. Thus, the new exchanges are usually based on topics or subject areas, not on individuals, while the older ones continue to be exchanges of individual scholars nominated by the sending side.

By November 1973, the time of the second meeting of the joint commission, projects for cooperation had developed in many areas; on a few topics, such as chemical catalysis and energy sources, joint research was actually underway. In other areas, such as water resources and the production of protein by microbiological means, progress was disappointingly slow, in large part because of the ignorance of past work and institutional strengths and weaknesses by the other side. Under agreements in environmental protection, over 160 specialists made exchange visits in 1973, while studying sixteen major subject areas—including air and water pollution, pest management, wind erosion, noise abatement and control, urban planning, wildlife studies, oceanography, the genetic effects of pol-

7. "U.S.-Soviet Cooperation to Focus on Six Areas," *Science News* 102, no. 85 (5 August 1972), p. 85.

lutants and legal means of protecting the environment. In agriculture some problems were encountered in gaining access to relevant Soviet economic data. However, the two sides have agreed to do research on forecasting production and consumption of major agricultural products, integration of agroindustrial complexes, crop and livestock management, mechanization of agriculture and soil science.[8] Exchanges in transportation include cooperative investigations of bridge and tunnel construction, cold weather and high-speed problems in railway transport, the safety and efficiency of civil aviation, marine transport technology and automobile traffic safety.

In all these areas the prospects for the future appear to be good. The exchanges, rather than being primarily plans for the future, are now gradually acquiring the foundation provided by actual on-going research projects. The forward movement has been impressive in both government-to-government exchanges and contracts between American private companies and the Soviet State Committee on Science and Technology or Soviet ministries.

SCIENTIFIC-TECHNOLOGICAL EXCHANGE AND HUMAN-RIGHTS ISSUES

Among the most sensitive of the problems which plague Soviet-American scientific relations is that of political or human-rights issues as factors influencing the course of the exchange programs. Should Soviet treatment of dissidents—in particular, of dissident scientists —be considered a relevant factor governing the decisions of American officials and scientists about the scope and degree of scientific cooperation?[9] It is obvious to Western observers that Soviet scientists have been among the most prominent of Soviet dissidents; of these scientists who have frequently been critical of the Soviet government Andrei Sakharov is the best known in the West, but there are many others. Should their freedom to travel abroad, to accept invitations to engage in cooperative research, to emigrate if they wish or to hold their positions at home be topics for discussion between the Soviet and American administrators of the scientific exchange?

Among American scientists there is a full spectrum of opinion on these questions, ranging, on the one hand, from those who stoutly maintain that a clear division between science and politics should be made and, on the other hand, to those who say that since scientists can no more escape their moral and social obligations than can other citizens, they must make their protests against injustice known.

The first group would say that science is science, not politics. To them the introduction of human-rights demands into scientific exchange discussions is not only inappropriate for science itself, but even counterproductive, in the long run, to the goal of easing international tensions with a concomitant expansion of human rights. Their argument is that the ultimate beneficial effects of continuing scientific contacts would surely outweigh the few short run improvements which might be gained through

8. For a report on problems and progress in agriculture, see, "U.S.-U.S.S.R. Detente: Bumpy Progress on the Agricultural Front," *Science* 183 (22 March 1974), pp. 1175–1176.

9. "Soviet-American Science Accord: Could Dissent Deter Detente?" *Science* 180 (6 April 1973), pp. 40–41.

protest—particularly when one considers that the likely outcome of a long series of political protests to Soviet authorities would be a curtailment of the exchange program.

The scientists on the other end of the spectrum—the active supporters of the Soviet dissidents—would say that not only must scientists express their political views, but that they have a particular obligation to do so, since they have a unique leverage as a result of the Soviet government's need for Western technology. Furthermore, the critics maintain, fruitful scientific exchanges rest on the assumption of free flows of information and personnel; to the critics, the attempt to conduct exchanges in the absence of such freedoms is to maintain a hypocrisy.

In order to gain some perspective on these very difficult issues—which will almost certainly remain with us during the coming years—we should step back to view the past attitudes of scientists toward such questions and also consider some of the likely outcomes of alternative patterns of response. First, it is important to make a distinction between science and technology when we speak of the role of politics in exchange programs. Science is traditionally an international subject transcending political boundaries, while technology has often been restricted by governments. We will all grant, I think, that a government which raises barriers to the propagation of knowledge in pure mathematics or physics violates the ethic and the practice of science in a way that a nation which tries to prevent the export of a technical innovation —say, a computer or a missile— does not. This distinction—which may at first glance seem obvious —should be kept in mind as we attempt to solve the knotty problems of the degree to which scientific and technological exchanges should be subject to political controls. I am much more reluctant to link political issues to scientific exchanges than I am to technological ones.

Historically speaking, scientists have usually attempted to keep problems of science free from international tensions and political disputes. There have been instances of individual scientists maintaining fruitful contacts concerning their research topics even during a war between two nations. Whenever this effort has failed, with science displaying the passions of political disputes, the usual result has been damage both to science and, subsequently, to political relations. During World War I, for example, groups of scientists in Germany, Britain and France engaged in such recriminations through published manifestoes and public protests that even many years after the war the wounds were not entirely healed. One of the results of this friction was serious damage to postwar European science. Almost no one looking back on these events would believe that the protests had led to good results, however heartfelt they were at the time.

It is also clear from history that the levelling of charges by one side opens the way for the other side to respond in kind. There are certainly aspects of American society which might become new targets for Soviet criticism if the situation becomes increasingly polarized, as it was during the Cold War. What, for example, would be the likely outcome if Soviet authorities—in response to American protests against the treatment of dissident scientists or the adoption of the Jackson Amendment—advanced as a condition for continuing detente the granting of amnesty by the United States government to the thousands of American young men who refused to serve in the Viet Nam War and who, consequently, are now living abroad in exile or at home in hiding? Although the Soviet treatment of dissident scientists and the American treatment of evaders of war are not comparable phenomena in many ways, the Soviet authorities could argue with rather good logic that American policies toward those who refused to serve involve issues of intellectual freedom related to scholarship and science; they know that at least some of those exiled Americans were science students who are being deprived, for political reasons, of appropriate places to study and work in their homeland.

Both the goals of increasing human rights in the Soviet Union and the granting of amnesty to Americans who refused to serve in an unjust war are very worthwhile ones. I am not sufficiently naive, however, to believe that involving these issues in discussions of scientific exchanges could cause fundamental changes of policies on these questions. I say this even though I think that eventually there will be an amnesty in the United States. Belief in a fundamental increase in human rights in the Soviet Union requires a different order of optimism, but in the very long run I think it is also justified. Continuing scientific exchanges will be one contribution toward that goal.

There is yet another reason for being cautious about imposing strong ethical conditions upon scientific exchanges with the Soviet Union. Americans tend to be highly selective in making their ethical protests, so much so that some skepticism about the degree to which these protests are based on universal principles, as opposed to old Cold War attitudes, is justified. The Soviet Union is by far not the only country in the world where intellectual freedom is under heavy restrictions. If we intend to insist on tying detente with the Soviet Union to human-rights issues, then we must ask ourselves what similar issues should we raise in our relations with racist regimes in Africa or with the right-wing military governments in Europe and South America. Furthermore, who really knows just what the position is of scientists and intellectuals in China? Some people would answer that we should be consistent and apply ethical conditions in all such instances. If this application is consistent and rigorous, however, the most likely result would be a world considerably more dangerous than the one in which we presently live. Surely, the adoption of an ethical stance which brings the world closer to a position in which warfare—including the use of nuclear weapons—becomes more likely is, in the final analysis, unethical.

The argument which I have made up to this point may seem to support the position that science and politics are entirely separate categories and that protests by scientists against practices in the Soviet Union have no place. On the contrary, I am convinced that a clean separation of science and politics or ethics is theoretically impossible, practically unwise and morally indefensible. In my opinion, the introduction of ethical issues into discussions of scientific exchanges with the Soviet Union is occasionally very helpful—especially on the unofficial level between individual scientists, but sometimes even between the official administrators of the programs. An example of a protest on the official level which I believe was entirely appropriate was the September 8, 1973 cable sent by President Philip Handler of the United States National Academy of Sciences to President Mstislav Keldysh of the Soviet Academy of Sciences; in his telegram Mr. Handler expressed his concern over the fate of Andrei Sakharov, the Soviet physicist and foreign associate of NAS, who was the object of a severe political attack in the Soviet Union.[10] It is clear that dissidents, such as Sakharov, need the attention of their foreign colleagues for protection. However, official protests—as opposed to individual actions—can be made only rarely if they are not to lose their value or even to become destructive. The main leverage which American officials have when they express their displeasure is the severing or reduction of contacts and exchanges—an action which would not only eliminate that leverage, but would also do much further harm to both sides.

The fact that science and ethics cannot—and should not—be entirely separated, but instead will frequently meet in painful encounters, can be illustrated in several ways. The most obvious is to point out that even scientists who make the strongest arguments in favor of an absolute separation of questions of fact from questions of value usually abandon this position when they confront the topic of the ethics of scientific research itself. In his popular book *Chance and Necessity*

10. "In the Sakharov Matter, Understanding is Sought in an Exchange of Cables," *News Report, NAS, NRC, NAE* 23, no. 9 (November 1973), pp. 1–2, 7.

Jacques Monod, the French biologist and Nobel laureate, concluded that there is only one value that is inherent in science: the value of objective knowledge itself. Therefore, the one set of ethics which a scientist must defend *qua* scientist is that set of principles necessary to gain knowledge, such as free access to information, the right to communicate with other scientists freely and the right to question the assumptions reigning in his area of investigation. A very strong case can be made that this particular set of ethical rules necessary for gaining knowledge is more frequently violated in the Soviet Union than in any other of the five or six leading nations of the world.

If it is true that the ethic of objective knowledge is particularly frequently attacked in the Soviet Union, then it is inevitable that scientific exchanges between that country and other nations will be somewhat difficult. A Western scientist who travels in the Soviet Union and defends the right of his Soviet colleagues to go to foreign scholarly congresses or to accept an invitation to lecture in a Western university—rights he knows have frequently been denied—is not being politically provocative in the way he would be if he attacked Soviet foreign policy or the structure of Soviet government. He is commenting on matters which fall within the area of his expertise as a specialist, for he knows that fruitful scientific research requires such forms of communication and that the particular Soviet scholars he names would be able to make genuine contributions if they were permitted to exercise these rights. Western scientists would be remiss as representatives of their professions if they engaged in far-reaching exchanges with Soviet scientists without pointing out that an advancement of science is dependent on the removal of existing barriers to communication and travel.

The more one reflects on these problems the more it becomes clear that the maintenance of scientific exchanges with the Soviet Union presents Western scientists and science administrators with an entire range of acute moral dilemmas of a type which they are not accustomed to meeting. If we—knowing that only Western attention and publicity can preserve Soviet scholars who appeal for Western support in their efforts to defend themselves or to increase their own freedom—turn our backs on our colleagues, we are not only at least partially responsible for the fates of those individuals, but we are also failing to serve the needs of science itself. On the other hand, if we deeply involve ourselves in these struggles and present the Soviet government with a series of increasingly insistent demands, we are almost surely going to fall into the hypocritical position of demanding from the Soviet Union what we demand from no other nation— as there are many cases of repression of scholarship in the world —and, even more seriously, we are very likely to cause the Soviet government to reject angrily those demands and to constrict or to sever the existing exchange programs. The result of such a loss of scientific contacts would be twofold: the obstruction of knowledge and the exacerbation of international tension. Again, one must insist that a policy which, in the long run, increases the possibility of military conflict can hardly be termed ethical, however meritorious the original intentions contained in that policy may have been.

Although this dilemma is a difficult one, it is hardly the first thorny problem in Soviet-American relations. Dealing with it can be facilitated by making several important distinctions, starting with the one between protests by American individuals and those by official administrators. It is obvious that individuals can react more quickly and with greater latitude than those persons who must represent governmental policies. Furthermore, religious and ethnic issues which arise in relations with the Soviet government are more appropriate for unofficial consideration than they are for governmental representation. The 150 scientists from the National Institutes of Health, including three Nobel laureates, who recently signed a petition declaring that their readiness to welcome Soviet scientists in the United States was "impaired" by Soviet treatment of scientists were acting as individuals.[11] In a country, such as the United States, where public opinion must be carefully considered in the making of policy, these statements have influence, and there are signs that officials in the Soviet government realize this.

On the official level a rather different type of request for changes in Soviet practices is appropriate. It seems to me, for example, to be entirely justified at this time to point out to the Soviet government that the large quantitative increase in scientific exchanges with the US which the USSR evidently desires cannot be made truly successful unless there are a number of correlative qualitative improvements in the possibilities for communication and con-

11. "Briefing: U.S.-Soviet Pacts Threatened by Scientists," *Science* 180 (1 June 1973), p. 934.

tact. For instance, there are serious travel restrictions on American scientists in the Soviet Union, including prohibitions on travel to large areas, and requirements to stay close to home cities. For Soviet scientists similar restrictions exist in the United States, imposed—according to the American government—as retribution for the Soviet regulations. Although these mutual prohibitions seemed irrational and tedious in the past, so long as the exchanges between the Soviet Union and the United States were minimal, the rules were tolerable. Any contact at all is certainly better than no contact. If, however, genuine and meaningful scientific and technological exchanges on a large scale are to occur between the two countries, then, as NAS President Handler observed: "This nonsense must cease—on both sides."[12] Many other similar areas of potential improvement exist, such as better and prompter postal and cable communication between scientific institutions and individual

12. Philip Handler, "The Moscow Agreements and U.S.-Soviet Scientific Relationships," *News Report, NAS, NRC, NAE* 22, no. 7 (August-September 1973), p. 8.

scientists, fuller exchange of data on agricultural and technological subjects and, especially, wider possibilities for the exchange of personnel named as scholars whose work is particularly interesting by the side extending the invitation.

In conclusion, I would like to underscore the optimism which I have met in discussions with the officials administering exchanges in science and technology between the United States and the Soviet Union. During the past two years a range of scientific contacts has been established between these two nations that is greater than it has been since the 1930s; furthermore, it seems likely that the level of the thirties will be surpassed. However, many problems remain, some of them inherent to science and technology, but many more dependent on the course of international relations. We are now entering a period of optimism tempered with realism in which the rate of the expansion of exchanges will rest, to a large degree, on the willingness of the two sides to face openly a number of problems and to find solutions to them emanating from a spirit of accommodation.

* * *

QUESTIONS AND ANSWERS

Q: I get a feeling from the speakers that Americans are being had unilaterally in these exchanges—that is, we are educating the Soviets in the fields they deem to be important, while the Soviet government seems to take pleasure in frustrating our scholars. Furthermore, I would question the speakers' statements about the mutually equal value of exchange information. The Soviets are squarely behind the eight ball today in terms of productivity—a great technology lag

further exacerbating their problems. They are so far behind that they currently deem it absolutely essential to buy our technology rather than to develop their own. In view of the fact that the exchange programs give the Soviets access to the technology and information which they feel are so sensitive and necessary, why do we accept frustration of our efforts in the program?

A: I disagree very much with the thesis that these exchange programs are beneficial to the Soviet Union, but not to the United States. There are many ways of illustrating this. First of all, American private companies are enthusiastic participants in the exchanges. They are very eager to have relations with Soviet industries, and I'm sure that their eagerness does not issue from a spirit of philanthropy, but from the conviction that there is a profit to be made. I feel certain, then, that the benefit in a strictly economic sense is certainly two-way.

So far as knowledge is concerned, again I doubt very much that the thesis can be made that only the Soviets are benefiting from the exchanges, unless one defines knowledge in some special way that relates only to technology. That is, American exchangees are getting a great deal of knowledge in fields other than technology.

However, for a moment, let's restrict the question to technology and then ask: in which specific area of exchange does the Soviet Union benefit a lot more than the United States? It is not nearly so easy to answer as it might appear at first glance. Some people would maintain that, as a result of wider exchange, the Soviet Union is becoming evermore dependent on Western technology while in the West the rate of innovation is actually accentuated. It has been found that whenever a certain computer or technical innovation is sold to the Soviet Union, the next generation of that computer or innovation is already on the line in American factories. Therefore, it can be argued that this general stimulation has at least the potential of creating a dependency relationship. If I were to regard the situation from the Soviet point of view, I'd be very worried about becoming dependent upon Western technology.

A (Kassof): Just to add a comment, speaking not of the commercial relationships between the United States and the Soviet Union, but of exchanges on the scholarly and scientific level, the evidence is simply contrary to the questioner's suggestion. We very carefully follow the reports from academic and scientific hosts in the United States who have spent a year or a semester working with Soviet scientists. As I indicated in my address, the benefits tend to be mutual, no matter where the location of the exchange happens to be. Obviously, not in every case, but in the majority of cases, young Soviet scientists working in university laboratories in the United States are making equal, and in many cases team, contributions. Finally, I would add the observation that in the best kind of scientific and technological exchange—which occurs more frequently than one might suppose—the contribution is made not to one side or the other, but to the general advancement of knowledge. This kind of division of scientific labor is beneficial for everyone.

The USSR and Security in Europe:
A Soviet View

By Vladimir L. Bykov

ABSTRACT: During the Soviet-American summit meetings of 1972 and 1973, the two governments expressed their desire to contribute to the reinforcement of peace in Europe. Behind this sentiment—which at first sight may seem to be a stereotyped diplomatic formula, as presented in the concluding communiques of both summits—lies a turning point of great historic significance. For the first time in the twenty-seven years of the postwar period of international relations the Soviet Union and the United States agreed on the possibility of, and need for, joint efforts in building a stable European peace. Such agreement would have been inconceivable in the not too distant past, when the Cold War completely held sway. Having crossed this line, the two countries cannot but be aware of the responsibility stemming from their actions. Any retreat would not only tell negatively on the fundamental interests of the two nations, but would also darken the prospects for an all-European settlement. The normalization process of Soviet-American relations affects many problems of a global and local nature, including those which have no direct connection with Europe. However, the Soviet Union proceeds from the firm belief—confirmed by the harsh lessons of recent history—that the ensurance of lasting security and peaceful cooperation among European countries with different social systems is the core of detente. Europe was the scene of the most bitter and destructive wars ever known to humankind; it is this same Europe which can now emerge as an example of the success of peaceful coexistence.

Vladimir L. Bykov is presently Counselor of the Soviet Embassy in Washington, D.C. He was on the first tour at the Embassy of the USSR in the United States from 1964 to 1969. Mr. Bykov holds the degree of Candidate of History since 1971. His academic research has been primarily on the problems of Soviet-American relations in the postwar period. Presently, he is in charge of the European Section of the Embassy. Mr. Bykov, who was born in Kharkov, Ukraine, USSR in 1932, graduated from the Moscow Institute of International Relations in 1957.

IN 1917, while drafting the founding, basic document of Soviet foreign policy—the Decree of Peace—Vladimir I. Lenin wrote: "We shall welcome all clauses containing provisions for good neighbourly relations and all economic agreements; we cannot reject these."[1]

This decree embodied the fundamental principles of Soviet foreign policy, a policy of peace and friendship among nations. Lenin's contribution to peace was so considerable that the Norwegian Social Democratic Party nominated him for the 1917 Nobel Peace Prize. In their citation they wrote: "To date, Lenin has done more than anybody else for the triumph of the ideas of peace. Not only does he propagate peace fervently, he also takes steps to achieve it."

Throughout its history the USSR always proceeded from the feasibility and necessity of international cooperation and peaceful settlement of world problems. There is no thinkable alternative to this approach with regard to Europe. In the foreign policy of the Soviet Union, both historically and currently, no other approach has ever been tried, unless we were provoked to act otherwise in order to defend the national security and the existence of the USSR.

TOWARDS A SYSTEM OF SECURITY:
A RETROSPECTIVE OF SOVIET
EUROPEAN POLICY

Less than five years after the emergence of the Soviet Union, it proposed a general reduction in armaments and armies to ensure peace and the security of all peoples. Soviet diplomacy worked persistently

for European security throughout the thirties. In December 1933 the Central Committee of the All-Union Communist Party adopted a decision to strive to establish a system of collective action against any aggression. On the initiative of the Soviet Union and some French political leaders, talks were held on setting up a collective security system through the signing of a regional pact, named the Eastern Pact. Even after Munich—when the threat from Nazi Germany loomed larger—the Soviet Union insisted that the aggressor could be curbed and war prevented through cooperation among the Soviet Union, Britain, France and other countries being threatened. Just a few months before the Second World War the Soviet Union proposed an agreement to Britain and France, based on the mutual obligation of each country to render immediate aid in case of Nazi aggression, for a period of five to ten years.

Scarcely were the guns of the Second World War silenced before the Soviet Union resumed its drive for strengthening peace and security in Europe. For example, in January-February 1954—at the Berlin conference of the foreign ministers of the Soviet Union, the United States, France and Britain—the Soviet government proposed concluding an all-European treaty on collective security in Europe. Somewhat later, in November 1954, the Soviet Union proposed an all-European conference aimed at the setting up of a collective security system in Europe. In 1955 the Soviet Union again proposed a collective security system in Europe. In November of that year the USSR came up with a proposal to conclude a nonaggression pact among the existing military and political groupings in Europe as an intermediary

1. V. I. Lenin, Collected Works (London: Lawrence and Wishart, 1960–1970), vol. 26, p. 255.

step towards an all-European treaty on collective security on the continent.

Finally, in July 1966, at a conference in Bucharest, the Soviet Union and six other socialist countries proposed the convening of an all-European conference on security and cooperation. Their proposal was outlined in the *Declaration on Strengthening Peace and Security in Europe,* which was adopted by the conference. This was the biggest, joint postwar contribution of the socialist countries to working out a program for strengthening European security. Then followed the meetings of the Warsaw Treaty countries in Budapest—March 1969—and Prague—October 1969—which made specific suggestions about an all-European conference.

On March 30, 1971, the Twenty-fourth Congress of the Communist Party of the Soviet Union (CPSU) proclaimed a comprehensive peace program—or, as the West called it, Brezhnev's six-point program. It covered the most important problems of contemporary international relations and proposed practical ways of dealing with them. In this program special attention was devoted to Europe.

The basic thrust of this long range program is to perpetuate the major achievements of European development since the end of World War II—that is, twenty-five years of peaceful life. The basic specific requirement for the realization of this task requires, in the Soviet view, final recognition of the territorial changes which took place in Europe as a result of the Second World War. Other Soviet goals in Europe were defined as follows:

—to bring about a radical turn towards relaxation of tension and peace on the continent;

—to insure the convocation and success of an all-European conference;
—to do everything to insure collective security in Europe.[2]

Habit is said to be second nature. Thus, becoming accustomed to using military terminology during the Cold War years, Western journalists and experts coined the expression peace offensive when commenting and reporting on the proposals of the Soviet Union and other socialist countries for peace and security in Europe. Since Western commentators and experts acknowledged, then, that the Soviet Union and other socialist countries in Europe were conducting a peace offensive, they should also acknowledge now—if they are to be fair and objective—that the peace offensive was not a fleeting factor—based on considerations of the moment—in Soviet foreign policy, but that it constituted the very essence of the Leninist foreign policy of the Soviet state.

The specific results of this peace offensive are quite obvious today. Significant changes have come about in the relations of the socialist countries with the Western European countries—with France, one of the first countries to adopt the course of constructive cooperation among states with different social systems, the Federal Republic of Germany, Italy and others. Among the most significant indications of the improvement in international relations are the treaties concluded by the Soviet Union, Poland, the German Democratic Republic and other socialist countries with the Federal Republic of Germany (FRG). All

2. See, *Twenty-fourth Congress of the Communist Party of the Soviet Union, 30 March-9 April 1971* (Documents of Novosti Press Agency, Moscow, 1971), pp. 37–38.

of you know that these treaties are based on the recognition of the inviolability of the existing frontiers and contain commitments to refrain from the use of force in international disputes.

Moreover, the European conference is a concentrated expression of the positive changes. The following facts: (1) that this conference, for which the progressive forces of the continent worked so long, took place; (2) that practically all the European countries, the United States and Canada participated in it; and (3) that matters related to European peace and security and to peaceful cooperation were jointly discussed, are in themselves a considerable gain.

The Soviet European initiatives, as outlined at the Twenty-fourth Congress of the CPSU, are not limited to the direct proposals mentioned above. The Soviet approach to the future of Europe also includes the readiness to have a simultaneous annulment of the Warsaw Treaty and the North Atlantic Treaty Organization (NATO) or, as a first step, the dismantling of their military organizations. The European-related policy also includes the readiness of the USSR to promote the establishment of nuclear-free zones in various parts of the world and a desire for nuclear disarmament of all states in possession of nuclear weapons and for the convocation of the conference of five nuclear powers—the USSR, the USA, the People's Republic of China (PRC), France and Britain—for this purpose.[3]

Since the United States is actively involved in the security arrangements with its allies in Europe—and since it is an inseparable participant of the postwar settlement in Europe

3. Ibid.

—most of the proposals of the peace program of the Twenty-fourth Congress of the CPSU, as related to Europe, might well fall into those areas of the USA-USSR dialogue in which we can work together with all interested European nations.

LESSONS OF THE PAST AS SOURCES OF SOVIET EUROPEAN POLICY FOR THE FUTURE

The historic outline of the major European initiatives of the USSR is absolutely essential for understanding the present Soviet approach to Europe, as well as Soviet-American relations as related to European matters. Especially important in this respect are the lessons of World War II which influenced, to a very substantial extent, the formulation of Soviet European policies in the postwar period.

If the entire population of Europe were to be polled today on the question of whether the inhabitants of Europe want another war, the overwhelming majority would respond with a no. Europeans know the meaning of war from bitter experience. Twice, in the course of a relatively short period of time, Europe has been the epicenter of world wars which caused both vast losses of life and material destruction. More than 20 million lives were lost by the Soviet Union, which bore the brunt of the war. Poland lost 6 million; Yugoslavia, 1.7 million; Britain, 375,000; the United States, more than 400,000—even though the war was not fought on its territory; France, 576,000; and the Netherlands, 200,000.

All over Europe there are monuments to millions of people who died in two world wars fought within the life span of one generation. Europe itself is a graveyard of almost 50 million who were carried away by only the Second World War. There is not a shade of unwarranted pathos in the statement that the European continent, by its history, is the largest monument on earth to those who fell fighting or unarmed.

In this respect it is appropriate to quote the statement made by Soviet Foreign Minister Andrei A. Gromyko at the opening of the European Conference on Security and Cooperation in Helsinki in July 1973. This statement exactly reflects the Soviet feeling towards the lessons of World War II:

I think, we will be correctly understood when we say that we shall do everything possible so that the sacrifices made to achieve victory will not have been in vain; so that the results of the war which our people waged under such strain and with selflessness, alongside their allies in the anti-Hitler coalition and many other nations—victims of fascist aggression—will not be undermined; and so that that war will be the last war not only for the Soviet people, but for all the other peoples of Europe. This is our lofty duty to those who fell, to those living, and to the coming generations.[4]

The cooperation between the countries of the anti-Hitler coalition, which was shaped during the war years, could have become an important factor in ensuring truly peaceful development in Europe. Such was the spirit and the letter of the Potsdam agreements. Unfortunately, detente in Europe was held back for more than two decades.

It is better not to speak about this situation now. After all, no one holds power over the past; history cannot be remade. However, one can, and must, draw lessons from the past for the sake of the present and the future.

4. Andrei Gromyko, *A Lasting Peace for Europe* (Moscow: Novosti Press Agency, 1973), p. 9.

In the nuclear age the peoples of Europe cannot but strive for reliable security guarantees. Europe in general, and its Western sector in particular, is the most densely populated part of the world. More than 600 million people inhabit the limited territory of Europe. The ancient European land is a repository of truly innumerable material and spiritual values: a multitude of beautiful cities and towns with modern living conditions, seats of culture and of scientific and technological thought, countless numbers of artistic and architectural treasures, priceless ancient memorials and the highest level of agricultural development. As a result of historical development, within the narrow confines of Europe there is the highest concentration of people and of the greatest achievements of human civilization. For all that, not Eastern, but Western and Central Europe, is the most thickly populated and, therefore, most vulnerable in a contemporary nuclear-rocket war.

Not very long ago the Stockholm International Peace Research Institute estimated that the world stocks of nuclear weapons of all categories now amount to about 50,000 megatons—or about fifteen tons of TNT per man, woman and child. That is about two and a half million times the strength of the bomb dropped on Hiroshima. So, the very nature of the threat of war has become entirely different. What can be done to prevent another war? What can be done to ensure a stable peace and reliable security for all peoples of the world, including Europeans? How can we go about creating conditions for the equal cooperation of all countries on the continent?

There are politicians in the West who claim that peace can be today ensured only if the NATO countries have weapons that at least equal, in power and quantity, the armaments of the Warsaw Treaty Organization. However, this equilibrium-of-fear theory leads directly to a very dangerous and highly expensive arms race. Yet, the arms race, far from removing the threat of war, increases it.

Fully aware that the arms race is like a slope leading into an abyss, many historians, diplomats and scholars in the Western countries are proposing various projects for a future Europe. Some of them sketch the European situation in the next ten to twenty years on the basis of an Atlanticized Europe, sometimes with the addition of Japan. Others build up their plans around the vague model of a Europe of nations. There are theories under which the national and state sovereignty of European countries will dissolve in supranational formations on a continental scale. There are also plans for producing, within the NATO framework, a European component with its own nuclear weapons. This, it is claimed, would bring the peoples of Europe peace and security.

EUROPE OF THE FUTURE

The Soviet Union envisions Europe of the future as a continent of peace where aggression is ruled out for one and all.

General Secretary of the CPSU Central Committee L. I. Brezhnev expressed the feelings and wishes of the entire Soviet people when he said that we call for overcoming the consequences of the tragic past of Europe not in order to forget it, but in order to ensure that it will never be repeated. Our hope is that trust and mutual understanding will make it possible to gradually overcome the division of the continent into military-political groupings. Relations between all European states should be based on peaceful and mutually beneficial cooperation. In our mind, the building of such a Europe accords with the best interests of all nations, including the United States.

The Soviet Union would like to see a large all-European network of economic, scientific and cultural cooperation which would constitute a reliable material consolidation of peaceful relations among states. However, it is necessary to display a responsible and serious approach to the problems still confronting us. No one should yield to the temptation of instructing others how to manage their internal affairs. Internal practices and laws axiomatically constitute the threshold of each state at which others must stop.

Were we to take the path of imposing our practices upon other countries—be it in the field of economic affairs or in the field of social philosophy—those who are trying to persuade us to adopt alien laws, morals or customs would probably object. This is understandable. Sometimes events reach the point at which attempts are made to arrogate the right of deciding who, how, in what capacity, within what time-limit and specifically where matters of emigration from this or that country should be resolved. The Soviet Union vigorously rejects such an approach.

The question which involuntarily comes to mind is whether those who behave in this fashion seriously think that only the Soviet Union —or only the socialist countries— is interested in detente, while others only do a great favor by consenting to hold talks on such matters. Anyone interested in the improvement of the international climate knows well that this is not so, that this process is reciprocal and determined by the common interests of the parties and, above all, by the interests of the peoples. The main thing today is not to let the poisoned atmosphere created around trumped-up matters overshadow the major tasks faced by us—in particular, by the USSR and the USA.

Detente in Europe, as elsewhere, obviously requires a military relaxation. Accordingly, the Soviet Union —as is known—is prepared to take practical steps to reduce armed forces and armaments in Central Europe as early as by 1975. Our state constructively and realistically approaches, in all seriousness and responsibility, the Vienna negotiations on the measures of military relaxation. An agreement on the reduction of armed forces and armaments would unquestionably be a further major step improving the political situation in Europe and helping to install in the continent an atmosphere of trust, goodwill and peaceful cooperation.

On the basis of political and military security, equal economic, scientific, technical and cultural cooperation—multilateral and bilateral—we could make considerable headway. In particular, it would be possible to establish useful contacts and links between the different economic groups in Europe, notably between the CMEA and the EEC. In the words of General Secretary of the CPSU Central Committee L. I. Brezhnev:

We believe it is high time to start working out the European program of economic and cultural cooperation. In this connection there arises a question: is it possible to find a basis for some forms of businesslike relations between currently existing European trade-economic groups—the CMEA and the EEC? I think it is, if the states-members of the EEC will try not to discriminate against the other side and will contribute to the development of natural bilateral contacts and European cooperation.[5]

When presenting a paper on European security and the Soviet Union, one cannot but note with satisfaction that the United States in recent years repeatedly expressed its desire to contribute to the consolidation of peaceful conditions in Europe so that the continent never again becomes a battleground of the nations of the world. This is clearly the message of the joint Soviet-American communique signed at the Moscow summit in May 1972. Both countries have committed themselves to make further efforts ensuring a peaceful future for Europe, free of tensions, crises and conflicts. They agreed that the territorial integrity of all states in Europe should be respected. This statement is really one of historic importance and certainly the result of a pragmatic approach of the United States leaders to the situation in Europe—that is, an approach based on the understanding of European realities.

Certainly, one can see that new trends in Europe are sometimes not to the liking of everybody. Some say that this process of detente in Europe is too fast, that we should proceed in a more cautious way—slowly. What can we say to that?

Twenty five years of Cold War were a huge waste of time—as it is now almost everywhere acknowledged—and, as human beings, we unfortunately do not live too long. It was a tremendous waste of energy, of resources and of money —all spent in vain. For these reasons, we should now recover from the unfortunate times as quickly as

5. *Pravda,* 16 March 1974.

possible and move ahead to eliminate any chance of returning to them
again. The further away we are from
those Cold War years, the more
secure peace will be.

Others, especially American
"Atlanticists," try to caution the
policy makers of Western European
nations and the United States that
the Soviet Union, in persuing detente in Europe, aims to push the
United States out of this continent,
leaving Western Europe "helpless."
A new catchword—Finlandization
—is increasingly used in that respect
to describe the alleged goals of the
USSR in Europe.

Against the background of Soviet
past and present policies in Europe,
it is crystal clear that this is a false
conception which is politically provocative in the worst sense. Every
serious statesman and scholar will
not find any strong argument to support it. Let me, for example, refer
to the opinion of George F. Kennan
—with whom we frequently disagree conceptually and factually in
the interpretation of Soviet foreign
policy. In his recent analysis of
Finlandization he evaluates this
theory as unfounded and completely
misapplied.[6]

Opponents of durable peace and
good neighborly cooperation in
Europe are to be found elsewhere,
as well. We cannot overlook the fact
that Peking's political and propaganda line in European matters is
aimed at reviving the Cold War
spirit in Europe and at supporting
the forces opposing detente. Thus,
there is nothing surprising about the
fact that these forces readily join
hands with Peking.

In his time, FRG politician Strauss
published a book titled *Call and*

Response. He wrote in it that the
Maoists' anti-Soviet policy is "useful
rather than harmful." Indeed, the
forces represented by the author
benefit by this policy quite substantially. "This is why," Strauss wrote,
"our interests temporarily coincided
with those of the Chinese."

The course of developments has
shown that the positions of the
opponents to detente in Europe and
of the Maoists continue to draw ever
closer together and that the characteristics these positions have in
common are no longer temporary,
but remain unchanged. This follows
from the original attitude of the
Chinese leadership to the USSR's
and other socialist countries' agreements with the FRG and to the
all-European conference and its
decisions. The Chinese leaders seek
to discredit the idea of collective security in Europe, as well as
each real step along the road to
strengthening peace and security on
our continent. This cannot but evoke
public concern. Thus, one can see
that the path to achieving real peace,
understanding and security on the
European continent is not all that
rosy.

"The present period is a complex
and contradictory one," pointed out
General Secretary of the CPSU
Central Committee L. I. Brezhnev in
his speech in Alma-Ata in March
1974. Furthermore, he noted that:

Reaction is trying wherever it can to
launch counterattacks, if only on individual sections, to hold back the process
of relaxation of international tension and
complicate the solution of pressing problems. Actively used for these purposes
are many organs of the bourgeois press,
radio and television which deliberately
distort the meaning of our policy, report
events untruthfully and resort to time-
worn cliches of anti-Sovietism.[7]

6. See, George F. Kennan, "Europe's Problems, Europe's Choices," *Foreign Policy*
14 (Spring 1974).

7. *Pravda*, 16 March 1974.

THE TASKS AHEAD

There is still a lot to do in Europe. Permit me to go over some problems which still demand attention and all-out efforts:

—How can the process of detente in Europe be accelerated and further extended?

—What are the most effective forms of struggle to frustrate the attempts of all those groupings or states—European and non-European—who continue to resist the current process?

—Detente in Europe must not be confined only to the political sphere, but must also involve the military sphere. How are we to overcome obstacles in the way of a considerable reduction in the numerical strength of the armed forces and armaments now existing in Europe? How is Europe to be advanced along the way of disbanding blocs and how is the formation of new regional military groupings to be avoided?

—Economic integration is continuing and is even intensifying in both the capitalist and socialist parts of Europe. What is to be done to prevent this integration from developing into a greater division of Europe, which could pose a fresh threat to its security by strengthening certain negative influences?

—What is the role which public opinion can, and must, play in order that the strengthening of the political foundations of security in Europe can result in unprecedented development of cooperation in the economic, scientific and technical fields?

—How can we further develop and intensify cultural and informational exchanges and relations between men, as well as exchanges of spiritual values and social experience?

—What are the measures to be recommended for the achievement of better mutual understanding and the preservation of the cultural and moral face of Europe in all the diversity of its social systems and world outlooks, while displaying respect for national sovereignty?

—What role can a permanent body set up by the all-European conference of states play? Moreover, in which spheres should it concentrate its efforts to continue the beginnings which have been made and to consolidate the emergent detente among all the European states—in particular, seeking to make them take a fresh and more positive look at their relations with each other?

Even this partial list indicates the great amount of work to be done.

We in the Soviet Union are optimistic. In our multinational state exceptionally great importance is attached to questions of equality and friendship of different nationalities —of which we have about two hundred, speaking approximately one hundred different languages. We believe that the ideals of peace, the equality of nations and good neighborliness should become ever more deeply rooted in international relations. There should be no place for the propaganda of hatred, aggression, militarism, the cult of violence, of racial or national superiority and other ideas or notions which are incompatible with the goal of rapprochement and cooperation between nations or with the UN Charter or with universally accepted moral standards.

Social Stratification: 1969–1973

By THOMAS E. LASSWELL AND SANDRA L. BENBROOK

THE authors have been asked to summarize developments in social stratification over the past five years and to comment on the current state of the subdiscipline. Interested readers are referred to the earlier works published in THE ANNALS by Lasswell[1] and by Murphy.[2] The present authors have attempted to modify and extend those statements in the light of current developments rather than to write a discrete essay.

The most immediately noticeable feature of the current literature on social stratification—including social class and social mobility—is its great volume. As far as the United States is concerned, this may be due in part to the publication explosion and to the general expansion in the number of persons involved in academic disciplines and research during the period covered. The breakthroughs in theory, procedures and concept development do not seem from this perspective to be more impressive than the comparable ones which occurred in the two preceding five-year periods.

Scientific research and publication in the area of social stratification outside the United States is a different story. While it

1. Thomas E. Lasswell, "Social Stratification: 1964–1968," THE ANNALS 384 (July 1964), pp. 104–134.
2. Raymond J. Murphy, "Some Recent Trends in Stratification Theory and Research," THE ANNALS 356 (November 1964), pp. 142–167.

Thomas E. Lasswell, Ph.D., Pomona, California, is Professor of Sociology at the University of Southern California, where he has been teaching since 1959. He has been Visiting Professor or Professor at the University of California at San Diego, Northwestern University, Grinnell College and Pomona College. He is the author of Class and Stratum: An Introduction to Concepts and Research *and of numerous articles in the field of social stratification. He is a member of the Research Committee on Social Stratification of the International Sociological Association.*

Sandra L. Benbrook is a Doctoral Student in Sociology at the University of Southern California, where she received her A.B. degree in anthropology. Specializing in the studies of social stratification and demography, she is a National Institute of Mental Health trainee in the demography of social disorganization and is affiliated with the Population Research Laboratory at the University of of Southern California.

This article was prepared with the assistance of: Barbara Dietrick, L. Kay Gillespie, Anne Silver and Margaret Cramer. Portions of this article are to be presented as a paper to the Eighth World Congress of Sociology in Toronto, August 1974.

is true that there has been a publication explosion abroad—although to a more modest degree than in the United States in absolute quantity—and a proportionately great increase in the number of interested academics in other countries, the growth of published and unpublished research projects in the area of social stratification, social class and social mobility appears to have accelerated markedly. Even though the greater part of this article has been devoted to work done in the United States, this should be construed in part as an artifact of the accessibility of published materials rather than as a judgment of the importance of foreign contributions.

The interest of Eastern European scholars in social stratification —quite evident at the meetings of the Seventh World Congress of Sociology in Varna in 1970 —has been inferred from the sharp increase in the number of publications, particularly in the area of social mobility. The International Sociological Association's Research Committee on Social Stratification met in Rome in December 1972. The meetings were focused almost entirely on procedures for the study of social mobility, with the goal of making the respective studies of national mobility patterns more comparable. This laudatory goal was pursued to the extent that there was only incidental discussion of fundamental concepts and theories of social stratification or social class, and it was further decided to limit invitations to the Warsaw meeting in 1974 to researchers involved in national mobility studies.[3]

The extensive literature in the area of social stratification prohibits this article from being exhaustive. To a large extent, the selection of articles mentioned here has been made in terms of our personal interests; hence, it may not represent fairly all of the interests of concerned scholars. This article has been organized around contemporary concepts, theory, research procedures and research findings reported in the sociological literature on social stratification, social class and social mobility.

CONCEPTS

It is most feasible to attempt to simplify the terminological confusion in the field by arbitrarily distinguishing its two most central concepts, social classes and social strata and asking the reader to accept our diacritica, even though he or she may be uncomfortable with the labels we have chosen. The terms are sometimes used synonymously in the literature and occasionally reversed; instances are found in which either term has been made operational by the use of very specific measures of socioeconomic status or by occupational scales alone.

We shall use the term social strata to refer to any abstract

Stratification: Perspectives on the Second Generation of National Mobility Studies," *American Sociologist* 9 (February 1974), pp. 18–25. Featherman's article comments parenthetically that Lasswell's 1972 report for the United States failed to cite the replicate study of mobility by Featherman and Hauser. Lasswell takes this opportunity to direct the reader's attention to D. L. Featherman and R. M. Hauser, "Design for a Replicate Study of Social Mobility in the United States," in *Social Indicator Models*, ed. K. Land and S. Spilerman (New York: Russell Sage, listed in Featherman's 1974 article as forthcoming).

3. The Rome meeting has since been reported in David L. Featherman, "Toward Comparable Data on Inequality and

categories of any population which have been distinguished from one another and scaled or ranked. The scaling or ranking may be either subjective or objective. It may be done intuitively or it may have been accomplished by stringent, precise criteria. Its key feature is the inequality of population categories, whether it is a subjectively perceived inequality or an objectively measured unidimensional or multidimensional inequality. Stratum consciousness may be present in the subject population or, on the other hand, the bulk of the population may be totally unaware of the distinctions being made by a research scientist.

We shall use the term social class to refer to identifiable segments of a population who have distinguishable social motives, differing concepts of social welfare and different concepts of justice or propriety. Again, the incumbents of social classes may not be aware of these differences. Social classes may be in conscious conflict or, on the other hand, they may contribute to either the functionality or dysfunctionality of a society while their constituents are individually unaware of any class membership. The key concept is distinguishable values.[4] When one class of people has survival as a primary value and another has the exercise of power as a primary value, there may be little overt conflict. If two classes have differing secondary values, but aspire to the same primary values, in a zero-sum game, conflict may become overt. To the extent that social classes are unequal on any dimension, social stratification

may be said to exist. When social classes are conceptualized as unequal on some dimension, social strata is the more general of the two concepts, and social class stratification exists.

Conceptions of social justice centered on the differential access of different social classes to material or symbolic values have been described in the classical writings of Plato, Karl Marx, Max Weber and Charles Dickens. For Plato a society was merely the state in which every person accepted his class status, valued the achievement of his socially prescribed norms and exercised his capacities to achieve his appropriate goals. In Plato's utopian society no conflict exists. Marx, on the other hand, ascribed the same values to all members of society, envisioned justice as absolute rather than distributive and predicted disorganization and conflict until a utopian state was achieved in which, presumably, every person would behave according to universal norms in pursuit of the same values; however, his description of that state is at best nebulous. Both concepts—as also do those of Weber and Dickens—add surplus meaning to our arbitrary definition of social classes. Indeed, this is more characteristic than not of the contemporary sociological literature.

Several contemporary writers have either explicitly or implicitly described differential class values as distinguishing among social classes. The numerous responses to Jensen,[5] and other writers responding to him, have pointed to the differential evaluation of genetic

---

4. Compare, Richard Todd, "A Theory of the Lower Class: Edward Banfield—The Maverick of Urbanology," *Atlantic* 226 (September 1970), pp. 51–56.

5. Arthur T. Jensen, "How Much Can We Boost IQ and Scholastic Achievement?" *Harvard Educational Review* 39 (Winter 1969), pp. 1–123.

characteristics as morally or ideologically wrong and have challenged the social justice of a caste or color-caste system of stratification. The notion of justice being distributed according to racial classes has been valued positively by some people and negatively by others; the ensuing popular struggle for a uniform, absolute access to social values has been documented by Ransford[6] and others.

It is relatively easy to observe and to classify behaviors and somatic phenomena: wherever or whenever social classes are determined by an evaluation of one of these kinds of observable differentials, its conceptualization can be made operational and data can be gathered and processed. Beliefs, sentiments, motives and values, at the other extreme, cannot be directly observed either by the general public or by the scientist and must be inferred from observations of other phenomena, such as events and behaviors. Concepts of social class based on hypothetical variables are impossible to validate by conventional scientific methods, even though logical arguments can be made from other evidence. Popularly, such concepts are based on sentiment or tradition. This difficulty will be apparent in the discussion of procedures, below.

Reporting on popular conceptions of social class, Morris and Jeffries found that:

People can place themselves in classes . . . [but] they disagree whether classes are important or clearly demarcated, that class awareness does not seem to affect class dissatisfaction, and that class dissatisfaction is not clearly related to class action.[7]

Reissman and Halstead argued that ideological opposition of sociologists in the United States to the existence of social classes in this country has resulted in several biases in research and literature.[8] Bates and Kelley interpreted the literature as person-centered, stating that:

It will be our claim that social strata whether they be classes, castes or estates amount to categories of individuals and are not structural elements of social systems.[9]

Social mobility has changed little in conceptualization during the past five years, even though there have been methodological changes. The concept continues to refer to the replacement and displacement of persons in functional social categories in societally centered theory. In person-centered theory it refers to the changes in the self-concepts or social significance of persons usually attributed to changes in social contexts. In the former instance it is made operational through the observation of demographic variables; in the latter it is made operational by career histories, the collection of intergenerational case studies of demographic data and individual aspiration and achievement scales.

6. H. Edward Ransford, "Blue Collar Anger: Reaction to Student and Black Protest," *American Sociological Review* 37 (June 1972), pp. 333–345.

7. Richard T. Morris and Vincent Jeffries, "Class Conflict: Forget It!" *Sociology and Social Research* 54 (April 1970), p. 306.

8. Leonard Reissman and Michael N. Halstead, "The Subject Is Class," *Sociology and Social Research* 54 (April 1970), pp. 293–305.

9. In Frederick L. Bates and John D. Kelley, "A Station Centered Approach to the Study of Social Stratification," *Louisiana State University Journal of Sociology* 2 (Spring 1972), pp. 22–47.

THEORY

Most of the literature in the time covered by this article is an exploration of, or extension of, or further definition of, existing theories. Parsons, for example, has updated his analytical theory in "Equality and Inequality in Modern Society: Or Social Stratification Revisited."[10] Abrahamson has provided some empirical support for the functional theory of stratification.[11]

Treiman has reviewed the current state of knowledge about the effects of industrialization upon systems of social stratification.[12] Combining some empirically well-established propositions with some which still require further testing, he examined: (1) the disruption of status characteristics in the population concomitant with industrialization, (2) the patterns of interrelations among status characteristics and (3) the kinds of relationships between characteristics and other aspects of social behavior in industrializing societies.

Haller and Saravia have presented a fragment of stratification theory in their "variable discrimination hypothesis."[13] They tested the possibility that the particular variables which discriminate among the statuses of family units at different levels of the stratification hierarchy were different from the variables which discriminate at other levels. Their empirical observations in Acucena, Brazil, supported this hypothesis.

The nature of class conflict—or the lack of it—was examined by several writers, among them Himes,[14] Ransford[15] and Portes.[16] Himes explored the "calculated racial violence" in the United States during the past fifteen years as a direct and inevitable result of the progressively restrictive alternative value-oriented possibilities for action among American blacks. Ransford has observed that the economic advancements of American ethnic groups over the past three decades only in part offset the disadvantages which are residual from a traditional color-caste system. Portes found that lower-class leftist action in Chile was more a protest against the upper class for irresponsible, unjust implementation of the existing system than a clear-cut, well-understood Marxian revolution.

An attempt to evaluate the empirical adequacy of the Davis-Moore and Parsonian functional theories of social stratification was made by Land, with the conclusion that the Davis-Moore model provides a more accurate representation of societies with a high degree of cultural uniformity and organiza-

10. Talcott Parsons, "Equality and Inequality in Modern Society: Or Social Stratification Revisited," *Sociological Inquiry* 40 (Spring 1970), pp. 13–72.

11. Mark Abrahamson, "Functionalism and the Functional Theory of Stratification: An Empirical Assessment," *American Journal of Sociology* 78 (March 1973), pp. 1236–1246.

12. Donald J. Treiman, "Industrialization and Social Stratification," *Sociological Inquiry* 40 (Spring 1970), pp. 207–234.

13. Archibald O. Haller and Helcio U. Saravia, "Status Measurements and the Variable Discrimination Hypothesis in an Isolated Brazilian Region," *Rural Sociology* 37 (September 1973), pp. 325–351.

14. Joseph S. Himes, "A Theory of Racial Conflict" *Social Forces* 50 (September 1971), pp. 53–60.

15. H. Edward Ransford, "Skin Color, Life Chances and Anti-White Attitudes," *Social Problems* 18 (Fall 1970), pp. 164–178.

16. Alejandro Portes, "On the Logic of Post-Factum Explanations: The Hypothesis of Lower-Class Frustration as a Cause of Leftist Radicalism," *Social Forces* 50 (September 1971), pp. 26–44.

tional interdependence, while the Parsonian model was a more accurate representation of societies with a low degree of cultural uniformity and interdependence.[17]

In *Social Differentiation and Stratification*, Eisenstadt concludes that:

In no society . . . is the process of stratification and strata formation merely an abstract aspect of social structure. . . . Stratification goes beyond this to the hierarchical ordering of social categories and groups, which is a basic component of people's self-identity and conceptions of themselves as members of society, of the symbolism of social order, and of the way in which members of society tend to see themselves vis-à-vis others.[18]

Eisenstadt's person-centered theory explains social stratification in symbolic, cognitive, perceptual, sentimental and interactional terms. The organization of every society involves the positing of focal points of activity, values and feelings—a societal myth in the anthropological sense of the term—which he calls centers. The assumed and ascribed nearness of persons to the center—or the centers—is the chief determinant of the stratification system in that society.

Probably the work of Sewell and his associates at the University of Wisconsin has come closer to developing a general theory of social mobility than any other material

from the past five years reviewed here.[19] The status attainment process described by them relates occupational and educational aspirations, intelligence, school achievement and several variables relating to family orientation to later educational, occupational and income variables. This middle-range theory neither supports nor refutes the kinds of grand theory discussed above. It is empirically constructed and does not necessarily concern itself with macrosocial theories or ideologies. The grand theories which have allowed for social mobility, either implicitly or explicitly—with the possible exception of Eisenstadt's remarks on the social dynamics of modern stratification systems[20]—have not devoted a great deal of special attention to it.

PROCEDURES

A review of the procedures used for the observations and analyses of the phenomena of social stratification confirms that there have been few marked changes in recent years. Warner's Index of Status Characteristics, the Bogardus Social Distance Scale, Hollingshead's Index of Social Position, a variety of multidimensional socioeconomic scales and a limited number of occupational scales—most often modeling on those used by the Bureau of the Census—are the basic tools used for the vast bulk of the studies. Haug and Sussman have been criti-

17. K. C. Land, "Path Models of Functional Theories of Social Stratification as Representations of Cultural Beliefs on Stratification," *Sociological Quarterly* 11 (Fall 1970), pp. 474–484.

18. S. N. Eisenstadt, *Social Differentiation and Stratification* (Glenview, Ill.: Scott, Foresman, 1971), p. 234; S. N. Eisenstadt, "Status Segregation and Class Association in Modern Society," *Sociology and Social Research* 54 (July 1970), pp. 425–440.

19. William H. Sewell and Robert M. Hauser, "Causes and Consequences of Higher Education: Models of the Status Attainment Process," *American Journal of Agricultural Economics* 54 (December 1972), pp. 851–861.

20. S. N. Eisenstadt, *Social Differentiation*, pp. 149–179.

cal of the measurement instruments currently in use.[21] Miller has expressed concern that preoccupation with methodological mechanics may cause scholars in the area of social mobility to lose sight of the purpose of their work: "few ideas and studies can withstand the forceful sophistication of contemporary methodologists"[22]; he quite accurately warned that "social mobility" and "status inconsistency" are being downgraded as operationally specific terms as a result of their indiscriminate use in the literature.[23]

An innovative procedure was used by Badaloni and Rizzi in a study done in Italy.[24] They developed a reflexive scale for determining the categorical statuses of respondents according to the respondents' patterns of ranking the general prestige of fourteen occupational categories. The researchers were able not only to locate clusters of respondents by their response patterns, but also to compute a distance factor between clusters in three populations. The distance computations were then used as a measure of the relative homogeneity of the respective populations.

A comprehensive study of social rank in six American communities resulted in a factor analysis of the findings. Factors of residence—

neighborhood, area, house—ascribed status—family educational and occupational status—marital background and achieved socioeconomic status were common to all of the communities, but a fifth factor varied by community and by age of the respondent. It was concluded that stratification systems are the effects of a dynamic process of social organization, maintaining a homeostasis that is somewhat unique for each community.[25]

Several innovations were developed for procedures for studying social mobility as distinguished from social stratification. Spilerman used a regression procedure allowing a heterogeneous population to be examined within a Markov framework.[26]

Hawkes pointed to the wisdom of conceptualizing mobility as the linkage between statuses rather than the difference between statuses.[27] Goodman used an index in the measurement of social mobility which incorporated the degree to which an individual's status tends to persist from its origin to a later observation point.[28]

In a critique of Svalastoga's notion of the "permeability" of social entities—openness to persons

21. Marie R. Haug and Marvin B. Sussman, "The Indiscriminate State of Social Class Measurement," *Social Forces* 49 (June 1971), pp. 549–562.

22. S. N. Miller, "The Future of Social Mobility Studies," *American Journal of Sociology* 77 (July 1971), p. 62.

23. Ibid., p. 65.

24. Mario Badaloni and Alfredo Rizzi, "Contribution to Cluster Analysis and Its Use for the Study of Occupational Prestige," (Istituto di Statistica e Ricerca Sociale "C. Gini," Universita di Roma, 1972).

25. Reta D. Artz, Richard F. Curtis, Dianne Timbers Fairbank and Elton F. Jackson, "Community Rank Stratification: A Factor Analysis," *American Sociological Review* 36 (December 1971), pp. 985–1002.

26. Seymour Spilerman, "The Analysis of Mobility Processes by the Introduction of Independent Variables into a Markov Chain," *American Sociological Review* 37 (June 1972), pp. 277–294.

27. Roland K. Hawkes, "Some Methodological Problems in Explaining Social Mobility," *American Sociological Review* 37 (June 1972), pp. 294–300.

28. Leo A. Goodman, "On the Measurement of Social Mobility: An Index of Status Persistence," *American Sociological Review* 34 (December 1969), pp. 831–849.

lacking specific ascribed characteristics—MacFarland called attention to the applicability of information theory procedures to mobility studies.[29] Such procedures, he noted, can be used on nominally scaled data—which, in fact, occupational data are. It should be pointed out that Svalastoga is by no means alone among the sociologists who have used procedures appropriate to ordinal or metric data on data which are nominally scaled.

The problem of Haller and Saravia was unique, although from one point of view it was not unlike that faced in the construction of a reflexive scale.[30] After they determined the strata existing in Acucena and the degree of crystallization of, and dispersion between, those strata, they measured appropriate status content variables within the strata and found that they did indeed discriminate differently at different levels of the status hierarchy.

In the same vein as Haller and Saravia, Jones and Shorter developed a ratio measurement of social status and observed the relative importance assigned to typically valued American social characteristics—such as education and income—by judges from three distinct cultural backgrounds. Their findings indicate that such procedures are justified in any study of social stratification or social class where the population is heterogeneous.

Boudon has published a collection of the possible procedures for studying social mobility.[31] In the second part of his book he has dealt with a number of models.

Finally, Strauss ignored the almost universal procedures for studying intergenerational occupational mobility to draw on the materials of history, fiction, biography and social anthropology to construct a dynamic model of American social mobility.[32] His primary concern was with the social meaning of mobility and its context.

FINDINGS

The paragraphs which follow are devoted to notes on selected findings from the literature of the past five years. The tremendous volume of literature makes it impossible to give an exhaustive catalogue of the findings; almost certainly, some important materials have been given insufficient attention or have even been missed altogether. The work of Glenn, Alston and Weiner[33] suggests the possible scope of such an undertaking; rather than following their excellent example, we have elected to give an overview of the literature, with examples, in several substantive areas.

Classes as styles of life: population categories distinguished by cultural criteria

The cultural perspective of social classes emphasizes the probability

29. David D. MacFarland, "Measuring the Permeability of Occupational Structures: An Information-Theoretic Approach," *American Journal of Sociology* 75 (July 1969), pp. 41–61.

30. Haller and Saravia, "Status Measurements."

31. Raymond Boudon, *Mathematical Structures of Social Mobility* (San Francisco, Cal.: Jossey-Bass, 1973).

32. Anselm L. Strauss, *The Contexts of Social Mobility: Ideology and Theory* (Chicago, Ill.: Aldine, 1971).

33. Norval P. Glenn, Jon P. Alston and David Weiner, *Social Stratification: A Research Bibliography* (Berkeley, Cal.: Glendessary, 1970).

that there are differences in shared sentiments of population categories and that these differences are, in fact, the determinants of social class. Critical sentiments may include feelings about the proper or appropriate relationship of persons to the production and consumption of material goods—as in Marxian theory; however, the general notion embraces a much broader range of variables.

There is, of course, a close relationship between sentiments and behaviors, as well as between cultural and social variables, even though they are conceptually quite distinct. Especially since the literature does not always make this distinction, items will be found in this section which might equally well appear in the section on associational and interactional findings and vice versa.

The most basic sentiment which can distinguish among population categories with respect to social strata or social classes is that it is proper, appropriate, right or legitimate to evaluate population categories unequally. The legitimacy of such distinctions may, in fact, be viewed with differential affect by different social categories.[34] The traditional literature tends to assume either that social class stratification is an upper class—or bourgeois—sentiment which is more or less tolerated by the lower classes or that the total population believes that it is right and proper for societies to be divided into social strata. In the past there appears to have been more empirical support for the latter as-

sumption than there has been for the former; current research tends to be congruous with the latter assumption, but is by no means definitive.[35]

Rytina, Form and Pease found, however, that in an industrial community acceptance of the ideology of the American opportunity structure varied situationally among income strata in direct correlation with the probability of gain from supporting the ideology.[36] The belief that different social strata have different ideologies about the distribution of power in the United States was tested by Form and Rytina in Muskegon, Michigan. They found that respondents with the highest income and education were most likely to conceptualize the power structure as pluralistic, but somewhat less likely to believe that it ought to be that way.[37] It should be pointed out, however, that the author's data show that the amount of education discriminates more powerfully than the amount of income among ideological beliefs—at least among white persons—and that the pluralistic description of the American power structure was generally considered best by a majority of persons in all income strata.

Schiller investigated the low pattern of socioeconomic achievement

34. That sociologists themselves question the legitimacy of recognizing social classes was mentioned above in Reissman and Halstead, "The Subject is Class."

35. Compare, Ian Bowen, *Acceptable Inequalities: An Essay on the Distribution of Income* (Montreal: McGill-Queen's University Press, 1970).

36. Joan Huber Rytina, William H. Form and John Pease, "Income and Stratification Ideology: Beliefs About the American Opportunity Structure," *American Journal of Sociology* 75 (January 1970), pp. 703–716.

37. William H. Form and Joan Rytina, "Ideological Belief on the Distribution of Power in the United States," *American Sociological Review* 34 (February 1969), pp. 19–31.

of children from welfare families and concluded that the predisposing variables were not individual capabilities or parental educational or occupational statuses, but a "constriction in opportunities" resulting from the poverty of the family of origin.[38]

Goldthorpe and his associates have examined the assumption— dating back to Frederick Engels —that as a working class person becomes more affluent, he comes to accept bourgeois social values, life styles and political ideas.[39] Their empirical findings did not support the thesis of disembourgeoisement as an unequivocally valid principle. It was shown that affluence did not affect working class life styles, aspirations for social contacts with middle class persons or the adoption of middle class social norms to any great extent.

That class-distinctive styles of life are accompanied by distinctive material furnishings and aesthetic tastes was confirmed in a study of the Detroit area by Laumann and House.[40] They found that living room styles are not only related to social status, but that persons who are more traditional in religious and marital-role attitudes are also more traditional in their selection of decor.

Sentiments about aesthetics are not the only cultural distinctions between social classes which have been studied in the past five years. Kohn and his associates did studies of class-oriented parental values for child rearing in Italy, Washington, D.C., and the United States in general.[41] The researchers found that middle class parents placed great emphasis on self-direction for their children, while lower class parents emphasized conformity. Since the occupation of the middle class father typically requires many daily decisions, he rears his son to make such decisions. The lower class father, on the other hand, is more likely to succeed in his work by following orders; therefore, he trains his child to conform. The national sample in the United States was confined entirely to employed men; it is possible that the lower lower class was inadequately represented.

Evans and Smith studied family decision-making patterns in different social strata.[42] They found a linear, positive relationship between the extent of syncratic—joint decision-making—style and socioeconomic status.

Using self-esteem as an intervening variable between social status and deviant behavior, Hewitt concluded that delinquency behavior— as any other behavior—was a joint

38. Bradley R. Schiller, "Stratified Opportunities: The Essence of the 'Vicious Circle,'" *American Journal of Sociology* 76 (November 1970), pp. 426–442.

39. John H. Goldthorpe, David Lockwood, Frank Bechhofer and Jennifer Platt, *The Affluent Worker in the Class Structure* (Cambridge: Cambridge University Press, 1969).

40. Edward O. Laumann and James S. House, "Living Room Styles and Social Attributes: The Pattern of Material Artifacts in a Modern Urban Community," *Sociology and Social Research* 54 (April 1970), pp. 321–342; Compare, also, David R. Morgan, "Community Social Rank and Attitudes toward Suburban Living," *Sociology and Social Research* 55 (July 1971), pp. 401–413.

41. Melvin L. Kohn, *Class and Conformity* (Homewood, Ill.: Dorsey, 1969); Melvin Kohn and Carmi Schooler, "Class, Occupation and Orientation," *American Sociological Review* 34 (October 1969), pp. 659–678.

42. Richard H. Evans and Norman R. Smith, "A Selected Paradigm on Family Behavior," *Journal of Marriage and the Family* 31 (August 1969), pp. 512–517.

product of individual dispositions and social structure.[43]

Language

Grimshaw has reviewed the major recent contributions to the study of language and social class in a recent survey essay.[44] He devoted a considerable amount of space to Bernstein's new works, and rightly so, since Bernstein literally devised the language in which scholars discuss language and social class. "Public language," "positional control" and "elaborated code" are all terms first used, as far as we know, by Bernstein in describing the ways in which people become "locked into" social classes by their linguistic patterns.

Interest in speech and language as indicators of social class has increased in the period under study. Bernstein and Henderson observed that middle class mothers place much greater emphasis upon the use of language for interpersonal relationships, while working class mothers are more prone to emphasize the use of language for the transmission of basic skills.[45] Stanley noted that some spoken sounds are considered to be ugly by well-educated people.[46] Osser and Endler found that there was a different choice of terms to express the same idea—for example, flat versus apartment, pram versus baby carriage—by upper class and lower class Canadian girls.[47] The upper class sixteen-year olds tended to choose words of British origin, while the lower class girls tended to choose words of American origin. Other writings confirm social class differences in speech patterns, both in the United States and elsewhere.[48]

Glenn has observed that class differences in political party affiliation in the United States, especially in the South, appear to have undergone measurable change in the last two elections. He concluded that this was true because white collar workers typically take a less conservative stand on some issues on which blue collar voters typically take a more conservative stand and vice versa. Conservative positions on civil

43. John P. Hewitt, *Social Stratification and Deviant Behavior* (New York: Random House, 1970).

44. Allen D. Grimshaw, "On Language in Society: Part I," *Contemporary Sociology* 2 (November 1973), pp. 575–585. The works reviewed were: Basil Bernstein, *Class, Codes and Control, I: Theoretical Studies towards a Sociology of Language* (London: Routledge and Kegan Paul, 1971); Basil Bernstein, ed., *Class, Codes and Control, II: Applied Studies towards a Sociology of Language* (London: Routledge and Kegan Paul, 1973); Jenny Cook-Gumperz, *Social Control and Socialization: A Study of Class Differences in the Language of Maternal Control* (London: Routledge and Kegan Paul, 1973); William Labov, *Sociolinguistic Patterns* (Philadelphia, Pa.: University of Pennsylvania Press, 1972); William Labov, *Language in the Inner City: Studies in the Black English Vernacular* (Philadelphia, Pa.: University of Pennsylvania Press, 1972).

45. Basil Bernstein and Dorothy Henderson, "Social Class Differences in the Relevance of Language to Socialization," *Sociology* 3 (1969), p. 120.

46. George Stanley, "Phonoaesthetics and West Texas Dialect," *Linguistics* 71 (July 1971), pp. 95–103.

47. Harry Osser and Norman S. Endler, "Lexical Choice and Social Class," *Language and Speech* 13 (October-December 1970), pp. 254–263.

48. Walter Brandis and Dorothy Henderson, *Social Class, Language and Communication* (London: Routledge and Kegan Paul, 1970); Frederick William and Barbara Sundine, "Negro Childrens' Speech: Some Social Class Differences in Word Predictability," *Language and Speech* 13 (July-September 1970), pp. 141–150; S. Suseendirarajah, "Reflections of Certain Social Differences in Jaffna, Tamil," *Anthropological Linguistics* 12 (October 1970), pp. 239–245.

rights, civil liberties, involvement of the United States in foreign affairs, law enforcement and punishment of criminals, for example, have been more widely supported by blue collar conservatives than by white collar conservatives.[49]

Different sentiments about sexual behavior have been associated with differences in socioeconomic statuses in contemporary studies. Maranell, Dodder and Mitchell tested Reiss's earlier hypothesis that among conservatives those of higher social status would be less sexually permissive than those of lower status, while among liberals the relationship would be reversed. Reiss's hypothesis was not confirmed by the Maranell study.[50]

Coombs and her associates studied the substantial and readily evident economic and educational disadvantages of premaritally pregnant couples in the Detroit area.[51] They found that such couples are not disproportionately from low status backgrounds. While their young age at marriage only accounts directly for part of their lifetime disadvantage, the consequent truncated education and lower occupational capabilities are associated with a significantly lower income than their postmaritally pregnant counterparts.

A study of sexual activities by Walshok attributes a rise in swinging behavior—that is, agreements between husband and wife to have sexual relations with other persons, usually at the same time and in the same place—to a shift in middle class social values and institutions.[52] Walshok has not made the term middle class operational, a not uncommon feature of the literature of social protest and social action. Some twenty three descriptive words or phrases were used to sensitize the reader to the author's concept of middle class; they include "status anxiety," "corporate lives," "shopping in shopping center," "changing jobs," "transient" and the like, but these diacritica do not seem sufficiently operational to define precisely an observable population. It does seem clear that Walshok is attempting to distinguish conceptually between classes by cultural criteria, however.

The tendency to use cultural or life style criteria for distinguishing among social classes is certainly not new. Very often when this is done, terms such as middle class are not made operational and sometimes not really defined at all. Historically, the Marxian term middle class refers to the bourgeoisie, which might better be called the upper class in the contemporary United States, since there is no remaining vestige of feudal aristocracy to complete the original Marxian paradigm. From a mathematical paradigm or a continuum concept middle class would seem to refer to a distinguishable category of persons on some ordered scale which

49. Norval D. Glenn, "Class and Party Support in the United States: Recent and Emergent Trends," *Public Opinion Quarterly* 37 (Spring 1973), pp. 1–20.

50. Gary M. Maranell, Richard A. Dodder and David F. Mitchell, "Social Class and Premarital Sexual Permissiveness: A Subsequent Test," *Journal of Marriage and the Family* 32 (February 1970), pp. 85–88.

51. Lolagene C. Coombs, Ronald Freedman, Judith Friedman and William F. Pratt, "Premarital Pregnancy and Status before and after Marriage," *American Journal of Sociology* 75 (March 1970), pp. 800–820.

52. Mary Walshok, "The Emergence of Middle-Class Deviant Sub-Cultures: The Case of Swingers," *Social Problems* 18 (Spring 1971), pp. 488–495.

contains at least one higher class and at least one lower class. This basic terminological confusion is not only found among studies, but unfortunately within studies.[53]

Hyman and Wright attempted to replicate a study of the probability that persons of different social statuses would be members of more or fewer voluntary associations. Their findings supported their earlier study—reported in 1958—and indicated that there had been a 7 percent increase in voluntary association memberships generally.[54] Hyman and Wright also noticed a sharp increase in the Negro membership of voluntary associations, even though they were slightly less likely to belong to such organizations than white persons.

A study of the Flathead Indians indicated that they lacked any positive sentiments about the association of educational achievement with social class.[55] Brockmann rationalized his findings in several ways, including the selective outmigration of the more highly educated Flatheads, the greater association of class status with life cycle than among Anglos, the absence of educational requirements for employment on the reservation and so forth.

In a study of the influences of social class origin on the attainment of graduate education and subsequent employment, Crane found that social class origin continues to influence a student's progress at the highest levels of the educational system and that it influences both the quality of education received and the opportunities available to the student upon graduation.[56]

Chiricos, Jackson and Waldo found social class differences in the imposing of criminal labels, especially on the older, black, poorly educated, previously convicted persons being defended by a court-appointed attorney.[57]

It does not seem impossible to construct a taxonomy of social classes with cultural diacritica distinguishing among the categories. Even though such a taxonomy is implicit in many studies—for example, Walshok's study, above—it has not been formally defined to our knowledge.

Social classes as communities: associational categories

Weber used the term *stunde* to refer to social enclaves of persons who not only had a common life style, but who were in frequent interaction with one another—or who could be in frequent interaction with one another if they chose to be—whose children married one another and who belonged to the same social clubs and organizations. Although the flow of interaction does produce an ordering of behavior and, consequently, senti-

53. Compare, Robert Coles, *The Middle Americans: Proud and Uncertain* (Boston, Mass.: Little, Brown, 1971).

54. Herbert Hyman and Charles Wright, "Trends in Voluntary Association Memberships of American Adults: Replications Based on Secondary Analysis of National Sample Survey," *American Sociological Review* 36 (December 1971), pp. 191–206.

55. C. Thomas Brockmann, "Correlation of Social Class and Education on the Flathead Reservation, Montana," *Rocky Mountain Social Science Journal* 8 (October 1971), pp. 11–17.

56. Diana Crane, "Social Class Origin and Academic Success: The Influence of Two Stratification Systems on Academic Careers," *Sociology of Education* 42 (Winter 1969), pp. 1–17.

57. Theodore G. Chiricos, Phillip B. Jackson and Gordon P. Waldo, "Inequality in the Imposition of a Criminal Label," *Social Problems* 19 (Spring 1972), pp. 553–572.

ments about ways of behaving, the concept of social classes as associational categories emphasizes interaction rather than cultural homogeneity.[58] Laumann and Hesslink have both continued their distinguished works from this perspective.

Laumann found—just as Goldthorpe discovered, with respect to affluence and cultural change (see above)—that the relocation of ethnic and religious groups does not result in the social melting pot posited by other earlier scholars.[59] Defining the social structure of a community as "a persisting system of social relationships," Laumann observed that the formation of friendship relationships followed socioeconomic status lines both within and outside of religious categories—Protestant, Catholic, Jewish—and within ethnic categories, even after three or more generations of residence in Detroit. The pattern of friendship choices cannot be explained simply by any of these variables alone, however. Laumann's book is more than a simple monograph on urban social networks. He and his associates relentlessly explored their methodological and theoretical tools and concepts. In our opinion, he has assembled one of the most important books during the period under study.

In general, we have avoided reviewing second editions of earlier works; an exception must be made in the case of Hesslink's *Black*

Neighbors.[60] Hesslink's extension of his earlier study continues to focus on patterns of social interaction. The book shows—in the current edition, however—the impressive impact of the mass society on local interaction patterns. Hesslink's work is primary and personal. While he reports some secondary information from public records, the intentional gathering of the data for the particular study at hand—a feature becoming increasingly rare in sociology—reassures the reader that the author's findings are both focused and complete and that the deductions about the relationship between social status and friendship choice are valid.

Phillips found that for lower class persons the magnitude of the relationship between social participation and clear-cut feelings—happiness—is greatest.[61] They have fewer opportunities for social participation.

Vorwaller reported that although the number of memberships in voluntary associations is accounted for by the status effects of social origins and destinations, vertical social mobility itself is not strongly related to affiliations with such associations.[62]

58. Compare, S. N. Eisenstadt, "Status Segregation and Class Association in Modern Societies," *Sociology and Social Research* 54 (July 1970), pp. 425–440.

59. Edward O. Laumann, *Bonds of Pluralism: The Form and Substance of Urban Social Networks* (New York: John Wiley and Sons, 1973).

60. George K. Hesslink, *Black Neighbors: Negroes in a Northern Rural Community*, 2nd ed. (Indianapolis, Ind.: Bobbs-Merrill, 1973); Compare, also, George K. Hesslink, "The Function of Neighborhood in Ecological Stratification," *Sociology and Social Research* 54 (July 1970), pp. 441–459.

61. Derek L. Phillips, "Social Class, Social Participation and Happiness: A Consideration of 'Interaction Opportunities' and 'Investments,'" *Sociological Quarterly* 10 (Winter 1969), pp. 3–21.

62. Daniel J. Vorwaller, "Social Mobility and Membership in Voluntary Associations," *American Journal of Sociology* 75 (January 1970), pp. 481–495.

Interaction with significant others was found to differ with social class in several kinds of situations. Devor, for example, reported that middle class children exert a greater socializing influence on their parents than do lower class children.[63] Musgrove discovered a difference in the degree of parental control over childrens' television viewing that varied with social class.[64] Rist observed ghetto children in school and found that teachers reinforced the class structure of the community by basing their expectations of performance on the social status of the students.[65]

The status attainment process

Years of careful study of the Wisconsin schools by William H. Sewell and his many associates have provided a wealth of information about the variables associated with the achievement of occupational and educational statuses.[66] A great number of variables—including parents' income, father's education, mother's education, father's occupation, parental encouragement, teachers' encouragement, peers' plans, academic ability and sex differences—have been defined operationally and their direct effects on educational and occupational achievement have been studied, as well as their aggregate effects in selected groups of variables labeled, "socioeconomic status" and "significant others' influence."

The findings of the Sewell studies are generally congruous with popular expectations: high socioeconomic status is associated with educational attainment after high school. Academic ability, high school performance, significant others' influence and educational and occupational aspirations are also positively related to socioeconomic status. Parental influence on education and occupational as-

63. Geraldine M. Devor, "Children as Agents in Socializing Parents," *Family Coordinator* 19 (July 1970), pp. 208–212.

64. P. W. Musgrove, "How Children Use Television," *New Society* 13 (20 February, 1969), pp. 277–278.

65. Ray C. Rist, "Student Social Class and Teacher Expectations: The Self-Fulfilling Prophecy in Ghetto Education," *Harvard Educational Review* 40 (August 1970), pp. 411–451.

66. Otis Dudley Duncan, David L. Featherman and Beverly Duncan, *Socioeconomic Background and Achievement* (New York: Seminar Press, 1972); Robert M. Hauser, "Schools and the Stratification Process," *American Journal of Sociology* 74 (May 1969), pp. 587–611; Robert M. Hauser, *Socioeconomic Background and Educational Performance* (Washington, D.C.: American Sociological Association, Rose Monograph Series, 1971); Ruth M. Gasson, Archibald O. Haller and William H. Sewell, *Attitudes and Facilitation in the Attaining of Status* (Washington, D.C.: American Sociological Association, Rose Monograph Series, 1972); Robert M. Hauser, "Disaggregating A Social-Psychological Model of Educational Attainment," *Social Science Research* 1 (June 1972), pp. 159–188; William H. Sewell, "Inequality of Opportunity for Higher Education," *American Sociological Review* 36 (October 1971), pp. 793–809; William H. Sewell and Robert M. Hauser, Causes and Consequences"; William H. Sewell, Archibald O. Haller and Alejandro Portes, "The Educational and Early Occupational Attainment Process," *American Sociological Review* 34 (February 1969), pp. 82–92; William H. Sewell, Archibald O. Haller and George W. Ohlendorf, "The Educational and Early Occupational Status Attainment Process: Replication and Revision," *American Sociological Review* 35 (December 1970), pp. 1014–1027; Eldon Wegner and William H. Sewell, "Selection and Context as Factors Affecting the Probability of Graduation from College," *American Journal of Sociology* 75 (January 1970), pp. 665–679.

pirations is greater than that of teachers, and gender alone explains one-half year more educational attainment for men than for women. The great importance of the Sewell studies is that they have replaced folklore with science and have contributed new information about the degree and the direction of influence of a wide range of factors on status attainment.

Of the studies done outside the Sewell group at the University of Wisconsin during the period under study, one of the most noteworthy is Collins' effort to fit the explanation of educational stratification in the United States to a more elaborate, grand theory instead of the constructed theory of Sewell.[67]

Rehberg, Schafer and Sinclair compared the Sewell model of achievement patterns with a model suggested by the work of Turner,[68] particularly with respect to sequence in the path of the variables, and found the Turner model more acceptable by the Simon-Blalock correlational procedures.[69]

Jencks and his collaborators developed a model of the process of occupational and adult income attainment which differs principally from the Sewell and Turner models in its inclusion of variables of genetic origin and variables related to the family of orientation absent in other models.[70] They found the present educational process in the United States inequitable.

Perrucci and Perrucci have continued their investigations of career success in engineering. The direct relationship between social origins and career success found in an earlier study of engineering graduates in the midwest was not found in a Pacific coast study, but social origins were found to influence educational achievement, which in turn influenced success.[71] Further study of a national sample revealed that social origins were directly related to success only among high-grade engineers from highly selected colleges.

Hauser found that the sex ratio—proportion of males to females—in specific high schools was positively related to educational aspirations of white high school seniors in Davidson County, Tennessee,[72] but concluded—in the face of a rather large literature maintaining that the social context of an entity has an independent effect on its constituents—that the observed effect was spurious, "speculative, artifactual, and substantively trivial." He went further to generalize on contextual studies as "a waste of time and effort," providing "no special insight into

67. Randall Collins, "Functional and Conflict Theories of Educational Stratification," *American Sociological Review* 36 (December 1971), pp. 1002–1019.

68. Ralph Turner, *The Social Context of Ambition* (San Francisco, Cal.: Chandler, 1964).

69. Richard A. Rehberg, Walter E. Schafer and Judie Sinclair, "Toward a Temporal Sequence of Adolescent Achievement Variables," *American Sociological Review* 35 (February 1970), pp. 34–48.

70. Christopher Jencks and Marshall Smith, Henry AcLand, Mary Jo Bane, David Cohen, Herbert Gintis, Barbara Heyns and Stephen Michelson, *Inequality: A Reassessment of Family and Schooling in America* (New York: Basic Books, 1972).

71. Carolyn Cummings Perrucci and Robert Perrucci, "Social Origins, Educational Context, and Career Mobility," *American Sociological Review* 35 (June 1970), pp. 451–463.

72. Robert M. Hauser, "Context and Consex: A Cautionary Tale," *American Journal of Sociology* 75 (January 1970), pp. 645–664.

processes determining group differentiation," and that "the sociological literature would benefit from their absence." Although Hauser's later justification of his sociological position is clear, the motivation for his polemics is not.[73]

Much of the Sewell work dealing with social-psychological factors of status attainment is built on the work of Haller and his associates.[74] Haller and Miller have provided a standard procedure for measuring occupational aspirations which has been thoroughly tested and validated. The procedure which Haller and Woelfel have devised for making operational the expectations of significant others and their effect on attitude formation is, as far as we know, unique. As does Sewell, Haller is replacing impressionistic sociology with science. Furthermore, he is making it possible to test social-psychological theories, such as symbolic interactionism, with a precision which has not been previously possible.

The effects of occupational and educational mobility on differential social strata, especially on ghetto and minority populations, continued to be explored by Miller and Roby, Reissman and Pen.[75]

Iutaka and Bock have questioned whether the model of status attainment or career mobility derived from studies of highly industrialized societies is appropriate for societies which are still in the process of industrialization.[76] Their study of Brazil showed that the model of career mobility was generally congruous with that of the United States. The principal differences between the two models were that fathers' last occupational status was more important in Brazil than in the United States, while fathers' educational status was found to be less important in Brazil. It is the impression of the authors that the industrialization process involves an increasing emphasis on status achievement through educational attainment, however, and that this will result in the future in a decreased emphasis on social origin.

Subjective perception of social class

Schreiber and Nygreen documented changes in the self-designation of social class by persons with different occupations over a period of two decades.[77] They observed

73. Compare, Allen Barton, "Allen Barton Comments on Hauser's 'Context and Consex,'" and "Hauser Replies," American Journal of Sociology 76 (November 1970), pp. 514–519.

74. Archibald O. Haller and Irwin W. Miller, The Occupational Aspiration Scale (Cambridge, Mass.: Schenkman, 1971); Archibald O. Haller and Joseph Woelfel, "Identifying Significant Others and Measuring Their Expectations for a Person," Proceedings of the XXII Congress of the Institut International de Sociologie (1969), pp. 395–429; Archibald O. Haller and Joseph Woelfel, "Significant Others, the Self-Reflexive Act and the Attitude Formation Process," American Sociological Review 36 (February 1971), pp. 74–87.

75. S. M. Miller and Pamela A. Roby, The Future of Inequality (New York: Basic Books, 1970); Leonard Reissman, Inequality in American Society: Social Stratification (Glenview, Ill.: Scott, Foresman, 1973); and Jan Pen, Income Distribution (London: Penguin Press, 1971).

76. Sugiyama Iutaka and E. Wilbur Bock, "Determinants of Occupational Status in Brazil," Social Science Information 11 (October 1972), pp. 213–222.

77. P. M. Schreiber and G. P. Nygreen, "Subjective Social Class in America: 1945–1968," Social Forces 48 (March 1970), pp. 348–356.

a drop of more than one-quarter in the number of employed persons designating themselves as working class in national samples between 1958 and 1968. The drop was much larger among persons engaged in manual work than among professionals, businessmen and white-collar workers who had previously identified themselves as working class.

It has often been either hypothesized or assumed that there was a linear relationship between self-esteem and social class. A study defining social class in terms of Hollingshead's Index of Social Position and comparing it with self-derogation—that is, "relatively intense characteristic negative affect evoked in a person by his global consideration of his personal qualities, achievements and behaviors" —supported such assumptions for a series of specific contextual variables: salience of social class, self-evaluation, perception of relative social class position, salience of correlates of social class for self-evaluation and lack of control and defenses.[78] In nine other randomly chosen items relating to context, the hypothesized relationship was not found.

A comparison of ISP scores with class awareness and class identification showed that they were strongly correlated, supporting the notion of congruity between subjective and objective measures of social position.[79]

Jackman and Jackman gathered evidence to test the relative validity of neo-Marxian and pluralist conceptualizations of social status in its objective and subjective perspectives.[80] They found: (1) that Americans do not recognize their association with the means of production as salient for subjective class identification; (2) that for American blacks, their blackness overpowers any achieved status in subjective estimations of their general status; (3) and that the status of one's social contacts mediates the relationship between objective status and subjective class identification.

Portes tested a correlational—personal frustration plus structural blame—and an interactional—personal frustration times structural blame—interpretation of leftist radicalism in Chile.[81] He found strongest support for the correlational interpretation.

Alexander concluded that differentiated perception of status is a general characteristic of any group.[82] He found that the higher a judger's status, the greater was the dispersion of his assignments of statuses to others. Lower status persons minimized the distance between themselves and the top; upper status persons maximized the distance between themselves and the bottom.

78. Howard Kaplan, "Social Class and Self-Derogation: A Conditional Relationship," Sociometry 34 (March 1971), pp. 41–64.

79. George W. Lewis, "A Research Note on Class Awareness and Class Identification and the Hollingshead Index of Social Position," Sociological Quarterly 12 (Winter 1971), pp. 90–94.

80. Mary R. Jackman and Robert W. Jackman, "An Interpretation of the Relation between Objective and Subjective Social Status," American Sociological Review 38 (October 1973), pp. 569–582.

81. Alejandro Portes, "On the Interpretation of Class Consciousness, American Journal of Sociology 77 (September 1971), pp. 228–244.

82. C. Norman Alexander, Jr., "Status Perceptions," American Sociological Review 37 (December 1972), pp. 767–773.

Socialization

Two articles are particularly concerned with the development of class and stratificatory concepts in school-aged children. Simmons and Rosenberg found that by the time they had reached the third grade, Baltimore school children had a comprehension of the American occupational prestige hierarchy which was generally reminiscent of the NORC scale.[83] Children through the twelfth grade did not appear to believe that equality of opportunity for status attainment actually existed in the United States. The majority of the children, however, aspired to higher occupations than those held by their fathers, with middle class children having the highest aspirations. The authors attributed aspirations for upward mobility in part to the children's keen awareness of differences in prestige.

Tudor broke class awareness into three dimensions—cognitive, behavioral and evaluative—and studied change along these dimensions in the children in the first through sixth grades of a public school system.[84] She found that cognitive awareness of social classes increased from slightly better than chance in the first grade to substantial cognitive awareness by the sixth grade, with females showing greater awareness than males. The behavioral dimension was actually also a cognitive dimension, but dealt with what class-identified figures would do—for example, an item on the scale would be "which of these [pictured] fathers went to college?" Findings on the evaluative dimension were not conclusive, undoubtedly due to a large extent to the deletion or alteration of items in the original scales by school officials.

Kerckhoff has examined the psychological and sociological research literature from the perspective of the relatively stable context in which a child learns social class identification and the relatively dynamic development of aspirations and expectations.[85] He presents a developmental thesis concerning the interaction of these kinds of variables.

Prestige, influence and power

Reference was made earlier in this article to Eisenstadt's model in which compliance to the central values of a society is rewarded by the differential allocation of prestige and deference. Svalastoga has presented a more complex model drawn from Danish data, adding the variables of occupational responsibility, occupational difficulty and subject's knowledge of specialized activities to the ideological interpretation of centrality.[86] Eisenstadt's model might be more adequately implemented from a methodological procedure suggested by Young, who associates the paths of information flow with the identification of prestige.[87]

83. Robert G. Simmons and Morris Rosenberg, "Functions of Children's Perceptions of the Stratification System," *American Sociological Review* 36 (April 1971), pp. 235-249.

84. Jeannette F. Tudor, "The Development of Class Awareness in Children," *Social Forces* 49 (March 1971), pp. 470-476.

85. Alan C. Kerckhoff, *Socialization and Social Class* (Englewood Cliffs, N.J.: Prentice-Hall, 1972).

86. Kaare Svalastoga, *The Determination of Occupational Prestige* (Copenhagen: unpublished, 1972).

87. T. R. Young, "The Cybernetics of Stratification: Prestige and the Flow of Information," *Sociology and Social Research* 55 (April 1971), pp. 269-284.

From their Brazilian data, Haller, Holsinger and Saravia conclude that isolation from the Euro-American urban societies may account for the prevalence of different conceptualizations of prestige hierarchies.[88] In other words, the more isolated the society, the greater the variation of the occupational prestige hierarchy from the classical NORC scale.

The transfer of power from individual persons to corporate entities in Western societies has been studied by Coleman.[89] Coleman accounts for the voluntary surrender of personal usage rights by an increase in benefit rights as the subject's control over his resources and behaviors is diminished through his transfer of usage rights to corporate entities—whether it be to a marriage partnership, an industrial corporation or a sovereign state. The subject must experience some change in consumer privileges, such as protection or corporate power, if he is not to experience a sense of frustration or degradation. Coleman presents strategies of withdrawal, coalition and reinterpretation as devices for maximizing personal gains and minimizing personal losses.

The two models of national political power which were developed earlier continued to be studied in this period: the power elite model and the pluralistic model. Domhoff opted for the power elite model.[90] Using smallest space analysis and graph theory, Laumann and Pappi examined consensus and cleavage in a small West German city which had a clearly identified elite.[91] It was discovered, however, that although clear-cut differences of opinion were found on five issues with which they were confronted, decisions tended to be identified with particular community influentials.[92]

From a different perspective, Hamilton undertook the task of determining whether political parties in the United States are formed along, or follow, the lines of occupational stratification—which he calls social class.[93] Not particularly surprisingly, he discovered that there are fundamental cleavages in sentiments about certain issues—welfare services, such as health insurance and guaranteed employment, racial integration and the like—but that these are not coincident with either party lines or the lines of occupational strata.

88. Archibald O. Haller, Donald D. Holsinger and Helcio Ulhoa Saravia, "Variations in Occupational Prestige Hierarchies: Brazilian Data," *American Journal of Sociology* 77 (March 1972), pp. 941–956.

89. James S. Coleman, "Loss of Power," *American Sociological Review* 38 (February 1973), pp. 1–17; James S. Coleman, *Power and the Structure of Society* (New York: W. W. Norton, 1973).

90. G. William Domhoff, *The Higher Circles: The Governing Class in America* (New York: Random House, 1970).

91. Edward O. Laumann and Franz Urban Pappi, "New Directions in the Study of Community Elites," *American Sociological Review* 38 (April 1973), pp. 212–229.

92. Compare, also, Robert Perrucci and Marc Pilisuk, "Leaders and Ruling Elites: The Interorganizational Bases of Community Power," *American Sociological Review* 35 (December 1970), pp. 1040–1057; Bruce H. Mayhew, "System Size and Ruling Elites," *American Sociological Review* 38 (August 1973), pp. 468–475; Maximilian H. vonBroembsen and Louis N. Gray, "Size and Ruling Elites: Effects of System Growth on Power Structures," *American Sociological Review* 38 (August 1973), pp. 476–478.

93. Richard F. Hamilton, *Class and Politics in the United States* (New York: John Wiley and Sons, 1972).

Class, race and ethnicity

The relationship between racial factors and class phenomena in the explanation of social behaviors has been of some concern in the period under study. Ransford and Hurst have continued with the exploration of the concept and operational definition of race-class phenomena.[94]

Laumann, using the criteria of social distance and friendship choices and a technique of smallest space analysis, discovered that friendships within a broad religious category—Protestant, Catholic, Jewish—were composed of persons in similar socioeconomic statuses. Ethnic differences also played a role in channeling friendship formation.[95] From a macro point of view, Lieberson theorized that the economic theory of social stratification cannot completely explain the social organization of an ethnically heterogeneous society.[96] Stratification and friendship were found to be weaker whenever economic strata were composed of different ethnic categories, confounding political processes.

Interracial marriage has been the focus of an important study by Burma, Cretser and Seacrest.[97]

While significant differences were found in the average occupational statuses of grooms and brides by ethnic or racial category, the average occupational statuses of intermarrying persons was approximately the same as that of intramarrying persons, between and within each ethnic or racial category. The earlier assumption that there would be differences is not valid, at least in the Los Angeles County sample.

Skin color criteria for mate selection were found to operate on a double standard in the District of Columbia.[98] While the traditional advantage of light-skinned Negro women over their darker counterparts in obtaining higher status husbands persists, blacker men were found to have increasingly more upward occupational mobility and advantages in mate selection.

Gordon has written a monograph on the determinants—including racial ones—of adolescent achievement orientation.[99] Olsen has written about power perspectives on stratification and race relations.[100] There have been numerous works on specific aspects of both black[101]

94. H. Edward Ransford, "Skin Color, Life Chances and Anti-White Attitudes," *Social Problems* 18 (Fall 1970), pp. 164–178; Charles E. Hurst, "Race, Class and Consciousness," *American Sociological Review* 37 (December 1972), pp. 658–670.

95. Edward O. Laumann, "The Social Structure of Religious and Ethnoreligious Groups," *American Sociological Review* 34 (April 1969), pp. 182–197.

96. Stanley Lieberson, "Stratification and Ethnic Groups," *Sociological Inquiry* 40 (Spring 1970), pp. 172–181.

97. John H. Burma, Gary A. Cretser and Ted Seacrest, "A Comparison of the Occupational Status of Intramarrying and Intermar-

rying Couples: A Research Note," *Sociology and Social Research* 54 (July 1970), pp. 508–519.

98. J. Richard Udry, Karl E. Bauman and Charles Chase, "Skin Color, Status, and Mate Selection," *American Journal of Sociology* 76 (January 1971), pp. 722–733.

99. Chad Gordon, *Looking Ahead: Self-conceptions, Race, and Family as Determinants of Adolescent Orientation to Achievement* (Washington, D.C.: American Sociological Association, Rose Monograph Series, 1972).

100. Marvin E. Olsen, "Power Perspectives on Stratification and Race Relations," in *Power in Societies*, ed. Marvin E. Olsen (New York: Macmillan, 1970).

101. Robert L. Crain, "School Integration and Occupational Achievement of Negroes," *American Journal of Sociology* 75 (January

and Mexican-American[102] class and status phenomena.

Congruence, consistency and crystallization

Landecker has investigated the theoretical underpinnings for understanding status congruence phenomena in social entities of varying degrees of class crystallization. He noted Simmel's position that persons with incongruous individual statuses increased the unity of a collectivity by "crossing boundaries" in various statuses. On the other hand, he noted Homans' conclusion that personal status in-

1970), pp. 593–606; Sidney Kronus, *The Black Middle Class* (Columbus, Ohio: Charles E. Merrill, 1970); Morris Rosenberg and Roberta G. Simmons, *Black and White Self Esteem: The Urban School Child* (Washington, D.C.: American Sociological Association, Rose Monograph Series, 1972).

102. Chandler Davidson and Charles M. Gaitz, "Ethnic Attitudes as a Basis for Minority Cooperation in a Southwestern Metropolis," *Social Science Quarterly* 53 (March 1973), pp. 738–748; Lawrence G. Felice, "Mexican-American Self-Concept and Educational Achievement: The Effects of Ethnic Isolation and Socioeconomic Deprivation," *Social Science Quarterly* 53 (March 1973), pp. 716–726; Leo Grebler, Joan Moore and Ralph Guzman, *The Mexican American People* (New York: Free Press, 1970); Armando Gutierrez and Herbert Hirsch, "The Militant Challenge to the American Ethos: 'Chicanos' and 'Mexican Americans'" *Social Science Quarterly* 53 (March 1973), pp. 830–845; Dale S. McLemore, "The Origins of Mexican American Subordination in Texas," *Social Science Quarterly* 53 (March 1973), pp. 656–670; Joan W. Moore, "Colonialism: The Case of Mexican Americans," *Social Problems* 17 (Spring 1970), pp. 463–472; Joan W. Moore, *Mexican Americans* (Englewood Cliffs, N.J.: Prentice-Hall, 1970); Fernando Penalosa, "The Changing Mexican-American in Southern California," *Sociology and Social Research* 51 (July 1967), pp. 405–417; William A. Rushing, "Class, Culture and Social Structure and Anomie," *American Journal of Sociology* 76 (March 1971), pp. 857–872.

congruities are incompatible with the notion of distributive justice in their perceivers, and the incompatibility is reduced by the cognitive replacement of incongruous statuses with congruous ones. Landecker concluded that Simmel's idea may be applicable to large groups while Homans' idea may apply to smaller groups. The process by which social cleavages are fostered in a collectivity by incongruity of status seems to vary more with the size of the collectivity than with its degree of class crystallization. In the Detroit area he found that there were greater differences in value judgments between status levels of a strongly crystallized collectivity than of a weakly crystallized collectivity. There has been much interest in status inconsistency during the period, as evidenced by the literature,[103] much of it extending the earlier work on the relationship between status inconsistency and political attitudes.[104]

103. See, for example, Steven Box and Julienne Ford, "Some Questionable Assumptions in the Theory of Status Inconsistency," *Sociological Review* 17 (July 1969), pp. 187–202; Uta Gerhardt, "Role Conflict and the Class Structure," *Sociology and Social Research* 55 (April 1971), pp. 285–296; John W. Meyer and Phillip E. Hammond, "Forms of Status Inconsistency," *Social Forces* 50 (September 1971), pp. 91–101; Joseph Berger, Bernard P. Cohen and Morris Zelditch, Jr., "Status Conceptions and Social Interactions," *American Sociological Review* 37 (June 1972), pp. 241–255; Elton F. Jackson and Richard F. Curtis, "Effects of Vertical Mobility and Status Inconsistency: A Body of Negative Evidence," *American Sociological Review* 37 (December 1972), pp. 701–713; William H. Form, "The Internal Stratification of the Working Class: System Involvements of Auto Workers in Four Countries," *American Sociological Review* 38 (December 1973), pp. 697–711.

104. See, for example, D. Stanley Eitzen, "Social Class, Status Inconsistency and

Segal asked for a clearer distinction between the effect of objectively perceived status inconsistencies and subjectively perceived status inconsistencies.[105] He suggested that the contradictory findings on the relationship between political partisanship, voting behavior and status inconsistency result from a failure to identify whether status inconsistency is the result of visibility of an individual's low status in one respect or the result of his personal awareness of an incongruous low status which is not visible to others. Obviously, the latter instance would be more likely to serve as a motive for stress-reducing behavior.

The delinquency rates for adolescent boys seems to be about the same for all social classes; however, high achievement motivation among lower class boys is associated with the highest official rates of delinquency, according to Gould.[106] His findings suggest that the subjective perception of status incongruities can extend to aspirations and, indeed, can be a factor in motivating behavior designed to reduce personal stress.

Broom and Jones speculate that status inconsistency is most stressful to individuals in societies "where most differentially valued statuses are ascribed rather than achieved, and when stress-reducing mechanisms are largely ineffective —the example *par excellence* is racial-ethnic status—it is ascribed, visible, and irreversible."[107] They found that in Australia, when achieved status characteristics were considered independently, status inconsistency did not significantly affect voting behavior, even though specified combinations of achieved statuses seemed to have some relationship—but not a statistically significant one—with such behavior.

The pervasiveness of kinship organization, the degree of socioeconomic development and the size or concentration of population were found to have little or no bearing on the political complexity of preindustrial societies, according to Abrahamson.[108] The variable which showed the greatest relationship to political complexity was the degree of social differentiation in the society.

Voting behavior

By and large, the studies of voting behavior during the past five years have continued to support the findings of earlier studies.[109] A

Political Attitudes," *Social Science Quarterly* 51 (December 1970), pp. 602–609; Alejandro Portes, "Status Inconsistency and Lower Class Leftist Radicalism," *Sociological Quarterly* 13 (Summer 1972), pp. 361–382; Marvin E. Olsen and Judy Corder Tully, "Socioeconomic-Ethnic Status Inconsistencies and Preference for Political Change," *American Sociological Review* 37 (October 1972), pp. 560–574.

105. David R. Segal, "Status Inconsistencies, Cross Pressures and American Political Behavior," *American Sociological Review* 34 (June 1969), pp. 352–359. Compare, also, Thomas S. Smith, "Structural Crystallization, Status Inconsistency and Political Partisanship," *American Sociological Review* 34 (December 1969), pp. 907–921.

106. Leroy C. Gould, "Juvenile Entrepreneurs," *American Journal of Sociology* 74 (May 1969), pp. 710–719.

107. Leonard Broom and F. Lancaster Jones, "Status Consistency and Political Preference: The Australian Case," *American Sociological Review* 35 (December 1970), pp. 989–1001.

108. Mark Abrahamson, "Correlates of Political Complexity," *American Sociological Review* 34 (October 1969), pp. 690–701.

109. David Berry, *The Sociology of Grassroots Politics* (New York: St. Martin's Press, 1970), explored party divisions and social class in England; compare, also, Colin A.

study by Bennett and Klecka did not show that voting behavior was more influenced by occupational status than by the voter's educational experience.[110] Olsen and Tully concluded from their findings in the Indianapolis Area Project that status inconsistency did not explain enough variation in preference for political change to warrant its retention as a variable.[111]

In Canada McDonald found that "the objective indicators of a person's status in society, with one exception, did not significantly increase the explanation of voting beyond that already explained by the main status variables of occupation, ethnicity, and religion."[112] The one exception observed was that middle class people with personal savings were more likely to vote conservatively.

Crime and delinquency

Frease found no direct relationship between social class and juvenile delinquency in Marion County, Oregon.[113] He did conclude, however, that college-bound middle class high school students suffer the greatest reaction formation in the face of failing grades, while lower class noncollege-bound students tend to become "declassed" when they are academically successful.

Box and Ford also report a contradiction to commonly-held notions that class differences are related to criminality.[114] They feel the conclusion can be justified "that the official construction of data on crime and criminals distorts the real social distribution of such behavior and types." Bytheway and May disputed their conclusions.[115]

Matsumoto compared a sample of junior and senior high school boys in Tokyo with a matched group in Nashville, Tennessee.[116] He found that while delinquency rates for specific classes in Nashville depended on the status structure of the local community, in Tokyo the delinquency rates of those from blue collar families were consistently higher than those of other social classes, regardless of neighborhood structure.

Bullington, Munns and Geis studied the attempt to lead ex-narcotics offenders into the acceptance of middle class values through a federally funded employment program and found that: "the lures of a legitimate, decent salary [$600 per month] and a prestige status alone appeared insufficient to insure middle class

Hughes, "Political Party Workers in Brisbane," *Australian and New Zealand Journal of Sociology* 5 (April 1969), pp. 32–39.

110. Stephen E. Bennett and William R. Klecka, "Social Status and Political Participation: A Multivariate Analysis of Predictive Power," *Midwest Journal of Political Science* 14 (August 1970), pp. 335–382.

111. Olsen and Tully, "Socioeconomic-Ethnic Status Inconsistencies."

112. Lynn McDonald, "Social Class and Voting: A Study of the 1968 Canadian Federal Election in Ontario," *British Journal of Sociology* 22 (December 1971), pp. 410–422.

113. Dean E. Frease, "Delinquency, Social Class, and the Schools," *Sociology and Social Research* 57 (July 1973), pp. 443–459.

114. Steven Box and Julienne Ford, "The Facts Don't Fit: On the Relationship between Social Class and Criminal Behavior," *Sociological Review* 19 (February 1971), pp. 31–52.

115. W. R. Bytheway and D. R. May, "On Fitting the 'Fact' of Social Class and Criminal Behavior: A Rejoinder to Box and Ford," *Sociological Review* 19 (November 1971), pp. 585–607.

116. Yoshio Matsumoto, "The Distribution of Juvenile Delinquency in the Social Class Structure—A Comparative Analysis of Delinquency Rates between Tokyo and Nashville," *Japanese Sociological Review* 20 (March 1970), pp. 2–18.

conformity."[117] James found no evidence of family, ethnic or class predispositions among fifteen- to nineteen-year-old heroin addicts in the London area.[118]

Religion and socioeconomic status

Two important studies indicated clearly that of the three major religious categories in the United States—Jews, Protestants and Catholics—Jews are found in disproportionately large numbers in the highest strata and Catholics are found in disproportionately large numbers in the lowest strata.[119] Both Goldstein and Featherman went on, after noting this empirical fact, to identify differential educational achievement rather than religion, per se, as the crucial variable in determining socioeconomic status. Featherman eliminated both religious and ethnic variables as directly responsible for income or occupational achievement.

Jackson, Fox and Crockett concluded from national sample data that:

(1) Protestants are more likely than Catholics of the same occupational origin to enter high status nonmanual occupations;

(2) Catholics are more likely than Protestants of the same origin to enter low status nonmanual occupations;

(3) Protestants are more often sharply up-mobile, and Catholics are more often sharply down-mobile.

These differences are small, but are not diminished by controls for ethnicity, region in which reared, age, generation and size of community in which reared.[120]

The differences in college aspirations of teenagers vary with (1) religion of their mothers and (2) religious composition of the schools they are attending, according to a study by Rhodes and Nam.[121] These differences persist even when the usual socioeconomic variables—and I.Q., also—are taken into account.

Sexual stratification

The rising consciousness of confirmed and suspected inequities in the prestige-reward patterns of American social organization has produced a number of studies of sexual stratification. The bulk of these are either exhortatory, polemical or purely descriptive. A sample of the exceptions are noted here.

Collins raised the argument that persons struggle for as much dominance as their resources permit and that the structure of social dominance will change as changes occur

117. Bruce Bullington, John G. Munns and Gilbert Geis, "Purchase of Conformity: Ex-Narcotic Addicts Among the Bourgeoisie," Social Problems 16 (Spring 1969), pp. 456–463.

118. I. Pierce James, "Delinquency and Heroin Addiction in Britain," British Journal of Criminology 9 (April 1969), pp. 108–125.

119. Sidney Goldstein, "Socioeconomic Differentials Among Religious Groups in the United States," American Journal of Sociology 74 (May 1969), pp. 612–631; David Featherman, "The Socioeconomic Achievement of White Religio-Ethnic Sub-Groups: Social and Psychological Explanations," American Sociological Review 36 (April 1971), pp. 207–222.

120. Elton F. Jackson, William S. Fox and Harry J. Crockett, Jr., "Religion and Occupational Achievement," American Sociological Review 35 (February 1970), p. 48.

121. A. Lewis Rhodes and Charles B. Nam, "The Religious Context of Educational Expectations," American Sociological Review 35 (April 1970), pp. 253–267.

in women's resources.[122] He then reviewed the low status of women in the labor force and those resources of males which are most unlikely to change vis-à-vis the related resources of women.

Coser and Rokoff have developed the argument that women are excluded from high status occupations because of "cultural mandate."[123] Women's roles are seen as generally perceived as complementary to, rather than competitive with, men's roles in high status positions. Conflicting cultural prescriptions about women's commitments to family activities are seen as disruptive to careers and not legitimate from the perspective of the high degree of commitment required to occupational performance.

Of the coeds sampled in an East coast university 77 percent said that they intended to have a career outside marriage—53 percent in stereotyped male professions—and 99 percent said they intended to marry.[124] Klemmack and Edwards reasoned from these data that current norms for pre-labor-force females include "role expansion" instead of role conflict between marriage and a career.

As did Klemmack and Edwards, Acker noted the need for a revision of the NORC scale of occupational prestige.[125] She raised a number of questions about the conventional concepts and operational definitions used in sociology which require revision of sociological studies in order to eliminate traditional sexism from their assumptions.

Epstein suggested that the ordering of occupational prestige is changing and that the social welfare and service professions will become more prestigious in the future.[126] The large numbers of women in such professions would mean that a rise in the prestige of the occupations would be concomitant with a rise in the status of women in general.

A somewhat different perspective of sociological problems of procedure has been noted by Glenn, Ross and Tully.[127] They addressed the issue of whether female intergenerational mobility resulting from marriage was comparable with male intergenerational mobility resulting from occupational attainment. Their findings showed that "marrying up" was no more common for women than rising occupationally from the preceding generation was for men, but that women are generally more mobile than men—both upwardly and downwardly.

122. Randall Collins, "A Conflict Theory of Sexual Stratification," *Social Problems* 19 (Summer 1971), pp. 3–22.

123. Rose Coser and Gerald Rokoff, "Women in the Occupational World: Social Disruption and Conflict," *Social Problems* 18 (Spring 1971), pp. 535–554.

124. David L. Klemmack and John N. Edwards, "Women's Acquisition of Stereotyped Occupational Aspirations," *Sociology and Social Research* 57 (July 1973), pp. 510–525.

125. Joan Acker, "Women and Social Stratification: A Case of Intellectual Sexism," *American Journal of Sociology* 78 (January 1973), pp. 936–945.

126. Cynthia F. Epstein, "Encountering the Male Establishment: Sex-Status Limits on Women's Careers in the Professions," *American Journal of Sociology* 75 (May 1970), pp. 965–982.

127. Norval D. Glenn, Adreain A. Ross and Judy C. Tully, "Patterns of Intergenerational Mobility of Females through Marriage" (Paper presented at the Southwestern Sociological Association, Dallas, Texas, 22–24 March 1973). Compare, also, Glen H. Elder, Jr., "Appearance and Education in Marriage Mobility," *American Sociological Review* 34 (August 1969), pp. 510–533; J. D. Martin, "A Comment on Whether American Women Do Marry Up," *American Sociological Review* 35 (April 1970), pp. 327–328.

Age stratification

The conceptualization of age categories as social strata is not warranted by any classical theory of American social class of which we are aware. On the other hand, demographic data—income, education, housing characteristics—show that a descriptive category of multidimensional socioeconomic characteristics varying with age suggests a precipitate change in social status at age sixty-five. Signs of emerging stratum consciousness among the aged suggests that studies in this area of interest will increase in the future.[128]

Health

Failure to carry out the prescribed roles for one's status may result in claims of illness as an effort to justify or legitimate that failure.[129] On the other hand, Meile and Haese have found that status incongruence is not significantly associated with the ordinary physiological symptoms which accompany other forms of stress.[130]

Rushing has found two distinct patterns in the relationship between social class and mental hospitalization.[131] He suggests that the earlier hypothesis that all social classes but the lowest have little difference in rates of mental illness, while the lowest class has a much higher rate, needs to be tested against a second hypothesis that there is a continuous relationship of social class to mental illness with the rate systematically increasing as class status drops, but with an extremely large increase for the lowest class. Rushing considers alternative explanations which support his positive finding on the second hypothesis in a Washington study. One possibility is that relative deprivation increases in a continuous, linear, inverse relationship to rise in social class. The sharp increase and break in linearity at the lowest class level may possibly be the result of the recognition of minimal life chances and, presumably, loss of hope.

Kohn proposed a unity of genetic, social, cultural, and physiological correlates of schizophrenia.[132] He argued that the conditions of life experienced by lower class persons

128. Compare, Matilda White Riley, "Social Gerontology and the Age Stratification of Society," *The Gerontologist* 11 (Spring 1971), part I, pp. 79–87; Matilda White Riley, Marilyn Johnson and Anne Foner, *Aging and Society, Volume III: A Sociology of Age Stratification* (New York: Russell Sage Foundation, 1972); Thomas Tissue, "Social Class and the Senior Citizen Center," *Gerontologist* 11 (Spring 1971), part I, pp. 79–87; Erdman Palmore and Frank Whittington, "Trends in the Relative Status of the Aged," *Social Forces* 50 (September 1971), pp. 84–91; Norval D. Glenn and Ted Hefner, "Further Evidence on Aging and Party Identification," *Public Opinion Quarterly* 36 (Spring 1972), pp. 31–47.

129. Stephen Cole and Robert Lejeune, "Illness and the Legitimation of Failure," *American Sociological Review* 37 (June 1972), pp. 347–356.

130. Richard L. Meile and Philip N. Haese, "Social Status, Status Incongruence and Symptoms of Stress," *Journal of Health and Social Behavior* 10 (September 1969), pp. 237–244. Compare, also, Glen H. Elder, Jr., "Occupational Mobility, Life Patterns, and Personality," *Journal of Health and Social Behavior* 10 (December 1969), pp. 308–323.

131. William A. Rushing, "Two Patterns in the Relationship between Social Class and Mental Hospitalization," *American Sociological Review* 34 (August 1969), pp. 533–541.

132. Melvin L. Kohn, "Class, Family and Schizophrenia: A Reformulation," *Social Forces* 50 (March 1972), pp. 295–304. Compare, also, the critique of this article by David Mechanic, "Social Class and Schizophrenia: Some Requirements for a Plausible Theory of Social Influence," *Social Forces* 50 (March 1972), pp. 305–309.

impair their abilities to deal resourcefully with stressful situations generally. The presence of predisposing genetic factors renders them particularly vulnerable to mental illness.

The distribution of obesity in society and the distribution of dieting behavior have received attention in the recent literature. Whitelaw found that earlier studies of obesity among British children showed no relationship with social class.[133] He then reported a more recent finding of a positive association between low social class and obesity of British children, a finding congruous with studies of English adults and American children. Whitelaw explained the preponderance of obesity in lower social classes by the increased proportions of carbohydrates and fats —used more frequently as a result of their relative cheapness—found in lower class diets.

Sports and leisure

A number of studies related leisure and sports activities to social status or social class during the period under study. Some of these appear in *Games, Sport and Power*, edited by Gregory P. Stone.[134] The literature thoroughly supports earlier findings that there is a positive correlation between the amount of sports participation or organized

leisure time activity and social status or occupational prestige.[135]

An impressionistic report of the differential behavior of middle class bar patrons and lower class bar patrons during the Calgary Stampede was more noteworthy for content interest than methodology. Ossenberg found that patrons of middle class drinking establishments exhibited more festival-related aggressive/expressive behavior than patrons of lower class drinking establishments during the festival.[136]

Finally, Phillips and Schafer found that athletes who take part in interscholastic sports are more upwardly mobile than their peers, help socialize lower socioeconomic status athletes into the middle class and tend to exceed comparable non-athletes in the achievement of their educational goals.[137]

Demographic documentation of social stratification

The simplest, and therefore often most attractive, procedure for breaking a sizeable population into

133. Andrew G. L. Whitelaw, "The Association of Social Class and Sibling Number with Skin Fold Thickness in London School Boys," *Human Biology* 43 (September 1971), pp. 414–420.

134. Gregory P. Stone, ed., *Games, Sport and Power* (New Brunswick, N.J.: Transaction Books, 1971); see, for example, Joseph Bensman, "Classical Music and the Status Game," pp. 217–218.

135. Doyle W. Bishop and Masaru Ikeda, "Status and Role Factors in the Leisure Behavior of Different Occupations," *Sociology and Social Research* 54 (January 1970), pp. 190–208; Rabel J. Burdge, "Levels of Occupational Prestige and Leisure Activity," *Journal of Leisure Research* 2 (Summer 1969), pp. 262–274; Glenn Morris, Richard Pasewark and John Schultz, "Occupational Level and Participation in Public Recreation in a Rural Community," *Journal of Leisure Research* 4 (Winter 1972), pp. 25–32.

136. Richard J. Ossenberg, "Social Class and Bar Behavior During an Urban Festival," *Human Organization* 28 (Spring 1969), pp. 29–34.

137. John C. Phillips and Walter E. Schafer, "Consequences of Participation in Interscholastic Sports: A Review and Prospectus," *Pacific Sociological Review* 14 (July 1971), pp. 328–338.

social strata is undoubtedly to use gradients of a single abstract characteristic taken from data already collected. It is ideal if there has been a demonstrated theoretical relationship of such a variable with other variables in some more general theory of social stratification. In the period under review, the most popular such variable still continues to be occupation. Marxian theory clearly links occupation to social class, but many of the contemporary studies which use this criterion make no effort to match occupational categories to the relationship of the incumbents to the ownership of the means of production in a society. In some studies, occupational category becomes the operational definition of social class or social stratum in the total absence of any theoretical rationale.

There has been what we think is a healthy trend in the study of status attainment. It involves the use of multivariate stratification models, often including social-psychological variables, as well as those stratification variables which have become more or less customary in the literature of the past few decades—occupation, education, residential area, income, wealth and the like. In many instances, newly constructed theory has supplanted simple collections of related descriptive data and has incorporated genetic, interactional and friendship choice data, broadening it far beyond the boundaries of raw demography. Sewell and Laumann and their associates have presented exemplary work of this kind.

Strictly demographic studies of social stratification have often been concerned merely with differential birth and death rates of different social strata,[138] or with rates of population growth in different strata, particularly in developing countries.[139] Of particular interest in the light of the growth of the women's movements in the United States is research on the involvement of women in the labor force in various parts of the world.[140]

All in all, theories constructed from demographic variables alone are not usually satisfying to students of social class and social stratification unless they are a part of some broader theory, such as functionalism or Marxian theory.

MOBILITY

In addition to the review presented by Dietrick below we would like to add a word about the widespread interest reflected in international and comparative studies of mobility.[141] The number of such

138. Geoffrey Hawthorn, *The Sociology of Fertility* (London: Collier-Macmillan, 1970; Evelyn Kitigawa and Philip M. Hauser, *Differential Mortality in the United States: A Study in Socioeconomic Epidemiology* (Cambridge, Mass.: Harvard University Press, 1973).

139. Donald F. Heisel, "Rapid Population Growth and the Social Structure," in *Are Our Descendants Doomed?* ed. Harrison Brown and Edward Hutchings, Jr. (New York: Viking, 1972), pp. 179–196; Stanford Quentin, ed. *The World Population Problems of Growth* (New York: Oxford University Press, 1972), see especially, "Economic and Social Factors Affecting Fertility," pp. 105–114.

140. Nadia H. Youssef, "Social Structure and the Female Labor Force," *Demography* 8 (November 1971), pp. 427–440.

141. Jones has commented on the urgent need for better data to implement studies in this area. See, F. Lancaster Jones, "Social Mobility and Industrial Society: A Thesis Re-examined," *Sociological Quarterly* 10 (Summer 1969), pp. 292–305.

studies reported to, and generated by, the Research Committee of the International Sociological Association is phenomenal.

Bock and Iutaka have been conducting studies in Brazil of diverse variables—such as the effects of residential mobility from rural to urban settings[142] and the effects of premarital pregnancy on social status in different strata[143]—in social mobility models.

Occupational and educational mobility in Costa Rica and Mexico were compared with those phenomena in the United States. It was found that those kinds of mobility produce intense normlessness in the two Latin American countries; that downward educational mobility produces feelings of powerlessness in all three countries; and the normlessness and powerlessness were more characteristic of the lower levels of occupational prestige in the Latin American countries than in the United States.[144]

In Sweden, upward social mobility was reported as affecting nuclear family cohesion negatively, especially when husband and wife were experiencing different degrees of mobility.[145]

Broom and Jones discovered that the growth rates of occupational mobility between fathers and sons were high in Australia when compared to data from Italy, but somewhat lower than those in the United States. Australia was found to have the highest rate of circulation mobility of the three countries, however.[146]

In Britain, Noble reported that social class is becoming a less important factor in achieving occupational status and power and questioned whether the concept of differential amounts of upward and downward mobility reported in the United States by Duncan and Blau is meaningful in Britain.[147] In England, Thompson examined the assertion that the type of secondary school attended was a nonfamily factor in social mobility which overshadowed all family factors.[148] Thompson found that, in fact, the type of school attended by a child had about the same effect on his upward mobility as the type of housing occupied by his family, although the housing effect is not reduced to the same degree when type of secondary school is controlled.

Procedures of studying occupa-

142. E. Wilbur Bock and Sugiyama Iutaka, "Rural-Urban Migration and Social Mobility: The Controversy in Latin America," *Rural Sociology* 34 (September 1969), pp. 343–355.

143. E. Wilbur Bock and Sugyama Iutaka, "Social Status, Mobility and Premarital Pregnancy: A Case of Brazil," *Journal of Marriage and the Family* 30 (May 1970), pp. 284–292.

144. Miles E. Simpson, "Social Mobility, Normlessness and Powerlessness in Two Cultural Contexts," *American Sociological Review* 35 (December 1970), pp. 1002–1013.

145. Everett Dyer, "Upward Social Mobility and Nuclear Family Integration as Perceived by the Wife in Swedish Urban Families," *Journal of Marriage and the Family* 32 (August 1970), pp. 341–350.

146. Leonard Broom and F. Lancaster Jones, "Father-to-Son Mobility: Australia in Comparative Perspective," *American Journal of Sociology* 74 (January 1969), pp. 333–342.

147. Trevor Noble, "Social Mobility and Class Relations in Britain," *British Journal of Sociology* 23 (December 1972), pp. 422–436.

148. Patricia Thompson, "Some Factors in Upward Social Mobility in England," *Sociology and Social Research* 55 (January 1971), pp. 181–190.

tional strata with respect to their permeability and a design which could be universally applicable have been described by McFarland.[149] His work has contributed to international thought in making studies of mobility in different societies more comparable.[150]

In the United States the effects of religious mobility on socioeconomic status were examined by Alston.[151] He reported that he found no difference in the occupational mobility of persons who remained in the same religious denomination and those who changed church memberships to the higher status denominations of Protestantism—that is, Presbyterian, Congregational and Episcopalian. A possible problem was indicated in that the majority of denominationally mobile persons were found to be females, and the suggestion was made that their mobility was a result of marriage rather than occupational aspirations. Bode found that neither the class status nor intergenerational mobility rates of Prostestants, Catholics or nonchurch members were significantly different. Nonmembers were similar in social rank to Protestants and showed comparable mobility.[152]

Additional studies of mobility in the United States have been made with regard to persons who are spatially mobile:[153] political preferences of mobile persons,[154] the voting behavior of mobile people,[155] the work satisfaction of mobile persons,[156] the participation of occupationally mobile persons in formal associations,[157] school achievement and intelligence[158] and the degree of involvement with relatives.[159]

NON-UNITED STATES AND COMPARATIVE STUDIES OF STRATIFICATION

The number of comparative studies of social stratification and the number published about other countries has increased substantially in the past five years. Several of these studies have been men-

149. David D. McFarland, "Measuring the Permeability of Occupational Structures: An Information-Theoretic Approach," *American Journal of Sociology* 75 (July 1969), pp. 41–61.

150. Compare, Theodor Geiger and David Glass, "Western European Mobility," *American Journal of Sociology* 76 (November 1970), pp. 520–523.

151. Jon P. Alston, "Religious Mobility and Socioeconomic Status," *Sociological Analysis* 32 (Spring 1971), pp. 140–148.

152. Jerry Bode, "Status and Mobility of Church Members and Non-Members," *Sociology and Social Research* 157 (October 1972), pp. 55–62.

153. Harrison C. White, "Stayers and Movers," *American Journal of Sociology* 76 (July 1970), pp. 307–324.

154. David Knoke, "Intergenerational Occupational Mobility and the Political Party Preferences of American Men," *American Journal of Sociology* 78 (May 1973), pp. 1448–1468.

155. James Alden Barber, Jr., *Social Mobility and Voting Behavior* (Chicago, Ill.: Rand McNally, 1970).

156. Barbara Laslett, "Mobility and Work Satisfaction: A Discussion of the Use and Interpretation of Mobility Models," *American Journal of Sociology* 77 (July 1971), pp. 19–35.

157. James M. Bruce, "Intragenerational Occupational Mobility and Participation in Formal Associations," *Sociological Quarterly* 12 (Winter 1971), pp. 46–55.

158. Jerome H. Waller, "Achievement and Social Mobility: Relationships Among IQ Score, Education and Occupation in Two Generations," *Social Biology* 18 (September 1971), pp. 252–259.

159. Michael Aiken and David Goldberg, "Social Mobility and Kinship: A Reexamination of the Hypothesis," *American Anthropologist* 71 (April 1969), pp. 261–270.

tioned earlier in this article. Some outstanding studies which have not been mentioned should be given recognition at this point. They include works by: Streib,[160] Uusitalo,[161] Atkinson,[162] Okedra,[163] Marulasiddaiah,[164] Balan,[165] Wisniewski,[166] Girod,[167] Mayer and Müller,[168] Bertaux,[169] Boudon,[170] Charvat,[171] Chekki,[172] Stagl,[173] Tominaga,[174] Andorxa,[175] Janicijevic,[176] Shanin,[177] Lissak,[178] Parker,[179] Connor,[180] Dumont,[181] Ferge,[182] Gerhardt,[183] D'Souza,[184] Hazelrigg,[185] Jacobson and Kendrick,[186] Darroch and Marston,[187] Marsh,[188] Wilkie,[189] Vogel,[190] Churchward,[191] Jones,[192] Korpi,[193] Machonin,[194] Palmore, Klein and Marzuki,[195] Portes,[196] Ramu and Wiebe,[197] Sharma,[198] Williamson[199] and Gella;[200] and collections by: Hope,[201] Plotnicov and Tuden[202] and Archer and Giner.[203]

160. Gordon F. Streib, "Social Stratification in the Republic of Ireland: The Horizontal and the Vertical Mosaic," *Ethnology* 12 (July 1973), pp. 341–357.

161. Hanu J. Uusitalo, "A Note About the Stratification Aspects of a Comparative Survey in Four Nordic Countries" (Report presented at the Conference of the Research Committee on Social Stratification, International Sociological Association, Rome, Italy, 18–20 December 1972); Seppo Pöntinen and Hannu Uusitalo, "Household Incomes in the Scandinavian Countries: A Multivariate Analysis," *Research Reports* 3 (Research Group for Comparative Sociology, University of Helsinki, 1974); Hannu Uusitalo, "On the Distribution of Income in Scandinavia," *Research Reports* 2 (Research Group for Comparative Sociology, University of Helsinki, 1973).

162. Maxwell Atkinson, "Social Isolation, Class and Social Mobility in Old Age," *Bevolking en Gezin/Population et Familie* 23–24 (March 1971), pp. 183–199.

163. J. D. Okedra, "The Relationship Between Unemployment of the Primary and Secondary School Graduates and the Socioeconomic Status of Their Parents in Ibadan, Nigeria," *International Review of Sociology* 1, no. 1 (March 1971), pp. 1–12.

164. H. M. Marulasiddaiah, "Caste Consolidation, Social Mobility and Ambivalence: A Case Study of Caste Hostels in Mysore State," *Indian Journal of Social Work* 31 (January 1971), pp. 391–399.

165. Jorge Balan, "Determinantes del Nivel Educational en Monterrey, Mexico: Un Analisis Multivariado," (Determinants of Educational Level in Monterrey, Mexico: A Multivariate Analysis), *Revista Latinoamericana de Sociologia* 6 (July 1970), pp. 262–292.

166. Wieslaw Wisniewski, "The Academic Progress of Students of Different Social Origin," *Polish Sociological Bulletin* 21 (1970), pp. 135–144.

167. Roger Girod, "Mobilite Sequentielle," (Sequential Analysis of Mobility), *Revue Francaise de Sociologie* 12 (January 1971), pp. 3–18.

168. Karl U. Mayer and Walter Müller, "Die Analyse von Mobilitatsrens: Anmerkungen zu Einer Kontroverse über Forschundsdesign un Patenanalyse," (The Analysis of Mobility Trends: Comments on a Controversy over Research Design and Data Analysis), *Kölner Zeitschrift für Soziologie und Sozial-psychologie* 24 (March 1972), pp. 132–139.

169. Daniel Bertaux, "New Perspectives on Social Mobility in France," *Quality and Quantity* 5 (June 1971), pp. 81–129.

170. Raymond Boudon, "Eléments pour une Théorie Formalle de la Mobilité Sociale," (Elements for a Formal Theory of Social Mobility), *Quality and Quantity* 5 (June 1971), pp. 39–85.

171. Frantisk Charvat, "Socialni Stratifikace a do Tedreticke Problematiky a Konketniho," (Social Stratification and Structure, Social Mobility and Change: Introduction into Theoretical Problems and Concrete Research), *Sociologiky Casopis* 7, no. 4 (1971), pp. 356–365.

172. Dan A. Chekki, "Social Stratification and Trends of Social Mobility in Modern India," *Indian Journal of Social Work* 31, no. 4 (January 1971), pp. 367–380.

173. J. Stagl, "Ingleichheit, Fuerhrung and Mobilitaet," (Inequality, Leadership and Mobility), *KAI* 1 (1970), pp. 13–35.

174. Den'ichi Tominaga, "Trend Analysis of Social Mobility 1955–1965," *Japanese Sociological Review* 21 (June 1970), pp. 2–23.

175. R. Andorxa, "Social Mobility and Economic Development in Hungary," *Acta Oeconomica* 7 (1971), pp. 25–45.

176. Milosav Janicijevic, "Newer Sociological Studies of Social Stratification and Mobility," *Sociologija* 11 (1969), pp. 95–128.

177. Teodor Shanin, *The Awkward Class* (Oxford: Clarendon Press, 1972).

178. Moshe Lissak, *Social Mobility in Israel Society* (Jerusalem: Israel University Press, 1969).

179. Frank Parker, "Class Stratification in Socialist Societies," *British Journal of Sociology* 20 (December 1969), pp. 355–374.

180. Walter D. Connor, "Juvenile Delinquency in the U.S.S.R.: Some Quantitative and Qualitative Indicators," *American Sociological Review* 35 (April 1970), pp. 283–297.

181. Louis Dumont, *Homo Hierarchicus: An Essay on the Caste System*, trans. Mark Sanisbury (Chicago, Ill.: University of Chicago Press, 1970).

182. Susan Ferge, "On Ways of Life in Hungary," *Sociology and Social Research* 57 (January 1973), pp. 222–235.

183. Uta Gerhardt, "Role Conflict and the Class Structure," *Sociology and Social Research* 55 (April 1971), pp. 285–296.

184. Victor S. D'Souza, "Changes in Social Structure and Changing Roles of Older People in India," *Sociology and Social Research* 55 (April 1971), pp. 297–304.

185. Lawrence E. Hazelrigg, "Religious and Class Bases of Political Conflict in Italy," *American Journal of Sociology* 75 (January 1970), pp. 496–511.

186. Barbara Jacobson and John M. Kendrick, "Education and Mobility: From Achievement to Ascription," *American Sociological Review* 38 (August 1973), pp. 439–460.

187. A. Gordon Darroch and Wilfred G. Marston, "The Social Class Basis of Ethnic Residential Segregation: The Canadian Case," *American Journal of Sociology* 77 (November 1971), pp. 491–510.

188. Robert M. Marsh, "The Explanation of Occupational Prestige Hierarchies," *Social Forces* 50 (December 1971), pp. 214–222.

189. James A. Wilkie, *Elitelore* (Los Angeles, Cal.: University of California Latin American Center, 1973).

190. Ezra Vogel, *Japan's New Middle Class: The Salary Man and His Family in a Tokyo Suburb* (Los Angeles, Cal.: University of California Press, 1971).

191. L. G. Churchward, *The Soviet Intelligentsia* (London: Routledge and Kegan Paul, 1973).

192. F. Lancaster Jones, "Occupational Achievement in Australia and the United States: A Comparative Path Analysis," *American Journal of Sociology* 77 (November 1971), pp. 527–539.

193. Walter Korpi, "Some Problems in the Measurement of Class Voting," *American Journal of Sociology* 78 (November 1972), pp. 627–642.

194. Pavel Machonin, "Social Stratification in Contemporary Czechoslovakia," *American Journal of Sociology* 75 (March 1970), pp. 725–741.

195. James A. Palmore, Robert E. Klein and Ariffin bin Marzuki, "Class and Family in a Modernizing Society," *American Journal of Sociology* 76 (November 1970), pp. 375–398.

196. Alejandro Portes, "On the Interpretation of Class Consciousness," *American Journal of Sociology* 77 (September 1971), pp. 228–244.

197. G. N. Ramu and Paul D. Wiebe, "Occupational and Educational Mobility in Relation to Caste in Urban India," *Sociology and Social Research* 58 (October 1973), pp. 84–91.

198. K. L. Sharma, "Caste and Class Consciousness in Rural Rajasthan: Some Sociological and Psychological Expressions," *Sociology and Social Research* (April 1970), pp. 378–387.

199. Robert C. Williamson, "Social Class, Mobility and Modernism: Chileans and Social Change," *Sociology and Social Research* 56 (January 1972), pp. 149–163.

200. Aleksander Gella, "The Life and Death of the Old Polish Intelligentsia," *Slavic Review* 30 (March 1971), pp. 1–27.

201. Keith Hope, ed. *The Analysis of Social Mobility* (Oxford: Clarendon Press, 1972).

202. Arthur Tuden and Leonard Plotnicov, ed. *Comparative Essays in Social Stratification* (Pittsburgh, Pa.: University of Pittsburgh Press, 1970); Arthur Tuden and Leonard Plotnicov, ed. *Social Stratification in Africa* (New York: Free Press, 1970).

203. Margaret Scotford Archer and Salvador Giner, ed., *Contemporary Europe: Class, Status and Power* (New York: St. Martin's Press, 1971).

Social Mobility: 1969–1973

By Barbara A. Dietrick

O F central importance to the study of stratification is the topic of social mobility. In societies where strata are arranged in a hierarchy, one may note that both individuals and groups change positions. Two kinds of mobility are conventionally distinguished: (1) intergenerational mobility—referring to the degree of difference between an individual's position and his parent's position—and (2) intragenerational mobility—referring to changes of position within an individual's single lifetime.

Most researchers define the process of social mobility in terms of occupational prestige, an outgrowth of studies following a unidimensional conceptualization of social mobility in contrast to a multidimensional interpretation of its effects in industrial Western societies.[1]

The notion that high mobility rates accompany industrialization has been challenged by Tuden and Plotnicov,[2] who suggest that mobility rates should be thought of in terms of cultural differences and distinctions between strata, and not in terms of the distinction between traditional and industrial society. Using Africa as an example, they assert that social mobility is greatest in a society where cultural differences are least salient and that social mobility is diminished by the presence of sharp differentiation between strata. Furthermore, they challenge the idea that industrialization is necessarily accompanied by a shift toward occupation as the primary referent of an individual's position in the society's hierarchy. They note that:

The question whether job is a primary point of social identification in black Africa remains open to empirical investigation. In fact, sufficient evi-

---

1. Compare, Seymour Martin Lipset and Reinherd Bendix, *Social Mobility in Industrial Society* (Berkeley, Cal.: University of California Press, 1960).

2. Arthur Tuden and Leonard Plotnicov, ed., *Social Stratification in Africa* (New York: Free Press, 1970).

Barbara A. Dietrick is a Doctoral Student in sociology at the University of Southern California and is affiliated with its Ethel Percy Andrus Gerontology Center. Specializing in the studies of social stratification and social gerontology, she is currently engaged in research of organizational dynamics of nursing homes in retirement communities.

dence exists to believe the Africans have not internalized Western evaluations and perceptions of occupation and career.[3]

Tuden and Plotnicov's challenge was supported by Kelley and Perlman.[4] They reported that the adaptation of a modern economic system by the Toro of Western Uganda may have decreased their rates of mobility.

While occupation may serve as a shorthand means of identifying other status characteristics in the industrialized Western countries, one cannot ignore the possible salience of other factors in determining degrees of honor, prestige or power in a society. An instructive case in point is caste—*jati*—mobility in India.[5] The means of *jati* mobility does not rest on alteration of occupation so much as on the casting off of ritually unclean practices, adjustment of the *jati's* origin myth and, very often, the acquisition of a new name. Such accomplishments are usually based on the accrual of political and economic power over several generations.

The following essay is a survey of the work done in the area of social mobility in the past five years, with the scope extending only to English language publications. The amount of attention given to this topic is astonishing; therefore, the present survey will be by no means exhaustive. As a matter of convenience, the topic has been divided into five subareas which follow the major topics of interest in the literature for these years.

The largest increase in the volume of research on mobility has been in the area of individual career mobility. It is likely that this increase is due to the increasing recognition that modes of stratification within an occupation may be as salient for the individual as is the position of his occupation in societal structure.

THE BLAU-DUNCAN MODEL

The work of Blau and Ducan has been universally noted as a landmark in the field of mobility and has been referred to by at least one researcher as an emerging "standard paradigm."[6] The basic model uses father's occupational status as a measure of family background. Family background has a causal influence on educational attainment, and both education and family background influence occupational attainment.

In the past five years considerable attention has been given to extending and elaborating this model. Family background has been enlarged to include race, national origin, urbanization, number of siblings and religion.[7] Further

3. Ibid., p. 25.

4. Jonathan Kelley and Melvin L. Perlman, "Social Mobility in Toro: Some Preliminary Results From Western Uganda," *Economics, Development and Cultural Change* 19 (January 1971), pp. 214–221.

5. David G. Mandelbaum, *Society in India: Change and Continuity*, vol. 2 (Berkeley, Cal.: University of California Press, 1970).

6. Jonathan Kelley, "Causal Chain Models for the Socioeconomic Career," *American Sociological Review* 38 (August 1973), pp. 481–493; Peter Blau and O. D. Duncan, *The American Occupational Structure* (New York: Wiley, 1967).

7. Otis Dudley Duncan, David L. Featherman and Beverly Duncan, *Socioeconomic Background and Achievement* (New York: Seminar Press, 1972); David L. Featherman, "Residential Background and Socioeconomic Career Achievements in Metropolitan Stratification Systems," *Rural Sociology* 36 (June 1971), pp. 107–124; David L. Featherman, "The Socioeconomic Achievement of White Religio-ethnic Subgroups: Social and Psychological Explanations," *American Sociological Review* 36 (April 1971), pp. 207–222.

intervening variables which link family backgound and and occupational attainment have been added to the model, including motivation, ability, appearance, migration, marriage and fertility.[8] Hope has published an insightful work on the relationship between social mobility and fertility, incorporating in his model the variables of class origin and class destination into a "Halfway hypothesis."[9]

It should be noted that the inclusion of motivation in a model of socioeconomic achievement is not a settled issue. Featherman reports constructing several path analytic models in which achievement motivations are included as intervening variables capable of explaining the link between socioeconomic origins or early career achievements and later socioeconomic attainments.[10] His data did not support any of the models. Hansen, in a study of Costa Rican youths, measured motivation as well as ability and structural variables.[11] He found support for a model which contained only structural and ability variables.

Spaeth has given attention to occupational attaining among male college graduates.[12] He reported that occupational prestige expectations were the strongest predictors of job prestige four years later. Hauser reported that academic achievement among secondary pupils is determined by socioeconomic background, through an association with intelligence.[13] Family background and intelligence influence aspirations through effects on grades, memberships in school organizations and perceived parental expectations.

Cross-national evidence of the utility of the Blau-Duncan model's emphasis on educational attainment as an intervening mechanism of status transmission is found in the reports of Balan on industrial Monterrey, Mexico,[14] and Cummings and Naoi on Japan.[15] Evidence from Haiti and Costa Rica[16]

8. Duncan, Featherman and Duncan, *Socioeconomic Background*; Alan E. Bayer, "Marriage Plans and Educational Aspirations," *American Journal of Sociology* 75 (September 1969), pp. 239–244; David L. Featherman, "Achievement Orientations and Socioeconomic Career Attainments," *American Sociological Review* 37 (April 1972), pp. 131–143; Glen H. Elder, "Appearance and Education in Marriage Mobility," *American Sociological Review* 34 (August 1969), pp. 519–533; William H. Sewell, Archibald O. Haller and George W. Ohlendorf, "The Educational and Early Occupational Status Attainment Process: Replication and Revision," *American Sociological Review* 35 (December 1970), pp. 1014–1027.

9. Keith Hope, "Social Mobility and Fertility," *American Sociological Review* 36 (December 1971), pp. 1019–1032. Compare, also, Keith Hope, ed., *The Analysis of Social Mobility: Methods and Approaches* (Oxford: Oxford University Press, 1972).

10. Featherman, "Achievement Orientations."

11. David O. Hansen, "Early Occupational Attainment Process in Costa Rica" (Paper presented at the Annual Meeting of the Rural Sociological Society, 1969).

12. Joe L. Spaeth, "Occupational Attainment among Male College Graduates," *American Journal of Sociology* 75 (January 1970), pp. 632–644.

13. Robert M. Hauser, "Schools and the Stratification Process," *American Journal of Sociology* 74 (May 1969), pp. 587–611.

14. Jorge Balan, Harley L. Browning and Elizabeth Jelin, *Man in a Developing Society: Geographic and Social Mobility in Monterrey, Mexico* (Austin, Texas: University of Texas Press, 1973).

15. William K. Cummings and Atsushi Naoi, "Education and Mobility: An International Comparison With Reference to Japan and the United States" (Paper presented at the Annual Meeting of the American Sociological Association, 1972).

16. Nan Lin and Daniel Yauger, "The Process of Occupational Status Attainment: A Preliminary Cross-national Comparison"

and Columbia[17] cautions us that the Blau-Duncan emphasis on education is only useful when applied to developed, industrialized nations. Another anomalous case is reported by Schiller, who found that differences in family background and ability could not explain differences between children from welfare families and the general population for socioeconomic achievement.[18] He suggested that the achievement lag of poor children is explained by inequality of opportunity along class lines.

POLITICAL BEHAVIOR

On the basis of Italian party preferences and sociopolitical attitudes, Hazelrigg and Lopreato formulated a theory of downward social mobility and political behavior.[19] Given middle class and working class structures in which conservative political behavior is normal to the middle class and leftist political behavior is normal to the working class, they asserted that:

(1) Associated with a status in each class are pressure to espouse political ideologies to the class—that is, if men experience downward mobility, then they are likely to be subject to political resocialization into the class.

(2) Men, however, are influenced by superior status in the sense that they tend to emulate behavior which gives them a sense of superiority over others. Thus, skidders are likely to emulate the political orientation of the more prestigeful class of origin, thereby mitigating the force of resocialization to which they are subjected as members of the working class.

(3) Therefore, the normal political behavior of skidders is intermediate between the behavior of persons in the class of origin and the class of destination.

(4) However, the efficacy of the resocialization factor varies inversely with the strength of the success ideology which (a) underscores individual responsibility for both failure and success; (b) promotes the hope of class reascent by accentuating the reality of existing opportunities; and (c) asserts the reality of distributive justice.

(5) It follows that: (a) if skidders hold a strong success ideology, they are likely to resemble their class of origin in political behavior; (b) conversely, if they have an image of limited opportunities, they are likely to resemble politically their class of destination.[20]

This theory is an expression of a larger general theory of political orientation and social mobility

(Paper presented at the Annual Meeting of the American Sociological Association, 1973).

17. Rodrigo P. Sandoval, *Dependency and Education in Columbian Underdevelopment* (Madison, Wis.: Land Tenure Center, 1973).

18. Bradley R. Schiller, "Stratified Opportunities: The Essence of the 'Vicious Circle,'" *American Journal of Sociology* 76 (November 1970), pp. 426–442.

19. Joseph Lopreato and Janet Saltzman Chafetz, "The Political Orientation of Skidders: A Middle-Range Theory," *American Sociological Review* 35 (June 1970), pp. 440–451.

20. Ibid., p. 450.

which asserts that the more easily upwardly mobile individuals are accepted socially by the old-timers of their class, the more likely they are to exhibit the political behavior appropriate to their new social class, and the greater the opportunity perceived for social reascent, the greater the likelihood that skidders will exhibit the political behavior normal to their class of origin.

Partial support for the theory has been reported by Barber,[21] Hopkins[22] and Thompson.[23] In a secondary analysis on voting preferences for the national elections of 1952, 1956 and 1960, Barber found that upwardly mobile individuals exhibit an intermediate position between those with high and those with low status for political participation and membership in the Democratic Party. The upwardly mobile "have adopted a certain measure of the attitude structure typical of those who inherit high status, but retain clear traces of the attitude toward politics that they learned in their youth."[24] Downwardly mobile individuals show an intermediate position between those with a stable high status and a stable low status for most politically relevant traits. Compared with those of a stable low status they show more interest in politics, conservatism, satisfaction with life and membership in the Republican Party. They are, however, more like those with low status than those with high status. With the exception of racial attitudes, Barber found no support for the notion that the mobile, particularly the downwardly mobile, are inclined toward political extremism.

Thompson found that upwardly mobile Americans are consistently less likely to be conservative than stable members of the middle class and that they are more likely to be conservative than stable members of the working class. In addition, males are more likely to approximate the politics of the class of destination than females.[25]

Hopkins reanalyzed the evidence of seven studies and found no statistically significant evidence to support the proposition that upwardly mobile sons of workers are more likely than stable members of the middle class to vote Republican.[26]

In an essay on the implications of social mobility for political change Davies asserted that affluent workers, per se, are unlikely to change their voting habits because of higher wages. Voting behavior is determined by work factors, tradition and life style. He noted that:

The implication of social mobility for political change is not that mobility necessarily brings with it a challenge to the political system but that the challenge comes from a recognition by the mobile that their identification in a society rests on interpretations of their role situations which are distinctly different from those which are held by the political elites.[27]

21. James A. Barber, Jr., *Social Mobility and Voting Behavior* (Chicago, Ill.: Rand McNally, 1970).
22. Andrew Hopkins, "Political Overconformity by Upwardly Mobile American Men," *American Sociological Review* 38 (February 1973), pp. 143–147.
23. Kenneth H. Thompson, "Upward Social Mobility and Political Orientation: A Reevaluation of the Evidence," *American Sociological Review* 36 (April 1971), pp. 223–235.
24. Barber, *Social Mobility*.

25. Thompson, "Upward Social Mobility."
26. Hopkins, "Political Overconformity."
27. Ioan Davies, *Social Mobility and Political Change* (New York: Praeger, 1970).

The French Revolution, for instance, most basically changed the legitimating symbols of the society. However, as long as differentiated roles persist, the concentration of power in society is likely to persist intact and, thus, to create less change for concerted action by a group.

INDIVIDUAL CAREER MOBILITY

Career mobility is individual movement up or down in some system of status or prestige during a person's lifetime. In a work organization, according to Pavalko, this movement is affected by "career contingencies"—which he identifies as age, sex and "career crunch."[28] Career crunch is defined as the situation in which one's expectations are out of phase with the options open to one. Forms which career crunch may take are individual ignorance; change in the pattern of work activities, such as technological innovation; organizational context alteration, such as an attempt by the organization to persuade an individual to redefine his role; change in the goals or reward structure of the organization; and organizational growth or lack of growth.

Sex as a factor in career contingencies has received renewed attention. Gross saw no change in the degree of sexual segregation in the occupational structure in the United States since 1900.[29] "Women's" jobs are regarded as having secondary significance by employers and incumbents; this attitude results in lower wages and a reluctance for promotion. Epstein, however, noted that among professional elites the double negative of being black and female form a positive matrix for a meaningful career.[30] Black women, it appears, have a greater opportunity to enter "women's professions" than do black men to enter "men's professions."[31]

Career mobility in the professions is strongly influenced by the colleague system and patterns of sponsor-protégé relationships. Together with interaction patterns within a professional structure which are incompatible with sex-role expectations and sex-typing of occupations, they serve to limit women from the upper reaches of the profession.[32]

Patterns of career mobility are also dependent upon the kinds of opportunities which are open to an individual to distinguish himself in an occupation. Zuckerman, in an investigation of age-stratification in American science, examined some of the linkages among the codification of knowledge in the sciences, opportunities of discovery and recognition and the age structure of the scientific elite.[33] She

28. Ronald M. Pavalko, *Sociology of Occupations and Professions* (Los Angeles, Cal.: F. E. Peacock, 1971), pp. 110–165.

29. Edward Gross, "The Sexual Structure of Occupations Over Time," in *The Professional Woman*, ed. Athena Theodore (Cambridge, Mass.: Schenkman, 1971).

30. Cynthia F. Epstein, "Positive Effects of the Double Negative: Sex, Race and Professional Elites" (Paper presented to the American Sociological Association, Denver, Colorado, 30 August–2 September, 1971).

31. E. Wilbur Bock, "Farmer's Daughter Effect: The Case of the Negro Female Professional," in *The Professional Woman*, ed. Athena Theodore (Cambridge, Mass.: Schenkman, 1971).

32. Cynthia Epstein, "Encountering the Male Establishment: Sex-Status Limits on Women's Career in the Professions," in *The Professional Woman*, ed. Athena Theodore (Cambridge, Mass.: Schenkman, 1971).

33. Harriet Zuckerman, "Age Stratification in American Science" (Paper presented to the American Sociological Association, Denver, Colorado, 30 August–2 September, 1971).

found that the physical sciences are better codified than the behavioral sciences. Greater codification leads to the possibility of important contributions at a younger age. Scientific elites of performance tend to be younger, and elites of office—who participate most actively in governing science—were older.

Perrucci and Perrucci pursued the question of identifying the conditions under which the ascriptive factors of social origins affect the postcollege success of engineering graduates.[34] They reported finding no relationship between origins and success after adjustment for scholastic marks, personal values and educational attainment. The values endorsed by engineers were related to the amount of salary received and the degree of technical and supervisory responsibility exercised. Engineers in larger organizations held positions of higher technical responsibility. College grades were linked to the level of technical responsibility attained and the degree of participation in professional activities.

The basic Blau-Duncan model has been extended to include occupation and income at several successive stages of the life cycle. Blau and Duncan proposed a modified causal chain in which occupation at any given time period in the life cycle is affected by occupation in the immediately preceding time period, but not directly affected by occupation in the more remote past. The causal chain is modified by education and family background at each successive stage. Duncan, Featherman and Duncan evaluated the model and rejected the causal

chain pattern as incorrect.[35] Using Princeton Fertility Study data, Featherman directly measured occupational status at different stages in the life cycle and tentatively rejected the model.[36] He proposed an alternative "historical model" in which occupation and income at any point in the life cycle are directly influenced by occupations and income received in the distant past. Kelley reanalyzed Featherman's data, rejected the "historical model" and concluded that:

A man's current occupation is the key to his future status; nothing else matters much. . . . A man's future income depends almost equally on his future occupation and on his current income.[37]

Jacobson and Kendrick looked at the work histories of Puerto Rican workers during a period of economic transition from an agricultural to an industrial base.[38] They reported that the growth of educational certification requirements which accompanied the rapid increase in school enrollment and literacy damaged career mobility opportunities for some workers. The institution of educational requirements reinforced ascriptive status and extrawork performance to the detriment of achieved status in the workplace.

MOBILITY AND ASCRIBED STATUS

That the possession of certain ascribed statuses can affect social

34. C. C. Perrucci and R. Perrucci, "Social Origins, Educational Contexts and Career Mobility," *American Sociological Review* 35 (June 1970), pp. 451–463.

35. Duncan, Featherman and Duncan, *Socioeconomic Background*.

36. David L. Featherman, "A Research Note: A Social Structural Model for the Socioeconomic Career," *American Journal of Sociology* 77 (September 1971), pp. 293–304.

37. Kelley, "Causal Chain Models."

38. Barbara Jacobson and John Kendrick, "Cohorts, Modernization and Social Mobility" (Paper presented to the American Sociological Association, Denver, Colorado, 30 August–2 September, 1971).

mobility is a well-known phenomenon. Duncan reported that a disproportionate number of Afro-Americans are poor because of their race.[39] He rejected the validity of the "vicious cycle of poverty" hypothesis for this group as an "intellectual obfuscation." Blacks who do have favorable origins cannot, as readily as whites, convert them into occupational achievement and income. Blacks with a better than average education can pass on educational attainment to their children, but cannot pass on occupational attainment or income. In 1961 the income gap between blacks and nonblacks was $3,790. Differences in family background accounted for only a quarter of this amount. Duncan concluded that:

If we could eliminate inheritance of race, in the sense of exposure to discrimination experienced by Negroes, the inheritance of poverty in this group would take care of itself.[40]

Crain reported evidence that Afro-American socioeconomic achievement is enhanced by attending integrated public schools.[41] He found that blacks who attended integrated schools had better jobs and higher income throughout at least three decades, which could not be explained in attainments of alumni of integrated schools. He explained this phenomenon in terms of access to information about employment opportunities through informal contacts.

Raymond reported that the economic status of Negroes in the United States improved during the 1940s when judged on an absolute basis.[42] He showed that the improvement was due to rapid upward occupational mobility rather than to geographical mobility.

Slater suggested that the high mobility rate of Jewish immigrants in America is a product of the group's capacity to capitalize upon economic trends upon their arrival in this country.[43] Their commercially oriented, culturally marginal background in Europe and their arrival during eras of commercial prosperity predisposed the new arrivals to economic success, regardless of their adherence to a scholarly tradition. She proposed that intellectuality as the cultural motivator of American Jews be rejected as a myth.

Census data and a study carried out in Pomona, California, show that although second generation Mexican-Americans have on the average a lower educational level than later generations, their average income is higher.[44] It is suggested that this discrepancy may be explained by a high proportion of relatively unacculturated descendants of Spanish colonial settlers who have been unable to translate higher levels of formal schooling into higher occupational and, hence, income levels.

Female intergenerational mobility is the subject of conflicting re-

39. Otis D. Duncan, "Inheritance of Poverty or Inheritance of Race," in *On Understanding Poverty: Perspectives from the Social Sciences*, ed. Daniel P. Moynihan (New York: Basic Books, 1969), chap. 4.

40. Ibid., p. 103.

41. Robert O. Crain, "School Integration and Occupational Achievement of Negroes," *American Journal of Sociology* 75 (January 1970), pp. 593–607.

42. Richard Raymond, "Mobility and Economic Progress of Negro Americans During the 1940s," *American Journal of Economics and Sociology* 28 (October 1969), pp. 337–350.

43. Mariam K. Slater, "My Son the Doctor: Aspects of Mobility Among American Jews," *American Sociological Review* 34 (June 1969), pp. 359–373.

44. Fernando Penalosa, "Education-Income Discrepancies Between Second and Later-Generation Mexican Americans in the Southwest," *Sociology and Social Research* 53 (July 1969), pp. 448–454.

ports. Walker and Bradley found that the prestige of an occupation is to some extent determined by the sex of the incumbent.[45] Prestige ratings for male-stereotyped occupations, blue collar jobs and positions requiring masculine attributes obtained lower ratings for female incumbents than for male incumbents.

Sewell reported that the educational chances for males are uniformly greater than for females at all socioeconomic levels.[46] The male advantage is greatest at the lowest levels and least in the top categories. Despite the advantages of higher grades and higher occupational aspirations, women must still contend with the low levels of teachers' and parents' encouragement and their own low levels of educational aspirations. On the other hand, DeJong, Brawer and Robin compared male and female patterns of intergenerational occupational mobility and found no major differences between males and females.[47]

Palmore and Whittington reported finding increasing gaps between individuals over sixty-five and younger groups for income, education, amount of time working, employment in the manufacturing sector and rate of suburban residence.[48] They suggested that the aged should be regarded as a minority group, implying that age has become a source of downward mobility in the United States.

CULTURE

In an earlier work Warner commented on the lack of association between the upper upper and lower upper classes.[49] Laumann and House presented a study supplying evidence that the nouveau riche need to validate their social positions in terms of home decoration,[50] following similar suggestions from Birmingham concerning their strain for recognition as "elite."[51]

Laumann and House interviewed individuals and noted the contents of their living rooms.[52] Using multidimensional scalogram analysis and smallest space analysis they established that household objects cluster and that the clusters can be located on a four dimensional graph of high to low social status and traditional to modern living room styles. They found that those with extreme political identities tend to have more extreme styles and are less likely

45. Catherine A. Walker and Donald S. Bradley, "Women and Occupational Prestige" (Paper presented at the Annual Meeting of the American Sociological Association, 1973).

46. William H. Sewell, "Inequality of Opportunity for Higher Education," *American Sociological Review* 36 (October 1971), pp. 793–809.

47. Peter Y. DeJong, Milton J. Brawer and Stanley S. Robin, "Patterns of Female Intergenerational and Occupational Mobility: A Comparison with Male Patterns of Intergenerational Occupational Mobility," *American Sociological Review* 36 (December 1971), pp. 1033–1042.

48. E. Palmore and F. Whittington, "Trends in the Relative Status of the Aged," *Social Forces* 50 (September 1971), pp. 84–91.

49. W. Lloyd Warner, *American Life: Dream and Reality* (Chicago, Ill.: University of Chicago Press, 1953).

50. Edward O. Laumann and James A. House, "Living Room Styles and Social Attributes: The Patterning of Material Artifacts in a Modern Urban Community," *Sociology and Social Research* 54 (April 1970), pp. 321–342.

51. S. Birmingham, "The Rugged Art of Social Climbing," *Vogue* 153 (May 1969), pp. 190–191.

52. Laumann and House, "Living Room Styles."

to mix styles. The former mode of analysis showed that those favoring modern styles tend to be non-WASP (non-White Anglo-Saxon Protestants) and to show upward intergenerational mobility. Those with traditional styles tend to be WASPs and not recently upwardly mobile. The latter type of analysis showed that upwardly mobile, non-WASPs seemed to be adopting traditional styles.

Birmingham reported that recognition as upper class is less likely to be found in charity work and membership in the better clubs than it was earlier.[53] Under the new rules for recognition, attention by the press is supremely important, but one no longer needs to hire a publicist. Some of the current favored paths toward recognition are giving one's society columnist Christmas presents, acquiring an easily recognized label or gimmick, identifying with big name friends and attending art openings.

Vorwaller found no evidence to support the hypothesis that the mobile individual will dissociate himself from his earlier social milieu.[54] Vertical social mobility exerts little effect on the number of affiliations which an individual may have with voluntary associations. Differences could be accounted for by the social forces associated with origin or destination statuses to which the individual is exposed.

Kessin found no evidence that intergenerational social mobility is related to disturbed emotional states or to decreased participation in solidary groups.[55] The exceptions to this finding were individuals who were very mobile, with the upwardly mobile showing lower community integration and higher rates of anxiety and psychosomatic symptoms.

Hauser and Featherman have summarized trends of occupational mobility in the United States during the period 1962 to 1970:

Intercohort net shifts in the male occupation distribution between 1969 and 1970 are similar to those observed over the past several decades. There were shifts toward employment as salaried professionals and managers, as laborers, and in farm occupations. In terms of the status hierarchy of occupations, these changes consist of a shift from manual to nonmanual occupations combined with shifts from lower to higher status occupations within both the manual and nonmanual groups.

Although definitive analyses of mobility trends await the outcome of the 1973 survey of "Occupational Changes in a Generation," we do not think that we have yet exhausted the usefulness of the indirect methods employed here. For example, one promising line of inquiry is based on a comparison of black and white mobility trends using the set of components developed here; and a second attempts to identify the ways in which changes in educational attainment have affected mobility patterns.[56]

53. Birmingham, "Social Climbing."

54. Darrel J. Vorwaller, "Social Mobility and Memberships in Voluntary Associations," American Journal of Sociology 75 (January 1970), pp. 481–495.

55. Kenneth Kessin, "Social and Psychological Consequences of Intergenerational Occupational Mobility," American Journal of Sociology 77 (July 1971), pp. 1–18.

56. Robert M. Hauser and David L. Featherman, "Trends in the Occupational Mobility of U.S. Men, 1962–1970," American Sociological Review 38 (June 1973), pp. 309–310.

Report of the Board of Directors to the Members of the American Academy of Political and Social Science for the Year 1973

MEMBERSHIP

MEMBERSHIP AS OF DECEMBER 31

Year	Number	% Increase Over 1962
1963	15,890	7.8
1964	18,191	23.5
1965	20,071	36.2
1966	21,043	42.8
1967	23,440	59.1
1968	25,158	70.7
1969	24,597	66.9
1970	24,544	66.6
1971	23,413	58.9
1972	21,963	49.0
1973	21,070	43.0

FINANCES

Our bank balance at the end of 1973 was $57,888.84.

SIZE OF SECURITIES PORTFOLIO

MARKET VALUE AS OF DECEMBER 31

1963	$415,091
1964	442,284
1965	491,817
1966	462,675
1967	481,123
1968	566,681
1969	539,083
1970	616,429
1971	612,046
1972	642,808
1973	533,024

*STATEMENT OF REVENUE AND EXPENSE FOR THE YEAR ENDED DECEMBER 31, 1973

REVENUES:

Dues and Subscriptions, net of agents' commissions and refunds	$247,350.35
Sales of Publications, net of discounts and refunds	26,407.15
Advertising Revenues, net of discounts	10,063.10
Royalty and Reprint Permission Revenue	7,581.06
Annual Meeting Revenue, net of refunds	2,293.57
List Rental Revenue	1,582.48
Revenue from Sale of Review Books	2,121.00
Miscellaneous Revenues	718.49
TOTAL NET REVENUES	$298,117.20

OPERATING EXPENSES:

Annals Printing, Binding and Mailing	$ 89,614.01
Shipping and Cost of Publications Sold	7,470.70
Salaries and Related Benefits	154,488.53
Telephone	1,577.57
Postage	8,765.09
Printing, Duplicating and Stationery	19,251.69
Supplies	2,390.50
List Rental and Exchange	2,690.68
Insurance	1,490.53
Depreciation	564.00
Annual Meeting Expense	9,560.72
Miscellaneous Expenses	13,512.38
TOTAL OPERATING EXPENSES	$311,376.40
NET OPERATING INCOME (LOSS)	($13,259.20)

MONOGRAPHS:

Expenses:	
Printing, Binding and Mailing	$ 29,017.61
Miscellaneous	19,317.75
Total Expenses	$ 48,335.36
Net Revenue from Monograph Sales and Grants	23,528.69
NET MONOGRAPH COST	$ 24,806.67
NET INCOME (LOSS)—PUBLICATIONS	($38,065.87)

* The Statement of Revenue and Expense for the year ended December 31, 1973 was prepared on the accrual basis of accounting whereas prior years' statements were prepared on a cash basis. This change prevents the presentation of a comparative statement for the current year. In future years a comparative statement will be presented on the accrual basis of accounting.

OTHER REVENUE (EXPENSE)

Interest and Dividends	$ 25,602.31
Investment Management Expense	1,120.57
Net Investment Income	$ 24,481.74
Gain on the Sale of Investments	16,456.68
NET OTHER REVENUE	$ 40,938.42
NET INCOME FOR THE YEAR	$ 2,872.55

PUBLICATIONS

NUMBER OF VOLUMES OF *The Annals* PRINTED

(6 PER YEAR)

1963	106,394
1964	115,416
1965	119,681
1966	133,056
1967	134,788
1968	147,631
1969	154,153
1970	145,456
1971	139,450
1972	138,852
1973	132,709

NUMBER OF VOLUMES OF *The Annals* SOLD

(IN ADDITION TO MEMBERSHIPS
AND SUBSCRIPTIONS)

1963	12,438
1964	15,247
1965	12,492
1966	18,063
1967	19,061
1968	13,072
1969	15,610
1970	14,143
1971	10,046
1972	16,721
1973	12,430

MONOGRAPHS PUBLISHED

Date	Subject	Number Printed	Number Sold	Complimentary Distribution
1962	#1–Behavioralism	15,225	5,368	9,757
1963	2–Mathematics	30,725	2,563	28,162
1963	3–Public Service	17,230	1,140	16,090
1964	4–Leisure	37,488	3,644	33,844
1965	5–Functionalism	44,459	2,631	41,828
1966	6–Political Science	21,067	5,646	15,421
1967	7–Urban Society	22,578	1,505	21,073
1968	8–Public Administration	25,311	2,180	23,139
1969	9–Design for Sociology	16,191	3,669	12,522
1970	10–International Relations Research	10,055	1,052	5,806
1971	11–Technology	12,167	354	3,175
1971	12–International Studies	7,609	346	3,758
1972	13–Diplomacy	7,090	263	2,972
1972	14–Integration	8,096	214	6,941
1973	15–Public Interest	8,001	101	6,804
1973	16–Urban Administration	20,066	152	17,489
1973	17–Language Studies	5,109	147	652

During 1973, the six volumes of THE ANNALS dealt with the following subjects.

January — Urban Change and the Planning Syndrome, edited by George Fox Mott, Managing Partner, Mott of Washington and Associates, Washington, D.C.

March — The Military and American Society, edited by Adam Yarmolinsky, Ralph Waldo Emerson Professor of the University, University of Massachusetts, Boston.

May — Blacks and the Law, edited by Jack Greenberg, Director-Counsel, NAACP Legal Defense and Educational Fund, Inc., New York, New York.

July — The Future Society: Aspects of America in the Year 2000, edited by Marvin E. Wolfgang, President of this Academy.

September — Income Inequality, edited by Sidney Weintraub, Professor of Economics, Wharton School of Finance and Commerce, University of Pennsylvania, Philadelphia.

November — The Energy Crisis: Reality or Myth, edited by Norman I. Wengert, Professor of Political Science, Colorado State University, Fort Collins, and by Robert M. Lawrence, Associate Professor of Political Science, Colorado State University, Fort Collins.

The following special supplementary articles were published in the March and July 1973 issues.

March — Continuity and Change in Recent Research on Social Institutions, by Robert M. Williams, Jr., Henry Scarborough Professor of Social Science, Cornell University, Ithaca, New York

July — Recent Developments in Archaeology, by Jeremy A. Sabloff, Assistant Professor of Anthropology and Assistant Curator of Middle American Archaelogy at the Peabody Museum, Harvard University, Cambridge, Massachusetts, and by Thomas W. Beale, Ph. D. Candidate in Anthropology, Harvard University, Cambridge, Massachusetts, and by Anthony M. Kurland, Jr., Ph.D. Candidate in Anthropology, Harvard University, Cambridge, Massachusetts.

Monograph #15, *Public Service Professional Associations and the Public Interest*, edited by Don L. Bowen, was published in February, Monograph #16, *Education for Urban Administration*, edited by Frederic N. Cleaveland and Thomas J. Davy, was published in June, and Monograph #17, *Language and Area Studies Review*, by Richard D. Lambert, was published in October.

The publication program for 1974 includes the following volumes:

January — Changing Congress: The Committee System, edited by Norman J. Ornstein, Assistant Professor of Political Science, The Catholic University of America, Washington, D.C.

March — The Information Revolution, edited by Donald M. Lamberton, Professor of Economics, University of Queensland, St. Lucia, Queensland, Australia.

May — Interest Groups in International Perspective, edited by Robert Presthus, University Professor of Political Science, York University, Toronto, Ontario, Canada.

July — USA-USSR: Agenda for Communication, edited by Marvin E. Wolfgang, President of this Academy.

September — Political Consequences of Aging, edited by Frederick R. Eisele, Assistant Professor of Social Policy, Pennsylvania State University, University Park.

November — Intergovernmental Relations in America Today, edited by Richard H. Leach, Professor of Political Science, Duke University, Durham, North Carolina.

The rotating summaries of social sciences disciplines, established in 1961, are being continued, as are the monographs.

During 1973, the Book Department of THE ANNALS published 521 reviews. More than three-fourths of these reviews were written by professors, 15 by college or university presidents, 12 by members of private and university-sponsored organizations, 8 by government and United Nations officials, active or retired. Most reviewers were residents of the United States, but some were residents of Great Britain, Israel, Africa, India, Canada and Argentina. Sixteen hundred books were listed in the Other Books section.

Two hundred and eighteen requests were granted to reprint material from THE ANNALS. Most of these went to professors and other authors for use in books under preparation.

MEETINGS

The seventy-seventh annual meeting, which was held in April 1973, had as its subject *The Future Society: Aspects of America in the Year 2000*, and continued the tradition of our gatherings with respect to the diversity of organizations represented by delegates, the size of the audiences and the interest displayed. Thirty-five embassies sent official delegations, as did 19 United Nations missions and 17 states, cities and agencies of the federal government. Delegates were also sent by 171 American and foreign universities and colleges and 131 international, civic, scientific and commercial organizations. Nearly 800 persons attended one or more of the sessions. The average attendance for a session was 675.

The theme of the seventy-eighth annual meeting, held April 5 and 6, 1974, at the Benjamin Franklin Hotel, Philadelphia, was *USA-USSR: Agenda for Communication*. This volume of THE ANNALS contains the papers presented at the meeting.

OFFICERS AND STAFF

Dean R. Jean Brownlee, Dr. Richard D. Lambert, Walter M. Phillips and Elmer B. Staats were reelected for another three-year term.

The Board also renewed the terms of its counsel, Henry W. Sawyer, III, and its auditor, John H. McMichael.

All of the Board officers were reelected, and both the Editor and Assistant Editor were reappointed.

Respectfully submitted,

THE BOARD OF DIRECTORS

Norman D. Palmer
Howard C. Petersen
Walter M. Phillips
Paul R. Anderson
Karl R. Bopp
Elmer B. Staats
Marvin E. Wolfgang
Lee Benson
A. Leon Higginbotham, Jr.
Richard D. Lambert
R. Jean Brownlee
Covey T. Oliver

Philadelphia, Pennsylvania
1 June 1974

Book Department

INTERNATIONAL RELATIONS AND POLITICAL THOUGHT

DEAN ACHESON. *This Vast External Realm. Thoughts Concerning the Making of Foreign Policy, Its Morality and Execution, and the Factors Making for Practical Relations Among Nations.* Pp. 298. New York: W.W. Norton, 1973. $9.95.

Selected, but not edited by the former Secretary of State's son, David C. Acheson, are speeches, university lectures, and published articles expressing the thoughts, aspirations, doubts and fears of the author after his departure from high office. His ideas were made public in *Foreign Affairs, The Yale Review,* and in graceful responses when receiving awards from learned societies. No longer in office and thus free of the demands of protocol, the Secretary's wit and candid characterizations are as revealing to the public at large as they are reminiscent and nostalgic for those who knew him personally.

A son of a minister, and a scholar of history, Acheson's long experience in government and in business gave him ample authority to lecture the students at Amherst College on "Ethics in International Relations." An eighteenth century diplomatist is quoted: "The negotiator must be a man of probity and one who loves truth; otherwise he will fail to inspire confidence." Acheson's own admonition was: "In foreign affairs only the end can justify the means; this is not to say that the end justifies any means, or that some ends can justify anything. . . . Our objective (end) is to foster an environment in which free societies may exist and flourish."

Candid as to his own reputation as a "cold warrior," in an address in Milwaukee Acheson referred to himself as "a warrior in the fray." His commander in the battles, President Truman, enjoyed Acheson's respect and admiration. Those attitudes were also reciprocated. In what is by far the longest essay in the book, entitled "The President and the Secretary of State," there is spelled out the daily effort of the Secretary to keep the President informed. Even greater pains were taken to accomplish this purpose when Acheson was abroad—the Truman-Acheson relationship was able to withstand and outlast the criticisms arising out of the Hiss affair and the accusations of Senator Joseph McCarthy.

On occasion, disappointed with the Congress, but more often and more sorely wounded by the press, Acheson obliquely defended both the elected executive and the elected legislature in observing that to read the public prints "would lead one to believe that we elect to public office the most zealous imbeciles bent upon every imaginable folly, extravagance, and disastrous adventure, determined to blight the hopes of the young, the poor and the disadvantaged, and probably venal into the bargain."

WILLARD BARBER
University of Maryland
College Park

GEORGE N. GORDON and IRVING A. FALK. *The War of Ideas: America's International Identity Crisis.* Pp. v, 362. New York: Hastings House, 1973. $7.95.

This is a lively book—controversial, and loaded deliberately with levity and sarcasm which may annoy many—on a very important subject that should get the attention of a wide audience well beyond the classrooms. Neither author claims to be an expert at foreign policy; but, rather, experts on "communications and persuasion, necessary subcomponents for understanding the issues . . . " (p. 100). I agree. (Dr. Gordon is presently chairman of the Department of Communications at Hofstra University; and Dr. Falk is professor of Communications at New York University.)

The main (not sole) thesis is that "a construction of peace (if it is ever achieved) will be evolved, not from old-time notions like peaceful coexistence but newer concepts derived in great measure from contemporary social psychological thinking" (p. 42).

One is tempted to quote many of the hard-headed criticisms, and to pursue some of them, but space makes this impossible. You will find here harsh criticisms of many things—our foreign policy; our official and semi-official information and propaganda efforts; much of social science data and research; the "mindless use" of information theory, cybernetics, games theory, decision theory and computerized wisdom; the "cant" of "international understanding"; cultural relations programs; Peace Corps; futurists; traditional American appeals to "higher morality";

the media; "chauvinistic do-goodism"; the Vietnam War; the educational system, and much else.

Let me quote to attract the readers the book deserves.

"Snatching defeat from the jaws of victory has become an American habit" (p. 75). ". . . Our foreign policy is a policy to sustain no consistent policy. Instead, we have consistent morals—that is, we always set out to do what is 'right' " (p. 90). ". . . We confused (and still confuse) our intentions with our objectives" (p. 132). "Ideas are weapons"; "truth" (in our propaganda) is a weapon but "a damn blunt one" (pp. 177–178, but see p. 320). Our propaganda results are either "useless" or "catastrophic" (p. 183). ". . . It is not only the ideals of liberalism that have failed, gone also is the implicit faith behind the old-time liberal's visions of social progress. In its place is arrogance" (p. 318).

The authors repeat throughout that American prestige is at the lowest point ever. They seem to favor a strategy of a modified Realpolitik, one dependent upon a limited entente with China and Russia—they do not consider, apparently, a united Europe as a superpower (p. 303). Chapter eight, "The Sound of Money," is very perceptive on the importance of trade and the international multi-corporate business community so much in the news today.

But I must report the authors do say: "The present moment is . . . potentially the finest in the history of the United States," if we can learn humility (p. 294). The best hope, it seems, "rests in a return to the same pragmatism that sustained us through the caprices of our first 200 years" (p. 320).

Chapter ten makes fourteen "Suggestions and Recommendations Anyway," but here we can fairly brief only a few, not necessarily the most important ones.

Decrease present foreign aid spending and channel some of the saved funds into low interest loans. From scratch, overhaul our official and semi-official propaganda agencies, including Radio Liberty and Radio Free Europe, and place them under one roof and one chain of command. The person in charge of the persuasive arm should be on parity with the Secretary of State in the "articulation" of foreign policy. Separate the persuasive arm of the Department of State from the diplomatic part. Don't put the direction of our international persuasion policies in the hands of American advertising, media, and public relations personnel. Don't expect too much from cultural relations programs.

The end papers quite appropriately are photographs of the porcelain "Mute Swans of Peace," replacing the dove symbol, which Nixon presented to Chairman Mao and the people of the People's Republic of China, significant to the authors who believe symbols are important.

RICHARD H. HEINDEL
Department of International
Relations
Pennsylvania State University
Middletown

ROGER E. KANET, ed. *The Soviet Union and the Developing Nations.* Pp. ix, 302. Baltimore, Md.: The Johns Hopkins University Press, 1974. $12.50.

The establishment of a major presence in the Third World during the past two decades has signified the USSR's emergence as a global power. No longer restricted in its diplomacy to the Eurasian land mass, the Soviet Union is now active from India to Cuba, from Egypt to Zaire. It has skillfully exploited regional animosities and Washington's previous penchant for military pacts with nations situated along the soft underbelly of the USSR, and offered its support as an alternative to the Western Powers. Through a combination of high powered salesmanship, showcase economic projects, and lavish arms aid, Moscow has assiduously courted key countries and helped to shape the evolution and politics of this vast area of newly independent, non-Communist nations.

The ten essays in this volume provide a great deal of information and a balanced overview of the Soviet record. The assessments are sober, the research is sound, and the analysis is consistently of high quality.

The two introductory chapters by Roger Kanet trace the role of the colonial question in Soviet ideology and policy under Lenin and Stalin, and the various ways in which doctrinal formulations have changed since 1953. They examine the reassessments by Soviet writers of previously unquestioned assumptions that, inter alia, national liberation movements will automatically develop into socialist movements, that the noncapitalist path of development will prevail in "progressive" states, and that heavy industry is essential for political independence. Arthur Jay Klinghoffer shows how the USSR has become more realistic in its expectations and approach to Black Africa. Justus M. van der Kroef expertly reviews the principal elements of Soviet policy toward Southeast Asia, highlighting the pragmatism of the Soviets in dealing with such diverse countries as North Vietnam, Indonesia, and the Philippines. Bhabani Sen Gupta focuses on recent Soviet policy in South Asia: the Soviet-Indian Treaty of August 1971; the Indo-Pakistani War of December 1971; the breakup of Pakistan and the creation of Bangladesh; the growing Soviet naval presence; and the quest for a "collective security" system in the Indian Ocean area.

The article on the Middle East (reproduced from *Problems of Communism*) by John C. Campbell covers familiar themes and has been overtaken by the October 1973 Arab-Israeli war. Rober Hamburg ties together the many strands of Soviet activity in Latin America, including relations with Cuba, and implies that, notwithstanding perennial American anxieties, they do not add up to very much in terms of influence or impact. Elizabeth Kridl Valkenier notes that the two decades of Soviet economic relations with the Third World are important because of "the solidification of relations into settled patterns" and the greater attention devoted by Moscow to correcting "the malfunctioning of the state sector" and to improving "the methods of state control" in order to enhance the chances and popularity of "socialist economics." Richard W. Manbach evaluates Soviet policy in the United Nations and sees "the existing Soviet-Third World alignment" as based "on convergent, not common, interests." As the Afro-Asian states come increasingly to dominate United Nations forums, politics there will become more complex, "and the great powers will become less able to perceive dominant strategies for themselves." Finally, Jan S. Prybyla observes that Soviet and Chinese aid programs have afforded the developing countries additional policy options.

ALVIN Z. RUBINSTEIN
University of Pennsylvania
Philadelphia

HAROLD B. MOULTON. *From Superiority to Parity: The United States and the Strategic Arms Race, 1961–1971*. Pp. xii, 333. Westport, Conn.: Greenwood, 1973. $12.00.

JOHN NEWHOUSE. *Cold Dawn: The Story of SALT*. Pp. vii, 302. New York: Holt, Rinehart and Winston, 1973. $7.95.

From Superiority to Parity: The United States and the Strategic Arms Race, 1961–1971, by Harland B. Moulton, is an attempt to follow the debate in this country throughout the decade of the 1960s concerning the nation's posture vis-a-vis the major challenge posted by the Soviet Union's expanded nuclear weapons arsenal and her improved delivery capabilities. At the outset of the race examined here, the United States had clear superiority in terms of the number of missiles available for targeting against the Soviet Union, and the sophistication of the U.S. arsenal was vastly superior to that available to the Kremlin. The so-called "missile crisis," presumably favoring

the Soviets, had been a major issue in the 1960 presidential campaign, but the Kennedy administration soon acknowledged that the dire forewarnings of 1960 were unfounded. Instead of a Soviet lead, there was considerable U.S. superiority in the early 1960s. Much of the book discusses the various efforts engaged in by the Kennedy and Johnson administrations to maintain a comfortable lead over the perceived main adversary in the strategic field. The key figure in this effort was Robert McNamara, Secretary of Defense throughout much of the period covered. Large sections of the book are consumed by an almost verbatim report of the Secretary's major speeches and his statements before the various congressional committees dealing with military appropriations.

The book is well written and interesting, although the novice in the field will have some initial difficulty in mastering the technical jargon, which is abundant throughout the book. My most serious objections to the book fall into two categories: First of all, the book only covers part of the period its title lays claim to; the detailed analysis really stops with 1969, while the two remaining years are covered in an overview, which is well written and interesting, although too short to do real justice to the important developments during this period. In this overview section, the author also engages in some rather passionate criticism of Pentagon dissemination of misinformation concerning U.S. capabilities, ostensibly for the purposes of enhancing its "clout" with Congress. While much can be said about such tactics (which surely do exist), the harshness of the critique somewhat mars the author's otherwise scholarly style.

A second criticism refers to Mr. Moulton's use of sources. Most of the source material is taken from the records of the various congressional committees involved in military budgeting in this period. This is clearly extremely important source material, but it should be pointed out that there also exists a considerable academic literature on this subject, and a little more reliance on these sources might have brought in additional perspectives and insights. As it now stands, the book tends to depict a sparring match between Secretary McNamara, on the one hand, and the Joint Chiefs of Staff, part of the Pentagon bureaucracy, and congressional committees, on the other hand. This kind of narrative tends to overlook the many subtleties, indeed contradictions, found in the groups examined (although it should be noted that the author analyzes the differences among the three major services within the military fairly well).

A rather serious problem arising from the author's focus is the extended paraphrasing of statements given by McNamara, the Joint Chiefs, and members of congressional committees. This is not really necessary; explanatory footnotes, or direct—if limited—quotes, could do the job equally well, and would leave more room for the author's own analysis, which is rather lacking in many sections of the book.

Despite the criticisms indicated above, I find Harland B. Moulton's book interesting and informative. Its value is enhanced by a bibliography, good—if limited—footnoting, and an index.

John Newhouse's *Cold Dawn: The Story of SALT* is an extremely interesting and timely book. It describes the major events leading up to the SALT agreement, which was signed by President Nixon and Party Chief Leonid Brezhnev in a historic ceremony in Moscow in May 1972. The book brilliantly analyzes the decision making process within the U.S. government which preceded the final agreement. It is, understandably, much less thorough on the procedures on the Soviet side; after all, the Soviet Union is a rather closed society, and this factor is of particular importance in anything that deals with strategic matters and military decision making and planning. In analyzing the U.S. side, however, Mr.

Newhouse is brilliant; and he convincingly shows that U.S.-Soviet negotiations—difficult as they were—in some cases paled before the sustained, and sometimes bitter, controversies within the U.S. government, with various agencies taking positions often quite contradictory to others, and primarily for reasons of agency prestige and limited gain. It is this masterful insight into the dynamics of decision making in the U.S. which makes Newhouse's book more interesting than Harland B. Moulton's effort, although the latter was primarily concerned with an overview rather than an in-depth treatment of a complex, but, nevertheless, limited topic.

While the agencies in Washington maneuvered, the SALT delegation, headed by Gerard C. Smith, had a vested interest in success, and often acted on this basis. The delegation's efforts were immensely aided in the latter stages of the negotiations by the opening of the so-called "back channel," in which Henry Kissinger and Soviet Ambassador Dobrynin negotiated directly, occasionally involving the President and Mr. Brezhnev as well. Paradoxically, this back channel stimulation to the SALT delegation's endeavors came at the expense of Smith's position in the talks; towards the end, things were happening in the back channel that the delegation did not know about, and this caused occasional embarrassment and much anger among the men in the field in Helsinki and Vienna. Against this backdrop of conflict stands Henry Kissinger, masterfully calling up position papers and memoranda from a slave-driven group of bureaucratic experts. In the end, the White House adviser was very much in charge of getting the agreement, a feat which has of course been matched by his many accomplishments since.

Mr. Newhouse's book is also superior in its description of the actual negotiations and thus represents investigative reporting at its best. The author obviously has good sources "all over the map" of U.S. defense planning and military strategy. Perhaps this kind of inside information prevented Mr. Newhouse from footnoting his rich text in any detail; this lack of documentation is one of the few criticisms one might raise. Another problem is the extremely technical jargon used in the book, although this problem is mitigated by an introductory chapter, which is useful in explaining many of the terms used. The problem of jargon cannot readily be laid at the author's door; he is dealing with agencies that seemingly thrive on tongue-twisting acronyms, so often confusing to the layman. It is to Mr. Newhouse's great credit that he has made good, readable sense out of a welter of confusing interagency struggles in the extremely important decision to reach a limited agreement with the Soviet Union. The book is further strengthened by an appendix containing the text of the treaty itself. There is also a good index.

TROND GILBERG
Pennsylvania State University
University Park

THOMAS G. PATERSON. *Soviet-American Confrontation: Postwar Reconstruction and the Origins of the Cold War.* Pp. xi, 287. Baltimore, Md.: The Johns Hopkins University Press, 1973. $12.50.

In March 1944 Ambassador Averell Harriman wrote: "I am impressed with the consideration that economic assistance is one of the most effective weapons at our disposal to influence European political events in the direction we desire and to avoid the development of a sphere of influence of the Soviet Union over Eastern Europe and the Balkans" (p. 36). In the next four years, as Professor Paterson's richly documented study reveals, American statesmen in Washington proceeded to carry out Harriman's advice. Fully conscious of American economic strength, the Truman administration sought to influence Russian policy by dangling—and eventually denying—a postwar loan, abruptly terminating Lend-Lease, cutting back

Soviet-American trade, halting UNRRA relief supplies to Eastern Europe, and gradually restricting loans and trade to countries within the Soviet sphere. These attempts at economic coercion were counterproductive, Paterson argues, hastening Moscow's construction of an iron curtain. Elsewhere, in Western Europe, the Near East, West Germany, through dominance of the United Nations, International Monetary Fund, and World Bank, American economic diplomacy was more successful. At least half the world would subscribe to American principles of multilateral trade. Secretary Byrnes summed up American policy in September 1946: "We must help our friends in every way and refrain from assisting those who either through helplessness or for other reasons are opposing the principles for which we stand" (p. 120). According to Paterson, even the Marshall Plan was put forward in such a way as to preclude Russian (and Eastern European) participation. Because the United States alone had the economic resources to bring about postwar reconstruction, and because Washington used this power as a weapon rather than a tool, Paterson places major responsibility for the Cold War on the Truman administration.

Paterson has written an important book. The research is exhaustive, for Paterson has examined more manuscript sources than any other historian of the early Cold War. (His bibliographic essay is the best guide to unpublished manuscripts that this reviewer has yet encountered.) The tone is also commendable. While clearly "revisionist" Paterson displays none of the shrill dogmatism that has unfortunately characterized much of the recent scholarly debate on Cold War origins. No economic determinist, Paterson is careful to include bureaucratic politics, historical "lessons," presidential "style," and a sense of national mission in his analysis of American diplomacy. Nor does he hesitate to criticize Russian attitudes and behavior. In sum, *Soviet-American Confrontation* is an excellent work, clearly written and handsomely printed. It elevates Cold War historiography to a new level.

JOHN GARRY CLIFFORD
Department of Political Science
University of Connecticut
Storrs

GEORGE H. QUESTER. *The Politics of Nuclear Proliferation.* Pp. ix, 249. Baltimore, Md.: The Johns Hopkins University Press, 1973. $11.50.

This book should solidify George Quester's reputation as one of the very best writers on modern strategic problems. It consists of a series of eighteen case studies on the factors underlying the nuclear policy of seventeen countries and the International Atomic Energy Authority. Quester summarizes a tremendous amount of material with the lucid reasoning, scepticism of conventional wisdom, and superb writing which are becoming his trademark, using the currently fashionable bureaucratic politics approach with sophistication and restraint. The result is an excellent introduction to the subject for novices which also will cause both governmental and academic specialists to rethink some accepted notions. Everyone will not accept his arguments that, for example, India can become the sixth nuclear power without triggering more proliferation, that Israel needs nuclear rumors but not explosions, that cheap American-enriched uranium has prevented proliferation, that we may see a nuclear race between Argentina, Brazil, and Chile in the 1980s, and that South Africa opposes proliferation but will not sign the Non-Proliferation Treaty; but all will find them stimulating. This is an important book, and I only hope that its university publisher will give it enough publicity so that it can achieve the wide dissemination it deserves.

Quester has done superbly what he set out to do. It may be unfair to criticize him for not attempting more, but I believe it would have been a better book it he had been more ambitious. The usual strategy for this type of study is to have country specialists write separate chapters. Quester has scarificed the specialized knowledge which this technique elicits, presumably for the advantages of the single author, focusing the cases on the same questions and facilitating comparison. Unfortunately, the book exhibits only the first virtue; it has almost no comparative material, and no attempt has been made to put these cases together to suggest general trends or patterns. As a result, it is likely to have a short shelf-life for policymakers, since events will date its historical materials. There is no general analysis to allow the reader to apply them to other cases and to changing circumstances, and no indication of how the past experiences of one country may help explain the future actions of another. No one can foretell the future completely, but the analyst must furnish the intellectual tools which will make it more comprehensible. When Dr. Quester decides to tackle this task, the results undoubtedly will be illuminating.

ROY E. LICKLIDER
Department of Political Science
Douglass College
Rutgers University
New Brunswick
New Jersey

WARNER R. SCHILLING et al. *American Arms and a Changing Europe: Dilemmas of Deterrence and Disarmament.* Pp. vii, 218. New York: Columbia University Press, 1973. $12.00. Paperbound, $3.95.

There is widespread recognition that the United States has confronted a difficult dilemma in reconciling its superpower strategic relationships with the preservation of a security commitment to Western Europe. This problem has become especially acute in recent years in an "era of negotiation" with the Soviet Union accompanied supposedly by the construction of "partnerships" with allies in Europe and elsewhere. This volume, based on a study prepared for the United States Arms Control and Disarmament

Agency, provides an analysis of the continuing American effort to preserve a "balance of power" in Europe while seeking agreements designed to minimize the prospects for conflict between the United States and the Soviet Union. As the authors succinctly state the problem: "Policies designed to maintain the security of Western Europe have frequently strained the stability of the Soviet-American strategic balance, and policies designed to improve the stability of the Soviet-American balance have seemed to threaten the security of Western Europe" (p. 5).

Included in the volume is a generally sophisticated, if somewhat dated, analysis of the evolving superpower strategic environment and its implications for European security. While much of the detailed discussion of technological developments by both the Soviet Union and the United States, as well as the treatment of SALT-I, has been superceded by the signing in May 1972 of the ABM Treaty and the Interim Agreement on Offensive Missiles, the authors conclude, quite perceptively (p. 49), that a consequence of the development of MIRV technology will be increased interest by the superpowers in counterforce doctrines. In fact, new technologies available, especially to the United States, now make possible the development of strategic and battlefield tactical weapons of unprecedented accuracy and thus enhance the prospects for at least a limited counterforce posture and conceivably the reduction of collateral, or unintended damage. However, the analysis contained in the volume might have been improved by a more detailed treatment of the implications of new technologies for deterrence both at the superpower level and in Europe. While the authors conclude that tactical nuclear weapons may play a greater role in future European security, they make no mention of the range of new technologies for nuclear and conventional weapons or the implications of such technologies for arms control in Europe.

Another deficiency of the volume lies in the absence of a detailed analysis of the major Europe-related issues of the SALT. These include the so-called forward based systems (FBS)—for example, tactical aircraft based in Western Europe designed principally for support of NATO forces but capable of reaching Soviet territory on a one-way mission, no transfer of technology agreements designed to limit U.S. assistance to European nuclear forces, or nuclear-free zones in Europe. The FBS issue was raised repeatedly by the Soviet Union, and rejected by the United States, during the first phase of the SALT, and has been an object of concern to Europeans in the present strategic arms control negotiations. The FBS issue, like the technology transfer and nuclear free zone issues, is fraught with potentially divisive implications for the European-American relationship and deserves extensive treatment in a study of arms control in Europe.

Engaging in an exercise in futurology, the authors developed eight models setting forth alternative security arrangements for Europe. These range from Soviet dominance to a position of increased power for the United States. The volume contains a systematic analysis of patterns of political-strategic interaction for each model and its implications for arms control in Europe. They conclude that a model called "Two Spheres Europe," which closely approximates Europe in the early 1970s, is likely to endure for the remainder of this decade. The Soviet Union will oppose any erosion of its hegemony in Eastern Europe, and the United States will seek to preserve a residual security guarantee for Western Europe. Each superpower will continue to guarantee the security of its European allies against armed attack by the opposing superpower or its allies. Further erosion in the credibility of the United States nuclear guarantee to Western Europe through the achievement by the Soviet Union of "demonstrable superiority," or the unilateral reduction by the United States of its defense commitment would lead the NATO allies toward a model called "Big Finland Western Europe," in which the states of Western Europe would become highly susceptible to Soviet influence.

Appropriately, the authors conclude that the "Atlantic Community must therefore remain the organizing concept for American and Western security until the Europe that lies between the superpowers becomes again an autonomous, self-maintaining subsystem in world politics, or until Western Europe by itself becomes such a system" (p. 155).

In their concluding chapter the authors offer four general guiding principles for United States arms control policy in Europe (p. 186): (1) a military posture on both sides that neither threatens nor invites an all-out attack; (2) a political commitment by both sides to the territorial status quo clear enough to deter the use of force; (3) recognition by both sides of the need to restrict military operations until political leaders can identify and hopefully resolve problems and miscalculations that led to hostilities; and (4) a deliberate effort by both sides to develop military doctrines and postures that permit each to exercise restraint without jeopardizing military security.

However laudable such objectives, the problems of translating them into specific arms control agreements, as we have seen in the ongoing SALT and the negotiations for mutual and balanced force reductions in Europe, are formidable. Equally difficult will be the development of a consensus between the United States and Western Europe on the level of forces, the sharing of burdens, and the framework for defense in an era of rising defense costs and reluctance to increase military budgets both in Western Europe and the United States. Without such a consensus, it will become increasingly difficult to preserve the "balance of power" in Europe based upon criteria for defense planning and arms control set forth in this excellent analysis of European security and American policy in the 1970s.

ROBERT L. PFALTZGRAFF, JR.
Tufts University
Medford
Massachusetts

AFRICA, ASIA AND LATIN AMERICA

OTON AMBROZ. *Realignment of World Power: The Russo-Chinese Schism under the Impact of Mao Tse-Tung's Last Revolution.* Pp. vol. I, 338; vol. II, 406. New York: Robert Speller & Sons, 1972. $12.50 per vol.

These two volumes provide the most comprehensive coverage up to 1972 of the Russo-Chinese schism from the standpoint of Taiwan, which the author, like General Douglas MacArthur, accepts as the West's "unsinkable aircraft carrier." Ambroz defines realignment, which to him is the product of this schism, as the substitution of a multipolarized world for the bi-polarized world that emerged from World War II. In reality, it is the subtitle—the Russo-Chinese Schism—rather than realignment, which is the substance of this work. As the kaleidoscopic events and the author's arguments fluctuate, it is often difficult to determine whether the schism produced the realignment or the realignment merely aggravated the schism. The schism, according to Ambroz, is "the most important event in the second half of this century."

The author's thesis is bolstered by numerous references and an extensive bibliography, unusual for a journalist. It would be a herculean task to check the accuracy of these references, many of them from Yugoslav, Latin American, Russian, and other sources. I should like, however, to call attention to one significant omission pertaining to dialectical materialism. Ambroz deals with the alleged deviation from Leninism of the Soviet-trained Marxist scholar, Yang Hsien-ch'en, in the spring of 1964, which brought him into disrepute with Mao. Yang's interpretation of the basic law of social development—"two combine into one" —as a single conceptual whole, was said to be at variance with Lenin's early pronouncement, *razdvoyeniye yedinogo*—"one divides into two"—to which Mao subscribed. Mao, and apparently Ambroz, were unaware that Yang's definition was based on a later interpretation by Lenin, *Ucheniye o yedinstve protivopolozhnostyei* (Theory of the Unity of Contradictions). See *Tolkovyi Slovar*, edited by D. N. Ushakov (Vol. I, p. 706).

Time and again Ambroz repeats his thesis that Maoist China is a giant on feet of clay (Vol. I, p. 219) and that Mao will be swept away by history (Vol. II, p. 109). Maoist leadership, in his opinion, is a gerontocracy—rule by the old generation—which is inherently unstable and must inevitably collapse. The impression is given, however, that Ambroz is still more antagonistic to the Tsarist Russian and Soviet regimes. As he states in his preface: "One of the few positive contributions of Maoist China was her reminder to the world of Soviet colonialism, not only in Asia, but also in Europe, from Riga and Koenigsberg to Chisinau (Bessarabia)."

The Sino-Soviet schism, as presented in this work, is basically ideological. As was the case with theology, ideology is now in the process of undergoing its "reformation." The great upheaval in Western Christendom in the sixteenth century resulted in the formation of various Protestant denominations (churches) in Europe, led by Luther in Germany, Calvin and Zwingli in Switzerland, Cranmer in England, and John Knox in Scotland. Monolithic Communist ideology likewise has split into many Communist "denominations," led by Tito in Yugoslavia, Dubcek in Czechoslovakia, Ceausescu in Rumania, and Mao Tse-tung in China.

Ambroz is an unqualified anticommunist regarding both the Soviet and the Chinese versions of that ideology. He attributes the hardships that beset both revolutionary regimes to the fact that the leaders in both countries, Lenin and Mao, as compared to Marx and Engels, were outright amateurs in economics. As Mao himself proudly conceded, he was only a political and military man: "I am fundamentally incompetent on economic construction and I do not understand industrial planning" (Vol. II, p. 99). The new Chinese cultural revolution, proclaimed by Mao in February 1974, which is beyond the scope of this work, once again indicates that the Chinese leader's emphasis is not on economics (production, tonnage, and the like), but on ideology.

IVAR SPECTOR

Professsor Emeritus
The Institute for Comparative
and Foreign Area Studies
University of Washington
Seattle

CHING PING and DENNIS BLOODSWORTH. *Heirs Apparent.* Pp. 236. New York: Farrar, Straus and Giroux, 1973. $7.95.

Several volumes have been written about the top leadership in China, particularly about those close to Mao; and much has been published on the problem of succession. *Heirs Apparent* deals with both of these topics, but is unique for several reasons. First, it reads like a novel; the authors even use nicknames and narrate stories and rumors. Second, the Bloodsworths eschew the bibliographic materials on Chinese leaders and draw their information from personal sources, though they support their main themes with documentary evidence. Third, they focus on the intimate personal relations of those in the top decision-making hierarchy in China.

The main thesis of *Heirs Apparent* is that interpersonal bonds are crucial in China. They have always been more important than formal rules of conduct, argue the Bloodsworths; this was again demonstrated during the Cultural Revolution when private negotiations at the top brought an end to factional fighting. Whoever succeeds Mao, they assert, will have to manipulate with precision numerous associates.

Whether such a hypothesis can be proven is questionable due to the dearth of reliable information about what goes on in meetings—much less informal encounters—of the top leaders in China. Nevertheless, the Bloodsworths seem eminently qualified to attempt to prove such a view—or at least write a book about it. Ching Ping was born of a political family in Peking; her father was a confidant of Sun Yat-sen. Dennis is a journalist with many years' residence in Asia and experience with the China scene. The Bloodsworths demonstrate throughout this book that they have considerable inside information about China's rulers—albeit much of it is hearsay.

They begin with a very brief background to the problem of succession and present a kaleidoscopic glimpse into the lives of those close to Mao from before the Long March to the present. Then they deal with these people in greater detail; civilians are considered first, starting with the women: Chiang Ch'ing (Mao's wife), Yeh Ch'un (Lin Piao's wife), and Mrs. Chou En-lai and Mrs. Liu Shao-ch'i. They depict various jealousies among them, and describe Chiang Ch'ing as a woman with an inferiority complex who vented her feelings during the Cultural Revolution. The Bloodsworths note, however, that women in the Chinese Communist Party rise and fall with their husbands, suggesting that Chiang may not be around long.

They divide the civilian men into three groups: (1) the young Shanghai activists, (2) three "old hands" who survived the Cultural Revolution, and (3) Chou En-lai. In the first category are Yao Wen-yen, the writer whose articles launched the Cultural Revolution, and Chang Ch'un-ch'iao, who masterminded the violent phase of the movement in Shanghai. The Cultural Revolution is not over, the Bloodsworths contend; and these two figures may play a vital role in succession. The authors also unravel some close connections between these two and Chiang Ch'ing and an alleged family relationship between Yao and Mao.

Li Hsien-nien (the "Money God"), Nieh Jung-chen (the "Nuclear Monk"), and Kan Sheng ("Cloak and Dagger") are described as the three "old hands" who played a crucial role in China before the Cultural Revolution, survived this unsettling event, and are close to Mao or Chou. They also relate Kang's long personal relationship with Chiang Ch'ing (including his matchmaking role). The Bloodsworths assert that these three will certainly figure in the decision to choose Mao's heir.

They characterize Chou En-lai as a "man with five smiles" and elaborate on his versatility and ability to survive. It was Chou, they say, who mediated between the regional military and the Maoists to end the Cultural Revolution and who designed China's new policy toward the United States. They suggest that he complements Mao: Chou is the *ying*, Mao is the *yang* (two complementary forces in Chinese philosophy).

Next the authors examine the important military leaders in China. They begin by tracing the growth of the armies and the forging of loyalties in the 1920s which are still important today. They argue that personal relationships and followings are central in the military—as much as they were in warlord days. The Bloodsworths assert that the prerogatives of the People's Liberation Army in the wake of the Cultural Revolution are greater than at any time since 1949; hence, the military will be a factor in a struggle for succession.

In the last section of this book the Bloodsworths describe Mao's monumental role and his dream for China. They also speculate on what may transpire when he dies. They conclude that Chou En-lai will be able to fill the vacuum Mao's death will create and that he can cope with any instability or problems that might arise. However, the authors point out that we must look to some of the younger leaders to know who will rule China in the next generation.

The main criticism of this book is the frequent resort to guessing and speculation as well as some rather ridiculous storytelling. For example, the Bloodsworths relate one explanation of Lin Piao's death: Israeli intelligence sources learned of Lin's plot against Mao and informed the CIA; Nixon then told Kissinger to pass this information on to Chou En-lai. Nevertheless, they try to be objective about such tales; and they try to relate such accounts as well as their characterization of various subtle interpersonal relations to the ultimate problem of who will succeed Mao.

For a lively, fast reading treatment of problems of leadership and succession in China from largely informal sources, *Heirs Apparent* is recommended. One can also judge it from the point of view of the Tenth Party Congress convened just after this book was published and the new leadership chosen at this meeting. The Bloodsworths demonstrated some degree of prescience—except for Wang Hung-wen, who ended up third in the pecking order; he is not mentioned in this book.

JOHN F. COPPER
University of Maryland
College Park

JOHN DUNN and A. F. ROBERTSON. *Dependence and Opportunity: Political Change in Ahafo.* Pp. vii, 400. New York: Cambridge University Press, 1973. No price.

In summary, this represents a rich, in-depth, thorough study of an important and predominantly rural area in the interior of Ghana's southern region. The book's principal value, perhaps, is found in the effort to trace on the land of a relatively unknown entity, Ahafo—a fair distance from the well-covered Ghanaian national capital and its politics—a substantial segment of West Africa's march from colonial bondage to independence and beyond. In the course of that endeavour, we learn much about the social, economic, and political affairs of what might appropriately be described as a small-scale replica of any one of the newly independent states, viewed through the lens of local politics. But in other respects, the effort was less successful.

Most assuredly, the two collaborating authors have the professional qualifications to conduct the kind of social science inquiry the introduction suggests they set out to do. But there is much room to doubt whether the agreed arrangement allowed each to unfold his talents and expertise to the fullest extent. Although the book's title suggests a common theme for the political science and the anthropological investigations, the finished product itself tends to contradict such claim. Between the introduction and the inconclusive conclusion, a most impressive mass of facts pertaining to the Ahafo community is compressed into a mold which should give satisfaction to neither the political scientist nor the anthropologist. Incidentally, the nature of the unit, Ahafo, is never quite defined, which is significant in itself. Perhaps the two disciplines could not come to terms on the exact meaning of "community." But this is not important by itself.

If one is prepared to accept that government, administration, politics, economy, social life in general, at the level of a traditional "community" in West Africa, are disordered, inchoate, in spots chaotic, and held together mainly by legal pressures from legal-political agencies operating "from above," then this book is an appropriate introduction. If, on the other hand, one expects an identifiable thread, a theme, a social, political, or economic unity—by reference to which the vast mass of data can be ordered, the large number of personalities classified, indeed the nature of the political unit Ahafo revealed in a form substantive enough to facilitate further discourse and study—then at the very least, the book requires further explanation, a guide perhaps, from the authors.

The conclusion is indicative of the problem. As a summation it fails to do justice to the labors of two obviously very industrious investigators. In one respect alone, the conclusion is disappointing. In the introduction, the authors seem to set the stage for a grand debate concerning the possibility of "political value becoming localized in African political structures at all," and concerning the alleged attempt by unidentified persons "to define politics stolidly in terms of who get what, when, how, [sic]. . . ." On this subject, the authors argue that to proceed in that manner—as does Harold Lasswell—"is to ignore the pervasively relevant and altogether more fundamental question of just why this should be the pattern of distribution which is maintained." One's appetite whetted, his questions remain unanswered at the end of the book.

HENRY L. BRETTON
State University College
Brockport
New York

ALEXIS U. FLORIDI and ANNETTE E. STEIFBOLD. *The Uncertain Alliance: The Catholic Church and Labor in Latin America.* Pp. viii, 108. Coral Gables, Fla.: University of Miami Center for Advanced International Studies, 1973. $7.95. Paperbound, $4.95.

DONALD L. HERMAN, ed. *The Communist Tide in Latin America: A Selected Treatment.* Pp. vii, 215. Austin: University of Texas Press, 1973. $7.50.

Floridi and Steifbold's slender volume purports to study "the relationship between the Catholic church and the Catholic-oriented labor movement in the contemporary climate of turmoil in Latin America" at a time when both "are being rent by challenges to their established positions from both within and without" (p. 1). During the course of roughly four years' research, the authors have collected a wide variety of materials bearing on the diffuse and often contradictory currents of Latin American Catholicism. Brief surveys are presented on Catholic labor unions, on church positions on Marxism, social reform, and guerrilla priests; and sketches of how these phenomena ap-

pear in particular countries (for example, Peru, Brazil, and Mexico) are provided.

Unfortunately, none of these interesting phenomena is explored in either analytical depth or empirical detail. Instead, the authors present a compendium of ideological statements about the phenomena, with little or no explanation on their part. Thus, *The Uncertain Alliance* reads like the string of quotations that it is, with everyone from the Pope on down contributing his utterance on a plethora of issues, most of which are clearly unresolved. The unresolved issues (does the Church really have a future in Latin America? Do labor unions?), coupled with the strings of pronouncements and the lack of explanation, give this work an aura of triviality.

A typical example of the manner in which Floridi and Steifbold reduce important issues to trivia can be seen in their treatment of Helder Câmara. Câmara, the celebrated "Red Archbishop of Recife" in Brazil's poverty wracked Northeast, has been calling for "authentic Marxism" in the church as the way to eliminate poverty and provide justice. The questions raised by Câmara's existence are: How does he survive with only rebukes from a dictatorship which has driven all other Marxists underground, physically or politically? And how does the Pope, hardly a fellow traveler, tolerate a renegade archbishop? To the former question, the authors have no explanation. For the latter, they suggest that pontifical tolerance is "perhaps due to his (Câmara's) rejection of birth control for Brazil" (p. 33). End of analysis. In short, *The Uncertain Alliance* is a quintessential non-study.

The Communist Tide in Latin America is a collection of essays which deals with the entire Latin American Left, and not simply communist parties, as the title implies. Herman is concerned with developing two major themes: (1) "the influence of outside forces on the Communist movement and (2) left wing democratic regimes and the communist movement" (pp. 25–26). Apparently, the United States Department policy makers, whose policies towards Latin America Herman views as obsolete, provide the major constituency for this book. By presenting an up-to-date assessment of the principal competitors to the United States hegemony in Latin America, the editor hopes that more enlightened policy may be formulated (pp. 31–32).

This book contains the following essays: An introduction by Herman traces the growth of communism in Latin America from the Russian Revolution to the present, emphasizing the growth of Moscow line parties until the advent of Castro (the new breed), with the emphasis on the disarray in the Communist ranks at the present. Robert J. Alexander's "Impact of the Sino-Soviet Split on Latin American Communism" focuses on ideological and organizational party struggles in Peru, Chile, Guatemala, Venezuela, and Chile. His concluding point is that neither the pro-Chinese nor pro-Moscow communist parties are as politically significant as the Jacoben left, essentially Castro oriented parties. J. Gregory Oswald's "Essay on USSR Relations with Mexico, Uruguay, and Cuba" discusses the failure of Soviet trade and diplomacy, Cuba excepted. Herman's essay on Mexico is concerned with the penetration of Communists in the Cardenas regime. He attributes the decline of Mexican Communism mainly to events external to Mexico—for example, the Hitler-Stalin pact. An alternative explanation could be found in the evolution of the PRM (now PRI), the populist, but counter revolutionary, government party. John W. F. Dulles' analysis of the Brazilian Left is the liveliest piece in the book. In addition to a competent handling of the myriad of Brazilian left groups, Dulles captures the essences of major personalities and key situations with the view of an insider. Herman's concluding piece urges the support of emergent democratic regimes as a necessary alternative to communism or militarism. To the reviewer, this old style liberal dream is probably the least

likely political alternative for any Latin American country.

There are several implicit unifying themes which give coherence to these disparate essays. All of the authors concentrate on the more formal aspects of the left—that is, governments, political parties, and their ideologies. Not one of them focuses on social conditions within Latin America which have generated the Latin American Left. That is, they view politics as simply a thing of elites which is ironically one of the defects of orthodox Latin American communist parties. Not one of the authors considers the possibility that one of the major reasons for both a left and social ferment in Latin America is U.S. imperialism, whose political spearhead is precisely the State Department. In short, this work is a kind of leftover from that nostalgic era of the fifties, when political liberalism was a hothouse flower in the big garden of the Cold War.

EDWARD C. HANSEN
Queens College
The City University of New York
Flushing

NANCY FONER. *Status and Power in Rural Jamaica; A Study of Education and Political Change.* Pp. xx, 172. New York: Teachers College Press, Columbia University, 1973. $8.50. Paperbound, $3.95.

This book is a community study, with a difference. It has a focus. Foner does not tell us a bit about everything but rather a good deal about a few significant things in Coco Hill (a pseudonym), a rural community in Jamaica where she lived between July, 1968 and September 1969. She tells us that her original intent was to study the impact of nationhood and independence in a rural community (Jamaica became independent in 1962). "However," in her words, "as so often happens, preconceptions of what would be meaningful to the people involved were not correct" (p. xviii). Instead, she found herself exploring "just why education was so significant" to rural

Jamaicans. She had the courage to change directions even though a few months had gone by, and to get on with what concerned her hosts most deeply.

Foner found that status differentiation, unlike the caste system, was linked to income distribution. Of the 113 respondents to a survey, sixty-one mentioned income, financial position, life style, and occupation as determinants of social status; fifty-two mentioned behavioral or moral qualities. No one in the first group and only four in the second stated that "poor people—wage laborers—could be respectable" (p. 19). Power was dependent upon status. Occupational mobility was usually contingent upon economic advantage. Despite political change, the life chances of villagers had not improved. In this closed universe, education alone provided the rural Jamaicans the illusion of an opening. If the parents could not achieve the good life, perhaps their children, through education, could. Yet this too turned out to be an unrealistic expectation. Foner found that "success in sending children to post-primary school is closely linked to economic status" (p. 78). The schools were crowded and the children neglected. Teachers concentrated their attention on those whose parents were known to have the means and the ambition to encourage their children to do well and go on to higher education.

Yet, unlike the United States, the poor were not (as yet) thoroughly segregated from the rest of the community. Primary relationships were still of sufficient intimacy that they allowed for interpersonal quarrels, spite, and envy. If children of a particular family were accused of being less bright than others and it was said that they could not "pass examinations," this resulted in a "fuss" of limited nature. There still existed a common social context; the poor were experienced as real human beings and not reduced to a statistical category, a point Oscar Lewis emphasized in *La Vida* regarding poverty in India as being different in cultural meaning from poverty in the United States.

It is a pessimistic book. It is a sympathetic book. Written in the best tradition of community studies, it has a feel for its subject. One senses that empathy existed between the author and the rural Jamaicans.

BHAGWATI P. K. PODDAR
Environmental Quality Branch
Corps of Engineers
Portland
Oregon

IRWIN F. GELLMAN. *Roosevelt and Batista: Good Neighbor Diplomacy in Cuba, 1933–1945.* Pp. 303. Albuquerque: University of New Mexico Press, 1973. $12.00.

The title of this book is somewhat misleading, for the relationship between Roosevelt and Batista is not its central focus. Rather, the book deals mainly with the theme of its subtitle, Good Neighbor diplomacy in Cuba between the years 1933 and 1945. Its principal protagonists are the five men who served as U.S. Ambassador to Cuba during the four Roosevelt administrations—Sumner Welles, Jefferson Caffery, J. Butler Wright, George Messersmith and Spruille Braden. Utilizing memoirs, private papers, memoranda and data gathered during interviews, as well as the usual secondary sources, Gellman reconstructs and analyzes the ambassadors' differing interpretations of the Good Neighbor policy. His conclusion is that during their terms of service, "the tactics were altered," but "the fundamental objectives of the United States in the Western Hemisphere remained constant." Although troops were no longer used to maintain order, "the United States continued to work for stability . . . in order to protect American investments" (p. 5).

Gellman argues that the key concept of Good Neighbor diplomacy, "nonintervention," was interpreted very narrowly by Welles, who believed that anything short of landing troops on the island was permissible. As a result, Welles saw nothing incongruous between his role as the first "Good Neighbor" Ambassador and his efforts to get Machado to resign, his use of economic threats and his successful campaign to get Roosevelt to refuse recognition to the first Grau San Martin regime. Caffery, Welles' successor, also "chose to become an integral part of Cuba's political process" (p. 156). He strongly supported Batista because he regarded him as a stabilized force. Caffery also shored up Mendieta's shaky government by requesting the continued presence of American warships, influenced domestic sugar legislation to protect U.S. companies and played an important role in the impeachment of President Gomez.

Gellman argues, however, that the next three ambassadors, Wright, Messersmith and Braden, were strongly committed to nonintervention in domestic politics. Nevertheless, as a result of economic agreements elaborated during the Welles and Caffery years (when Roosevelt was somewhat confused as to the meaning of his Good Neighbor doctrine), the United States had so increased its economic penetration in Cuba that it was able to "(use) its economic power to influence decisions on the island" (p. 195). Thus, "assistance programs replaced political direction" (p. 196) while "stability continued to be the principal objective of the Democratic administration just as it had been under previous administrations" (p. 226).

Gellman also points out that in some ways any course of action pursued by the United States in Cuba would invoke considerable criticism. This is because after years of overt intervention in Cuba, the island's politicians —both the incumbents and the opposition—had grown accustomed to asking and expecting the U.S. Ambassador to intervene in their respective behalves. When Roosevelt's last three ambassadors refused to participate in Cuba's domestic political battles, they were thus severely criticized by those groups desiring intervention as aiding and abetting the side that did not wish their help.

Despite the attention to detail,

Roosevelt and Batista: Good Neighbor Diplomacy in Cuba, 1933–1945 is a very readable book, in part because the author has successfully combined his facts with interesting and clearly stated analyses of the data. Gellman's book thus is a welcome addition to the literature on United States-Cuban relations.

SUSAN KAUFMAN PURCELL
Department of Political Science
University of California
Los Angeles

PETER F. KLARÉN. *Modernization, Dislocation, and Aprismo: Origins of the Peruvian Aprista Party, 1870–1932.* Pp. xi, 189. Austin, Tex.: University of Texas Press, 1973. $8.50.

Peter Klarén has developed an appealing thesis on the origins of the American Popular Revolutionary Alliance (APRA) and its major political expression, the Peruvian Aprista Party. Despite the status of Aprismo as one of the best known forces of the Latin American "democratic left," Klarén notes that most interpretations evaluate the movement almost entirely in terms of the personal magnetism of its founder and leader, Victor Raúl Haya de la Torre who was born in 1895. To sustain his view of the importance of social and economic factors in the development of Aprismo, Klarén uses published primary sources and local archives to trace changes in the region of the important northern city of Trujillo, birthplace of Haya de la Torre. In 1850, sixty-four properties occupied the agricultural land of the Chicama Valley; by 1927, there were only three. The mammoth Casa Grande corporation of the Gildemeister interests controlled seventy-seven percent of this land. Casa Grande also operated its own port at Malabrigo, through which it exported sugar and imported goods needed by its plantation population. Traditional landowners, large and small, found themselves displaced. Local merchants lost control of trade, and the towns and cities of the region stagnated. Migrant Indians from the sierra and their children became a captive labor force. The political influence of the Gildemeister interests in Lima cemented the domination of the Casa Grande over the Trujillo region.

Klarén asserts that the case of the Trujillo area was similar to that of Lima, the central sierra, and other parts of the north under the impact of United States and British capital in the late nineteenth and early twentieth centuries. Foreign interests dominated mining, petroleum, commercial agriculture, commerce, manufacturing, and other economic activities in these areas. In response, Haya de la Torre, as a student political leader in Lima and as an exile in the 1920s, formulated a political program that drew upon the experience of his native Trujillo—in particular, the diminished position of its middle class. Klarén holds that Haya became the political leader of those "dislocated and frustrated by the rapid breakup of the traditional society." Anti-imperialism, *indigenismo*, and state intervention in the economy became major parts of Aprista ideology, while Trujillo became APRA's home base for attempts to gain the presidency via elections in 1931 and revolt in 1932. Klarén notes that since 1931 APRA has obtained most of its support from the "sugar-producing belt of the north coast and the mining centers of the northern and central sierra." The party has remained weak in regions where the local economy has lacked ties to foreign markets and capital.

Klarén's thesis remains incomplete, despite the appeal of its logic. Part of the book is a weak chronicle of Haya's life and Peruvian politics. The influence of the experience of the Trujillo region on Haya's politics is not shown to be more significant than that of his student days in Lima or his travels in exile. The comparison in the final chapter of APRA's origins with the genesis of political movements elsewhere in Latin America is skimpy. Such large concepts as "modernization" and "dislocation" remain undefined. Klarén unfortunately does not explore the very important question of how the Peruvian elite outside of the Trujillo region accommodated to foreign investment and related economic change. One hopes that Klarén's continued research in Peru will lead him to further refine his ideas.

ARTHUR SCHMIDT
Department of History
Temple University
Philadelphia

NGO VINH LONG. *Before the Revolution: The Vietnamese Peasants under the French.* Pp. viii, 276. Lawrence, Mass.: The MIT Press, 1973. $12.50.

Mr. Ngo Vinh Long, a former resident of rural Vietnam and currently enrolled in two programs at Harvard University, has written and translated an unusually relevant and, at times, disturbing series of essays. His work about and by the peasants and literati of Vietnam during the French colonial period (1880s–1945) forces the reader to assess and reassess his understanding of a particular form of Western imperialism. It is his view that, in their contact with the French, the Vietnamese peasants, cut off from their traditional as well as colonial rulers by custom and language, were debased and terrorized by their many overlords.

The "civilizing mission" of France, as Mr. Long's analysis amply suggests and develops, inevitably runs counter to the morality and customs of a society older than France herself. The peasants, represented in the tome by a series of writings and novellas in the second part of the book, are no match in their confrontations with the maledictions of an overpowering technologically advanced colonial regime. They try to understand the forces molding their lives but can neither empathize nor reject the many forms of social and political change which invaded and formed their daily lives. Nevertheless the chroniclers and propagandists of the various aspects of the French colonizing experience detail their views in the guise of "documentary fictions" and "realist literature," for these semi-fictional forms of expressions are the only types permitted by the ruling authorities. And repeatedly, the Vietnamese intellectuals tell—with limited rancor and self-pity—of finding ordinary peasants slowly becoming anti-French and politically responsive to the injustices meted out to them in the name of modernization and Western welfare. Step by step, graphically and carefully, the author suggests the coming of a revolution by peasants against their various exploiters, both those of colonial origin—bankers, industrialists, plantation-owners, and so on—and those of local origin. In the nearly complete opus aptly titled "Who Committed This Crime?" on the subject of Vietnam's starvation era (1944–45), Tran Van Mai completes his comment with a poignant vignette of things to come:

In the midst of the famine I had to go up to Hanoi on personal business. By accident, I met a Frenchman who was an old classmate of mine. I told him of the miserable situation of the population. "I know everything," replied my friend in a voice that revealed both anger and hopelessness. I know that Va-Re (Varet) and his superiors . . . are all pigs. Don't tell me about it anymore. I'm terribly ashamed. (p. 276)

The lesson of 1944–45 was one taught to the Vietnamese over many decades. Mr. Long details the nature of the debilitating colonial process when peasants were made to endure high taxes while being forced to purchase various products from the French, were involuntarily required to acquiesce in the expropriation by foreigners of their communal lands, and were compelled to borrow short and long-term loans in order to produce food staples while literally pawning their wives and children.

Having read this sad work, one does not find it difficult to be persuaded that there was and is a direct correlation between a colonial presence amidst a large indigenous population and the miseries which are the harbinger of revolution.

RENÉ PERITZ
Slippery Rock State College
Pennsylvania

LEON E. STOVER. *The Cultural Ecology of Chinese Civilization: Peasants and Elites in the Last of the Agrarian States.* Pp. 274. New York: Pica Press, 1974. $10.00.

The treatment of Chinese civilization in this volume is an interpretive analysis by a cultural anthropologist who spans the entire sweep of human experience from the stone age to the present. The peasants and elites of the subtitle are portrayed as the two major components of traditional China, set apart in rural and urban sectors characterized respectively in terms of folk culture and high culture or the great tradition. The first two chapters describe the primitive horticultural village, the "Green Circle," which was conquered by a warrior elite in the Bronze Age and harnessed as the energy base for the Great Society (ta-$t'ung$) of the high culture agents. The next seven chapters deal with folk culture from the perspectives of ecology, economy, politics, kinship, class, religion, and world view. Chapters ten through sixteen treat high culture in a parallel fashion, and a final chapter outlines briefly why the conversion from folk society to mass society in contemporary China marks the end of the Agrarian State. As one might expect in a work of such broad scope, some chapters are more adequate than others, early sections being the most substantive. Illustrative detail is supplied by extensive quotation from well-known works such as the short stories of Lu Hsun and Lao She, the autobiography of the last Manchu emperor, the Sacred Edict of the K'ang-hsi Emperor, and even the observations of Arthur H. Smith. A chapter on "Games Chinese Play" is an excursion into personal interactions based on the author's dissertation research as a participant observer among some Chinese residing in New York City.

The gap between the peasantry and the elite is heavily stressed. Village culture had its own independent origins in tribal culture before it was "captured" by civilization, at which point village culture became incomplete. The social contract which resulted from this state of affairs was one in which the peasantry supported the elite in return for being allowed to maintain their own culture. Atomized into conjugal family units, locked in a hostile and suspicious competition with their neighbors, the peasants were incapable of communal solidarity. Despite stratification by occupation and wealth, the peasantry lacked a link to the elite because there was no middle class. Peasants, whether in villages or in urban areas as part of a coolie proletariat, were a corporate class of commoners defined in terms of nonprivilege and nonparticipation in imperial politics. In historical times, the peasantry continued to practice their modified neolithic way of life, little changed except that iron tools replaced stone in their hoe agriculture.

In his rigid polarization of society into two exclusive groups, Stover has accepted the social model embodied in the sumptuary law of the Confucian state. By so doing he has simply defined away some of the most interesting questions of Chinese social organization. The vertical ties of religious, military, clan, economic or governmental hierarchies which linked the peasant to the elite are deemphasized and the organizing potential of secret societies, peasant rebellions and religious movements is not acknowledged. Indeed, the stress on a closed peasant village overlooks the view that the marketing system was the true unit of local culture.

This book invites controversy and criticism. Its argument is set out in the form of a series of provocative definitions with little substantiation and almost no documentation (there are no footnotes). The volume originated as lessons in cultural anthropology presented to students at Tokyo University in 1963–65, when the author was charged with interpreting traditional Chinese culture in light of the ideas of Julian H. Steward, his teacher at Columbia. The result is an analysis which is not sufficiently developed to find

acceptance as it stands, but which is too broad and ambitious to be ignored. An additional difficulty is that some readers may find the style of this book offensive. The author is irreverent and even flip in the coining of phrases—for example, "The Mighty Dragon and the Local Snakes" (central and regional power). An excellent feature, worthy of the widest emulation, is a brief outline of ideas which preceded the first chapter.

EDWARD L. FARMER
University of Minnesota
Minneapolis

TAI SUNG AN. *The Sino-Soviet Territorial Dispute.* Pp. 254. Philadelphia: The Westminster Press, 1973. $8.95.

The Korean researcher, Tai Sung An, evidently undertook his study to prove that the ongoing Sino-Soviet cold war is largely territorial in origin—which undoubtedly it is—and not ideological. Joining other books like those of Doolin and Keesing, *The Sino-Soviet Territorial Dispute* gives the reader a comprehensive background in the history of the territorial arrangements between the two countries, going all the way back to the seventeenth century and leading by painful stages up to the present era of border clashes and helicopter intrusions.

An appendix contains over a dozen documents, including a famous 1689 Treaty of Nerchinsk and the partial text of the 1881 Treaty of St. Petersburg. A well-annotated map (pp. 48–49) is most helpful in pinpointing the disputed areas. The text contains a brief but pithy discussion of the young Soviet republic's relations with China. The author notes how the Lenin government had "hasty second thoughts backing away from their generous 1919 and 1920 pledges, taking advantage of political chaos in China." In other words, he explains how the Lenin regime repudiated the 1920 Karakhan Manifesto, which had promised restoration "forever" to China of all its territories seized under the czars, as the Soviets clung to these territories and maintained the Russian hold over the Chinese Eastern Railway in Manchuria.

The book provides a handy review of the more recent period of Sino-Russian differences. Starting with the establishment of the Maoist regime in Peking in 1949, Mr. An shows how relations with the USSR never reached those peaks of friendship proclaimed so fulsomely in the media of the two countries up to 1960. Even in 1950, when the Soviets and the Chinese signed the Treaty of Friendship, Alliance, and Mutual Assistance on the eve of their cooperation in the Korean War (1950–53), Mao regarded the treaty as symbolic of the fact that the "Soviet Union had not yet fully renounced the traditional czarist expansionism." The post-Stalin (1955) restoration of Dairen and Port Arthur to Chinese sovereignty was not a friendly gesture on Russia's part, notes the author, but a "relinquishment" forced upon a weakened Soviet after Stalin's death, the result of the exertion of "heavy pressure" on Moscow by Peking.

As to the causes of the 1969 border clashes, the author seems to lean toward the theory that it was the Soviets who instigated them and that they stood to gain the most from the skirmishing. It is China who is the weaker of the two adversaries, and the author predicts, with anti-Maoist vehemence, that China will remain in this disadvantaged position until Mao leaves the scene and, along with the Chairman, the Maoist guerrilla-war strategy. Post-Maoist China will have to replace this outworn, doctrinaire strategy with military professionalism, he argues. Some readers may object to this hypothesis by pointing out that the Maoist guerrilla strategy still strikes terror in the camp of any potential invader, who might consider futile the occupation of a country rife with pockets of concealed guerrilla marauders.

The author refers to the length of the serpentine Sino-Soviet border as 4,150 miles whereas Soviet Foreign Minister Gromyko a few years ago gave the figure of 4,592. How these contending figures are arrived at would be interest-

ing to know. Also, while Mr. An correctly mentions that 600,000 square miles of former Chinese territory are presently under Soviet sovereignty, he does not estimate the area of the territories immediately adjacent to the USSR and the Chinese People's Republic—an area of around 50,000 square miles —which has been the subject of the latest phase in the Sino-Soviet border talks that have dragged on since 1969.

ALBERT L. WEEKS

New York City

RICHARD C. THORNTON. *China, the Struggle for Power, 1917–1972.* Pp. x, 403. Bloomington, Ind.: Indiana University Press, 1973. $15.00.

The three parts of this book—the development of Chinese Communism from 1917 to 1941, the American experience in China from 1941 to 1949 and the internal politics of the Chinese Communists from 1949 to 1972—have all been studied by numerous scholars and several works on each topic have long been available to the public. The justification for yet another book on these topics now rests on whether the author has broken new ground substantively or analytically over the old materials.

Against this criterion, the most justifiable portion of this book is the first part which covers the development of Chinese Communism from 1917 to 1941. By utilizing new data hitherto not available to other scholars—particularly the archives of the Chinese Nationalist Party (KMT) on Taiwan —Mr. Thornton has clarified several parts of the early history of the Chinese Communist Party (CCP) such as the Tsunyi Conference of 1935 and Mao's split with Chang Kuo-t'ao shortly after that. A particularly informative account is given by Thornton on the synchronization of CCP's policy toward the KMT with the Soviet Union's global strategy from 1937 to 1941. Thornton corrects a prevailing misconception about the CCP's alleged "independence" from Moscow during this period. However, in one instance, Thornton has unjustifiably challenged existing works on Chinese Communist history. This concerns the so-called "Li Li-san Line" of 1929–1930. Thornton's contention that the urban uprisings initiated by Li Li-san were instigated by Li alone, in contradiction to the directives of the Comintern (p. 24, pp. 30–33), is not convincing. He does not mention—as other scholars did—the ambiguous directives that the Comintern sent to Li which led the latter to embark upon a new wave of abortive military actions against the KMT. On page sixty-six, the name of Mao-Tse-tung's youngest brother, Mao Tse-t'an, is wrongly given as Mao Tse-ching.

Thorton's account and analysis of the American experience in China and the CCP-KMT relationship from 1941 to 1949 are not so informative or full of insight as his discussions on the early history of the CCP. His narrations seem to be all geared toward the contention that the defeat of the KMT on mainland China was largely due to blunders of the United States and the post-war strength of the CCP largely due to Soviet aid that reversed the hitherto military superiority of the KMT (p. 207). The bias of Thornton's analysis here is exemplified in this startling statement: "As long as the National Government could sustain its military position, the impact of other important factors, such as skyrocketing inflation due to growing shortages of food and goods, the reduction of morale, and corruption of government officials, all could be borne without too much hardship" (p. 212).

But the most controversial and dubious part of Thornton's book is the last part, on the internal politics of the CCP from 1949 to 1972. This is mainly due to Thornton's two underlying frames of reference. First, the gist of China's internal politics after 1949 is seen mainly as struggles for personal power. Second, factional alignment within the CCP are said to center around China's policy toward the Soviet Union. Thus Thornton states in the book that Mao initiated the communes in 1958 in order "to redress the imbalance of political power against himself" (p. 245) and the "transfer downward" (hsia-fang) policy was motivated by Mao's desire to put his own men into the vacated provincial seats (p. 258). Mao, according to the book, used the militia as a Trojan horse to dilute regional military power (p. 255). Thornton states, but does not substantiate, the contention that "a primary issue which acted as the implicit touchstone for coalescing domestic factions was China's relationship with the Soviet Union" (p. 244). In addition, most interpretations in this portion of the book are poorly documented; they are mainly speculations or at best inferences. Yet Thornton often treats them as if they were self-evident truths (see, for example, his discussion on the Kao-Jao affair, pp. 226–227). Furthermore, Thornton often uses secondary sources uncritically—such as the analysis on the alleged foreign policy debate between Lo Jui-ching and Lin Piao by Zagoria and Ra'anan, or columnist Jack Anderson's report about the Soviet Union's threat to open a second front on the Sino-Soviet border in Sinkiang so as to prevent Peking from aiding Pakistan in the Indo-Pakistani War of 1971. Both these sources need to be examined critically and carefully before they are made part of a scholarly analysis. On the whole, this last part of Thornton's book must be read very carefully and with much skepticism.

In the final analysis, the book is flawed by Thornton's not providing a larger context for the power struggles that he describes; Thornton implies that leaders of the CCP coveted power for power's sake.

ALAN P. L. LIU
Department of Political Science
University of California
Santa Barbara

FREDERIC WAKEMAN, JR. *History and Will: Philosophical Perspectives of Mao Tse-tung's Thought.* Pp. 392. Berkeley: University of California Press, 1973. $12.75.

History and Will is an ambitious attempt to explain Maoism, the course of the Chinese Communist movement over the last several decades, and the Great Proletarian Cultural Revolution by probing deeply into Mao's philosophical thinking. The central concern is the origins of the tenets of Maoism, especially Western sources. The author also details how Mao adapted Western philosophical ideas to China.

Wakeman endeavors, as he himself admits, to combine two disparate themes: history—which he defines as bureaucratic routinization—and will—Mao's permanent revolution. This—in addition to the fact that the reader must fit together pieces of his disjointed analysis, make the transition between variegated theses in Western philosophy, and then relate them to Chinese thinking—makes this book difficult reading for the layman.

Wakeman also employs linguistic analysis to explicate various philosophical concepts in the context of their language. This is done particularly in the case of Chinese philosophical positions. Thus, the reader requires not only a good background in Western philosophy but also some knowledge of the Chinese language.

Nevertheless, the scholar will appreciate Wakeman's subtle and frequently penetrating analysis of the Western roots of Chinese Communism, apart from Russian Communism. Also laudable is the author's elucidation of the reasons behind Mao's theory of permanent revolution and the causes of his departure from the Soviet model of Communism.

Assembling a wide array of data and arguments, Wakeman begins with an appraisal of Mao's intellectual background and different aspects of Mao as a leader. Hence, the author entitles the first section, "Montages." He views Mao as a revolutionary, a dictator, a legislator, and an image-seeker. Wakeman contends that Mao has sought to liberate man from his alienations—to identify with the entire community "without transplanting bourgeois democratic commonplaces like legislative chambers into society in formation."

In section II, "Transition to Ideology," Wakeman examines the Chinese influence on Mao's intellect and the basis for the formation of Maoist Communist ideology. He gives special emphasis to China's early thinkers, vitalism of the nineteenth century, and Kang Yu-wei. Mao, he notes, found much in Chinese traditional philosophy that was anachronistic in modern China, at least the new China Mao envisioned. Nor did Mao find Kang Yu-wei truly revolutionary. This explains, according to Wakeman, why the influence of Western thought on Mao was so intense—yet Mao was very much a nationalist.

It is precisely the reconciliation of this contradiction which Wakeman strives to detail and document. Section III is therefore an analysis of the impact of pre-Marxian Western philosophical writings on Mao. Here the author builds on the thesis that Mao's philosophical maturation—which ultimately determines the course of the revolution, the building of modern China, and much more—is influenced directly by Western thought rather than through the intermediary of Russian Communism.

Wakeman gives special attention to Immanuel Kant's rationalism and Friedrich Paulsen's idealism. Kant's influence, he says, was especially strong in the realm of voluntarism and moral philosophy, and came to Mao through the youth movement in China in the early 1900s. According to Wakeman, Mao—who, he says, posed as less of an intellectual than he really was—and other Chinese scholars saw Kant as an emancipator of the ego. Paulsen's idealism reached Mao via its translator, Ts'ai Yuan-p'ei, and gave Mao justification for placing the will over the intellect.

In section IV entitled "Necessity," Wakeman describes Mao's intellectual conversion to socialism and Marxism. He observes that one of Mao's adamantly espoused personal beliefs—the authority of the will over the intellect—was found in Karl Kautsky's concept of class conflict. Marx's elaboration of the concept of class struggle also appealed to Mao; however, Mao was impelled to alter drastically the meaning of class in applying Marxism to China. And, according to Wakeman, Mao saw Marxian philosophy as merely another kind of Social Darwinism, scientific theodicy, and intellectualism; thus, he drew the concept of practice from Wang Yang-ming and employed it to revise Marx.

In the fifth and final section, "History and Will," Wakeman tries to harmonize the central themes of this book. He asserts that the Maoist notion of will in history came from Marx; Mao put it in the context of revolution. But Mao's pragmatism led him to see contradictions in situations that Marx did not. Thus he deviated from Marx in various ways—to become a heretic or an original thinker. Mao, for example, holds that the superstructure—that is, laws and government—can influence the infrastructure—forces of production—via the will.

In the last part of this section Wakeman proffers an explanation of the Great Proletarian Cultural Revolution in terms of Maoist ideology, especially contradictions and permanent revolution, and the apotheosis of Mao. In this way he brings Mao's intellectual development up to date.

History and Will is a work that is stimulating, but painstaking reading. It is an attempt to trace the philosophical perspectives of Mao Tse-tung to the West, and to elucidate how Mao applied his intellectual views to revolution in China. It is further an effort to explain recent Chinese history and the Cultural Revolution in terms of their philosophical rationale. This, indeed, takes a writer with courage, or some measure of rashness. Wakeman has either exaggerated the intellectual basis of Mao's impact on China, or he has proven it. In the opinion of this reviewer, it is the latter.

JOHN F. COPPER
University of Maryland
College Park

STEPHEN R. WEISSMAN. *American Foreign Policy in the Congo, 1960–1964.* Pp. 325. Ithaca, N.Y.: Cornell University Press, 1974. $13.50.

As a case study of American relations with the Third World, Weissman has undertaken to examine American policies and assumptions in the Congo. He believes that Americans feared the Congo after independence would proceed through chaos to Communism. Because of that archetypical cold war conviction, and because American policy in Africa was primarily a reflex of American NATO relations, Americans favored and paralleled Belgian paternalism and interventionism. American policy progressed from early determination to protect white lives, white interests, and white-owned property to interference with Congolese politics. Diplomatic pressures, attempted tutelary bargaining, and support for Belgian initiatives gave way to CIA meddling and finally culminated in Operations Dragon Rouge and Dragon Noir, the paratroop drops on Stanleyville and Paulis.

The literature on American foreign relations contains very little on relations with African states in any era. That fact, and the real merits of Weissman's book, make it essential reading despite the redundance of its organization. Weissman has thoroughly explored published materials, including some United Nations documents, an important source far too often overlooked by historians of American foreign relations. Published materials are augmented by interviews with former policymakers in State and with "individuals with good 'agency' contacts" who communicated the CIA's role. All of this has resulted in an unusually fine account of the course of Congolese politics and of the evolution of American policy from the unsympathetic, conservative Eisenhower Republicans through the enthusiastic liberals of Kennedy's years to the interventionary liberals of Johnson's era.

Finally, though, the book is a curious mixture of naiveté and scholarship. The earnest conclusion that the United States and especially the Eisenhower Republicans failed to understand African nationalism lacks the impact and explanatory power that it possessed ten years ago. Weissman verges at times on begging questions, perhaps in attempts to predispose the reader to accept what will come, as in these statements: "In retrospect it was likely that the Congo would become a focus of Cold War competition" (the third sentence in the introduction); and "The two superpowers would certainly be alert to any opportunities or dangers which developed in a significant country like the Congo" (p. 28). In sum, the reader will find intelligent estimations of specific United States-Congo policies and relations side by side with too narrow acquaintance with broader perspectives of American foreign relations—a narrowness of knowledge which undercuts his breadth of generalization as to American relations with the Third World.

THOMAS H. ETZOLD
Department of History
Miami University
Oxford
Ohio

RICHARD D. WOLFF. *The Economics of Colonialism: Britain and Kenya, 1870–1930*. Pp. xi, 203. New Haven, Conn.: Yale University Press, 1974. $9.75.

In the unending discussion over the nature of the colonial relationship between the conquered peoples and the European powers of the nineteenth and early twentieth centuries, the question of the degree and type of economic exploitation maintains a prominent position. Wolff provides a useful analysis of the colonial economy of Kenya as his contribution to the debate, contending that late nineteenth-century Britain drew significant economic benefits from its colonies, advantages that would not have been available if the captive territories had not been part of the British Empire. Wolff recognizes the argument that the amount of the

benefit added to Britain's economy was small in relationship to the total, but that nonetheless the size of the contribution did not mean that it was insignificant.

To demonstrate this reasonable hypothesis, Wolff analyzes Kenya's economy from the period immediately preceding the colonial period up to about 1930. There is a satisfactory chapter explaining the precolonial period, but the book's main value lies in the subsequent discussions, beginning with the basic decision setting the stage for Kenya's often stormy development—the utilization of European settlers as the main component of agricultural development. Thus, land had to be taken from the African owners, who were relegated to a secondary role in development. The subsequent logical step was the determination of the particular crops to exploit, and Wolff carefully explains the various private and public experiments attempted to solve the difficult problem of finding profitable export commodities. Crops like coffee, then in short supply within the British Empire, were the natural outcome of this heavily subsidized government effort. Once suitable crops were available, the European plantation owners required an abundant—and cheap—supply of labor, thus leading to programs designed to force Africans from their existing patterns of labor. The various techniques utilized—including direct and indirect taxes and the seizure of land—and the unduly heavy burden thus falling on Africans are fully detailed.

Wolff convincingly proves that by the late 1920s the system was, from the then British point of view, a success. Africans, forced by myriad government pressures, had become the necessary cheap labor source that allowed Kenya's economy to provide what Britain required. This oppressive exploitation of Kenya's African peoples created an increasing bitterness that led to the troubled period of the 1950s within the colony and to the eventual downfall of the European settlers' dominant position within Kenya's political and economic life.

NORMAN ROBERT BENNETT
Boston University
Massachusetts

EUROPEAN HISTORY AND POLITICS

JAROSLAV KREJČÍ. *Social Change and Stratification in Postwar Czechoslovakia.* Pp. xiv, 207. New York: Columbia University Press, 1972. $11.00.

VLADIMIR V. KUSIN. *Political Grouping in the Czechoslovak Reform Movement.* Pp. xii, 224. New York: Columbia University Press, 1972. $11.00.

These two books are parts of a series entitled "Political and Social Process in Eastern Europe," written under a grant of the Social Science Research Council by a group of social scientists in Great Britain. Both authors are post-1968 exiles from Czechoslovakia, now associated with British universities— Krejčí with the University of Lancaster and Kusin with the University of Glasgow. They explore different aspects of Czechoslovakia's postwar development until the "Prague Spring" in 1968, when various groups both within and without the Czechoslovak Communist party, pressured and cajoled the party leadership under Alexander Dubček to try to reform the country's political, social, and economic system in a manner to give Czechoslovak communism a "human face."

The two books, however, do not rehearse the course of the reform movement, which was cut short by Soviet invasion of Czechoslovakia in August of 1968, but rather explore its underlying causes. Krejčí, who is an economist by training, analyzes the transformation of the Czechoslovak society as a result of World War II and the Communist takeover in 1948. Although he presents a mass of statistical information about the transformation, he does not relate it to the reform movement. In the short conclusion to his book, however, he offers his general

opinions about the movement. Kusin, who was originally a journalist, looks beyond the monolithic facade of Czechoslovakia's society under communism and identifies seven groups, which in different ways and for different reasons participated in the reform movement: workers; farmers; intelligentsia; youth and students; nationalities and minorities; and societies, clubs, and churches.

The two volumes partake of the nature of case studies, which are helpful to the specialist but are of limited use to the general reader. The two books bear a heavy imprint of their authors' marxist training. In marxist fashion, Krejčí and Kusin envision history as a product of impersonal but quantifiable forces, rather than as a resultant of actions, both individual and collective, of flesh-and-bone men. The leaders of postwar Czechoslovakia are not identified, nor are its ordinary citizens described. Historians of Czechoslovakia and students of communism will greatly benefit by Krejčí's and Kusin's books, but the general reader interested in the Czechoslovak political "springtime" in 1968 had better turn to contemporary journalist accounts or Galia Golan's scholarly volumes for information about its origins, course, and tragic end.

VICTOR S. MAMATEY
Department of History
University of Georgia
Athens

OTTO J. MAENCHEN-HELFEN. *The World of the Huns: Studies in their History and Culture.* Edited by Max Knight. Pp. 640. Berkeley, Calif.: University of California Press, 1973. $20.00.

The nature of the literary sources is such that the political history of the European Huns must be studied largely from the vantage point of their impact upon the Roman Empire. However, the more complex questions of Hunnic origins, geographic distribution, and social history require a far broader approach, correlating widely dispersed archaeological material from the Eurasian steppe with evidence culled from Chinese, Iranian, Altaic, Slavic, and Germanic philology. Possessed of a remarkable philological competence and a deep and sensitive knowledge of Eurasian art and archaeology, Otto Maenchen-Helfen devoted the larger part of his scholarly career to this enormous field of research. At his death in 1969, he left an unfinished manuscript of a major study of the Attilanic Huns, which is published here as essentially a collection of separate essays on various aspects of Hunnic history and civilization. A detailed political narrative, preceded by a survey of the nature of the literary evidence, is followed by a series of richly illustrated chapters treating economy, society, warfare, religion, art, race, language, and the question of proto-Huns in eastern Europe. Several questions of detail, such as religious motifs in Hunnic art, are examined in appendices, while an extensive and extremely valuable bibliography concludes the book. The author's work is supplemented by an essay on the Roman Empire at the time of the Hunnic invasion written by Paul Alexander and aimed at supplying a background for the general reader.

In fact, the reviewer would hesistate to recommend the present volume to such a reader. Like Franz Altheim's monumental *Geschichte der Hunnen*, it was conceived as a series of penetrating examinations of individual problems rather than as a work of synthesis. Thus the long chapter devoted to political history consists largely of detailed analysis of the sources and extended discussion of chronological questions. In this context, the preliminary chapter on the literary sources is too general and overemphasizes the view that Ammianus Marcellinus' portrait of the Huns is distorted by Hunnophobia. Maechen-Helfen tends to be overly polemical towards certain of his modern predecessors as well. At times, this can be misleading. In his caustic rebuttal of the opinion that the Huns did not work metal, he neglects to mention that his own view has been preceded in print by Altheim (*Geschichte der Hunnen:* I, 201).

The individual essays on aspects of Hunnic culture vary greatly. Obviously the most finished and most successful are the exhaustive examination of the evidence for the language of Huns and the chapter on warfare, which will long remain a fundamental study of the contribution of the steppe to the transformation of military tactics and equipment in the later Roman Empire. On the other hand, the treatments of Hunnic art and religion are disappointing. There is no attempt to define Hunnic art or the role of the Huns in the dispersal of nomadic animal motifs among the Germans. The entire chapter is largely a complete catalogue of Hunnic cauldrons and gold diadems. The discussion of religion gives a good account of Sarmatian cult objects but leaves the reader with no idea of the nature of Hunnic religious conceptions or even of what deities were worshipped. The examination of sacral kingship is partially vitiated by the mistaken opinion that the Persians viewed their kings as divinities and by a fundamental misunderstanding of the significance of "god" as a royal epithet in Graeco-Roman and thence Parthian and Sassanid royal ideology. Maenchen-Helfen's treatment of the ethnic composition of the Huns is a valuable summary of recent eastern European palaeoanthropological research; but the reader looks in vain for a clear statement of the historically important controversy over the identity of the Huns with the Hsiung-Nu of the Chinese sources.

Despite its uneven quality, *The World of the Huns* is a major contribution to Hunnic studies and to later Roman history in general. Nonetheless, E. A. Thompson's *A History of Attila and the Huns* remains the book to recommend to the beginner, while the advanced student will commence his work with Altheim's controversial, but always stimulating, *Geschichte der Hunnen*.

J. RUFUS FEARS
Department of History
Indiana University
Bloomington

WILLIAM E. ODOM. *The Soviet Volunteers: Modernization and Bureaucracy in a Public Mass Organization.* Pp. ix, 360. Princeton, N.J.: Princeton University Press, 1973. $14.50.

The Society of Friends of Defense and Aviation-Chemical Construction (*Osoaviakhim*) was founded in 1927, and during the decade following became the largest mass, public, voluntary organization in the U.S.S.R. Odom's case study of Soviet civilian defense deals with *Osoaviakhim's* goals, organization, processes and growth. His treatment is conducted in full view of conceptual tools, facts and generalizations about bureaucratic organizations in general, problems of modernization in less-developed countries, and, of course, Soviet history of the 1920s and 1930s. The book is important for the light it throws upon this type of organization and for the implications of *Osoaviakhim's* formation and performance for the mobilization of populations in other developing societies.

The role envisaged for *Osoaviakhim* by the Soviet leaders originated in general Bolshevik doctrines about organizing the masses, integrating the military with civil society, struggling against cultural, especially technological, backwardness in the population, and in their concern within a hostile capitalist environment to provide elementary military training to large portions of the population without having to withdraw them from the labor force. Specific, publicly-recognized goals for the organization were: (1) tap otherwise unavailable resources of labor, materials, and money; (2) provide training in military technology, especially that linked with chemicals and aviation; (3) create an organization and attitudes that would, by encouraging widespread participation, make large masses of the population "administratively accessible"; and (4) enlist the *Osoaviakhim* membership's assistance in raising the general awareness of the probable character of future war and military technology. An additional pair of "factional" goals were: (5) the Soviet military's desire to control certain industries and gain access for its manpower needs to the Soviet population; (6) the aim of Stalin's faction among the party leaders to diffuse and restrict the military's control over these resources. In 1935 a secret decree from Stalin restated *Osoaviakhim's* goals, restricting its concern largely to more direct adaptation of civilian skills and resources to military use.

Among the specific activities of *Osoaviakhim* units were study circles, corners (for display of equipment and charts), small-bore ranges, training teams and detachments, clubs (for aviation and marksmanship), schools (for flying, parachuting, gliding), paramilitary formations, camps (for advanced training and recreation), laboratories and experimental plots (to show the advantages of chemical fertilizers and other things), and profit-oriented enterprises (a publishing house, a national lottery, crop dusting and pest control by plane).

As in all Soviet organizations, policy formation and control were in the hands of the party, which faced the difficult task of inducing, without any substantial reward, the individual Soviet citizen to give up his scarce income and leisure to defense activities. Disinterest and neglect at the higher levels of cadre control, and apathy, dissimulation, and "paper membership" at lower levels (13,000,000 reported members in 1935, perhaps half of which were illusory) were perennial problems. In characteristic Soviet fashion, excessive demands from the center met with evasion, misappropriation, the forming of "family groups," and other manifestations of "localism" at the peripheries of the system. Notwithstanding these rough edges—interpreted in terms of the outcome of struggles between different levels of power—it is Odom's judgement that *Osoviakhim* had considerable success in reaching intended goals.

The book is a work of informed and creative scholarship showing impressive command of the Soviet scene and displaying sophistication in assessing the relevance of the observed facts to general theoretical models in contemporary social science. Chapters fifteen and sixteen, on the operation of power relations inside and through this bureaucratic organization, are especially rewarding. In them Odom describes the specifically Soviet form of bureaucratic vicious circles, documenting his conclusion that there have been a lot of politics in *Osoaviakhim*.

H. KENT GEIGER
Department of Sociology
University of Wisconsin
Madison

FREDERIC SPOTTS. *The Churches and Politics in Germany*. Pp. ix, 419. Middletown, Conn.: Wesleyan University Press, 1973. $15.00.

It is quite a surprise to see that the first comprehensive monograph on the relationship between religious and political institutions in modern West Germany has been written by a young foreign-service officer of the United States Department of State. Mr. Spotts' first book is a masterpiece of incisive analysis and lucid writing style. This in itself is not so special. What makes Mr. Spotts' achievement so extraordinary is the complexity and the very contemporary nature of his subject matter.

In the major thesis of his book, Frederic Spotts contends that, since the Protestant and Catholic churches were the only major German institutions to survive the holocaust of Hitler's Third Reich relatively intact, they played a very major role in the reconstruction of West German political democracy. The churches were able to utilize their great traditional social prestige and political influence in the political vacuum created by the collapse of the Third Reich to help mold political attitudes and institutions in modern West Germany. In so doing, they were, in the long run, Mr. Spotts contends, only undermining their political influence. The new spirit of pragmatism, cooperation, and reconciliation, which so greatly characterized German political and religious institutions, not only

created positive roots for the only lasting period of liberal democratic government in German history, but also brought forth in its wake the increasing secularization of German thought and institutions. Thus, it was only natural that, in time, the purely confessional aspect in German political and social life, especially among West German Catholics, would have to diminish to a very great extent. This, in Mr. Spotts' view, was indeed a very favorable development. It was a very pleasant change from the churches' negative stance against political democracy and their unrelieved emphasis on confessional politics throughout the entire earlier period of German history.

Spotts' book presents a very positive view of modern German political and religious institutions, and he is very optimistic about the future of political democracy in West Germany. His book will no doubt become a seminal work in modern German historiography.

DR. JOHN S. WOZNIAK
Dunkirk
New York

WALTER STRUVE. *Elites against Democracy: Leadership Ideals in Bourgeois Political Thought in Germany, 1890–1933*. Pp. 486. Princeton, N.J.: Princeton University Press, 1973. $20.00. Paperbound, $9.75.

As the title indicates, Mr. Struve's volume concerns itself with the problem of elites versus democracy in German political thought from the fall of Bismarck to the rise of Hitler. The introductory chapter, which traces the development of an "open—yet authoritarian—elite" from the beginning of the nineteenth century, is weak, and depends almost entirely upon secondary works. The names of the brothers Gerlach, Stahl, and others are not even mentioned. The same is true of the following chapter, entitled "Intellectual Traditions." What Mr. Struve has to say about Nietzsche or the circle of Stefan George is lacking both in depth and comprehension.

The second part of the work is devoted to the right-wing elitists. The pages on Spengler, Edgar Jung, and Hans Zehrer are adequate and discerning. Obviously, the idea of elitist leadership had a greater appeal to the neo-conservatives; hence, their writings disseminated the ideology through wide sections of the bourgeoisie and the landed gentry. But here too we encounter an unbalanced picture. Count Hermann Keyserling is given a full chapter, whereas Heinrich von Gleichen and Max H. Boehm are not even mentioned. Of the neo-conservative journals, only *Die Tat* receives full treatment, while *Der Ring* and *Das Hochland* are neglected.

Obviously, elitism reached its most efficient performance in the German army, and I am in agreement with what Mr. Struve has to say on this subject (pp. 378–380). But surely he should have emphasized the fact that the elitism of the army was far more decisive in shaping the destiny of Germany than the philosophical bubbles of Spengler, Jung, Jünger, and Zehrer.

The final chapters of the book are entitled "The Sources of National Socialist Elitism," and it is here that I find myself in serious disagreement with Mr. Struve's study. It seems far fetched to point to an affinity between Nazi elitism and liberal elitism. Space forbids a discussion of this proposed parallel, but its incongruity should be obvious. That the Nazi party permeated all levels of society is certain; there was a black sheep in every family, as the saying went during the days of the Third Reich. Moreover, it is misleading to state that the Nazi party could lay claim to "the principle of an open elite." In the first place, the application of the premise of racial purity excluded millions from belonging not only to the open elite but also from mere citizenship. The example of Milch, quoted by Mr. Struve, was an exception that did not invalidate the devastating effect of racial anti-semitism. In the second place, one cannot overlook the favorable consideration given to the early members of the Nazi party, Hitler's old cronies, the so-called *Alte Kämpfer.*

Finally we come to the rigorously applied practice of the *Gleichschaltung* (synchronization) by means of which all organization, from the university to the city blocks, was under the leadership and supervision of a dedicated party member. The gestures toward the establishment of a socialist façade were limited to such offerings as the *Kraft-durch-Freude* vacation trips, the one-plate Sunday dinners, and the *Winterhilfe* — palliative measures which had no effect on the social structure. For the rest, if there was socialism, it was a socialism produced by terror, whereby all members of the community were equally alarmed. I am unable to agree with Mr. Ralf Dahrendorf's conclusion, shared by Mr. Struve, that the National Socialist movement produced an unintended but inevitable social revolution. It was Germany's military defeat that produced this revolution by annihilating the aristocratic East-Elbian ruling class, by destroying old fortunes and creating new ones. The figure of Willy Brandt could never have risen to the top in pre-1933 Germany, nor would a woman have been elected president of the parliament. Such changing attitudes are a result of the disillusionment with nationalism and imperialism which took root among the German youth after 1945. Finally, I have serious doubts about the way in which Mr. Struve uses his source material in this chapter. He alternates between Hitler's public speeches and his private conversations with Rauschnigg or his table companions. But we know that Hitler's public utterances are not to be taken at their face value. For the Führer, lying was a way of life. Campaign promises were only conjuror's tricks to mesmerize his audiencies, and were carefully attuned to their hopes and their fears. Here he succeeded all too well, but the historian must not be taken in by Hitler's speeches. His articles of faith might have been enumerated as a belief in racial imperialism, and an implicit trust in his own infallibility. When, in the end, these were proved to be false assumptions, he refused to relinquish them, maintaining that the German people were not equal to his greatness.

In spite of so many and so fundamental reservations, I should judge that Mr. Struve's book may fill a gap in our literature on Germany. Its value lies in the spadework he has undertaken and in the very valuable hints included in his footnotes.

GERHARD MASUR
Sweet Briar College
Virginia

GILLIAN SUTHERLAND. *Policy-making in Elementary Education, 1870–1895.* Pp. 370. London: Oxford University Press, 1973. $21.00.

In the 1870s and 1880s English elementary education presented a ridiculous spectacle of warring factions, principles, ideas, and devices. At the head stood an education department which was not a department but a Committee of the Privy Council, operating through a staff of inspectors (HMIs) who, to a great extent, did not inspect; of examiners who did most of the work; and clerks who, being definitely of a lower class, did the drudgery. Some schools, set up by local boards under the act of 1870, were supported by local taxes (rates), fees from parents, and subsidies (grants-in-aid) from the central government. Rival schools—voluntary schools—were maintained by religious denominations, mainly Anglican, supported by their own subscriptions, but also by grants-in-aid and by fees from parents. In some places no board schools existed; in others, both kinds. In some places schools were operated by other authorities under child labor laws, the children attending part time in order to earn the right to work part time.

Throughout, the denominational schools stonewalled against the expanding boards schools. Hampered by bureaucrats and by a "conscience clause" which permitted parents to withdraw their children during religious instruction, they could not easily compete. Their attitude was typically upper-class, a fear that the masses might get too much education. Lord Norton expressed this idea when he protested against the "education of children *out of* rather than *in* the station in which each of them happens to be born." The more political last third of the book shows this philosophy in action.

Gillian Sutherland has courageously hewn a path through these complexities. It clearly appears that progress came largely through cautious and partial bureaucratic pressures, little by little. Parliament produced no substantial reforms after 1870 but only grudging bits and pieces which, however, added up—in the end—to a large measure of free and compulsory schooling. In fact, the whole story is one of an incredible amount of tinkering, bureaucratic and political. The author moves about with assurance and discrimination through a wide range of official and personal sources. It is a worthy achievement to have kept such a difficult subject under firm control without sacrificing the reader's interest.

CHESTER H. KIRBY
Brown University
Providence
Rhode Island

ANTONY C. SUTTON. *Western Technology and Soviet Economic Development, 1945–1965.* Pp. ix, 482. Stanford, Calif.: Hoover Institution Press, 1973. $15.00.

Just when Congress is presented with the financial quid pro quo of détente with the Soviet Union, Antony C. Sutton's third volume has made a timely appearance. His extensive documentation of Soviet dependency upon Western technology represents a major scholarly contribution, one meriting the attention of both Soviet specialists and Western policy-makers. As in previous volumes, Sutton demonstrates the pervasive role of Western prototypes and technical assistance in the postwar development of Soviet technology. Those few cases of indigenous innovation in the USSR have typically been "scaling-up" operations where a "classic" Western technology is mastered and then raised to an unprecedented scale of production. Furthermore, Sutton's evidence lends considerable weight to the arguments of Western specialists that this lack of technological dynamism is a direct consequence of Soviet economic institutions.

In considering the merits of this book, however, one must distinguish between its demonstration of Soviet borrowing and the conclusions that Sutton draws from such evidence. He claims to have substantiated the hypothesis that " . . . by far the most significant factor in the development of the Soviet economy has been its absorption of Western technology and skills. . . . " Unfortunately, verification is always more difficult than enumeration, and Sutton's intuition is hard to reconcile with econometric studies suggesting the minimal contribution of technical progress to Soviet economic growth. Certainly, one should be skeptical of Sutton's conclusion that, denied access to Western technology, Soviet growth would cease.

The book's major flaw is its policy conclusion that the West should deny the Soviet Union its present access to modern technology. The merits of such a policy are doubtful since the author probably exaggerates the costs to the Soviet Union and clearly ignores blockade costs for the West. Since Western technology has become international through specialization and the multinational corporation, the denial of Soviet access would necessarily be a collective decision of Western nations. To preclude indirect transfers, an effective technology blockade would have to exclude "strategic" trade with Eastern Europe and perhaps the Third World. Many policy-makers would regard those political costs as prohibitive. Even assuming the political feasibility, there are economic costs to consider. Restrictions on the free exchange and sale of information would inhibit technological dynamism in the West as well. If Western technology is as valuable to the USSR as Sutton suggests,

then his policy would also require governmental policing of corporation activities since one can imagine the proliferation of illicit transactions in prototypes and information. Finally, Sutton's own analysis indicates that the USSR is doomed to technological backwardness and will never attain Western levels of productivity and economic power. Why then should the West impose a technology blockade for such doubtful benefits? If socialism would always need to maintain a small corner of capitalism in order to learn "correct prices," then that corner would be even more necessary to develop "tomorrow's technology."

DONALD W. GREEN
University of Pennsylvania
Philadelphia

UNITED STATES HISTORY AND POLITICS

JOHN J. BROESAMLE. *William Gibbs McAdoo. A Passion for Change: 1863–1917.* Pp. xii, 304. Port Washington, N.Y.: Kennikat, 1973. $15.00.

Colorful and controversial, the career of William Gibbs McAdoo offers unique opportunites for examining the complexity of Wilsonian progressivism. Although McAdoo was raised in antebellum Georgia, a member of a distinguished family declassed by war, his personal ambition allowed little time for lost causes. After attending the University of Tennessee, he began an Alger-like climb in business that gained him a reputation as one of New York's leading business promoters and, with his marriage to young Eleanor Wilson in 1914, even won him the boss's daughter (this union, Broesamle writes, brought him closer to President Wilson but did not endow him with the omnipotence many imagined). After managing Wilson's first campaign, McAdoo served as Secretary of the Treasury from 1913 through 1918. Despite an impressive record in the cabinet, McAdoo—like Alexander Hamilton before him—failed finally to achieve the presidency. But in seeking the nomination in 1924, he continued to play a central role in Democratic Party politics.

In this carefully researched study of a portion of this career, John Broesamle judiciously assesses McAdoo's contribution to Wilson's cause. Following two brief chapters on McAdoo's youth and business career, the author devotes the bulk of his narrative to the legislative and policy issues that consumed the Treasury Secretary's prodigious energies: the Federal Reserve Act, agricultural credit, Pan American trade, and the shipping crisis at the outbreak of World War I. While praising McAdoo's solid record, Broesamle is not uncritical. McAdoo, for example, "seriously overrated" the Farm Loan Act of 1916. Nor does he claim too much for his influence in shaping legislation. On several controversial points he notes that available evidence allows no solid conclusions: concerning the roots of McAdoo's fear that Wilson might prove too friendly to Negroes; or the motives behind McAdoo's abortive proposal for a highly centralized and ostensible conservative National Reserve System with headquarters at the Treasury Department.

Although Broesamle provides useful new information, if no significant revision, his study has several shortcomings. Originally a doctoral dissertation, it retains some less happy features of the genre: a flat and sometimes wooden style; an often mechanical inclusion of half-digested quotations from the writings of McAdoo and others; and a greater attention to details than to their broader implications. Listless as biography, it conveys less of its subject's motives and personality than McAdoo's *Crowded Years* (1931), an autobiography covering the same period. In stopping in 1917 (with no second volume promised), Broesamle omits not only McAdoo's later presidential bid but also such war-related issues within the period as loans to belligerent nations, Bryan's resignation, and the campaign of 1916. If thus not the "complete assessment" nor the "definitive" study

claimed on dust jacket blurbs, this scholarly study nonetheless provides a well-balanced look at an important facet of policy-making in the Wilson era.

ROBERT C. BANNISTER
Department of History
Swarthmore College
Swarthmore
Pennsylvania

PETER GRAHAM FISH. *The Politics of Federal Judicial Administration.* Pp. xi, 528. Princeton, N.J.: Princeton University Press, 1973. $20.00. Paperbound, $9.75.

The district courts, the backbone of the federal judiciary, have often been neglected in the more general concern over constitutional and legal issues decided at a higher level. The lower courts not only play an important work-horse role; at times they say the first word and often the last word concerning the law.

Originally, the district courts were not so much parts of a whole as separate isolated, independent, decentralized and individualistic entities. The district judges "became lions on their relatively remote thrones." A need arose to centralize and uniformize the administrative side of the judiciary, to establish agencies for house-keeping, statistics, budget, and personnel standards. The layman might suppose that the administration of the federal courts is an automatic and self-executing process. From Professor Fish we learn that the federal judiciary, like the academic and ecclesiastic worlds, has by no means been immmune to the proliferation of institutions and organizations so vital to the American way of life. What is amazing is how anyone can get any serious work done with so much organizational activity going on.

This book is a study of the administrative system of the federal judiciary and treats in detail the birth of the Judicial Conference (1922), the Administrative Office Act of 1939, the Federal Judicial Center, the circuit conferences and the circuit councils, as well as the judiciary's relations with Congress, cooperation between bench and bar and judicial lobbying.

The result is a well written, well researched doctoral dissertation, of interest principally to administrative scientists and members of the judicial and quasi-judicial professions. It is difficult to conceive that this thorough examination of the broom closets of Mount Olympus—the unglamorous side of judicial existence—has left any stone unturned.

At times one wonders what is the problem or the issue. More detailed case studies representing the various forms which conflicts have taken would have given more meat to a generally abstract treatment. There is also room for greater coverage of such problems as ethical standards and procedures for removal, mentioned only in passing, or of more substantive questions such as proposals for a National Court of Appeals, problems of jurisdiction, and federal-state court relationships. Finally, the book assumes on the part of the reader a passionate interest in the details of administrative organization in general more than any particular concern for the judiciary as such.

DAVID M. BILLIKOPF
New Canaan
Connecticut

PAUL W. GATES. *Landlords and Tenants on the Prairie Frontier: Studies in American Land Policy.* Pp. v, 333. Ithaca, N.Y.: Cornell University Press, 1973. $12.50.

For over thirty-five years, Paul Wallace Gates of Cornell University has produced a steady stream of articles and books on the public land policies of the United States. With only minor exceptions, his publications are based on original research in such sources as the voluminous manuscript records of the General Land Office in the National Archives, the unpublished records of railroads and private land companies, local land records, and manuscript collections relating to settlers, speculators, debtors and creditors. Besides his own

prodigious research, Professor Gates has had a number of billiant students who have explored various aspects of public land history.

Landlords and Tenants on the Prairie Frontier consists of nine articles published in 1939 to 1962 in various learned journals and are "offered here in the hope of providing a better understanding of the functioning of our national land system in the prairie states prior to the adoption of the Homestead Act." Professor Gates explains further that "The essays originally designed to focus on a particular facet of the subject have been revised somewhat to make them more up to date but have been permitted to remain as units . . . Following each essay is a bibliographical note indicating the important studies that have appeared since the essays were first published" (p. vi).

A general theme running throughout the essays is the question of the extent to which the legislation of the federal government accomplished the objects which the framers of the legislation intended. Under the federal system, over 2,000,000 farms were created in the public land states by 1880, of which seventy-six percent were owner-operated. While conceding that such an operation may be considered an overall success, he nevertheless maintains that the system was characterized by considerable malfunction.

One of the principal sources of malfunction was the role played by speculators and land companies. Although he points out that the speculators and land companies provided credit and promotional activities not otherwise available, Professor Gates believes there are definite connections between these activities and tenancy. "I have placed the emphasis upon the difficulties met by actual settlers in gaining ownership of public land; my concern has been to examine the intent of the framers of the laws as shown by their public utterances and their private actions—which were sometimes at variance with each other—to determine whether the legislation was carried out as intended and to determine the effect of the legislation and the administrative interpretations on the development of the West" (p. 9).

Professor Gates carries out his stated purposes admirably. Although his works are known to specialists, they deserve an even wider audience, and it is certainly to be hoped that the reprinting of these essays will achieve better dissemination. The Cornell University Press is to be congratulated not only for producing a volume of significant content, but also a book esthetically pleasing to the eye. *Landlords and Tenants* is a welcome addition to the literature on the public domain.

HARRY L. COLES
The Ohio State University
Columbus

KATHRYN GRIFFITH. *Judge Learned Hand and the Role of the Federal Judiciary.* Pp. vii, 251. Norman: University of Oklahoma Press, 1973. $8.95.

The title of this book does not convey its broad focus. Professor Griffith examines the influences on Learned Hand, analyzes some various strands in his judiciary philosophy and practice, and finally comes to an understanding about Hand's place in American political thought. It is an ambitious task, and the fact that the author does not entirely succeed on all points by no means vitiates the worth of the book.

Griffith is at her best in setting forth Hand's jurisprudence. The heart of the book explicates Hand's views on the role of judges in the American system, his arguments for judicial self-restraint, and the unusual interpretation that Hand gave to the Bill of Rights. His theory of statutory interpretation is also considered. Griffith relies quite heavily on standard commentaries by such scholars as Pritchett, McCloskey, Jerome Frank, and Judge Charles Wyzanski, but she also follows Hand through several lines of cases in such areas as freedom of speech and obscenity rulings. The author has done a good job in analyzing Hand's conception of the role of the judge and his arguments for judicial self-restraint. Griffith feels that Hand was very much influenced by American pragmatism, as well as by such earlier commentators as James Bradley Thayer, and the relevance of these influences is clearly established. Griffith also takes care to present the arguments of Hand's critics, though it is clear that she is sympathetic to many of his positions.

This book is much less satisfactory as an attempt to place Hand's legal thought in its broader context. In particular, the chapters on "the world of Learned Hand" would benefit greatly from the use of primary manuscript sources. I believe Hand's papers are still restricted while an authorized biography is written, but there are letters available in other collections which would give the reader a better feel for the private man. Hand's personal elitism, as opposed to his public endorsement of democracy, could thereby be made more explicit. Hand's social background and his political contacts and friendships with Theodore Roosevelt Progressives would also be revealing territory for a wider study than this.

In summary, this is a useful treatment of a very important and influential figure in American law. The book needs to be supplemented by more detailed studies, particularly of the private man.

EDWARD A. STETTNER
Department of Political Science
Wellesley College
Wellesley
Massachusetts

ALENZE L. HAMBY. *Beyond the New Deal: Harry S. Truman and American Liberalism.* Pp. viii, 635. New York: Columbia University Press, 1973. $12.95.

This book is a worthy addition to the excellent Columbia University *Contemporary American History Series*, edited by William E. Leuchtenberg. Mr. Hamby, at the time of writing an associate professor of history at Ohio

University, has given us a fascinating study of Harry Truman and his administration. In twenty-three chapters, many with fetching titles, Mr. Hamby examines in detail the relationship between President Truman and the New Deal liberals—those devoted followers of Franklin Roosevelt who had a hard time accepting and trusting the leadership of one so inexperienced, so much the court-house politician, and so lacking in the FDR charisma. Although the author expressly disclaims this volume as a comprehensive history of the Truman era, it seems to this reviewer to be almost that, for no important episodes are omitted, though treated always in their relation to the problem of liberalism—that is, the Cold War; Henry Wallace, the Wallace Progressive Party, and the Communists; McCarthyism; the Marshall Plan; the United Nations and Korea; the Truman Doctrine; civil rights; and all the others.

The special attention to liberals and liberalism requires some understanding of the meaning of these terms, and Mr. Hamby insists that "the concept of liberalism, while somewhat slippery, is hardly as unmanageable as many historians seem to assume." His introduction is an excellent essay on liberalism as it has changed with the course of history. It "has not been a set of programs but rather a persuasion built around a belief in human reason and dignity. Through the centuries, liberals have shared a commitment to freedom, equal justice, and equal opportunity. . . . Liberals have always distrusted power and privilege, have usually felt an emotional sympathy for the exploited and underprivileged, and have believed that enlightened social or economic policies can rehabilitate even the lowest elements of society" (p. xiii). He points out how that concept has been applied or redefined with changing developments, from the nineteenth century concept of "a powerful, activist state affirmatively promoting the welfare of its citizens," to a struggle against political bosses and

"an effort to curb the power of giant corporations," to the New Deal's reform legislation, political coalition, and dependence upon strong presidential leadership. "Twentieth-century liberalism required a president with the charisma to dramatize and virtually embody the cause of reform, a political leader who could mobilize a progressive coalition with the sheer force of his personality."

How the liberals and Harry Truman adjusted to one another is the main theme of the book, an adjustment or understanding that came about largely through the development of the *Vital Center* (Part II, twelve chapters, deals with this development). This meant that American liberalism, which Hitler had persuaded to consider fascism more abhorrent than communism, now "opposed the totalitarianism of the left as completely as it did the totalitarianism of the right, . . . gave liberalism a definition more in line with its historical meaning and preserved it as an important, if not triumphant, force in American politics" (p. 505). In a sense, the adjustment of Harry Truman to this concept of the *Vital Center* came quite naturally and easily. "He was a party man whose career reflected the course of the mainstream of the Democratic Party in the twentieth century. . . . His views changed accordingly, not because of simple political cynicism, but from a broadening of contacts and perspectives which, combined with the political pressures of the underprivileged and with his own sense of fairness and decency, impelled him towards liberalism" (p. 508). And so Truman and the liberals got together. "Thrown into partnership by a whim of history, Truman and the liberals coexisted uneasily but in a manner which reinforced each other's tendency toward increasingly advanced progressivism" (p. 515).

The book is a balanced, objective account of the Truman era; it has all the paraphernalia of sound scholarship—sixty-eight pages of notes, a bibliography of seven pages, and an index of twenty-eight pages—and it is written in such good English that it is a pleasure to read.

CLARENCE A. BERDAHL
Professor of Political Science,
Emeritus
University of Illinois
Urbana-Champaign

LOUIS HARRIS. *The Anguish of Change.* Pp. ix, 306. New York: W. W. Norton, 1973. $7.50.

With the election of John Kennedy in 1960, many of us hoped that the United States was entering an era of political change—one of progressive leadership. This hope was nourished somewhat by President Johnson's successes in the domestic fields of civil rights and poverty in 1964 and 1965. Then came Vietnam, domestic violence, inflation, slowing of the civil rights movement and the election of Richard Nixon in 1968. Nixon's election was widely interpreted as a conservative shift by the electorate. Indeed, Scammon and Wattenberg in *The Real Majority*, published as an analysis of the 1968 election, described the electorate as nonyoung, non-black, non-poor, non-urban and generally middle-of-the-road minded. By their analysis, the bulk of American voters are distinctly status quo oriented, and not likely to vote for presidential candidates who are openly sympathetic to blacks, the poor, the young and other groups they see as marginal in our society. They warn us clearly that the electorate would not tolerate avowedly liberal candidates and programs. In *The Anguish of Change* (a somewhat dramatic title) Louis Harris relies on data gathered by his polling organization during the sixties and early seventies. He tells us that American politics is changing and that the forces of change are within the electorate. It is his contention that the principal reason we have failed to make many of the needed adjustments in the policies of both public and private institutions is that the leaders of those institutions have failed to perceive the need for innovative leadership. Harris tells us that during a time of rapid accomplishment, Americans have lost

faith in their public and private institutions and the leaders of these institutions. He suggests that these leaders have failed to grasp the need for change. They have not realized that there is a substantial segment of the American public that will support leaders who have the courage and foresight to lead them in the direction of constructive change.

Harris detects potential support for change in two areas of American life. First, he finds that there are particular segments of the population who are more favorably disposed to support change. These are the young, college educated, prosperous middle class people. Others which he finds particularly susceptible to change are women, blacks and the young who have not yet entered the economic mainstream. In general he found these groups to be more ready than other elements of the population to support programs of peaceful coexistence with the Soviet Union and China, racial equality, assistance to the poor, and environmental controls. Two groups which we have come to regard as more conservative—union members and non-college youth—Harris sees as much less conservative and more amenable to change than we have thought in recent years.

The second major area in which he detects potential support for change is distinguished not by social group, but rather by issue identification. He thinks that there is support for change which cuts across group lines in a number of issue areas. Lower income people who generally tend to be older and more status quo oriented are more concerned with better health care programs than with just raising their incomes. People in all social categories are disturbed by increasing violence and they want more security, but not necessarily at the price of repressive police practices which diminish their freedoms.

In short, Harris thinks that Scammon and Wattenberg are wrong. He sees potential support for change in American life and politics if innovative leaders apply steady, educative pressure for constructive change.

The book is well written, with several interesting sidelights concerning events in which Harris was personally involved with each of the last three administrations. Criticisms of the work have to be considered marginal. Social scientists might well wish for slightly more sophisticated statistical analysis. Comparisons of raw percentages leave one wondering what differences there may have been in the question asked in 1966 as compared with those asked on a similar subject in 1972. However, the time spread and the variations in questions clearly obviate correlation or regression analysis, or whatever.

Nor is the age factor made entirely clear. When Harris refers to "youth" and "the young" we are never quite sure whether he means people under fifty years of age, or just those thirty or under. He seems to slide back and forth across age category lines in several instances. Early in the book when he identifies the conservative poor, he rather glibly assumes a congruence between those over fifty years of age and people who have incomes of less than $5000 per year. This is a tricky assumption, since obviously there are many people over fifty who earn more than $5000 per year and who are conservative.

All in all, this book is well worth the reading—for both the layman and the social scientists. Yes, perhaps even for the practicing politician.

CHARLES P. ELLIOTT
East Texas State University
Commerce

LARRY E. IVERS. *British Drums on the Southern Frontier.* Pp. xiv, 274. Chapel Hill, N.C.: University of North Carolina Press, 1974. $12.50.

As its subtitle indicates, this work is a detailed study of the military aspects of colonization in Georgia's formative years, 1733 to 1749. Written by a Vietnam veteran who utilizes his own experiences in military life to good advantage, the study is earmarked by both the strengths and weaknesses which characterized the author's earlier book, *Colonial Forts of South Carolina, 1670–1775.* There is ample evidence of careful research in both manuscript and printed sources, although the author occasionally fails to cast an adequately critical eye on the reliability of his materials. Likewise, the book is strengthened by Ivers' appreciation of military life on the frontier, and his grasp of the intricate details of garrison life, skirmish tactics, and the like.

James Oglethorpe is obviously the central figure of the narrative, and his abilities and complex personality figure largely in the ongoing deterioration of Anglo-Spanish relations following Britain's occupation of the disputed territory between South Carolina and Florida in 1733. The years between this initial British thrust and the outbreak of the War of Jenkins' Ear in 1739 were marked by Oglethorpe's efforts to consolidate his position in Georgia through establishment of strategically placed settlements and attempted encroachments on South Carolina's trade relations with the Indian tribes of the region. Once war came, Oglethorpe, despite traits such as impulsiveness which detracted from his ability as a military leader, proved his mettle by repulsing Spanish attempts to overrun Georgia. He returned to Britain shortly afterwards, but his courage and energy had laid the groundwork for Georgia's transition from an outpost of military settlement to full-fledged colonial status.

The essentials of these developments are covered in a fashion which leaves little room for criticism of the work as a factual account. Nonetheless, a number of factors detract from the study and result in its falling far short of its potential. Ivers' writing style is marked by turgidity, redundancy, and awkward or nonexistent transitions. His interpretations do not dovetail with the narrative as they should, and at places he shows a propensity to force his story when information is lacking. The proofreading is atrocious. Misspelled words, beginning with "implimentation" for implementation on the third line of the preface, greet the reader at every turn, and the book contains more than an acceptable leaven of grammatical errors as well. It is intolerable that a reputable university press and an author should permit so many mistakes to pass the proof stage unnoticed. There is the raw material of sound scholarship here, and there is no denying the book's contribution to the literature of colonial history, but ordinary care and more careful revision of the manuscript prior to publication might have made this a considerably stronger monograph than it is.

JAMES A. CASADA
Department of History
Winthrop College
Rock Hill
South Carolina

DOUGLAS EDWARD LEACH. *Arms for Empire: A Military History of the British Colonies in North America, 1607–1763.* Pp. xiii, 566. New York: The Macmillan Company, 1973. $14.95.

In *Arms for Empire*, Douglas Edward Leach narrates the military history of Anglo-America from the founding of Jamestown to the end of Pontiac's Rebellion. This is the story of how the various English colonies defended themselves against Indians, French, and Spanish. During the early years of settlement, the colonists adopted the militia system which they had known in England. Every adult male was required to attend periodic trainings and acquire some familiarity with the use of firearms. The militia system served as a defense system for direct attacks on settlements and provided the manpower pool out of which expeditionary forces were drawn.

In 1689 began the series of intercolonial wars between the French and the English, with the occasional participation of the Spanish, which disrupted the New World colonies. The French and the Spanish in North America were actually too weak to pose a serious threat to the existence of the English colonies, and the English were too disorganized to dispatch a successful offensive which could have eliminated either of their opponents. Consequently, these wars were mainly a series of raids and counter-raids on frontier settlements and posts.

During the 1740s, the English government finally attempted to direct the American war effort, but poor coordination, communications, and leadership yielded no permanent results. Finally, in the 1750s, William Pitt (the Elder) provided English troops, ships, money, and leadership which eventually defeated the French and reduced the Spanish threat to English North America.

Besides a detailed narrative of battles and campaigns, Professor Leach has contributed a brief but searching analysis of the impact of war on the English colonies. Leach shows the disruptive effects of war on the colonial economy, the constant fear of Indian raids on the frontier, and the changes in the political system which the war effort produced. In addition, the author discusses important topics often neglected in surveys of the colonial wars—conscription, prisoners, conscientious objection, veterans affairs, and civil-military relations. In the concluding chapter, the author summarizes the impact of the colonial conflicts and points to them as a major contributory factor in the coming of the American Revolution.

Although specialists may quarrel over certain aspects—the lack of analysis of the socio-political composition of the colonial soldiery or the superficial treatment of Indian-white relations—most scholars will agree that Professor Leach's impressive scholarship provides excellent coverage of a vast subject while suggesting topics requiring further investigation. The general reader will be delighted by an entertaining narrative which provides a solid introduction to the military history of colonial America.

RANZ C. ESBENSHADE
Department of History
University of New Hampshire
Durham

ALISON GILBERT OLSON. *Anglo-American Politics, 1660–1775: The Relationship Between Parties in Eng-*

land and Colonial America. Pp. vi, 192. New York: Oxford University Press, 1973. $7.50.

The author has undertaken the task of relating the role of political factions in mainland colonial America to that of their counterparts in England during most of the colonial period. She advances, however, a "suggestive essay" (p. xi) rather than a Namier-type study.

Olson proposes that Anglo-American politics passed through four important stages. In the first one, to the 1670s, the English government and groups in opposition to it for the most part left the colonies alone. The 1670s reversed this trend. Governmental attempts to reform colonial administration worked to shore up dissident groups in America, hitherto legally powerless to promote change and worked against colonial governors. "To tighten the colonial ties with England would be popular; to appoint enemies of the local governors to office would be the beginning of a popular, pro-English administration" (p. 68).

During the third period, from William and Mary to Walpole's rise to power, party struggle in America became a matter of "spoils and interests rather than tenaciously held beliefs" (p. 76). Various colonial groups maneuvered for imperial favors among the English parties, who would help the colonists in local affairs. In the process, the American groups tended to identify with either the Whigs or Tories in England.

This relationship broke up in the fourth period, from the 1730s to the Revolution. Bolingbroke and Pulteney, who led the opposition to Walpole in the 1720s, partially cooperated with opposition groups in the colonies. But when the Bolingbroke group thought to humble Walpole by working with lesser London merchants, it lost colonial rapport. The merchants, hostile to their colonial counterparts, made transatlantic cooperation impossible.

From the 1730s on, the English opposition used colonial issues purely for domestic political gain. The colonists in

reaction went their own way. Despite Chatham's and Rockingham's seemingly "pro-American" stance in the heated 1760s, their tactics "elicited a cynical sneer from some colonial politicians, and profound doubts about the British party system from others." Unfortunately, "the informal partisan associations so essential to empire were dead" (p. 181).

The above summary, because of space limitations, barely sketches the book's thesis, and omits many of the author's thoughtful and provocative suggestions. Specialists will undoubtedly find faults in such a general work, but they should remember that the author intended only to advance possibilities. She has advanced many in a bold endeavor to forge into a cohesive whole the complex and seemingly incohesive pattern of Anglo-American politics during the colonial period.

FRANKLIN B. WICKWIRE
University of Massachusetts
Amherst

ERNEST N. PAOLINO. *The Foundations of the American Empire: William Henry Seward and U.S. Foreign Policy.* Pp. xii, 235. Ithaca, N.Y.: Cornell University Press, 1973. $9.75.

KENNETH J. HAGAN. *American Gunboat Diplomacy and the Old Navy, 1877–1889.* Westport, Conn.: Greenwood Press, 1973. $11.50.

The first of these books is an attractively written account of Seward's views on certain aspects of foreign policy, as articulated from the 1850s and pressed forward during his term as Secretary of State. Setting his narrative in a modish procrustean framework which emphasizes the concept of "empire" as "global commercial hegemony," Paolino suggests in his title and argues in his conclusion that Seward laid the egg McKinley hatched. But between hypothesis and conclusion, research triumphs and the facts obtrude: as successive chapters deal with the international telegraph, rationalization of the international monetary system, and the problems of Alaska, the Caribbean and Panama, and the Far East, the Secretary's policy is shown to center on the expansion and protection of trade, a reasonably decent respect for the autonomy of distant countries, and equal opportunity for all (pp. 162, 179, 194). Such aims, founded on a faith in commerce as the great agent of advancing civilization, would seem to have small connection with a war to free Cuba or with Philippine annexation. Nor, indeed, were they original with Seward, dating back as they did through his mentor J. Q. Adams to the early years of the republic.

In the decades after Appomattox, the Navy, sharing this national faith, returned to its traditional function as a "police of the sea" (Paolino, p. 194n), and devoted itself to the expansion of commerce and the protection of citizens and property in the "semi-civilized" areas of the world. Within certain self-imposed limits of time and place, these activities—perhaps better described as "showing the flag" than as "gunboat diplomacy"—are well described by Kenneth Hagan. The attitudes of the officer corps are considered; the world cruise of Robert Shufeldt, probably the central figure of the period, is discussed in detail, as are operations in China and Latin America. The "coal-pile" problems posed by the coming of steam are, for once, intelligently handled. The coming of a new age is foreshadowed in the isthmian canal question, European technological advance, and the Panama intervention of 1885. To some, the omission of the Samoan imbroglio, the Korean opening, the activities of the European Squadron, and the problem of the protection of missionaries, may make the study appear a Hamlet without the Prince; at the least, Rosencrantz and Guildenstern seem to have sunk without trace. But the research is solid and has turned up much useful information, and one may hope the author will go on to investigate what went before and after the period he has dealt with here.

JAMES A. FIELD, JR.
Department of History
Swarthmore College
Pennsylvania

PAUL T. RINGENBACH. Tramps and Reformers, 1873–1916: The Discovery of Unemployment in New York. Contributions in American History, number 27. Pp. xi, 224. Westport, Conn.: Greenwood Press, 1973. $10.50.

JOHN D. BUENKER. Urban Liberalism and Progressive Reform. Pp. vii, 299. New York: Charles Scribner's Sons, 1973. $8.95.

Given the enormous quantity of published material on the nature and source of reform in the early twentieth century, it is not unfair, I think, to judge new books about this period in terms of how effectively they extend our horizons. On this basis, the two books under consideration rate mixed reviews. While both are absolutely competent within their own parameters, neither raises the exciting issues that breathe life into the study of social change.

Paul Ringenbach's Tramps and Reformers is a literate and well-researched account of how New York City's organized charities slowly altered their perceptions of the tramp. Convinced that jobs were readily available to those who were willing to work, charities groups villified and rejected tramps in the 1870s and eighties. The tramp was a scourge whose weak will and immoral self-indulgence conjured up visions of lawlessness and threats to established order. To be out of work was a crime for which the penalty was jail and a warm place to sleep at best, or whipping and a quick removal to the next town. Charity, in the form of food or money, would only encourage more tramps and was to be stringently avoided. As Ringenbach says, "the idea that men could not find work was absurd." But repeated economic depressions finally forced charities societies to recognize that unemployment was a social problem of which the tramp was only the most visible victim. After the depression of 1893, reformers began to seek ways of averting unemployment and the tramp became a less threatening figure.

Ringenbach presents a rich panorama of evidence, together with some beautiful illustrations from contemporary periodicals, and the book rewards careful reading. Awareness of the relationship between unemployment and the disintegration of the American dream filters through the material. Changing social consciousness emerges not only in the ways tramps were treated by judges and police as opposed to organized charities and housewives, but also in alterations in the meaning of the word itself. Yet the book remains, finally, an assessment of the ideas of a small group of people about a much larger group. No attempt is made to deal with the sociology of the tramp; with the exception of a brief excursion into lifestyles, Ringenbach, like the reformers, fails to distinguish job hunters from those who chose to tramp; we learn little of how tramps themselves changed over the years, or how they responded to changing public attitudes. One irrespressible question remains— were there any female tramps?

Like Ringenbach, John Buenker explores only formal relationships. In his ambitious *Urban Liberalism and Progressive Reform*, Buenker sets out to demonstrate that in seven crucial states, urban political machines—made up largely of what he calls "urban new stock" immigrants—supported liberal reform legislation. Each of four chapters on welfare legislation, economic regulation, political reform and culture follows the same pattern. Buenker begins with a brief discussion of the significance of the issues for the period; moves to an equally brief statement of

how machine politics would benefit by reform; and spends the bulk of the chapter describing specific laws, as they emerged in the state by state legislative turmoil. A final chapter attempts to justify his relatively favorable interpretation of the boss and the machine. Buenker concludes that "urban new stock lower class support for reform . . . was nationwide in scope."

I have difficulty with this conclusion for a variety of reasons. In the first place, the connection between immigrants and the machines remains as cloudy as it ever was. To argue that machine politicians supported reform legislation because they thought it would attract immigrant votes, as Buenker does, is not to prove that immigrants favored reform legislation. The link is especially tenuous here because Buenker deals largely with Irish politicians and people, to a lesser extent with Germans, rarely mentions the Italians or the Jews, and never talks about the Poles. He does not discuss the lines of communication between immigrants and bosses nor does he look at the tensions that emerged from the conflict between the immigrants' need for social change and the machine's desire to maintain its power.

Secondly, Buenker's failure to define reform adequately leads him to treat all Progressive period legislation as though it were of equal value to both machine and immigrant. Perhaps because Buenker tried to do too much, this book degenerates into little more than a chronicle of laws and bills that were or were not supported by machine politicians from a variety of states. The subtlety of political battles disappears; the influence of other pressure groups is not to be found; and the machine politician emerges as a fighter for legislation whose compromises and effects remain obscure.

Finally, Buenker's organization is faulty. Because the book is structured around categories of legislation and not around the politicians themselves, no coherent picture of any one machine and its attitudes towards a spectrum of legislation emerges. Names and dates tumble out of the pages in confusing disorder. Can anyone remember if Boston's Lomasney supported minimum wage legislation from the beginning of Chapter two to the end of Chapter five when we are told that he was instrumental in killing state aid to parochial schools? And what does the machine's antagonism to Yankee supervision of parochial schools have to do with its support for a torrent of state-supervised social welfare legislation?

The major problem here, as with Ringenbach's *Tramps and Reformers*, is that definitions of reform and reformers rest on conceptions of desirable goals. Since neither author deals critically with the goals of his protagonists, the machine remains a proponent of whatever legislation will keep it in power, and the charities society an antagonist of all laws that encourage vagrancy. Ringenbach and Buenker have contributed useful ammunition to the battle over the origins of Progressive period legislation, but the smoke-screen surrounding definitions of reforms remains intact.

ALICE KESSLER HARRIS
Hofstra University
Hempstead
New York

BERNARD SCHWARTZ. *From Confederation to Nation: The American Constitution, 1835–1877.* Pp. xi, 243. Baltimore, Md.: The Johns Hopkins University Press, 1973. $10.00.

Bernard Schwartz is a distinguished professor of law and author of an acclaimed five-volume commentary on the United States Constitution, among other works. Here he has brought his learning to bear in an apparent attempt at synthesizing constitutional development from the ascension of Chief Justice Roger B. Taney through Reconstruction. Schwartz's thesis is conveyed by his title and stated plainly in the Preface (x-xi): Before 1835 "the primary constitutional concern had been to draw the line between the authority of the nation and the power remaining to the states. . . . The Constitution which emerged from the Civil War and Reconstruction established a federal predominance which dwarfed even the doctrine of national supremacy developed by Marshall. The United States was now emphatically a nation, and not a mere confederation of states."

Schwartz's format is traditionally institutional in that he considers systematically each of the three branches of the federal government, then examines relations between them. The theme of national growth is most convincingly presented in the earlier parts of the book, where Schwartz treats the Taney Court. Schwartz has a high estimate of Taney and claims that the old Jacksonian has been generally misunderstood when presented as negative and pro states' rights. Taney's introduction of judicial restraint enhanced the Court's power, ultimately; and his "Court's articulation of the police power concept was a necessary complement to the expansion of governmental power that was an outstanding feature of the Jacksonian period" (p. 16). Schwartz regards the *Dred Scott* decision as an aberration in which the paralysis of the other two branches of government over the territorial question tempted Taney and his colleagues unwisely to abandon their characteristic judicial restraint. Within his nationalizing theme, too, Schwartz quibbles with Professor Stanley Kutler's portrait of a "judicial nadir" during Reconstruction. *Ex parte McCardle* "stands virtually alone" as a significant case in which the Court backed off from Congressional intimidation (p. 185).

Unfortunately, Schwartz's theme is not sustained. Toward the conclusion, in fact, his conventional emphasis upon the postwar decline of the Court and Presidency seems to contradict the theme. In this sense the book does not succeed as a synthesis. Specialists will find little new, although students and the "general educated public" should find it a handy survey. The research is curious: Schwartz cites his cases at law, familiar histories and biographies, and a number of interesting fugitive letters he found while browsing at New York autograph dealers; but he cites no article literature at all. The writing is generally clear and forthright. Schwartz blunders in noting that Preston Brooks beat Charles Sumner "within an inch of his life" (p. 81), but otherwise the book seems clean and factual.

JACK TEMPLE KIRBY
Miami University
Oxford
Ohio

HAROLD C. SYRETT, ed. *The Papers of Alexander Hamilton: January-July 1795; July-December 1795*. Vols. xviii and xix. New York: Columbia University Press, 1973. No price.

The two latest volumes in Harold Syrett's magnificently thorough edition are confined to the single year 1795. At the end of January, Hamilton carried out his previously announced intention of resigning as Secretary of the Treasury. After winding up his affairs he left Philadelphia and acquired a house and office in New York City, so as to resume his law practice.

As with every year in Alexander Hamilton's whirlwind life, this was a busy one in which he ran through quill pens, ink and paper at a prodigious rate. In his final weeks at the Treasury we find him dealing with a score of correspondents on matters of detail, and also compiling a long essay, theoretical and practical, on the "Public Credit." The editors point out that Hamilton's valedictory report has been neglected by historians. This is a pity, since he devoted a good deal of thought to proposals for paying off the national debt out of current sources of revenue. He has, so to speak, not been given credit, by his associates or by posterity, for a cogent and reasonable series of recommendations for American financial policy that have little connection with Ultra-Federalism.

Back in New York, he seems to have had almost no time for purely professional activities. He wrote a long defense of his old funding system. He was frequently consulted by George Washington and by his successor Oliver Wolcott. The President sought his advice on such problems as whom to appoint as Secretary of State—to replace the disgraced Edmund Randolph—and what to do about Lafayette's son, who had turned up in America with a tutor. The embarrassment for Washington was that his friend Père Lafayette, out of favor with the French revolutionary government, was in jail. Perhaps Hamilton told the President what he wished to hear. Certainly Washington depended on him. Hamilton, for example, rushed into action like a one-man vigilante team to refute a newspaper accusation that the President had been drawing more salary than he was entitled to. He challenged a Republican enemy, John Nicholson, to a duel, and put his personal affairs in order—nine years too early, as it happened: the duel was averted.

Above all, Hamilton threw himself into the controversy surrounding the commercial treaty which John Jay had concluded with Great Britain. In response to a worried plea from Washington he sent an exhaustive clause-by-clause analysis of the Jay Treaty. He followed up with a set of no less than twenty-eight essays, signed "Camillus," supporting the Treaty against its main opponents.

These forays make up the bulk of both volumes. They show Hamilton's splendid talent for legal tussling. He shared the President's view that while the Jay Treaty was not exactly a triumph for American diplomacy, failure to approve it would be disastrous. So with a parade of erudition and of courtroom techniques he presented the anti-Jay group as ignoramuses, fools and rascals. There is, however, no indication that Hamilton was merely pleading a case on behalf of an administration he had recently left. Here we see him as a sincere Federalist. In common with Washington, it is clear that he genuinely believed in the policies the government had pursued since 1789:

commercial stability, growth in trade and industry, adequate taxation, a desire to settle on moderate terms with the mother country, an assumption that the French were more unreliable than the British, and a passionate conviction that the Jeffersonian Republicans were dangerous men. For Hamilton, as for many of his contemporaries, these were alarming times. He and they smelled conspiracy, sedition, even treason in the air. But being a person of naturally combative temperament, Hamilton conveys to us a sense of his delight in verbal warfare. Consummately self-assured, he knew who were the heroes and the villains. He had already identified Senator Aaron Burr as a man to watch—and mistrust.

MARCUS CUNLIFFE
University of Sussex
England

TOM E. TERRILL. *The Tariff, Politics, and American Foreign Policy: 1874–1901.* Pp. ix, 306. Westport, Conn.: Greenwood Press, 1973. $12.00.

This book focuses on the struggles over the tariff in the Gilded Age, 1874–1901, when old issues were no longer effective, and when the two political parties competed on almost equal terms for public support.

During the 1800s both parties, seeking to widen their coalition, decided that an expansion of foreign trade was vital to the national economy. How was the expansion to be accomplished? Perhaps the tariff would provide an answer. The struggle continued until the elections of 1894 and 1896 indicated that the deadlock had been broken, the Republicans had emerged as the dominant party, and protectionism had become the national policy.

These are the problems with which Professor Terrill wrestles, relying principally on government documents and contemporary newspapers, in another volume of the series *Contributions in American History.* Since he does not attempt to analyze the economic effects of the tariff but, rather, the effect which the political leaders thought the tariff would have, he devotes most of his 200-plus pages to the arguments presented by James G. Blaine, David Wells, Samuel Randall, Frederick Frelinghuysen and others as they sought to find an acceptable policy.

The threads of the tariff tapestry were many and varied—the general issue and the specific problems; the free list; the size of duties; barter; agricultural versus industrial products; reciprocal trade agreements; the North versus the South; the East versus the Mid-west; tactics; problems of trade expansion; individual positions; inter- and intra-party debates; and so on. Those who are interested in this period will find this book very useful.

A larger audience will be aware, though Terrill does not make this point, that these problems also have recent significance. Reciprocal trade agreements were debated again in the 1930s and the 1970s; the balance of trade is a current problem; the issue of the Panama Canal is still with us; a Latin American customs union is as much of a problem as it was in 1889; and most-favored-nation treatment plagues Richard Nixon as it did Grover Cleveland and Benjamin Harrison.

Although "American foreign policy" is given a full third of the book title, it plays a less important role in the discussion. It is always in the background—tariffs do imply foreign trade—but it is not emphasized as are the domestic problems of the tariff. One chapter is devoted to the first Pan-American Conference. Hawaii, the Isthmiam Canal, Cuba, and the American merchant marine and navy are repeatedly mentioned but not stressed. Likewise, the Gilded Age was the era when American nationalism was beginning to stir, yet little is said about this as a period of nationalistic adolescence.

There are a few minor errors: "Colombia" is mis-spelled on page ninety-one and "Wanamaker" on page 137; there is an unnecessary "sic" on page twenty-nine.

Far outweighing these are seventy-four pages of bibliographical notes, a great help to anyone who wishes to follow the path made by Professor Terrill.

DONALD G. BISHOP
Department of Political Science
Slippery Rock State College
Pennsylvania

ELÉMIRE ZOLLA. *The Writer and the Shaman: A Morphology of the American Indian.* Pp. viii, 312. New York: Harcourt Brace Jovanovich, 1973. $12.50.

ROBERT M UTLEY. *Frontier Regulars: The United States Army and the Indian, 1866–1891.* Pp. xv, 462. New York: Macmillan, 1973. $12.95.

When early European migrants made their way to the New World, they brought with them not only their families, worldly possessions, and frustrations and aspirations, but also their heritages forged through centuries of evolution. Even though Scotsmen, Frenchmen, and others brought to America cultures whose differences were magnified back home, they approached the native American inhabitants of the continent with the shared belief that Europeans were superior beings and native Americans were uncivilized and savage remnants of an age long since past. It is this European mentality, and its tenacious grasp on generations of American writers unable to approach Native Americans as equals under God, that is the subject of this unusual and provocative book by Elémire Zolla of the University of Genoa.

Here, indeed, is a volume that should be of interest to a wide audience of American scholars. It is no narrow analysis of a few great writers and their impact on the nation's view of red Americans. Rather, the volume is an encyclopedic analysis of major and minor European and American writers who, for four centuries, played a role in defining, analyzing, and interpreting Indians on the American scene. *The Writer and the Shaman* is the result of a lifetime of interest and scholarship; it is overwhelming in its dimensions. For the first time, this volume brings together a synthesis of the ideas that made possible a program of genocide that lasted for centuries. Particularly impressive are two chapters—one analyzing the Puritan mentality, especially the little-studied missionaries John Eliot and David Brainerd, and the other chronicling the evolution of the publication of Indian literature in the United States. The volume allows the reader to rediscover Jonathan Edwards' belief that the devil brought Indians to America to create a demonic empire safe from all Christian influences and William Robertson's belief that Indians suffered from undeveloped intellects and a crudeness unknown to Christian society. Dozens of other writers pass in review as Zolla brilliantly weaves their considered judgements into a fabric of massive misunderstanding.

Without a doubt, *The Writer and the Shaman* is an important publication and will be read, enjoyed, and contemplated by an ever-growing public interested in insuring that the Indian's future is not a duplication of the past. However, because the volume is encyclopedic in dimension, it is not easy reading and will not be a best seller; it is a reference work that will be used again and again by scholars who will be constantly indebted to a great European scholar, Elémire Zolla, and a competent translator, Raymond Rosenthal.

Frontier Regulars is the ninth volume in the series *The Wars of the United States.* In many ways, it is the best volume to appear thus far in the series. If anyone heretofore doubted the contention that Robert Utley is a first-rate historian, all doubts should be dispelled by reading this masterpiece. No war in American history presents a historian with more organizational problems than do the one thousand or more campaigns fought all over the West between various tribal groups and innumerable Army commanders leading blue-clad cavalrymen and foot soldiers. A veritable myriad of battles and guerilla actions fought on terrain as dissimilar as the combatants themselves faces the historian brave enough to attempt telescoping the whole story in one volume. Yet, Utley not only covers the story completely, but also he does so in a style that is both understandable and scintillating. Even more impressive is the author's ability to organize the full story without the military historian's proclivity for repetition and without giving undue weight to any one theatre of operation. Here is a full story of an incredible moment in military history presented by a mastercraftsman.

Throughout the volume, the author never tries to hide the fact that the real hero is the U. S. Army—and it is refreshing to read a book that does not blame the Army for all the woes plaguing America. He correctly asserts that politicians and their constitutents are the real policy-makers, not the military. However, when a scapegoat is needed to explain corruption, excess, or inefficiency, the military is usually the handiest villain on which to vent understandable frustrations. The Army had a job to do in the West—a job neither sought nor enjoyed—and it undertook the shameful charge of killing or subjugating unwilling tribesmen the best way it knew how. And Utley is quick to point out that Indains were worthy military opponents by stating that "man for man, the Indian warrior far surpassed his blue-clad adversary in virtually every test of military proficiency" (p. 6). It is apparent, though, that the author often stretches fact a bit in defense of the Army, especially when discussing charges that soldiers desired total Indian annihilation. ". . . it seems clear that most officers tried hard to spare women and children" (p. 51), he wrote; "testimony showed conclusively that the troops, with several exceptions, had made every effort to avoid harming noncombatants" at Wounded Knee (p. 407). However, it is also clear, in an abundance of published testimony, that the charge of genocide levied against many

soldiers has not been levied without substantial corroboration.

Despite a minimum amount of overstatement and a neglect of available primary source materials, *Frontier Regulars* is an excellent book that deserves to be read and comtemplated by all who are interested in the history of America's first citizens. Indians appear intelligent, resourceful, and brave as they engaged a powerful nation bent on concluding four hundred years of relentless military pressure. After all is said and done, if I can paraphrase one of Utley's ideas, Indians lost the war because the whites won it and not because they failed to offer a heroic defense of their homeland and heritage.

ARTHUR H. DeROSIER, JR.
East Tennessee State University
Johnson City

WOODROW WILSON. *The Papers of Woodrow Wilson, 1905–1907.* Edited by Arthur A. Link. Vol. 16. Pp. viii, 598. Princeton, N.J.: Princeton University Press, 1973. $20.00.

Here is another volume in an important series featuring a prototypical figure in twentieth century American leadership. Wilson was not alone among academics who thought themselves fit to lead a raucous and competitive democracy. Nicholas Murray Butler would also have been glad to rule over it in what he imagined to be its best interests. But Wilson, son of a defeated Confederacy, saw with amazing clarity the challenge facing a would-be elite. It would have to think nationally. It would have to woo and charm the masses. And it would have to hammer out principles able to bring together a core of efficient, decisive administrators. In 1905 and 1906 Wilson was mainly absorbed in trying to forge an academic instrument at Princeton for the production of such leaders.

Wilson's coming glory is here mainly foreshadowed by the famous speech by George Harvey of *Harper's Weekly,* February 3, 1906, before the Lotos Club, proposing Wilson as a Democratic candidate for President. Neither

Harvey nor Wilson made secrets of his conservative principles. Harvey was ironic respecting "the general reformation of the human race now going on by executive decree," meaning Theodore Roosevelt's. But, Harvey urged, there would soon have to be a "breathing spell," one which would require a leader combining "the activities of the present with the sober influences of the past" (p. 300). He offered Wilson.

The Princeton president was cautious but interested. He asked Harvey for the names of persons supporting him. Harvey cited Henry Watterson of the Louisville *Courier-Journal*, Thomas F. Ryan, the financier, and Adolph S. Ochs, of the New York *Times*. Harvey worked with James Smith, Jr., New Jersey political boss, to groom Wilson for the United States Senate as one who could help slow down reform momentum. Wilson finally, working closely with Harvey, concluded to bow out temporarily in order not to upset delicate alliances affecting the future.

How, then, does this acknowledged conservative, antipathetic to William Jennings Bryan, at one with southerners committed to the supremacy of the white race (p. 288), opposed to socialism, and dedicated to "old fashioned morals" and religion emerge as a Progressive? For one thing, it is today fashionable to derogate Progressives as conservative or reactionary, as in the well regarded "Kolko thesis." But, secondly, there is no necessary contradiction between conservatism and reform. Wilson, by fighting successfully for a tutorial system at Princeton, in opposition to lecture-and-booklist routines, played a progressive role. His fight to abolish upper-class eating clubs and to group undergraduates more fraternally through colleges also broke democratic ground and stirred resentment among influential alumni.

Also important was Wilson's remarkable awareness of the public as being both conservative and progressive. He follows a talk by New Jersey reformer Everett Colby by pointing out that "private welfare is somewhat involved in public welfare," and that Tammany favors to constituents are not to be discounted (pp. 215–217). Wilson approves the insurance investigations of the time as a sign of "social virility," though the investigations struck at elite figures in finance. His resentment of Republican "paternalism" did not prevent him from hosting President Roosevelt at an Army-Navy game played at Princeton. And though Wilson solicited "gentlemen" for Princeton's faculty, and advocated impeccable standards of deportment, he also approved "newspaper English" as "generally terse and clear and right to the point" (p. 115). Wilson learned, and learned from voters who later helped him forge his "New Freedom" program.

LOUIS FILLER

Antioch College
Yellow Springs
Ohio

RAYMOND E. WOLFINGER. *The Politics of Progress*. Pp. vii, 416. Englewood Cliffs, N.J.: Prentice-Hall, 1974. $10.95.

As a research assistant for Robert A. Dahl at Yale University, Raymond E. Wolfinger was a participant-observer in New Haven city hall for a year in 1957–58. Combining this research experience with information drawn from forty-nine unstructured interviews with major political figures in New Haven (conducted by Dahl and Nelson W. Polsby during the same time period), two sample surveys of registered New Haven voters (directed by William H. Flanigan), and city voting data, Wolfinger has written a case study of local politics that takes its place among the best of this genre.

The urban specialist will find especially valuable Wolfinger's specific focus on urban renewal, as well as his general review of machine politics in America. The study, however, is bound to enjoy a much wider audience, since Wolfinger is concerned with several broad topics of interest to political scientists, including ethnic politics, leadership, and the pluralist-elitist dichotomy.

Although Wolfinger provides evidence relevant to the pluralist-elitist controversy, he finds the debate "limited and dull." Neither theory is very useful to him in his analysis of urban renewal in New Haven, for both reject the importance of individual politicians. To pluralist Arthur F. Bentley, the government is just a "registration clerk"; to the elitists, politicians are but toadies of the social-economic establishment. In contrast, Wolfinger explains urban renewal as "a function of individual ambition, not of interest group pressure."

Wolfinger's story, then, becomes the story of the driving ambition of one man: Richard C. Lee, former public relations officer at Yale and mayor of New Haven from 1953 to 1969. According to Wolfinger, Lee was guided more by the anticipated reactions of the New Haven electorate than by private groups. In one episode, for instance, Yale lost a land decision because of Lee's desire "to avoid appearing soft on Yale in the eyes of the electorate." The successes of New Haven urban renewal rested in large part, Wolfinger believes, on Lee's talent for publicity and on his popularity.

Wolfinger notes that few mayors are apt to match Lee's ambition, skill, and lengthy tenure—sixteen years compared to most mayors who are lucky to stay in office as long as four years. Thus he recommends turning to "less heroic" models of urban leadership—namely, professional municipal officials whose incentive structure emphasizes "not jealous defence of routine but rather a venturesome ambition" and a cosmopolitan outlook.

Since Wolfinger stresses the individual in this study, he might have made greater use of the recent literature on personality and politics. Yet this does not detract greatly from his careful examination of New Haven politics and the key linkage between the mayor and his electorate. Those accustomed to the excellence of Wolfinger's legislative research will not be disappointed by his book on local politics.

LOCH K. JOHNSON
Department of Government
Ohio University
Athens

SOCIOLOGY

ERNEST BECKER. *The Denial of Death.* Pp. ix, 314. New York: The Free Press, 1973. $7.95.

Someone has recently commented that "If we know nothing of the far side of death, we know all too little of the near side." Ernest Becker's book presents us with a moving evocation of the near side of death. The author contends that fear of death is endemic in man and places its origin in early childhood when "terror" results from looking death full in the face. In a book which the author describes as "a bid for the peace of my scholarly soul, an offering for intellectual absolution; . . . my first mature work," a serious effort is made to synthesize Freud, Kierkegaard, Norman O. Brown, and Otto Rank. When the race is over, Kierkegaard and Rank are in the vanguard with Freud and Brown bringing up the rear. Freud comes off poorly for what Becker describes as his "basic mistakes," while Brown is faulted for "fallacies so obvious that one is shocked. . . ." Kierkegaard and Rank emerge as true psychoanalysts, and thus it is not surprising in this philosophic scheme of things that psychoanalysis as a therapeutic system similarly gets short shrift. Contending that "neurosis is normal" and that "even psychotic failure represents only a little additional presentation in the routine stumbling along life's way," Becker joins the therapeutic nihilists in supporting Rank who contended: "Psychology as self-knowledge is self-deception."

Becker has rewritten Freudian psychoanalysis and replaced sexuality with fear of death as the motivating force in human behavior. Whether this change destroys the corpus of psychoanalysis or simply modifies it a bit is a decision which each reader must make for himself. It is unfortunate that Becker's psychoanalytic mentor is Paul Roazen, whose detective story, *Brother Animal: The Story of Freud and Tausk*, evoked my antipathy in this journal (November, 1972). If one adds to this the fact that Becker ends up synthesizing psychoanalysis and religion, the reviewer becomes even more uncomfortable.

It is hard to discover what is left of psychoanalysis when a new and presumably "corrected" vision of man's nature is presented, and when its therapeutic superstructure is held suspect. Perhaps it is fairer to say that Becker has offered a new personality theory which borrows some of its underpinnings from classical psychoanalysis while really opting for something very different in ideology in the final meld.

Still, when all is said and done, Becker has written an interesting and scholarly book. I don't agree with much of what he has written, but I found the book provocative and continuously stimulating. Becker's book undoubtedly will make for many arguments and, anyway, that is what the intellectual world is all about.

MORTON LEVITT
Department of Psychiatry
School of Medicine
University of California
Davis

BARRY BLUESTONE, WILLIAM M. MURPHY and MARY STEVENSON. *Low Wages and the Working Poor.* Pp. 215. Ann Arbor, Mich.: The Institute of Labor and Industrial Relations, The University of Michigan—Wayne State University, 1973. $4.95.

DENNIS P. SOBIN. *The Working Poor.* Pp. 194. Port Washington, N.Y.: Kennikat Press, 1974. $8.50.

These two recent books hopefully herald the redirection of attention away from the culture of poverty of the 1960s toward critical problems in the distribution of wages and working conditions. Bluestone, Murphy, and Stevenson provide the reader with a macro-level analysis of low wages based upon the Survey of Economic Opportunity (SEO) national sample of 1967. Sobin, on the other hand, aims to provide a more micro-level analysis, including 108 in-depth interviews with members of working poor. The first study is heavy on data analysis with an abundance of tables, charts, and graphs. The latter study includes very few tables and the author is more interested in understanding the meaning of work among his low-skilled black respondents.

Bluestone, Murphy, and Stevenson provide the reader with a model of the determination of wages developed within the framework of the dual economy. Low-wage workers are defined as those workers working at or below $2.25 per hour who worked at least thirty hours in the survey week and at least forty weeks in the preceding year. Thus, they are distinguished from the working poor—a group defined by a family income below the poverty line.

Recognizing the obvious impact of racism and sexism on the wage structure, the authors carry out their analysis separately for each race-sex group. They find, not surprisingly, that seventy-seven percent of black female full-time, full-year workers are low-wage; 51.3 percent of black male full-time full-year workers are low-wage; 58.8 percent of white female workers are low-wage; while only 21.2 percent of white male workers are low-wage. Extensive analysis is done on the effects of education, occupation, industry, residence in large SMSAs, migration, and health limitations. Education had a positive effect on wages but only within each age-sex group. With schooling held constant, industry was an important factor in the determination of wage differentials and supported the authors' thesis of dualism in the industrial structure. Their conclusion focuses upon the necessity of restructuring the peripheral sector where the industries are characterized by "small firm size, labor intensity, low profits, low productivity, intensive product market competition, lack of unionization and low wages" (p. 29).

In *The Working Poor*, Sobin fails to define his terms. Working poor, low-wage worker, unskilled worker, workers in dead-end jobs, are all used interchangeably throughout and nowhere is a clear, concise definition developed for these terms. In his all-black sample there are seventy-six workers in hospitals or manufacturing plants in three cities with about fifteen cases per plant. Thus, there can be no analysis of the situation at any one plant, and in spite of the two hour interviews, very little is revealed in the book of any in-depth meaning of work for these respondents. In fact, much of the argument of the book focuses upon the issues of race—the black heritage, discrimination against blacks, the black family, the black ghetto, and community protests — basically providing the reader with a rehash of the concerns of the 1960s. Furthermore, although sixty-one per cent of his sample are women, the discussion focuses primarily on the meaning of work and low wages for men.

In his conclusion, Sobin argues for policies such as humanizing work, upgrading skills and jobs, new job titles, and higher wages for entry-level jobs. Most of this discussion, however, could just as well have been written about the automobile workers in Detroit where the average wages per hour were already $2.90 in 1963 and the analysis of Bluestone *et al* reveals no low-wage workers in 1967.

Both books conclude by locating the problem in the jobs themselves rather than in the individuals who hold them. Discrimination is also viewed as an important aspect of the problem, although Sobin ignores the case of white women. Bluestone, Murphy and Stevenson present a much more sophisticated analysis of low-wage jobs leading up to their conclusion that the solution is not simple but will require basic restructuring of the economy itself. Sobin's humanistic approach is needed but more rigorous analysis is necessary; owner-managers of marginal textile firms in the South cannot be expected to upgrade jobs and increase entry-level wages if that means that they will be forced out of business.

SALLY BOULD VAN TIL
Department of Sociology
University of Delaware
Newark

ROBERT BROWN. *Rules and Laws in Sociology*. Pp. vii, 181. Chicago: Aldine Publishing Company, 1973. $7.95.

ANTHONY D. SMITH. *The Concept of Social Change: A Critique of the Functionalist Theory of Social Change*. Pp. vii, 198. London: Routledge and Kegan Paul, 1973. $6.00. Paperbound.

In *Rules and Laws in Sociology*, Brown attempts to clarify the confusion which he maintains has resulted from the failure of sociologists to distinguish between the search for social rules and regularities and the search for sociological laws. He attempts to clarify the complex relationship between a scientific interest in rule-oriented behavior of people and laws about behavior. He maintains that, because of the failure to distinguish between rules and laws, many sociological inquiries lead to a discovery of mere social practices rather than of social laws. The confusion results from the fact that many key sociological concepts—such as discrimination, minority, prejudice, alienation, delinquency and relative deprivation—are in fact policy-dependent or relational, not sociologically useful definitions.

Sociologists must search for satisfactory operational specifications which will produce definitions which refer to measureable properties of scientific interests. Brown argues that a large proportion of sociological problems are so ill-formed that they can never receive a useful solution. Of those which are well formed, many do not require an independent law-explanation, but simply one in terms of rule-following or rational goal-seeking.

Brown suggests that ill-formed questions, pseudo statements, and untestable theories are generated by sociologists by a common misuse of variable analysis—"the method, that is, of establishing and analyzing correlations of variables where the distribution of variables is determined by a survey or questionnaires. The misuse arises both from lack of constraints on what is to count as a variable, and from the attempt, in the absence of any directly relevant theoretical background, to discover causally significant correlations." Brown further maintains that "most of the high correlations we find will not be of scientific interest because they are not related to any reputable hypothesis or theory. We cannot discover sociological laws by mere correlation-hunting even though testable hypotheses seem to be in short supply."

The reason many of the procedures of sociologists insure the discovery of social regularities rather than social laws is that much of the subject matter of sociology consists of the rule-oriented behavior of people. Sometimes, sociologists must also explain the presence, origin, operations and success of social rules or conventions themselves, and this must be done with statements of law.

General directives cannot be given to sociologists as to where and when they ought to look for social laws, but if sociologists have well-formulated problems which require law-like explanations, the problems themselves should show where to seek the answers. Policy-dependent terms are only one kind of context-dependent terms. The use of context-dependent terms insures that sociologists will have severe problems in making cross-cultural comparisons and in establishing law-like generalizations.

Genuine laws, if formulated, will be derived from theory. A theory must refer to a set of nonobservable events and properties which can be used to explain observable data. Brown does not think that the search for such universal social laws is necessarily doomed to fail. It is not impossible for laws to be constructed. The fertile ground for sociologists lies between empty social generalizations on the one hand and patternless ethnography on the other.

The sentence structure of Brown's book is confusing and obscuring rather than simple and concise. The book is poorly edited and makes difficult reading. However, the basic argument presents a major challenge to sociologists, and will probably become a classic critical statement in sociological theory construction.

The Smith book represents an attempt to critique functional theory by demonstrating its inablity to deal adequately with social change. Smith presents a general brief summary of functional analysis and then equates it with what he calls neo-evolutionism. He maintains that the functionalists have revised social evolutionism, focusing on the tendency to embrace an endogenous paradigm of change. That is, he maintains that the dominant tradition in western thought has been to see change as normal continous upward-spiralling, irreversible, immanent, and explainable in any society in terms of internal processes.

As an alternative, Smith poses an exogenous paradigm wherein change is associated not only with the process of diffusion as used by early anthropologists, but also in a broader sense so that diffusion constitutes only one aspect of an exogenous model. The exogenous model recognizes influences upon the system of both social and physical environment. Social change can be analyzed only in terms of the influences which the histories of environment, crises, and neighboring societies exert. In order to critique "neoevolutionism" as a paradigm for explaining social change, Smith does not distinguish between universal or general evolution which is temporal and non-spatial; and specific evolution which is temporal and spatial and therefore specifically deals with exogenous factors in the analysis of the given cultural system. Functionalism as developed by some scholars is indeed a non-temporal, non-spatial form of analysis and as such may explain the existence of given cultural items more readily than cultural change. The paradigm of contemporary functionalists generally emphasizes the open systems model so that change, which can be traced to exogenous forces, is in fact most easily explained. Few functionalists envision the closed system model which Smith portrays vividly in order to embark on his critique of functionalism.

BRENT T. BRUTON
Department of Sociology and
  Anthropology
Iowa State University
Ames

EDMUND J. GLEAZER, JR. *Project Focus: A Forecast Study of Community Colleges.* Pp. 239. New York: McGraw-Hill, 1973. $9.50.

DAVID S. BUSHNELL. *Organizing for Change: New Priorities for Community Colleges.* Pp. 237. New York: McGraw-Hill, 1973. $9.50.

These two books are the end product of Project Focus, a nationwide study of community colleges, funded by the W. K. Kellogg Foundation. The purpose of the study was to determine community college objectives and the necessary strategies to achieve these goals. The recommendations of the study presumably are to be used as policy guides for the American Association of Community and Junior Colleges (AACJC) and its institutional members. Gleazer, the Executive Director of the AACJC since 1958, provides a holistic view based largely upon impressions gathered in a ten month tour during which he interviewed 1500 persons located in thirty institutions in twenty states. Bushnell, Director of Research for Project Focus, has carved out the more mundane task of providing factual background and statistical data for those who are to establish future new priorities for community colleges.

Gleazer addresses himself to a wide range of problems and issues. To the question "Who goes to community college?" his answer is simple—everybody. But "high on the priority list of community colleges must be improved services for the increasing number of minority group students." As to what kinds of changes in structure and outlook are needed in community colleges, his response is that they need a new view of education that "looks first to the needs of students (rather than to tradition) in determining forms for building, curricula, administration, teaching, and learning." Particularly intriguing is his discussion of "Who calls the shots?" It is a masterful piece of nodding to all concerned groups: state legislatures, state boards of education, boards of trustees, faculty, and students. He ultimately avoids an answer by concluding that it is "an open question."

A clue to the frustrating evasiveness of much of the book is afforded the reader by the first two quotations, one (unidentified) facing the title page and the other (by "a student") preceding the first chapter. They are the kinds of quotations that permit literally any kind of interpretation the reader wants to bring to them. A more specific inconsistency is found on page ninety-nine in which he refers to students as "excellent judges of the value and effectiveness of instructional programs." This is followed on page 119 with a wistful admission that the student is really faced with a dilemma. He does not really know what educational objective he should pursue. "He is uncertain. He wants to hedge his bets, to keep his options open." Furthermore, Gleazer points out that "appropriate yardsticks" are for the most part not yet available to measure output. The question still remains. Can faculty and staff legitimately buck this kind of professional obligation—that is, evaluation and assessment—on to students?

On the more positive side, both Gleazer and Bushnell speak optimistically and with considerable righteous pride about the accomplishments and future thrusts of community colleges. And they particularly stress the need to enroll the students at their present level of learning rather than lay upon them a predetermined and inappropriate academic curriculum. In this connection, one wishes that Gleazer in particular had expanded upon his one page treatment of "the relation of education to social problems."If these new thrusts are indeed followed, perhaps the community colleges "can contribute toward a social revolution characterized not by disruption and disorganization, but by greater individual freedom, competence in vocations of worth, and responsible citizenship." These are worthy goals for educators at all levels—including those in community colleges.

STANLEY P. WRONSKI
Michigan State University
East Lansing

THOMAS J. COTTLE and STEPHEN L. KLINEBERG. *The Present of Things Future: Explorations of Time in Human Experience.* Pp. 290. New York: The Free Press, 1974. No price.

Works dealing with time and the notion of temporality abound in the literatures of philosophy and physics. Here we have an attempt by a psychotherapist and a sociologist to come to grips with this question in its relation to the behavioral sciences. The result is thoroughly enjoyable reading which at times gives rise to further questions of importance, as well as new insights into supposedly worked-over material. This is especially true of the examination of social class and the presentations of time prespectives in Tunisian society. While certain of their expositions of metaphysical theories of time and their often rather sweeping generalizations concerning radical or revolutionary action would benefit from some qualifications, the authors do nonetheless develop fair summary views of past work in these fields. Drawing on widely-dispersed materials, they have further attempted to present an integrated view of what is happening in cultural, sociological and psychological studies of time perspectives. This alone would be a worthy project, but the authors have gone beyond this by integrating life studies to counterbalance and complement the rather impersonal aspects of statistical reporting. This mesh of objective and subjective reporting, though certainly making for more lively reading, does present problems, as the conclusions drawn from the life studies are never, even in the explanatory appendix, adequately grounded.

The book is divided into three parts. The first is an overall presentation of the material, combining an excellent introductory summary of how men come to form and trust their personal views of the future with an example of this process in the form of a life study. The second section deals with the development and maturation from early childhood through adult life of temporal experience as seen in relation to sex distinctions, social roles and cognitive growth. The third section discusses social and cultural forces which shape men's views of their personal existence by influencing their understanding of possible present actions as seen in the perspectives of future time.

The conclusions the authors arrive at are not meant to be original: their identification of freedom with the development of notions of past, present, and future has often been given and rarely questioned in some other disciplines. What is of interest in this work is the authors' presentation of how this develops in concrete instances. Freedom allows for action because, at least in the western world, the individual is able to understand that he has personal dignity. Both allow him to get beyond an all-encompassing *now*, to draw from the past, and to construct a future. And this future is in turn tied to a larger cultural notion of time. The merit of this book is that it gives us a number of insights into how this fundamental human achievement takes place.

JOSEPH BIEN
Department of Philosophy
University of Missouri
Columbia

ANTHONY GIDDENS. *The Class Structure of the Advanced Societies.* Pp. 336. New York: Barnes & Noble, 1973. $8.00.

An English critic, reviewing a book recently, remarked that he did not know whether or not its author was a good writer. All he knew was that anyone who managed to finish it was a good reader. Something of the sort might be said about this latest effort of Anthony Giddens, lecturer in sociology at Cambridge University. In this case the book is very much worth finishing, even though hard labor is required. Although the separate sentences do not lack lucidity, the argument is so "closely textured" (the author's own description) that one is never permitted to nod. We are told, for example, that a society without classes is not necessarily a classless society, that there is a fundamental difference between class awareness and class consciousness, that primitive communism and feudalism are both pre-class societies, that class relationships can exist in a classless society, that a classless society presupposes an advanced economy, and that a society can have a governing class without a ruling class. All this is fair enough—and the author's dialectical skill is spectacular—but the distinctions are delicate indeed.

Whether contemporary sociological theory is in a state of crisis or of torpor, Giddens believes that a new departure is needed, one stemming directly from the problem of class, which he regards as central to the enterprise. Accordingly, he treats Marx's theory of class, Weber's critique of Marx, and the critiques also of Dahrendorf, Aron, and Ossowski, refutes the criticisms of these latter three (he is especially hard on Dahrendorf), offers his own criticisms of Marx, and devotes the remainder of the book to the construction and elaboration of his own "structuration" theory.

Granting Giddens his premise that class, which is only one kind of social differentiation, is the most important kind, and granting also that advanced societies, rather than society itself, are the preferred focuses of sociological inquiry—both of which are debatable— he has made a significant, if highly abstruse, contribution to the literature.

ROBERT BIERSTEDT
Department of Sociology
University of Virginia
Charlottesville

DAVID G. GIL. *Unravelling Social Policy: Theory, Analysis, and Political Action towards Social Equality.* Pp. xvii, 171. Cambridge, Mass.: Schenkman Publishing, 1973. $6.95. Paperbound, $3.65.

David Gil has applied a systems approach to social policy in a searching, logical fashion, but admittedly from a clearly announced stance aimed at "structural social change toward an egalitarian, humanistic social order." Having nailed his banner to the masthead, he questions not at all the assumptions behind it, but follows this fashionable value system now increasingly implicit in Western democracies and underlined by the New Left. Whether such values are adequate to make functional a highly technological, resource-scarce nation of over 200,000,000 undergoing rapid societal change and in competition (whether it likes it or not) with two massive totalitarian dictatorships—not to mention a frightened Western Europe—is simply not questioned.

Within the parameters of the values which he employs in his system with a "policy science" approach, he does a most thorough job of exploring possible benefit/costs for a holistic (rather than piecemeal) approach to social welfare as part of the politico-economic-value system, as it most surely is. Using

"Mother's Wages" as a test case for applying his conceptual scheme, he concludes approximately that "Parent's Wages" would better advance his values.

In an epilogue, Gil realistically concludes that the time is not yet ripe for any macro-internal societal order switch—especially in our present nonegalitarian world. This is a useful book taking the often feeble do-gooder approach to welfare and forcing such ideas to face "reality" in a systematic fashion. "The Cambridge Syndrome" approach of Banfield and Moynihan which suggests that "everything we do makes things worse" would perhaps applaud Gil's rigorous logic but quite possibly question his values. It would be an interesting exercise to use societal-survival values based on stratification/status (meritocracy?) and put a segment of social policy through the careful systems analysis employed here.

W. WENTWORTH ELDREDGE
Dartmouth College
Hanover
New Hampshire

Alvin W. Gouldner. *For Sociology: Renewal and Critique in Sociology Today.* Pp. 480. New York: Basic Books, 1974. $10.95.

Alvin Gouldner's *For Sociology* is a collection of his essays which "have been selected with a view of clarifying the emerging vectors in my work." Somewhat more explicit indication of the book's primary intent may be gleaned from the jacket blurb, which we may assume was written by or at least had the approval of the author. "In *For Sociology*, Professor Gouldner both broadens the critique of *The Coming Crisis* and goes beyond it. In the title essay, 'For Sociology,' and in 'The Politics of the Mind,' he formulates his ideas for resolving the 'crisis' . . . and suggests fresh directions for a renewed critical sociology."

If the collection was intended to represent trends in Gouldner's life and work, one wonders why the essays were not arranged in the order of their publication or composition. They stretch from 1955 to 1973, but are ordered with no regard to age.

In terms of the order in which the essays were written or first published, Gouldner's intellectual biography divides into three periods: (1) the period extending through 1960 in which he was more or less objectively interested in ideas or was engaging in talmudic casuistry with respect to such ethical questions as reciprocity and benevolence; (2) the period of the 1960s in which he was engaged in vigorous unmasking and debunking activities against classical sociologists such as Max Weber or against friends and contemporaries such as Howard S. Becker—this period culminated in *The Crisis* where, in the name of reflexive sociology, debunking was generalized into a sociological way of life; (3) the period of the 1970s marked by agonized reactions to criticism of *The Crisis*.

As sociology's most talented exterminator, Gouldner's responses to critics—some of whom have recourse to his own tactics—have special interest. Among other things, critics of *The Crisis* have found it negativistic, failing to offer viable alternatives to the theories it destroyed, substituting ideology for objective analysis and being preoccupied with ideas about reality rather than with reality in a manner—and this particularly infuriated Gouldner—that amounted to navel gazing. Gouldner counterattacked by accusing his critics of ideology: "Touraine's and Zeitlin's standpoint is objectivistic, which is to say: it is an ideology about objectivity that expresses a false consciousness" (pp. 88–89). He questions the motives of his critics: "My impression . . . is that Zeitlin's defence of social science, his autistic need to defend it from non-existent attacks as mere ideology, actually derive from his anxieties about Marxism" (p. 93). He also accuses his critics of deliberate distortion and malice:

Such a shameless misrendering of my views should make it clear that this issue of the

A.J.S. was more nearly an act of war than of justice. Establishment critics have done just about everything, short of book-burning, to discredit the *Crisis*. Indeed, one of them, Jackson Toby, who is quoted by Lipset, scurrilously suggests that my motive in writing the *Crisis* was money (pp. 142–3).

To anyone observing that the contest between Gouldner and his critics seems to be a simple case of Gouldner's norm of reciprocity and the master debunker is being given a dose of his own medicine, Gouldner would possibly answer: not at all, he criticizes others because they are shabby hypocrites, flaunting their arrogant self importance while his critics are jealous aggressors, sadistically inflicting suffering on a sensitive soul.

Turning to Gouldner's proposal for a reconstructed sociology, the book gives a very different impression depending on whether one reviews the essays in the order they were first written or in the order that they are reassembled in *For Sociology*. As the essays are reassembled, *For Sociology* conveys the impression that Gouldner is on his way toward "Cuban and Chinese Marxism, both [of which] converge with a Hegelian Critical Marxism far more than with a 'scientific' socialism" (p. 444). But read in the order they were biographically produced, the essays seem to indicate that Gouldner is on his way back to a relatively pure form of Hegelianism. Hegel, who thought the highest type of man was the philosopher, would certainly have approved of Gouldner's suggestion that a sound basis for reflexive sociology can only be established by an intellectual community: "I want . . . to stress the sheer primordiality of establishing a community and the priority of a theoretical collectivity for all efforts at rational theorizing" (p. 96). Hegel would have been delighted by Gouldner's increasing inclination to erase the lines between "think" and "thought about" and the tendency to visualize both as evolving toward freedom."The ultimate end of our social theory and social praxis is human fulfillment and liberation" (p. 101).

Hegel would surely have applauded the following declaration:

Higher and prior to research, there is *reflection*. The sociologist should first conduct a dialogue with himself and others to see what he already knows. . . . This hardly seems worth saying. . . . My own impression, however, is that more often than not, that is not done even by those respectful of the claims of sociological theory. . . . There is absolutely no case on record in the history of sociology in which a sociologist is known to have systematically pondered the meaning of 'is' (p. 110).

But Hegel contemplated the meaning of "is," which he called "being." And the more he thought about "being," the more it included everything and, hence, nothing in particular. Thus the reflective process conjured up the antithesis of "being," or "non-being." But now thought had a real problem with a contradiction to overcome which it managed in the synthesis: "becoming." And so it came to pass that the world evolution toward freedom and liberation got underway. All of which is certainly worthy of a

Sociological Dialogue

Q

Tell me brother what is what—
Sitting on your chamber pot—
Arms akimbo, eyes, a-glazing,
Are you really navel gazing?
Is it true or is it not?

A.

Though bad mouth critics look askance
It flows from the reflexive stance
To see in navels a connection
With infra-structures and reflection
Of vast domains of relevance.

DON MARTINDALE
University of Minnesota
Minneapolis

EVELYN M. KITAGAWA and PHILIP M. HAUSER. *Differential Mortality in the United States: A Study in Socioeconomic Epidemiology*. Pp. vii, 255. Cambridge, Mass.: Harvard University Press, 1973. $9.00.

Kitagawa and Hauser present in this volume the salient findings of three researches, a Matched Records Study of death certificates and 1960 Population Census schedules, an investigation of longitudinal differential mortality data, 1930–1960, by census tracts for Chicago, and an analysis of special tabulations of 1959–61 deaths by cause.

The volume presents the results of monumental research and should serve as reference material of the best sort. This study shows rather sharp differentials in mortality of socioeconomic groups which indicate that "the goal of equal opportunity for all, so deeply ingrained in American ideology, tradition, and law, is still to be implemented in the realm of life itself—the achievement of equal opportunity for survival."

Among whites, and to a lesser extent among nonwhites, the education differential in mortality is acute in the United States. White males, between the ages of twenty-five and sixty-four, who had completed less than five years of school had an age-adjusted mortality ratio of 1.15 compared to a low of 0.70 for men with at least four years of college, a differential of sixty-four percent. For white females, the corresponding mortality ratios were 1.60 and 0.78 respectively, a differential of 105 percent!

Differentials in mortality for age-sex groups by income were in many cases even larger than they were by education. However, as the authors point out "the income differentials may be quite misleading because the very high mortality of the low-income groups—especially for persons under age sixty-five—no doubt reflects in part a reverse causal path in which the approach of death causes 'lower than normal income' during the year preceding death." As expected, both education and income mortality differentials were reduced when the effect of each variable was examined while the other was controlled. The wish for long life may best be fulfilled by getting a Ph.D. and a large income.

Those males who had no work experience between 1950 and 1960 had much higher mortality than those who had worked. For example, "White males, 25 to 64, with a mortality ratio of 2.04, experienced mortality more than twice as great as that of those with work experience. . . . Clearly the higher mortality of the men without work experience since 1950 suggests that they were men who were unable to work because of incapacitation or illness which adversely affected their longevity. . . ." We might add that as with income and mortality there is very likely a reverse causal path in play here also. Not only does illness or incapacitation lead to nonworking and higher mortality, but unemployment—of short and, particularly, of long duration—may lead to deterioration of health and higher mortality.

Mortality rates by cause of death were, of course, found to be negatively associated with education. The lesser educated had considerably higher mortality, often twice as high, not only for various infectious and degenerative diseases but also for the violent causes of death such as motor vehicle accidents and suicide (the available data clearly support this latter conclusion for white males only). However, there are some interesting reversals in the general pattern of socioeconomic differentials. For instance, among white women cancer of the breast is positively associated with education. This differential is probably related to the different prevailing patterns of fertility and breast feeding by socioeconomic class; curiously, however, mortality from cancer of the uterus, ovary, fallopian tube and broad ligament is negatively associated with education. On the other hand, among white males mortality from cancer of the prostate is ninety-five percent higher for the at-least-one-year-of-college compared with the less-than-eight-years-of-school-completed group.

An examination of differential mortality by race showed, among other things, that whereas the life expectancy at birth, 1959–61, for white males and females was 67.6 and 74.7 years respectively, for Negroes it was 61.3 and 67.2

years, while for the Japanese males and females it was 74.4 and 80.4 years! These data clearly indicate that there is much room for improving the health and life conditions not only of Negroes but also of whites.

Decades ago Emile Durkheim clearly established that the condition of being married affords considerable protection against the risk of suicide, especially for the male. One may conclude from the present study that the blissful state of matrimony wards off to a good extent other lethal forces as well. Undoubtedly, in part, the lower mortality of the married compared with the mortality of the single, widowed, and divorced is due to preselectivity—the healthy are more likely to become married, and less likely to become widowed or divorced. However, the mortality differentials by marital status for whites and nonwhites, for each sex, are much too great to be wholly accounted for in terms of preselectivity.

After examining parity differentials for ever-married white women, the authors conclude that "these data suggest that very high fertility per se—independent of socioeconomic status—may shorten a woman's life." And that "the reasons for restricting family size . . . can be bolstered by a significant additional reason—reduction of female mortality." A pro-natalist, which this reviewer is certainly not, may argue, however, that to achieve the greatest reduction in female mortality, women should bear three children each. When standardized for age and education, the mortality ratios of women with two, one, or no children ever borne to them are respectively six, seventeen, and twenty percent higher than those who had borne three children.

Some of the main conclusions of the authors are that "the lowest socio-economic class has continued to experience a much higher level of mortality and has shown no relative gain in recent decades"; at least fifteen nations have longer life expectancies at birth than the United States and this "is undoubtedly in large measure a reflection of the high mortality of the disadvantaged in the nation"; the unconscionably high mortality of the Negroes and Indians "constitutes stark evidence of their underprivileged status"; and "perhaps the most important next gain in mortality reduction is to be achieved through improved social-economic conditions rather than through increments to and application of bio-medical knowledge."

This reviewer contends, however, that given the socio-political realities of American life, "effective egalitarianism —the ability to survive—duration of life itself" may perhaps be enhanced even more through effective delivery and application of biomedical knowledge currently available. Better yet, reductions in mortality may be most efficaciously brought about by joining improved social and economic conditions with effective delivery of health services— including preventive measures—to all.

SURINDER K. MEHTA
University of Massachusetts
Amherst

MARY H. MANONI. *Bedford-Stuyvesant: The Anatomy of a Central City Community.* Pp. 118. New York: Quadrangle, New York Times Book Co., 1973. No price.

This slim volume is a by-product of a larger investigation of organized criminal activities in Brooklyn's Bedford-Stuyvesant (Bed-Stuy) area, of which Manoni was director of research. In the course of this study, she became interested in Bed-Stuy as the largest black ghetto in the country, and in its viability as a total community.

Bed-Stuy was a stable, largely Jewish, residential area until blacks and Puerto Ricans began to move into it after World War II. Today its quarter million population consists of blacks, eighty-four percent; Puerto Ricans, twelve percent; and whites and others, four percent. These people inhabit extensive slums now; more than one in five is on public assistance; much business and industry have vacated the area, causing a high incidence of unemployment; private and public institutions, especially schools and health delivery systems, have deteriorated. Many recent migrants are from the rural south, and are largely untrained for either urban residence or industrial employment.

Manoni reports on these all too familiar matters in short chapters, touching briefly on population changes, housing, ghetto schools, joblessness, broken families, poverty, and welfare. She devotes several chapters also to policy gambling, drug addiction, and other criminal activities which flourish in Bed-Stuy.

Her collection of data was based largely on reading and observation, without resort to more sophisticated methods of research. On the whole, she is sensible in presentation of her material, and sympathetic with the people of Bed-Stuy. She writes in plain or non-technical language for general rather than academic readers.

Her major conclusion is largely intuitive rather than derived from her investigation. She chooses to believe that Bed-Stuy is in the process of a "turnaround" from a disorganized into a more stable community. Indicators of this "are there if you take the trouble to look." She finds them in various private and public enterprises that are involved in improvement programs: The Bedford-Stuyvesant Restoration Corporation, the Neighborhood Improvement Program, community health programs, housing projects, cultural institutions such as the Billie Holiday Theater, and others.

One may wish with her that these community-building institutions function effectively, especially for the second generation of Brooklyn dwellers; but her data are grim evidence of the difficulties that beset them now and in the near future.

JOHN SIRJAMAKI
State University of New York
Buffalo

ARTHUR MITZMAN. *Sociology and Estrangement: Three Sociologists of* *Imperial Germany.* Pp. xii, 376, x. New York: Alfred A. Knopf, 1973. $12.50.

Even after a century and a half of the emergence of sociology as a new perspective on society and its eventual institutionalization and professionalization, the question of the origin and rationale of sociology has interestingly been eliciting new answers. In this study, Arthur Mitzman argues that the prime urge of the nineteenth-century founders of sociology was not a dispassionate, scientific, and objective study of society so much as it was a passionate, humanistic, and subjective understanding as well as the preservation of those values which have always sustained and imparted meaning to social existence but were now facing annihilation under the onslaughts of modernity.

With historical and sociological insight, Mitzman analyzes the writings of Toennies, Sombart, and Michels, three of the "founding spirrts" of sociology, who, despite differences in their training and scholarship, shared "a common heritage, a common experience, and a common aversion." They "were estranged from a world that had become alien and uncontrollable"; they accounted for the "abhorrent mechanization of life"; and they put forth in their ways the ideals of "community," "autonomous creative spirit," and "altruistic socialism" respectively, which they did in the tradition of the "sorrowing prophets" of the century, and at a cost of sacrificing their promising careers.

Times have proved the accuracy of their diagnosis and prognosis. In the state of social chaos and personal meaninglessness following from industrial and bureaucratic modernity which have increasingly been engulfing some of the materially advanced countries of the present age, foreboding only their eventual self-destruction, the ideas of these prophetic pioneers could well serve as a beacon light for social and personal survival and fulfilment, a view upheld by Mitzman too.

Also, for those societies which are

designated in contemporary social sciences as backward or developing, the understanding and far-sightedness of such scholars as aptly depicted by Mitzman could be of significant worth in that they could provide some of the ways of averting the pitfalls of ultra-materialistic civilization while imbibing their positive achievements, and combining them with their own "values, happiness, and mutual welfare," as Mitzman would say.

Lastly, this social-historical critique by Mitzman contains many insights into the complex origins of sociology and its development through complicated social circumstances. For those particularly interested in the interrelation of civilization and the disciplines which study it, including the currently emerging explorations in the sociology of sociology, this work by Arthur Mitzman should be valuable reading.

SANTOSH KUMAR NANDY

Toronto
Canada

JON PYNOOS, ROBERT SCHAFER, and CHESTER W. HARTMAN, eds. *Housing Urban America*. Pp x, 597. Chicago: Aldine Publishing, 1973. $25.00.

One picks up this four-pound book of nearly 600 pages in ten-point type containing fifty-one essays and hopes that this may be, as the dust-jacket proclaims, the "balanced and comprehensive review of the full range of housing problems in urban America today." This might then be the book to dam up the flood of publications with which it is impossible to keep pace. It is probably the first compilation on housing that includes in its bibliography items from *Esquire, Trans-Action, Daedelus, OSTI Press*, and a series of journals like *Society, Social Problems*, and *Social Policy*.

The essays are presented under five headings: Politics, Social Aspects, Economics, Production, and Policies and Programs. There are some excerpts from recognized authorities, such as Chester Rapkin, Nathan Glazer, Her-

bert Gans, and Dick Netzer. There are also excerpts from governmental documents such as the report of the National Commission on Urban Problems. The editors and their colleagues supply other articles.

The editors state that their bibliography is limited to books published since 1960, with a few exceptions, but their bibliography includes a book published in the 1960s which is a reissue of a book first published in the 1940s. A long footnote refers to several articles by Kain and Quigley entitled "Measuring the Value of Housing Quality" (1970) with no reference to the pioneer work of the Committee on the Hygiene of Housing of the American Public Health Association, chaired by the magistral Dr. C.E.A. Winslow. In the 1940s, this committee issued three monographs on standards of healthful housing, including not only *Construction and Equipment of the Home*, but also *Planning the Neighborhood*, which was reissued in 1960. Again, an article on community power structures cites as "groundwork for comparative studies" material from sociological journals of the 1970s. This article seems to have been much discussed among nine of the editors and their associates. One finds no reference to Robert Dahl's *Who Governs?* (1961), looked upon by political scientists as a seminal and original contribution.

To the editors, the rent strike as a form of citizen participation was an important contribution of the 1960s. The effort of the city manager of Cambridge, Massachusetts, to relate the Model Cities Program to general city government was an example of the efforts of the dominant oligarchy of wealthy landowners—including two great universities—to dominate an innovative social program. If one accepts the parti-pris of the editors, this collection is of some use, but it is not the "balanced and comprehensive review" proclaimed by the publisher.

CHARLES S. ASCHER

International Representative
Institute of Public Administration

RAY C. RIST. *The Urban School: A Factory for Failure. A Study of Education in American Society.* Pp. ix, 265. Cambridge, Mass.: The MIT Press, 1973. $12.50.

Elementary school teachers are reported to base their views of student academic potential on a variety of socio-economic factors and then treat children in ways that establish and maintain levels of academic achievement that are tied to the teacher's original perceptions.

Author Ray C. Rist uses a participant-observer method to study the first few school years of a group of St. Louis ghetto children and suggests that "the inequality of American education is accounted for, not so much by differences between schools, but by how the same school treats different children."

He suggests that unequal opportunities are most evident in the classroom where teacher-student interactions, seating arrangements, and everyday activities keep the poor and the black "in their place."

The teacher's self-fulfilling prophecy for student accomplishments starts with kindergarten registration, is developed and reinforced by the student's inability to gain access to the teacher's time and talent, and is cemented into place by second grade with groups of tigers, cardinals, and—of all things—clowns.

Rist reports that the most pervasive thought within the school was that large numbers of children would not "make it" in American society. This was understood by the school establishment to be a problem resulting from depressing levels of poverty, predominance of one-parent families, lack of parental concern, and the lack of reading materials in the home. "So long as the source of failure of the student was held to be outside the structural and bureaucratic domain of the school itself," Rist asserts, "then the school and its practices were not called into question."

Interspersing his narrative with teacher comments and items of interest, the author weaves an account showing an institutional web—school system, teachers' college, teachers—that creates and enforces conditions trapping children with goals and roles that are likely to remain with them for the rest of their school career and thereafter. The schools, he says, perpetuate the social class structure of the society and the ultimate solution to this problem is to be found in the political arena.

The major portion of the book is a chronological school diary of selected events that elaborate on these themes. This is followed by a more in-depth analysis of two "doing well" and two "doing poorly" students.

One assumes that a study of this duration would result in massive documentation but the reader is never given any standard by which the author selected one anecdote or observation over another. One would feel more comfortable knowing the author's original thoughts and how they changed over the three-year period. Instead, the reader is presented with a brief, not totally convincing note on the credibility of applying anthropological perspective to the school scene.

At the end of the first year, the kindergarten teacher says to Rist: "When you find the secret of how these children learn, let me be the first to know." While this was not the intent of Rist's report, it is the critical question. Rist has pinpointed some rather powerful indicators that appear to effectively limit the ability and opportunity of children to learn. His book is worthwhile reading for those who believe that American society and its schools could be made better.

TEDD LEVY

Norwalk
Connecticut

BARRY SUGARMAN. *The School and Moral Development.* Pp. 285. New York: Barnes & Noble, 1973. $13.50.

"Moral education is and always has been a dangerous profession, as the careers of Socrates and Jesus indicate." But, believes Barry Sugarman, it goes on informally and badly when it lacks attention, and with some attention, can or could be a venture as worthwhile as it is urgent. His goal is to see the emergence of "the morally-educated person" or MEP. The MEP is "defined . . . by his concern for other people, his adept social skills and competence in functioning in his environment, his fair-mindedness and strength of character—all of this in addition to the universalistic quality of his moral thought."

We do not have many MEPs, if the testimony of the public is taken seriously. The moral morass of Vietnam and the malaise accompanying Watergate are taken as international and domestic political symbols. High crime rates, delinquency, vandalism, unconcern, anomie—all these are cited as further evidence of decline. Remarkably, until recently—though there were nineteenth century precedents before confusion set in—there had been little attention to education in morals or values in schooling. With the decline in parochial schools, and the confusion resulting from Supreme Court decisions on prayer—decisions which actually charter and encourage certain kinds of moral education—large numbers of people are worried.

Still, Sugarman claims that his is the first work to collate the evidence on how moral education occurs in the modern school. He was working out of an English base when he wrote, though he also took American empirical studies into consideration. His is a valuable compilation, summary, and extrapolating argument. Traces of the profession's jargon—input and output, for example—are here, but for the most part he writes clear and lively prose about bewildering and sometimes deadly topics.

Few elements of education escape his summarizing scrutiny: the home (where love-oriented life must be combined with consistent rules, he thinks), the context in society—with special emphasis on the media, the relations of classrooms, and the formal and informal structures of the school are all taken into account. Sugarman offers no easy solutions. Since his is a wholistic view of personality and character in society, he cannot be simplistic. Too many matters have to be balanced or kept in creative tension.

The suggestions are very mild and complex; hardly a trace of utopia enters in. We can be somewhat better off than we are; that seems to be the message. Critics say, "it could never work." "But how well does the existing system work?" Sugarman serves up evidences, clues, and a sense of the old college —or elementary school—try.

MARTIN E. MARTY
University of Chicago

STEPHAN THERNSTROM. *The Other Bostonians: Poverty and Progress in the American Metropolis, 1880–1970.* Pp. xiv, 345. Cambridge, Mass.: Harvard University Press, 1973. $12.00.

During the past generation, the field of mobility studies, formerly dominated by sociologists, has been invaded by historians. Among the earliest intruders, and the most prolific of the group, is Stephen Thernstrom, presently a professor at Harvard. In 1964, Thernstrom published *Poverty and Progress,* a study of social mobility in Newburyport, Massachusetts, from 1850–1880. In many ways the Newburyport study was pathbreaking, but it was also open to the criticism that Newburyport and Thernstrom's sample were unrepresentative of other American cities and their occupational structures. The result is this study of Boston which attempts to "treat all of the major social elements of a great metropolitan center over a span of nearly a century" (p.4). The core of *The Other Bostonians* is a sample of 7,965 males, drawn from the 1880 U. S. manuscript census, Boston city marriage records for 1910, local birth records for 1930, the 1958 city directory, and a 1963 interview survey of Cambridge and Belmont, Massachusetts residents. From this data,

Thernstrom attempts to answer a number of "critical questions about social structure and social processes in the community"(p. 2).

Thernstrom's analysis of the data yields a number of conclusions that can be summarized as follows: (1) during the years from 1880 to about 1920, Boston experienced a vast in-out migration, the size of which is only hinted at by the net migration figures; since 1920, however, the migratory current has slowed although the population is far from stagnant; (2) the character of the migrant flow has changed: in the first decades of the study the working class population was most transient and the upper-middle class most persistent; since about 1920, this pattern has reversed itself; (3) during the years from 1880–1970, the Boston occupational structure has maintained a constant level of fluidity—in each generation about four out of ten men ended their careers in an occupational stratum different from that in which they first worked and about six of every ten advanced beyond their father's occupation; (4) family social class background influenced career patterns but not enough to prevent a "striking" amount of working class mobility; (5) foreign birth constituted a disadvantage in terms of mobility although there were important differentials between groups. Catholics more than other groups tended to "skid" to lower levels after making an occupational advance, while Jews had the highest rates of occupational mobility; (6) due to discrimination, the experience of blacks within our society has been "different in kind" from that of immigrants, and they experienced virtually no improvement in occupational position from the late-nineteenth century to the beginning of World War II; marked changes, however, have occurred for blacks within the past generation; and (7) comparisons between the findings from Boston and those from other cities reveal much less variance, regardless of size and type, than "is commonly believed." Thernstrom's analysis leads him to con-

clude that "The American class system . . . allowed substantial privilege for the privileged and extensive opportunity for the underprivileged to coexist simultaneously" (p. 258).

This summary does scant justice to Thernstrom's extensive labors with his sample and the implications he draws from it concerning the American social structure. But however diligent and ingenuous Thernstrom has been, there are a number of questions about his approach that will cause readers to regard his conclusions with caution. While he is disarmingly frank about weaknesses in his analysis, in his coding procedure, and in his sampling (see especially Appendix A), these admissions do not seem to have hindered Thernstrom's willingness to draw wide-ranging conclusions. Especially troubling is the small size of Thernstrom's samples which form the basis for his conclusions on occupational mobility. Equally disturbing is Thernstrom's last chapter which finds a "striking consistency of pattern" between his findings on mobility in Boston and those of other scholars on other cities. The demonstration of "striking consistency of pattern" depends on whether or not the reader is prepared to accept percentage differences ranging up to twenty-one points as significant or insignificant. There is also, of course, the danger of generalizing on the basis of studies using different coding patterns and different occupational classifications. Given Thernstrom's willingness to make comparisons between his findings and those of other mobility scholars, it is difficult to understand why he chooses to ignore the result reported by Peter M. Blau and Otis Dudley in their "massive and authoritative study" (Thernstrom's words), *The American Occupational Structure.* Such a comparison would have added further depth to his comparison.

To make these criticisms, however, does not detract from the immensity of Thernstrom's efforts nor the significance of his findings. *The Other*

Bostonians will undoubtedly set the standard for forthcoming mobility studies as has *Poverty and Progress* for the last generation.

JACOB BELKIN
JOEL A. TARR
Carnegie-Mellon University
Pittsburgh
Pennsylvania

ECONOMICS

IRMA ADELMAN and CYNTHIA TAFT MORRIS. *Economic Growth and Social Equity in Developing Countries.* Pp. xiv, 257. Stanford, Calif.: Stanford University Press, 1973. $10.00.

This detailed statistical examination of the interrelationships observable among a variety of characteristics of developing countries represents a direct continuation of the authors' earlier study, *Society, Politics, and Economic Development: A Quantitative Study* (Johns Hopkins Press, 1967), and can be properly evaluated only in juxtaposition to the aims and accomplishments of the earlier work.

In the earlier book, Adelman and Morris discovered certain consistent patterns of quantitative relationships among various social, political, and economic indicators of development for a sample of seventy-four Third World countries stratified into three subsamples by level of overall development. Their statistical findings emphasized the progressive differentiation of social, political, and economic institutions at the core of the development process, generating the rudiments of a general theory of the development process and suggestions for a reorientation of development policy.

The present book extends this statistical analysis to a consideration of the relationships between social, political, and economic development, on the one hand, and political participation and income distribution, on the other. These two indicators of social equity have been selected for special study because of the authors' interest in determining the degree to which the fruits of development in the Third World have been shared among the population at large. They conclude: "The frightening implication of the present work is that hundreds of millions of desperately poor people throughout the world have been hurt rather than helped by economic development. Unless their destinies become a major and explicit focus of development policy in the 1970s and 1980s, economic development may serve merely to promote social injustice" (p. 192).

While considerable independent evidence tends to corroborate this conclusion and the policy guidelines that stem from it, the procedures by which it is arrived at in the present study are open to serious question. The general statistical technique used by the authors is analysis of variance. Factor analysis was the specific method selected in the earlier book, and discriminant analysis and hierarchical-interactions analysis are relied on in the present book. In each case, the seventy-four country sample—stratified into low, medium, and high levels of development—is examined with respect to the interrelationships prevailing among specified sets of independent and dependent variables. Reservations as to the reliability of the authors' conclusions appear to stem not so much from the technique itself as from the means by which they derive the data and the manner in which they interpret the statistical results.

The independent variables used in the present study consist of some forty-eight social, political, and economic development indicators, which the authors spend half the book defining and which formed the basis of their analysis in the earlier book as well. In fact, the actual data used are derived from the earlier book and thus suffer from the same defect: the numerical estimates of each development indicator for the seventy-four country sample are graded rankings of countries based on a survey of "experts" in the field.

The dependent variables are political

participation as defined and operationalized in Appendix A, and income distribution defined in terms of percentage shares by population groups. As in the case of the estimation method used for development indicators, political participation was "quantitatively" estimated on the basis of the authors' a priori judgments of each country's ranking. The specification of national income distributions, too, required certain interesting estimating procedures, since many countries in the sample provide only partial measures; even so, the authors were forced, in this instance, to restrict the country sample to forty-three due to the lack of adequate data.

Whatever the imperfections of the data themselves, it is the interpretation of the results of the analysis that is most debatable. The statistical tests were cross-sectional in nature, covering a stratified sample of countries at a particular moment in history—circa 1960. On the basis of the different relationships prevailing at various strata, however, the authors develop an argument concerning the relationship between characteristics of development and social justice *over time*. The implicit presumption is that economic development is a unilinear phenomenon, experienced in similar fashion by all developing countries. This popular view that development is a single phenomenon, to be experienced "sooner or later" by every Third World country, has been placed in serious doubt by recent research.

Although this study has shortcomings, they cannot detract from the fact that Adelman and Morris have written a highly imaginative and relatively sophisticated work in a sadly neglected area of economics. Their work stands as a milestone on the road to heightened understanding and control of the development process.

EDWARD VAN ROY
State University of New York
Stony Brook

WALLACE N. ATHERTON. *Theory of Union Bargaining Goals*. Princeton, N.J.: Princeton University Press, 1973. $9.50.

Like Gaul, a model of collective bargaining can be divided into three parts: the employer's objectives, the union's goals, and the process by which any conflicts are resolved. The book is devoted solely to the theory behind the union's choice of objectives. In this effort, Atherton attempts a reconciliation of the Arthur Ross-John Dunlop debate: is trade union behavior (especially regarding wages) best viewed as "political" or "economic" in nature?

The author develops his model through a series of progressive complications. First, a simple "economic" model is developed, characterized by the assumption that all members of the union's workforce have the same preferences about objectives. This assumption is then dropped and a "politico-economic" model is developed in which various groups have differing preferences, among which the leadership chooses according to dictates of its and the union's survival. Finally, this model is enriched by adding uncertainty and lack of perfect information, in the face of which the union leadership makes decisions. At that point, we have a model which incorporates both economic and political influences on the union's choice of objectives in an uncertain world.

The model is drawn together in axiomatic fashion once the author reaches the "politico-economic" stage, but the book remains fairly easy and even pleasant to read. Atherton has taken care to indicate the actual counterparts in the real world of many of his institutional and behavioral assumptions about unions. The non-mathematical reader will still derive considerable benefit from this book.

Although Atherton has deftly interwoven the best of Ross, Dunlop, and other theorists of union behavior, the resulting model is still only a partial theory. As the author observes, a variety of aspects of union behavior have been left out: conflict resolution procedures other than collective bargaining, weapons other than the strike, and so on. But more important, in my view, is the fact that as it stands, the model is basically static and (at least politically) competitive in nature. A company and a union—or small numbers of either or both—and the union's antagonistic membership groupings slug it out in an apparently "hard" economic environment. As wage developments in recent years suggest, it is imperative that we develop a more general theory of how the whole wage structure rises through the conscious, recognized, and perhaps even formalized interdependence of great blocs of industries and unions. How do historically venerable and economically powerful wage or "tandem" relationships arise and perpetuate themselves?

These questions were not, of course, the author's objectives for analysis. However, the ultimate model of *Theory of Union Bargaining Goals* contains fruitful ideas for beginning that larger inquiry into the dynamics of wage structure. For the present, this book provides a considerable advance over earlier, even more partial, models of union decision-making in collective bargaining.

JAMES G. SCOVILLE
Department of Economics
Institute of Labor and Industrial
  Relations
The University of Illinois
Urbana

BRIAN J. L. BERRY. *The Human Consequences of Urbanization.* Pp. 205. New York: St. Martin Press, 1973. $9.95.

This book is a highly readable exposition on the process of urbanization in the twentieth century. The author's objective is to dispel the view that urbanization is the same process throughout the world, but rather that it has been produced by diverse circumstances in various countries and has produced different results. Explanations in the book can be understood by the general reader, yet are sophisticated enough to be appreciated by the specialist.

The reader is introduced to the "conventional wisdom" of present day urban theory through a detailed summarization of the nineteenth and early twentieth century thoughts on urbanization. Using this as a basis for discussion, the author plots the divergent paths of urbanization in North America, the Third World, and in post-war Europe.

Contemporary American social and economic changes have increased mobility and lowered urban density. Suburban growth around urban centers has intensified; fully two-thirds of Americans live in single-family housing. Here the American seeks shelter in his enclave of homogeneity: the suburban neighborhood where his neighbors are, like him, free from immediate status competition, free of ethnic or racial minorities; a safe area to be protected by legal, institutional and even illegal means from those that might intrude. Meanwhile, the core cities in America face abandonment by everyone except the poor. Minorities moving into vacancies in a white area accelerate the outmigration of whites. The greater the increase in the ghetto areas, the more rapid the decrease in the central city's total population. Furthermore, the communications media may have contributed to this movement by enforcing the universal perception of decaying central cities in the United States.

Public policies in the United States have reacted to strong economic forces with a complex set of uncoordinated, often contradictory, random policies and programs. Government action has involved the protection of the institutions of a free-enterprise, decentralized, market-oriented system with an unshakeable commitment to private ownership.

The biggest urban growth has occurred in the Third World where big city population increased nine-fold during the period 1920–60. The American and European urban experience involved gradual interdependent economic and social changes spanning more than a century. However, the Third World has had rapid urbanization with the lowest levels of economic development, education, nutrition, and health care. The author delineates the planning efforts in numerous Third World countries including separate sections for Communist China, Israel, and South Africa. The divergence of conditions in various countries further supports his thesis that the effects in human terms vary considerably from the twentieth century "conventional wisdom" typified by the North American experience.

Without an entrepreneurial class and private capital, development in the Third World has been government sponsored, involving foreign technical and economic assistance. Government planners have simply attempted to limit the migration to the large cities. Many countries have tried to develop the backward regions, such as northeastern Brazil and northern Thailand. The planning efforts of the Third World are described as being unconscious, uncoordinated, and even negative. Their aspiration of increasingly affirmative and effective planning will involve the adoption of policies and controls typical of the welfare states of Western Europe and the command economies of Eastern Europe and the Soviet Union.

The author has a more optimistic view of planning by the Europeans. While governments have had differences in the pattern and form of planning, their basic objective is the regional distribution of growth. European growth policies are designed to redress differences in the income and welfare of its citizens between regions of the country. They view growth as the basic means to achieve the social objectives of improved income, housing, education, health, welfare, and recreation. While the metropolitan areas in North America rot away, European public and private development have combined to preserve and reconstruct city centers that still dominate urban life. Documentation of planning in England, France, Sweden, Finland, Netherlands, the Soviet Union, and the Eastern European countries discloses varying circumstances and degrees of success.

The book is a unique overview of the entire gamut of urbanization. While the author's referential style in some chapters often seems tedious, it is probably necessary in summarizing the volume of theory from the past one hundred years. He is able to break through the mass of urban experience, isolating fundamental similarities and differences, leaving us with some degree of optimism for future changes in urban policy through political modification. It is an excellent consideration of the multifaceted conditions that have influenced the urban experience.

RUSSELL P. BELLICO
Department of Economics
Westfield State College
Massachusetts

WARD S. BOWMAN, JR. *Patent and Antitrust Law: A Legal and Economic Appraisal.* Pp. vii, 272. Chicago, Ill.: University of Chicago Press, 1973. $10.50.

Along with discussion about the much publicized issues of pollution, discrimination, inflation, unemployment and energy, a less well-known debate swirls about patent and antitrust law interactions. Bowman in this thorough volume has made a significant contribution to that debate.

His argument is relatively straightforward and can be summarized in four statements. (1) Invention and innovation increase consumer welfare. (2) Patents giving inventors the right to maximum monopoly returns for a limited period of time help motivate this consumer-oriented activity. Thus, there is no basic conflict with anti-trust law, which also has consumer welfare as its basic objective. (3) Patent monopoly requirements of tying contracts and other licensing restrictions are simply the means by which the inventor captures legal monopoly returns. (4) The conclusions of leading cases that such restrictions involve extension of monopoly beyond the patent grant consequently are erroneous.

A useful presentation of the pros and cons of patents is made, touching on the writings of Kenneth Arrow and Frank Knight. Basic themes and concepts of patent-antitrust interplay are addressed, including monopoly extension versus legal maximum profit maximization, leveraging, incipiency, foreclosing, exclusionary practices, patent pools and protection of competitors versus protection of the competitive process. Microeconomic analysis of monopoly and price discrimination are a core part of his work, along with a careful tracing of the key cases in patent and antitrust law relating to the subject.

In conclusion, the book can be particularly recommended for the specialist in this area. The dilettante might find more than he wanted to know about the issues.

HAROLD L. JOHNSON
Department of Economics
Emory University
Atlanta
Georgia

NAOMI CAIDEN and AARON WILDAVSKY. *Planning and Budgeting in Poor Countries.* Pp. xviii, 371. New York: John Wiley & Sons, 1974. $14.95.

The literatures—vast and ever increasing—on planning and on budgeting in poor countries are similar in that they are almost universally case studies, though some of them do attempt generalizations from the specific case examined; and secondly, planning and budgeting are invariably treated separately. The work under review is to be welcomed for it is a pioneering exception: It is not a case study of a country or of a set of countries, but on the basis of fieldwork in eleven underdeveloped countries—as diverse in size, structure, and political organization as Argentina and Nepal—it attempts to generalize to *all* poor countries; and it makes an effort to link and consider together plan implementation and budgeting. That we cannot conclude that the effort is entirely successful is of secondary importance. Caiden and Wildavsky are to be commended for making the effort and thus for

highlighting an important nexus of issues.

Chapters two to five, inclusive, contain their central thesis. Developing upon, and extensively expanding, ideas first suggested by Stolper *(Planning without Facts,* 1966, and *Comprehensive Planning in the Face of Comprehensive Uncertainty,* 1969), Caiden and Wildavsky argue that "from poverty stems uncertainty" (p. 47), that it is the very nature of poverty that it leads to greater relative uncertainty and a markedly reduced capacity to cope with such uncertainties. Information is poor, both in quantity and especially in quality: being poor where, by definition, resources are scarce, such societies operate on very tight margins so that they lack reserves, human and material, to fall back upon in emergencies; being relatively homogeneous, dependent excessively upon agriculture or upon single export commodities, such societies are subject to major vicissitudes in income and expenditures. In consequence, budgeting as it is known in the richer countries is almost unknown, despite the widespread *form* of an annual budget presented to parliament. "Extreme and extensive uncertainty which, when combined with severe scarcity of financial resources, narrows the time horizons of top officials to two or three months or less"(p. 95), leading to the widely observed phenomena of repetitive budgeting, elastic and highly cumbersome bureaucracies, and other things. Caiden and Wildavsky argue this case most persuasively, with a wealth of detail and illustration. This section alone justifies purchase of the book and should be required reading for those, scholars and administrators alike, concerned with the problems of the underdeveloped countries.

The rest of the book fails to achieve a similar high standard. We fail to see the purpose of chapter one ("Questions and Answers: The Literature of Solutions"), for readers of such a book would undoubtedly be familiar with the literature, and, for those not so familiar, the survey is not adequately detailed. The discussion of planning, chapters six to nine inclusive, is fundamentally unsatisfactory. While many of their detailed criticisms of planners—such as an excessive predilection for large demonstration projects or a failure to incorporate flexibility into the process—are valid, we find unacceptable their overall thrust that all planning is *inherently* deficient. The attempted contrast between budgeting which —while subject to improvement—is "good" and planning which is "bad" is quite unconvincing. Budgets and plans are surely not competitors, not mutually exclusive activities. Rather, a more reasonable approach might be to consider a budget as one of the methods of implementing a plan, so that coordinated budgeting and planning are needed. A budget raises and allocates resources and thereby "plans," whether on an ad hoc basis or on a long term overview. It is rare that abandoning an overall strategy and relying solely on day to day tactics will lead to optimal results—though it is equally clear that a rigid adherence to an a priori strategy, failing to adapt tactics to unforeseen changes in the environment, is equally undesirable. A budget is an instrument, not an end. To argue effectively against planning, one needs to argue explicitly that laissez faire—not an idealized laissez faire but one operating in a world of uncertainty and ignorance, of oligopolies and multinational enterprises—would be more effective in achieving the desired ends. Nowhere do Caiden and Wildavsky attempt this. This failure fundamentally affects the persuasiveness of their argument.

J.K.S. GHANDI

The Wharton School
University of Pennsylvania
Philadelphia

JOSEPH ALBERT ERNST. *Money and Politics In America, 1755–1775.* Pp. vii, 403. Chapel Hill, N.C.: University of North Carolina Press, 1973. $14.95.

This book is about the political and economic consequences of the Currency Act of 1764. This somewhat ambiguous law, which applied to the colonies south of New England, prohibited them from making new issues of paper money a legal tender. Several motives came together to produce the Act. To some extent it was the product of the tightening of control over the colonies which occurred in the years preceding the Revolution. But on a more mundane level it reflected the efforts of those British merchants who had extended credit in the colonies in the form of sterling-denominated loans to protect their economic interests.

The leading contributions of this book to political history are detailed accounts of the Currency Act Repeal Movement—which was centered in London with Benjamin Franklin taking a starring role—and the variety of attempts in the colonial assemblies to thwart or circumvent the law. The typical solution was to issue paper money which was not a legal tender, an expedient which probably worked well in practice. But the law undoubtedly constrained the colonial propensity to issue paper currency and may therefore have significantly increased political tensions.

A second strand of analysis is concerned with the economic consequences of colonial monetary policies. The emphasis is on the stability of exchange rates between colonial currencies and the pound sterling. Taking a somewhat unusual stance in a book about money and politics, Ernst assigns changes in the stock of money a minor role in producing exchange fluctuations. He points out correctly that the exchange rate was a relative price determined by the supply of and demand for foreign exchange. He argues that the major sources of fluctuations were changes in the market for colonial staple commodity exports, changes in colonial taste for imports, and frequent curtailments of the supply of English capital due to financial crises in London. In thus rejecting a crude purchasing power parity approach to exchange rates, Ernst has provided a useful framework for future research.

However, sophisticated purchasing power parity theorists would argue that behind the supply and demand schedules of foreign exchange lies, among other things, the level of prices in the colonies relative to England. Moreover, many would argue that the colonial internal price level would be strongly influenced by monetary emissions. Unfortunately, this channel of influence is generally ignored in Ernst's analysis. For this reason monetary historians who are strongly attached to the purchasing power parity theory are not likely to find the author's denigration of the role of money entirely convincing.

The analysis leaves an apparent contradiction between the economic unimportance of money and its political significance. Ernst achieves a reconciliation by arguing that the colonists were crude quantity theorists. Only what they believed to be important really mattered.

This book is written with the tools of the "old"—that is, non-quantitative, economic history. The appropriate method of research is, of course, not a question to be resolved here. However, one gets the strong impression that Ernst adopts the older methodology not so much because he is uninterested in quantitative questions but rather because he is more convinced by the opinions of well informed contemporaries than by economic arguments based on the surviving statistical data. At this point the correct choice of method still seems to be a matter of taste. Undoubtedly, both approaches can further our understanding of colonial economic history.

This is a well written book. It summarizes an immense amount of research carefully and lucidly. Although of most interest to political historians, it is a must on the reading list of any scholar contemplating research on the Revolutionary Era.

HUGH ROCKOFF
Rutgers University
New Brunswick
New Jersey

DON R. LE DUC. *Cable Television and the FCC: A Crisis in Media Control.* Pp. x, 289. Philadelphia, Pa.: Temple University Press, 1973. $10.00.

Cable television, as Professor Le Duc traces its development and the resulting regulatory responses, offers a fascinating example of the interplay of new technology, economic realities and regulatory processes within this nation's current political and social structure. But for Professor Le Duc, the overriding importance of his study is not historical. Rather, he views the cable controversy as only one of an ongoing series of such issues posed by continuing and fast-paced change in communications technology. "Waveguided or true laser transmissions could bypass cumbersome wired circuits to deliver an infinite number of messages directly to individual homes," he writes. "Cable interests will undoubtedly demand FCC intervention to protect the media structure from such destructive competition, but in view of the past history in this field, there is no reason to believe that restriction will be any more successful in that era than in this, or that any regulatory reaction based primarily on industry pressure will ever achieve any consistent society-based guidelines allowing communications evolution without continual crisis" (pp. 20–21). Thus, the basic concern of this book is with the future. Are there lessons to be learned from the tortured history of cable television that will be helpful in improving the processes by which the next and succeeding waves of technical change will be absorbed into the communications industry?

At the risk of severe oversimplification, the basic analytical framework over which Professor Le Duc stretches his detailed account of cable television during the past two decades is as follows. Cable television offers two fundamental advances in television communication. First, it can extend coverage to areas not reached by over-the-air transmission. And second, either in previously uncovered areas or those already served by broadcast television, it can expand vastly the number of options available to viewers, either by importing signals from other areas or by originating its own programs. The first function essentially serves the interests of broadcasters already in the industry; but the second represents a grave competitive threat. The Federal Communications Commission has never been simply a servant of entrenched industry interests, if for no other reason than that the industry itself is very diverse and has never coalesced into a unified interest group. But from its inception, the FCC has viewed its most important regulatory goal as promotion and protection of local broadcasting services, both in radio and television. The preoccupation with local service is, in turn, primarily a response to Congressional pressures on the Commission, since Congressmen have an eminently understandable interest in the welfare and goodwill of the independent radio and television stations in their districts. Efforts to harness the potential of cable television to this local service goal explain much of the behavior of the FCC. And as a final irony, the preference for network television shows, and the predominance of recorded music over community interest and locally originated radio programs make it obvious that the audiences do not share the FCC's sense of priorities regarding the services to be provided by the electronic communications media.

Professor Le Duc elaborates on his basic theme in a lucid and informative manner. But the only major policy recommendation his analysis leads him to is, in my mind, disappointing and inadequate. "All that seems necessary," he writes, "is an amendment to the Communications Act of 1934 expressly relieving the FCC of any responsibility for the economic welfare of the electronic mass media, an obligation it now discharges on the most tenuous of grounds" (p. 210). The simplicity of the proposal seems to belie the complexity of the problem. And such an abroga-

tion, unless coupled with an ending of the authority and responsibility to compel industry behavior designed to meet preordained "public" goals—that is, *de facto* abolition of the FCC as a regulatory agency—strikes me as a path to chaos, not reform. But this negative reaction in no way detracts from my admiration for the analytic, informative and thought-provoking qualities of Professor Le Duc's book.

WILLIAM L. BALDWIN
Department of Economics
Dartmouth College
Hanover
New Hampshire

ROY F. LEE. *The Setting for Black Business Development: A Study in Sociology and Political Economy.* Pp. vii, 249. Ithaca: New York State School of Industrial and Labor Relations, Cornell University, 1973. $7.00. Paperbound.

This is a poorly written book with some exceptionally good material. Therefore it poses certain problems for the reviewer. It would be easy to dismiss the book as mediocre but for the importance of the topic and the insights shown by the author in his analysis of a small part of the subject matter—that is, the federally funded programs of minority enterprises.

The book is divided into three convenient parts. The first one deals with the existing sociological and economic environment in the United States as it relates to minority groups. Part two is a history of black business development. It also describes and analyzes existing federal and, to a much lesser degree, local government programs designed to assist the development of black business enterprises. Part three provides detailed profiles of the black banker and black insurance executive based on questionnaire data of ninety-seven responses and compares these profiles with those of top executives of large corporations in the United States and India.

This book is an expanded version of Lee's doctoral dissertation—Part three in the book. It is an attempt to put his findings into a broader socioeconomic context; unfortunately, he has not succeeded. The book lacks cohesiveness due to the absence of an overall viewpoint or hypothesis. My main criticisms of the book, however, are the lack of rigor in definitions and unstructured and poorly supported arguments and conclusions which are untenable based on the data presented.

Instead of succinct analysis, the book appears to be a compilation of quotes from the writings of various people, notably DuBois, Washington, Cruse, Innis, and a few others. A scholarly book is not the one with the largest number of quotations and footnotes. While data should be carefully marshalled to make a point, supporting one's opinion with another opinion is simply tautological. For example, on the very first page of the book, Lee asserts that, in America, economic power and political power go together and that those without economic power have little or no political power. While the interaction of economic and political power is undeniable, Lee does not present any logic or historical reasoning to tell us how he came to establish the causal relationship between the two types of power. The book is similarly cluttered with "sociologese"—jargon which is often undecipherable and tends to confuse. The author frequently pontificates and makes sweeping statements, which he substitutes for objective reasoning, and expects us to accept these statements as "obvious facts" and, therefore, undeniable.

In another dimension, Lee shows fuzzy thinking when he talks about the way by which blacks can assume their proper share in the economic leadership of the country. Citing the example of successful black banks and insurance companies, Lee suggests that the increase in their ownership pattern is the only way to salvation. Apparently, Lee overlooks the fact that it is not the ownership of large corporations but the control which is more important, and that this control is not with the owners (stockholders) but with professional managers. Black banks control about $350 million in assets of a total of $400 billion by all the banks in the United States. Thus, blacks will not achieve any significant role in making any important economic decisions or increasing black employment in the United States even if their assets grow tenfold. To have any meaningful impact, blacks must assume or acquire positions of responsibility within the existing corporate structure. It is wishful thinking to believe that blacks can bring about any significant changes in the American economic system by creating competitive or even parallel business institutions.

The only redeeming feature of the book is the author's superb analysis of Nixon's programs for the development of minority enterprises and his proposals to improve their efficiency and alternatives for greater achievement of the objectives (pp. 119–162). I would strongly recommend this section for the careful study by all those who are interested in this area.

In conclusion, I believe the author would have been better off to write two or three short articles summarizing his major findings and presenting his viewpoint. Such an approach would have immensely helped his readers as well.

S. PRAKASH SETHI
University of California
Berkeley

KAREN ORREN. *Corporate Power and Social Change: The Politics of the Life Insurance Industry.* Pp. vii, 204. Baltimore, Md.: The Johns Hopkins Press, 1974. $10.00.

This is a good study in depth of the life insurance industry of Illinois—its motivations, politics, lending policies, and attempts to move toward more "social responsibility" in lending. The main title promises too much since the book does not contribute greatly to the broad question of whether the proper goal of large corporations in general is to look out for stockholders' interests or to accept lower profits in order to subsidize other groups.

The study starts out rather disappointingly with an introductory chapter that tends to deal with economics but fails to display enough knowledge of the subject. The author cites J. K. Galbraith on the alleged decline of competition, the ability of oligopolistic industry to administer prices at will, and the power of advertising to dominate the consumer. She does not seem to be aware that reputable economists have found evidence of quite the opposite nature. A rather strange statement is made (p. 8) that the prevalence today of retained earnings as a major source of corporate financing removes an important constraint on management "since profit levels previously had to remain high in order to insure a market for future securities." High profits are also a great help to the retention of earnings.

Professor Orren does much better in the areas of political science and empirical investigation. Her detailed analysis of insurance company lending in the Chicago area according to such factors as value of homes, density of population, urban or suburban location, race, and neighborhood condition is painstaking and impressive. Her interviews with insurance company executives, lobbyists, and politicians add interesting content.

The general feeling generated by the book is that even in a field such as life insurance, where cash flow is made dependable by long term contracts, it is not to be expected that there will be drastic departures from the principle of personal utility maximization. Insurance companies are probably characterized correctly as interested mainly in profits and growth. Social impulses of executives, on the other hand, are vague and variable.

Orren gives special attention to the Life Insurance Urban Investments Program under which two billion dollars was devoted to loans to improve the inner city. Conclusions as to its effectiveness are not easily drawn and differ from one observer to the next. While market interest rates were charged, loans were, to a degree, channeled into black ghettos previously unserved. But really hard core areas, with their rival gangs and general dilapidation, were found to be beyond help from this sort of program.

MARSHALL R. COLBERG
Florida State University
Tallahassee

GRANT L. REUBER et al. *Private Foreign Investment in Development.* Pp. 371. London: Oxford University Press, 1973. $17.75.

This book is a scholarly analysis of the economic effects of private foreign investment on economically backward countries. It is based primarily on new data collected by interview from eighty large manufacturing projects located in twenty-nine of the less developed countries. The authors also use the available statistical data on international investment from government sources and compare their own conclusions with those of others. The result is an informative summary of what is known about the economic effects of private foreign investment.

Private foreign investment is viewed in different ways. In developed countries, many advocate investment in less fortunate countries as a moral obligation or a form of charity. In the less developed countries, it is often viewed as a form of exploitation. The authors conclude that one of the principal steps that could be taken to assist less developed countries is to increase the supply of relevant statistical information.

The eighty projects studied are classified into three groups: industries producing for export, those producing for the local market, and those initiated at the request of foreign governments. There are numerous statistical tables contrasting the characteristics of these three groups. On the average, the government-initiated projects have had higher production costs than similar enterprises in the developed countries, and therefore probably were wasteful of resources. They were also more fully protected by tariffs and preferential taxes than the other types of projects. The most profitable projects were those that were export-oriented.

The taxes on the profits of the international companies, amounting in 1970 to between $3.2 and $4.0 billion, have contributed significantly to the economic resources of the less developed countries. Also, the principal sacrifice of the investing countries resulting from these foreign investments is the loss of those revenues. In addition, foreign-owned manufacturing firms alone employed 1.6 million persons in these countries in 1967. Almost all were local persons, and their wages were at or above prevailing rates.

The eighty projects provide little information on the major economic issue concerning private foreign investment—the effect on labor productivity. Although cross sectional estimates show clearly that GNP per capita is higher in those less developed countries which have larger amounts of private direct investment per capita, private investment and levels of income are interrelated. Private investment need not be the cause of the higher income. Still needed is an empirical study of the effect of the introduction of modern technology on the productivity of labor in these countries.

COLIN D. CAMPBELL
Dartmouth College
Hanover
New Hampshire

NEIL TRANTER. *Population since the Industrial Revolution: The Case of England and Wales.* Pp. 206. New York: Barnes & Noble, 1973. $13.50.

The stated intention of this book is "to serve as a brief introduction to the study of the population of England and Wales since the early eighteenth century. It aims to describe the pattern of population growth, and to examine some of its principal causes and consequences." To justify its appearance soon after the publication of several other excellent works on the subject, the author states his belief "that one of the greatest problems confronting anyone coming fresh to the study of English population history is the vast array of literature with which he must grapple" and announces as his main purpose "to attempt to draw together and summarize as much of this material as possible in one reasonably short volume." How successfully this purpose is served will depend on what aspects of the subject are of primary interest to the reader. One who is looking for a general overview of English demographic history as such—in terms of the growth and spatial redistribution of the population, fertility, mortality, international and internal migration, and aspects of population composition—is likely to find its contents rather skimpy. It serves better as a synthesis and critical evaluation of the literature on interrelations between population growth and the development of the English economy and society in the modern age. Different views of these interrelations found in the most important relevant works are succinctly and lucidly summarized and evaluated in the light of historical evidence. The author's own opinions and conclusions are a valuable supplement to this literature.

In chapters devoted to the sources of demographic data and methods of analysis and to the growth of the population between 1695 and 1939, the author takes the position that the defects of presently available data preclude any meaningful analysis of the components of population growth before the 1840s in terms of mortality, fertility, immigration, and emigration. The chapter on the causes of expansion of the population during the period of the initial demographic "take-off," between 1780 and 1850, appears to this reviewer as the most valuable part of the book. One of its useful features is the comparison of England's experience with that of other western European countries in this period. Noting a broad similarity of demographic developments in diverse economic circumstances, the author considers as a plausible explanation "an exogenous amelioration in the virulence of epidemic disease or an improvement in human resistance," possibly due to change in the climate. The chapter on the "demographic transition" between 1850 and 1939 and its causal explanation is less satisfying, especially in regard to the decline of mortality and the influences of economic and other factors in this respect. In fairness to the author, it should be noted that the mortality side of the history of the demographic transition has not received the attention it deserves in the literature which he attempts to summarize. It is a pity that the device of viewing England's experience in a European regional frame, employed so effectively in the preceding chapter, is hardly used at all in this one. The work is completed by two chapters dealing with the role of population growth and structural change as a causal factor in the economic, cultural, political, and social development of England. "In the course of industrialization and economic development," Tranter opines (p. 170), "the population variable has undoubtedly lost much of its autonomy and a good deal of its relative significance. Demographic trends have become much less dependent on the uncontrollable vagaries of nature and much more dependent on human control; and population itself has become much less vital an agent of economic change than it was in the preindustrial world. Yet despite this we would be well advised to continue treating the population factor as a potential force for social change."

JOHN D. DURAND
University of Pennsylvania
Philadelphia

RICHARD J. WARD. *Development Issues for the 1970s.* Pp. xiv, 282. New York: Dunellen, 1973. $15.00.

As the title of the book indicates, this study represents a conceptual approach to the various problems facing developing nations. A major objective of this work is to identify these problems and to take them to the conference table, the classroom and the public to induce free discussion and to suggest new approaches which might contribute to better understanding of the issues involved and perhaps contribute to their solution.

This study strikes a happy medium between pure historical description of concrete cases of development and an attempt to develop a broad generalized conceptual framework for analysis of problems of economic development. It is a pragmatic attempt to deal with specific issues and problems as they arise in the process of development. These problems are handled within the theoretical framework of existing hypotheses which belong to the category of "intermediate range" theories.

The author considers the 1960s a "decade of development" during which many developing nations achieved a considerable developmental progress. But many problems still remain and they are carried over into the 1970s. Despite considerable past successes, the gap in living standards continues to grow in absolute terms and the problems of income and social inequalities are not resolved.

This very timely volume is divided in three parts. Part one deals with the dramatic race between the growth of population and the increase in production of food. It describes the "green revolution" in agricultural production, population control programs, transformation of agriculture from subsistence-oriented to a surplus generating sector and a "residual" human factor with its elements of knowledge, innovation, drive and improved organization.

Part two is dedicated to current development problems and covers, among others, such important issues as social and income inequality, sharply rising debt service ratio, declining net aid, critical balance of payment pressures, defaults and need of multilateralism in aid.

The last part examines various planning strategies and potentials. It treats such issues as balance between "big push" and balanced development, identifying the highest yield programs, change in strategies of development, new approaches to the growth and development processes and future directions of research.

Numerous statistical tables containing up-to-date information on several aspects of economic development unavailable elsewhere greatly increase the value of this outstanding contribution in the field of economic development.

OLEG ZINAM

Department of Economics
University of Cincinnati
Ohio

OTHER BOOKS

ANDERSON, MARJORIE O. *Kings & Kingship in Early Scotland.* Pp. viii, 310. Totowa, N.J.: Rowman and Littlefield, 1974. $13.50.

ANDERSON, RALPH E. and IRL E. CARTER. *Human Behavior in the Social Environment: A Social Systems Approach.* Pp. v, 183. Chicago, Ill.: Aldine, 1974. $8.50.

AVINERI, SHLOMO. *Hegel's Theory of the Modern State.* Pp. vii, 252. New York: Cambridge University Press, 1974. $4.45. Paperbound.

AXELSON, ERIC. *Congo to Cape: Early Portuguese Explorers.* Pp. 224. New York: Barnes & Noble, 1973. $11.00.

BAILY, SAMUEL L. and RONALD I. HYMAN, eds. *Perspectives on Latin America.* Pp. 105. New York: Macmillan, 1974. $5.95.

BALDWIN, ROBERT E. and J. DAVID RICHARDSON. *International Trade and Finance: Readings.* Pp. v, 486. Boston, Mass.: Little, Brown, 1974. $6.95. Paperbound.

BARBER, JAMES DAVID. *The Presidential Character: Predicting Performance in the White House.* Pp. v, 479. Englewood Cliffs, N.J.: Prentice Hall, 1972. No price.

BARCK, OSCAR and NELSON M. BLAKE. *Since 1900.* 5th ed. Pp. v, 821. New York: Macmillan, 1974. $12.95.

BELOK, MICHAEL V. *Forming the American Mind.* Pp. 248. Mesa, Ariz.: Michael V. Belok, 1973. $8.00.

BENDIX, REINHARD, ed. *State and Society: A Reader in Comparative Political Sociology.* Pp. 656. Berkeley, Calif.: University of California, 1974. $17.50.

BENSMAN, JOSEPH and ARTHUR J. VIDICH. *The New American Society.* Pp. v, 306. New York: Quadrangle, 1973. $2.95. Paperbound.

BENT, DR. ALAN EDWARD. *Escape from Anarchy.* Pp. 212. Memphis, Tenn.: State University Press, 1972. $6.95.

BERGER, BRIGITTE, ed. *Readings in Sociology: A Biographical Approach.* Pp. 561. New York: Basic Books, 1974. $10.00. Paperbound, $5.95.

BERLE, PETER A.A. *Does the Citizen Stand a Chance?* Pp. ix, 127. Woodbury, N.Y.: Barron's Educational Series, 1974. $1.25. Paperbound.

BERNSTEIN, HARRY. *Dom Pedro II.* Twayne's Rulers and Statesmen of the World Series, no. 20. Pp. 267. New York: Twayne, 1974. $5.95.

BLUME, STUART S. *Toward a Political Sociology of Science.* Pp. ix, 288. New York: The Free Press, 1974. $9.95.

BONDANELLA, PETER E. *Machiavelli and the Art of Renaissance History.* Pp. 186. Detroit, Mich.: Wayne State University Press, 1973. $10.95.

BRAYBROOKE, DAVID. *Traffic Congestion Goes through the Issue-Machine: A Case-Study in Issue Processing, Illustrating a New Approach.* Pp. ix, 62. Boston, Mass.: Routledge & Kegan Paul, 1974. $11.75.

BROADFOOT, BARRY. *Ten Lost Years: 1929–1939.* Pp. iv, 390. New York: Doubleday, 1974. $7.95.

CAMERON, GORDON C. and LOWDON WINGO, eds. *Cities, Regions and Public Policy.* Pp. v, 337. New York: Longman, 1973. $15.00.

CAMPBELL, BERNARD. *Human Evolution.* 2nd ed. Pp. v, 469. Chicago, Ill.: Aldine, 1974. $12.50. Paperbound, $7.95.

CAPLAN, FRANK and THERESA. *The Power of Play.* Pp. 360. New York: Doubleday, 1974. $3.95. Paperbound.

CARLSON, RICHARD J., ed. *Issues of Electoral Reform.* Pp. v, 159. New York: National Municipal League, 1974. $3.50. Paperbound.

CARNEY, JAMES D. and RICHARD K. SCHEER. *Fundamentals of Logic.* 2nd ed. Pp. v, 428. New York: Macmillan, 1974. $8.95.

CARSTEN, F. L. *The Reichswehr and Politics, 1918–1933.* Pp. 440. Berkeley, Calif.: University of California Press, 1974. $4.25. Paperbound.

CARTER, APRIL. *Direct Action and Liberal Democracy.* Pp. 170. New York: Harper & Row, 1973. $9.00. Paperbound, $3.95.

CAUGHEY, JOHN. *To Kill a Child's Spirit: The Tragedy of School Segregation in Los Angeles.* Pp. viii, 255. Itasca, Ill.: F.E. Peacock, 1973. $4.95. Paperbound.

CAVAN, RUTH SHONLE, ed. *Marriage and Family in the Modern World: Readings.* 4th ed. Pp. 500. New York: Thomas Y. Crowell, 1974. No price.

CIPOLLA, CARLO M. *Cristofano and the Plague: A Study in the History of Public Health in the Age of Galileo.* Pp. 188.

Berkeley, Calif.: University of California, 1973. $7.50.

COHEN, ABNER, ed. *Urban Ethnicity*. A.S.A. Monograph Series, no. 12. Pp. v, 391. New York: Barnes & Noble, 1974. $16.00.

COHEN, STANLEY and LAURIE TAYLOR. *Psychological Survival*. Pp. 216. New York: Pantheon, 1973. $6.95.

COHEN, STANLEY and JOCK YOUNG, eds. *The Manufacture of News: A Reader*. Pp. 383. Beverly Hills, Calif.: Sage, 1974. $15.00.

COHEN, YEHUDI A., ed. *Man in Adaptation: The Biosocial Background*. 2nd ed. Pp. 522. Chicago, Ill.: Aldine, 1974. No price.

COHEN, YEHUDI A., ed. *Man in Adaptation: The Cultural Present*. 2nd ed. Pp. 602. Chicago, Ill.: Aldine, 1974. $15.00. Paperbound, $5.95.

COOK, CHRIS and JOHN RAMSDEN, eds. *By-Elections in British Politics*. Pp. ix, 399. New York: St. Martin's Press, 1974. $17.95.

COPPA, FRANK J. *Camillo Di Cavour*. Twayne's Rulers and Statesmen of the World Series, no. 24. Pp. 215. New York: Twayne Publishers, 1974. $5.95.

COWAN, PETER et al, eds. *The Future of Planning*. Vol. 1. Centre for Environmental Studies. Pp. 184. Beverly Hills, Calif.: Sage Publications, 1973. $8.95.

CREWE, IVOR, ed. *British Political Sociology Yearbook: Elites in Western Democracy*. Vol. I. Pp. 360. New York: Halsted Press, 1974. $15.95.

CURTIN, MARY ELLEN, ed. *Symposium on Love*. Pp. xii, 244. New York: Behavioral Publications, 1973. $9.95.

DAUBIER, JEAN. *A History of the Chinese Cultural Revolution*. Pp. vii, 336. New York: Random House, 1974. $2.45. Paperbound.

DAVIS, JAMES W., JR. *An Introduction to Public Administration: Politics, Policy, and Bureaucracy*. Pp. v, 336. New York: Free Press, 1974. $8.95.

DIXON, BERNARD. *What is Science For?* Pp. 256. New York: Harper & Row, 1974. $7.50. Paperbound, $3.95.

DOBROVIR, WILLIAM A. et al. *The Offenses of Richard M. Nixon*. Pp. 169. New York: Quadrangle, 1974. $3.00. Paperbound.

DOSA, MARTA L. *Libraries in the Political Scene*. Pp. xv, 226. Westport, Conn.: Greenwood Press, 1974. $12.50.

DUBOFSKY, MELVYN. *We Shall Be All: A History of the Industrial Workers of the World*. Pp. v, 557. New York: Quadrangle, 1974. $4.95. Paperbound.

DUIGNAN, PETER and L. H. GANN. *Colonialism in Africa, 1870-1960: A Bibliographical Guide to Colonialism in Sub-Saharan Africa*. Vol. 5. Pp. v, 552. New York: Cambridge University Press, 1974. $27.50.

DUVERGER, MAURICE. *Modern Democracies: Economic Power versus Political Power*. Pp. 198. Hinsdale, Ill.: Dryden, 1974. No price. Paperbound.

EHRLICH, THOMAS. *Cyprus, 1958-1967: International Crises and the Role of Law*. Pp. 164. New York: Oxford University Press, 1974. $1.95. Paperbound.

ELDEFONSO, EDWARD. *Issues in Corrections: A Book of Readings*. Criminal Justice Series. Pp. 372. Beverly Hills, Calif.: Glencoe, 1974. $5.95. Paperbound.

FARSON, RICHARD. *Birthrights: A Bill of Rights for Children*. Pp. vii, 248. New York: Macmillan, 1974. $6.95.

FERNS, H. S. *The Argentine Republic, 1516-1971*. Pp. 212. New York: Barnes & Noble, 1973. $10.00.

FEST, JOACHIM C. *Hitler*. Pp. v, 844. New York: Harcourt Brace Jovanovich, 1974. $15.00.

FICHTER, JOSEPH H. *One-Man Research: Reminiscences of a Catholic Sociologist*. Pp. v, 258. New York: John Wiley & Sons, 1973. No price.

FILL, J. HERBERT. *The Mental Breakdown of a Nation*. Pp. 136. New York: New Viewpoints, 1974. $6.95. Paperbound, $3.95.

FINDLAY, RONALD E. *International Trade and Development Theory*. Pp. x, 230. New York: Columbia University, 1973. $12.00.

FLEISCHER, HELMUT. *Marxism and History*. Pp. 160. New York: Harper & Row, 1974. $8.00. Paperbound, $3.95.

GATES, JOHN M. *Schoolbooks and Krags: The United States Army in the Philippines, 1898-1902*. Pp. xi, 315. Westport, Conn.: Greenwood, 1973. $11.00.

GELFAND, DONALD E. and RUSSELL D. LEE. *Ethnic Conflicts and Power: A Cross-National Perspective*. Pp. v, 354. New York: John Wiley & Sons, 1973. $8.95. Paperbound, $6.95.

GEORGE, PIERRE. *France: A Geographical Study*. Pp. v, 228. New York: Barnes & Noble, 1974. $12.75. Paperbound, $5.25.

GORDON, MARGARET S., ed. *Higher Education and the Labor Market*. The Carnegie Commission on Higher Education. Pp. xi, 629. New York: McGraw-Hill, 1974. $17.50.

GRAY, TONY. *The Orange Order*. Pp. 292. Levittown, N.Y.: Transatlantic Arts, 1972. $9.50.

HAFFNER, SEBASTIAN. *Failure of a Revolution—Germany, 1918-19*. Pp. 205. La Salle, Ill.: Library Press, 1973. $7.95.

HAIM, SYLVIA G., ed. *Arab Nationalism: An Anthology.* Pp. 255. Berkeley, Calif.: University of California, 1974. $12.75.

HALLOWELL, A. IRVING. *Culture and Experience.* Pp. iii, 434. Philadelphia, Pa.: University of Pennsylvania, 1974. $6.95. Paperbound.

HASKINS, JAMES. *Witchcraft, Mysticism and Magic in the Black World.* Pp. 168. New York: Doubleday, 1974. $4.50.

HIGGINS, HUGH. *The Cold War.* Pp. 141. New York: Barnes & Noble, 1974. $9.00.

HOETINK, H. *Slavery and Race Relations in the Americas: Comparative Notes on their Nature and Nexus.* Pp. 232. New York: Harper & Row, 1973. $13.50. Paperbound, $3.95.

HOUSE, PETER. *The Urban Environmental System.* Pp. 352. Beverly Hills, Calif.: Sage, 1973. $15.00.

IVANOV, MIROSLAV. *Target: Heydrich.* Pp. 292. New York: Macmillan, 1974. $7.95.

JAMES, JUDSON L. *American Political Parties in Transition.* Pp. xi, 273. New York: Harper & Row, 1974. $7.95.

JEFFERSON, LARA. *These Are My Sisters: A Journal from the Inside of Insanity.* Pp. 232. New York: Doubleday, 1974. $7.95.

JOHNSON, DOUGLAS, ed. *The Making of the Modern World: The World of Empires.* Vol. II. Pp. 415. New York: Barnes & Noble, 1974. $16.50.

JONES, ANN. *Uncle Tom's Campus.* Pp. ix, 225. New York: Touchstone, 1973. $2.95. Paperbound.

JONES, EUGENE W. et al. *Practicing Texas Politics.* 2nd ed. Pp. v, 467. Boston, Mass.: Houghton Mifflin, 1974. $5.95. Paperbound.

JUKIC, ILIJA. *The Fall of Yugoslavia.* Pp. 315. New York: Harcourt Brace Jovanovich, 1974. $8.50.

JUPP, PETER. *British and Irish Elections: 1784–1831.* Pp. 212. New York: Barnes & Noble, 1973. $12.50.

KAIL, F. M. *What Washington Said: Administration Rhetoric and the Vietnam War, 1949–1969.* Pp. 256. New York: Harper & Row, 1974. $16.50. Paperbound, $3.95.

KELCH, RAY A. *Newcastle: A Duke Without Money, Thomas Pelham–Holles, 1693–1768.* Pp. 232. Berkeley, Calif.: University of California, 1974. $12.00.

KIMBALL, SOLON I. and JACQUETTA H. BURNETT. *Learning and Culture.* Pp. v, 264. Seattle, Wash.: University of Washington, 1973. $6.50. Paperbound.

KIRKEMO, RONALD B. *An Introduction to International Law.* Pp. ix, 235. Chicago, Ill.: Nelson-Hall, 1974. $7.95.

LAWRENCE, D. L. *Don't Rock the Boat (U.S.S. Nasa).* Pp. 199. Houston, Texas: D. L. Lawrence, 1974. $10.00. Paperbound.

LENTIN, A. *Russia in the Eighteenth Century.* Pp. v, 139. New York: Barnes & Noble, 1974. $8.75.

LEWIS, PAUL G. and DAVID C. POTTER, eds. *The Practice of Comparative Politics.* Pp. vii, 352. New York: Longman, 1974. $9.00. Paperbound, $4.50.

LIFTON, ROBERT JAY. *Home from the War: Vietnam Veterans neither Victims nor Executioners.* Pp. 478. New York: Simon and Schuster, 1973. $3.95. Paperbound.

LITTELL, FRANKLIN H. and HUBERT G. LOCKE, eds. *The German Church and the Holocaust.* Pp. 327. Detroit, Mich.: Wayne State University, 1974. $15.95.

LOPEZ, ANDRE A. and JAN YOORS. *The Gypsies of Spain.* Pp. 143. New York: Macmillan, 1974. $12.95.

MACKINNOO, JAMES. *The History of Edward The Third (1327–1377).* Pp. vi, 625. Totowa, N.J.: Rowman and Littlefield, 1974. $20.00.

MARLOW, LOUIS. *Sackville of Drayton.* Pp. 300. Totowa, N.J.: Rowman and Littlefield, 1974. $12.50.

MARTINDALE, DON and EDITH. *Psychiatry and the Law: The Crusade Against Involuntary Hospitalization.* Pp. v, 194. St. Paul, Minn.: Windflower Publishers, 1973. No price.

MASON, H. P. and J. G. CAIGER. *A History of Japan.* Pp. 334. New York: The Free Press, 1974. $8.95.

MCCOY, F. N. *Robert Baillie and the Second Scots Reformation.* Pp. ix, 244. Berkeley, Calif.: University of California, 1974. $10.00.

MCNALL, SCOTT G., ed. *The Sociological Perspective: Introductory Readings.* 3rd ed. Pp. vii, 660. Boston, Mass.: Little, Brown, 1974. No price.

MCNAMARA, PATRICK H., ed. *Religion American Style.* Pp. vii, 408. New York: Harper & Row, 1974. $4.95. Paperbound.

MECHANIC, DAVID. *Politics, Medicine, and Social Science.* Pp. vii, 306. New York: John Wiley & Sons, 1974. $12.95.

MEYER, MICHAEL. *A Handbook for the Humanistic Astrologer.* Pp. 384. New York: Doubleday, 1974. $4.50. Paperbound.

MINTER, WILLIAM. *Portuguese Africa and the West.* Pp. 200. New York: Monthly Review Press, 1974. $2.95.

MOORE, WILBERT E. *Social Change.* 2nd ed. Pp. vii, 132. Englewood Cliffs, N.J.: Prentice-Hall, 1974. No price.

MORGAN, E. PHILIP, ed. *The Administration*

of Change in Africa. Pp. v, 420. Cambridge, Mass.: Dunellen, 1974. $15.00.

MORGAN, M. R. *The Chronicle of Ernoul and the Continuations of William of Tyre.* Oxford Historical Monographs. Pp. 204. New York: Oxford University Press, 1974. $14.50.

MOSS, MILTON, ed. *The Measurement of Economic and Social Performance.* Studies in Income & Wealth, no. 38. National Bureau of Economic Research. Pp. 605. New York: Columbia University Press, 1974. $17.50.

MUNRO, JOHN A. and ALEX I. INGLIS, eds. *Mike: The Memoirs of the Right Honourable Lester B. Pearson, 1948–1957.* Vol. II. Pp. 344. New York: Quadrangle, 1974. $12.50.

NAGATSUKA, RYUJI. *I Was a Kamikaze.* Pp. 212. New York: Macmillan, 1974. $6.96.

NANDA, B. R. *The Nehrus: Motilal and Jawaharlal.* Pp. 357. Chicago, Ill.: University of Chicago Press, 1974. $3.95. Paperbound.

NANUASHVILI, JAN V. *What Everyone in the Free World Should Know about Russia.* Pp. 386. New York: Vantage Press, 1973. $10.00.

NEUBECK, KENNETH J. *Corporate Response to Urban Crisis.* Pp. vii, 166. Lexington, Mass.: Lexington Books, 1974. $13.50.

The Official Associated Press Almanac, 1974. Pp. 1,040. New York: Quadrangle, 1974. $5.95.

OLDSON, WILLIAM O. *The Historical and Nationalistic Thought of Nicolae Iorga.* Pp. 135. New York: Columbia University Press, 1974. $10.00.

OSBORN, ROBERT J. *The Evolution of Soviet Politics.* Pp. vii, 574. Homewood, Ill.: Dorsey Press, 1974. $10.95.

PARK, GEORGE. *The Idea of Social Structure.* Pp. viii, 392. New York: Doubleday, 1974. $3.50. Paperbound.

PERRETT, GEOFFREY. *Days of Sadness, Years of Triumph: The American People, 1939–1945.* Pp. 512. Baltimore, Md.: Penguin, 1974. $2.95. Paperbound.

PETACCO, ARRIGO. *Joe Petrosino.* Pp. viii, 195. New York: Macmillan, 1974. $5.95.

PHILLIPSON, MICHAEL. *Understanding Crime and Delinquency.* Pp. ix, 210. Chicago, Ill.: Aldine, 1974. $7.50. Paperbound, $2.95.

PIRAGES, DENNIS C. and PAUL R. EHRLICH. *Ark II: Social Response to Environmental Imperatives.* Pp. viii, 344. San Francisco, Calif.: W. H. Freeman, 1974. $3.95. Paperbound.

POWERS, WILLIAM T. *Behavior: The Control of Perception.* Pp. vii, 296. Chicago, Ill.: Aldine, 1973. $8.95.

PREWITT, KENNETH and SIDNEY VERBA. *An Introduction to American Government.* Pp. vi, 630. New York: Harper & Row, 1974. $9.95.

PRYCE, ROY. *The Politics of the European Community.* Pp. vii, 209. Totowa, N.J.: Rowman and Littlefield, 1974. $6.75. Paperbound.

QUESTER, GEORGE H. *The Continuing Problem of International Politics.* Pp. vii, 272. New York: Dryden Press, 1974. No price.

QUINNEY, RICHARD, ed. *Criminal Justice in America: A Critical Understanding.* Pp. v, 448. Boston, Mass.: Little, Brown, 1974. $6.95. Paperbound.

QUINNEY, RICHARD. *Critique of Legal Order: Crime Control in Capitalist Society.* Pp. v, 206. Boston, Mass.: Little, Brown, 1974. $4.95. Paperbound.

RAINES, JOHN CURTIS. *Attack on Privacy.* Pp. 144. Valley Forge, Pa.: Judson, 1974. $4.95. Paperbound.

RAINWATER, LEE, ed. *Social Problems and Public Policy: Deviance and Liberty.* Pp. v, 437. Chicago, Ill.: Aldine, 1974. $15.00. Paperbound, $5.75.

RAINWATER, LEE, ed. *Social Problems and Public Policy: Inequality and Justice.* Pp. v, 456. Chicago, Ill.: Aldine, 1974. No price.

REYNOLDS, CHARLES. *Theory and Explanation in International Politics.* Pp. v, 367. New York: Barnes & Noble, 1974. $17.50.

ROAZEN, PAUL, ed. *Sigmund Freud.* Pp. 186. Englewood Cliffs, N.J.: Prentice-Hall, 1973. $6.95. Paperbound, $2.95.

ROBERTS, SAMUEL. *Survival or Hegemony? The Foundations Of Israeli Foreign Policy.* Pp. v, 162. Baltimore, Md.: Johns Hopkins Press, 1974. $7.50. Paperbound, $2.95.

ROSALDO, MICHELLE ZIMBALIST and LOUISE LAMPHERE, eds. *Women, Culture & Society.* Pp. viii, 352. Stanford, Calif.: Stanford University Press, 1974. $12.50. Paperbound, $3.95.

ROSOW, JEROME M., ed. *The Worker and the Job: Coping with Change.* Pp. ix, 208. Englewood Cliffs, N.J.: Prentice-Hall, 1974. $6.95. Paperbound, $2.45.

ROTHSCHILD, CONSTANTINA SAFILIOS. *Women and Social Policy.* Series in Social Policy. Pp. vii, 197. Englewood Cliffs, N.J.: Prentice-Hall, 1974. No price.

ROWAT, DONALD C., ed. *The Government of Federal Capitals.* Pp. vi, 377. Buffalo, N.Y.: University of Toronto, 1973. $15.00.

ROWBOTHAM, SHELIA. *Woman's Conscious-*

ness, Man's World. Pp. vii, 136. Baltimore, Md.: Penguin, 1974. $1.95. Paperbound.

RUSSETT, BRUCE M. *Power and Community in World Politics.* Pp. viii, 372. San Francisco, Calif.: W. H. Freeman, 1974. $10.00. Paperbound, $4.95.

SALAMAN, G. and K. THOMPSON, eds. *People and Organizations.* Pp. 423. New York: Longman, 1973. $12.50. Paperbound, $6.50.

SALVEMINI, GAETANO. *The Origins of Fascism in Italy.* Edited by Roberto Vivarelli. Pp. 450. New York: Harper & Row, 1973. $20.00. Paperbound, $4.95.

SCHEINER, IRWIN. *Modern Japan: An Interpretive Anthology.* Pp. ix, 270. New York: Macmillan, 1974. $4.25. Paperbound.

SCHNEIDER, DAVID M. and KATHLEEN GOUGH, eds. *Matrilineal Kinship.* Pp. vii, 761. Berkeley, Calif.: University of California, 1974. $22.50.

SERVICE, JOHN S. *Lost Chance in China.* Edited by Joseph W. Esherick. Pp. viii, 409. New York: Random House, 1974. $12.95.

SHAWCROSS, WILLIAM. *Crime and Compromise: Janos Kadar and the Politics of Hungary since Revolution.* Pp. 311. New York: E. P. Dutton, 1974. $10.00.

SERMAN, ROGER. *The Economics of Industry.* Pp. v, 426. Boston, Mass.: Little, Brown, 1974. $12.50.

SILK, LEONARD. *Capitalism: The Moving Target.* Pp. 159. New York: Quadrangle, 1974. $5.95.

SIMON, GERHARD. *Church, State and Opposition in the U.S.S.R.* Pp. v, 248. Berkeley, Calif.: University of California Press, 1974. $12.00.

SOMERVILLE, JOHN and HOWARD L. PARSONS, eds. *Dialogues on the Philosophy of Marxism.* Pp. vii, 420. Westport, Conn.: Greenwood Press, 1974. No price.

SOMIT, ALBERT. *Political Science and the Study of the Future.* Pp. 336. Hinsdale, Ill.: Dryden Press, 1974. No price.

STEIN, DONALD G. and JEFFREY I. ROSEN. *Basic Structure and Function in the Central Nervous System.* Pp. viii, 246. New York: Macmillan, 1974. $4.25. Paperbound.

STEIN, DONALD G. and JEFFREY I. ROSEN. *Motivation and Emotion.* Pp. v, 200. New York: Macmillan, 1974. $4.25. Paperbound.

SUCHLICKI, JAIME. *Cuba: From Columbus to Castro.* Pp. v, 242. New York: Charles Scribner's Sons, 1974. $7.95.

SUSSMAN, MARVIN B. *Sourcebook in Marriage and the Family.* 4th ed. Pp. vii, 389. Boston, Mass.: Houghton Mifflin Co., 1974. No price.

TOBACH, ETHEL et al. *The Four Horsemen: Racism, Sexism, Militarism and Social Darwinism.* Pp. 123. New York: Behavioral Publications, 1972. $7.95.

TOURAINE, ALAIN. *The Academic System in American Society.* Third of a Series of Essays Sponsored by the Carnegie Commission on Higher Education. Pp. xi, 319. Hightstown, N.J.: McGraw-Hill, 1974. $12.50.

TRIPODI, TONY. *Uses and Abuses of Social Research in Social Work.* Pp. 222. New York: Columbia University, 1974. $10.00. Paperbound, $4.00.

TYSSE, AGNES N. *International Education: The American Experience—A Bibliography.* Dissertations and Theses, vol. I. Pp. iii, 169. Metuchen, N.J.: Scarecrow Press, 1974. $5.00.

VAUGHAN, RICHARD. *Charles the Bold.* Pp. vii, 491. New York: Barnes & Noble, 1974. $28.00.

WAKEMAN, FREDERIC, JR. *Strangers at the Gate: Disorder in South China, 1839–1861.* Pp. 285. Berkeley, Calif.: University of California, 1974. $3.45. Paperbound.

WARNER, SAM BASS, JR. *The Urban Wilderness: A History of the American City.* Pp. vii, 303. New York: Harper & Row, 1973. $4.95.

WATT, KENNETH E. F. *The Titanic Effect: Planning for the Unthinkable.* Pp. vii, 268. New York: E. P. Dutton, 1974. $7.95.

WEINBERGER, PAUL E. *Perspectives on Social Welfare.* 2nd ed. Pp. v, 519. New York: Macmillan, 1974. $5.95. Paperbound.

WESTIN, ALAN F. and MICHAEL A. BAKER. *Databanks in a Free Society: Computers, Record-Keeping and Privacy.* Pp. vi, 522. New York: Quandrangle, 1974. $4.95. Paperbound.

WHISENHUNT, DONALD W., ed. *Delegate from New Jersey: The Journal of John Fell.* Pp. 209. Port Washington, N.Y.: Kennikat Press, 1974. $9.50.

WHITTAKER, JAMES K. *Social Treatment: An Approach to Interpersonal Helping.* Pp. 270. Chicago: Aldine Publishing, 1974. $9.75.

WILCOX, ALLEN R. *Public Opinion and Political Attitudes.* Pp. vi, 667. New York: John Wiley & Sons, 1974. No price.

WILKINS, BURLEIGH TAYLOR. *Hegel's Philosophy of History.* Pp. 193. Ithaca, N.Y.: Cornell University Press, 1974. $7.50.

WILLIAMS, JOHN B. *Narcotics and Drug Dependence*. Criminal Justice Series. Pp. vi, 422. Beverly Hills, Calif.: Glencoe, 1974. $7.95. Paperbound.

WILLIAMS, ROBERT E., PETER A. JANUS, and KENNETH C. HUHN. *NLRB Regulation of Election Conduct*. Labor Relations and Public Series, no. 8. Pp. 473. Philadelphia, Pa.: University of Pennsylvania, 1974. No Price. Paperbound.

WRIGHT, ERIK OLIN. *The Politics of Punishment: A Critical Analysis of Prisons in America*. Pp. 349. New York: Harper & Row, 1973. $12.95. Paperbound, $3.75.

Number
of Copies
paper cloth

—————— Social Goals and Indicators for American Society, Volume II
Sept. 1967, vol. 373, cloth

—————— Realignments in the Communist and Western Worlds
July 1967, vol. 372, paper

—————— National Character in the Perspective of the Social Sciences
Mar. 1967, vol. 370, paper

—————— Americans Abroad
Nov. 1966, vol. 368, paper & cloth

—————— The New Immigration
Sep. 1966, vol. 367, paper & cloth .

—————— American Civilization: Its Influence on Our Foreign Policy
July 1966, vol. 366, paper & cloth

—————— The Peace Corps
May 1966, vol. 365, paper

—————— Ethics in America: Norms and Deviations
Jan. 1966, vol. 363, paper

—————— Nonalignment in Foreign Affairs
Nov. 1965, vol. 362, paper

—————— Political Socialization
Sep. 1965, vol. 361, paper

—————— Latin America Tomorrow
July 1965, vol. 360, paper & cloth

—————— The Negro Protest
Jan. 1965, vol. 357, paper

—————— The Non-Western World in Higher Education
Nov. 1964, vol. 356, paper

—————— Africa in Motion
July 1964, vol. 354, paper

—————— Urban Revival: Goals and Standards
Mar. 1964, vol. 352, paper

—————— The Changing Cold War
Jan. 1964, vol. 351, paper

—————— Communist China and the Soviet Bloc
Sep. 1963, vol. 349, paper

● Quantity and wholesales discounts cannot be applied to this special offer.
● Shipping charges additional if payment is not received with order.
● Watch for other sales in future issues.

Please send me the volumes as indicated above.

☐ Enclosed is $————
☐ Please bill me

Name————————————————————————————————————

Address—————————————————————————————————

City————————————————State——————————————Zip———

THE AMERICAN ACADEMY OF POLITICAL AND
SOCIAL SCIENCE

3937 Chestnut Street   Philadelphia, Pa. 19104

INDEX

Kindly mention THE ANNALS *when writing to advertisers*

Origin and Purpose. The Academy was organized December 14, 1889, to promote the progress of political and social science, especially through publications and meetings. The Academy does not take sides in controverted questions, but seeks to gather and present reliable information to assist the public in forming an intelligent and accurate judgment.

Meetings. The Academy holds an annual meeting in the spring extending over two days.

Publications. THE ANNALS is the bi-monthly publication of The Academy. Each issue contains articles on some prominent social or political problem, written at the invitation of the editors. Also, monographs are published from time to time, numbers of which are distributed to pertinent professional organizations. These volumes constitute important reference works on the topics with which they deal, and they are extensively cited by authorities throughout the United States and abroad. The papers presented at the meetings of The Academy are included in THE ANNALS.

Membership. Each member of The Academy receives THE ANNALS and may attend the meetings of The Academy. Annual dues for individuals are $15.00 (for clothbound copies $20.00 per year). A life membership is $500. All payments are to be made in United States dollars.

Libraries and other institutions may receive THE ANNALS paperbound at a cost of $15.00 per year, or clothbound at $20.00 per year. Add $1.00 to above rates for membership outside U.S.A.

Single copies of THE ANNALS may be obtained by nonmembers of The Academy for $3.00 ($4.00 clothbound) and by members for $2.50 ($3.50 clothbound). A discount of 5 percent is allowed on orders for 10 to 24 copies of any one issue, and of 10 percent on orders for 25 or more copies. These discounts apply only when orders are placed directly with The Academy and not through agencies. The price to all bookstores and to all dealers is $3.00 per copy less 20 percent, with no quantity discount. It is urged that payment be sent with each order. This will save the buyer the shipping charge and save The Academy the cost of carrying accounts and sending statements. Monographs may be purchased for $4.00, with proportionate discounts.

All correspondence concerning The Academy or THE ANNALS should be addressed to the Academy offices, 3937 Chestnut Street, Philadelphia, Pa. 19104.